Introduction to International Economics

Catrinus J. Jepma
Henk Jager
and
Elise Kamphuis

FT Prentice Hall
FINANCIAL TIMES

An imprint of **Pearson Education**
Harlow, England • London • New York • Boston • San Francisco • Toronto • Sydney • Singapore • Hong Kong
Tokyo • Seoul • Taipei • New Delhi • Cape Town • Madrid • Mexico City • Amsterdam • Munich • Paris • Milan

Open University of the Netherlands
Heerlen

Pearson Education Limited
Edinburgh Gate
Harlow
Essex CM20 2JE
England

and Associated Companies throughout the world

Visit us on the World Wide Web at:
http://www.pearsoned.co.uk

First published 1996

ISBN 0 582 27765-5 PPR

British Library Cataloguing-in-Publication Data

A catalogue record for this book is
available from the British Library

Library of Congress Cataloging-in-Publication Data

Jepma, C. J.
  Introduction to international economics / Catrinus Jepma, Henk
Jager, Elise Kamphuis.
    p.   cm.
  Includes bibliographical references and index.
  ISBN 0-582-27765-5
    1. International economic relations. 2. International trade.
  3. International finance. 4. Balance of payments. 5. Commercial
policy. I. Jager, Henk, 1947–   . II. Kamphuis, Elise, 1965–   .
III. Title.
HF1359.J47   1996   96-3560
337—dc20   CIP

10 9
07   06   05   04   03

Set by 33 in Times
Printed in Malaysia, GPS

Contents

Tables

Figures

The International Business Programme

This volume, together with an accompanying study guide produced by the Netherlands' Open University (OU), forms an integrated 100 hour course, called 'Introduction to International Economics'. This course has been developed as part of a larger (1,720 hours, 42 credit points) OU higher distance teaching programme on International Business. There are no formal prerequisites to enter the programme; however, the programme's academic level should be recognised. The course materials have been carefully designed for distance teaching purposes, which means that the student should be able to comprehend the course contents without additional educational tools.

The International Business Programme has been specifically designed for junior and mid-career professionals. After completion of the programme, the candidates are qualified to enter the European Master of Business Administration Programme which has been organised by a number of European distance teaching universities.

The International Business Programme centres around the following themes:

- International Economic Relations; main modules: Introduction in international economics, International trade
- Business Administration; main modules: International financial management and accounting
- Management; main modules: International human resource management, International management, Strategic issues in a European context
- Institutions; main modules: International economic institutions, European economic integration

The International Business Programme is completed with a course called International Business Simulation, wherein students actively take part, as members of an international team of company executives, in an international computerised systems simulation.

Although the International Business Programme has been designed as an intellectually and conceptually integrated whole, the various underlying modules of 100 hours (3 credit points) each can also be studied independently. Separate modules or sets of modules can be purchased at the Netherlands' Open University, either with or without the right to additional tutorial support or to take an official exam.

For more information please contact:

xiv

Professor Catrinus J. Jepma or Mrs Elise Kamphuis
Coordinators, International Business Programme
Open University of the Netherlands, Department of Economics
P.O. Box 2960
6401 DL Heerlen
The Netherlands
Tel.: +31 45 5762724
Fax: +31 45 5762123
E-mail: elise.kamphuis@ouh.nl

Preface

The idea of producing a new introductory course on International Economics emerged from the initiative taken at the Netherlands' Open University (OU) to develop a 1,720-hours distance teaching programme in the field of International Business at university level.

A 100 hours course on 'International Economics' was needed as one of the introductory elements of the programme; besides, such a volume seemed to be missing in the international catalogue of textbooks on the issue, which are almost all significantly more sizeable and take a graduate student's rather than a businessman's perspective. Our aim was to develop a course for those who are interested in international economic relations primarily from a practical, business-oriented point of view.

The volume was developed with those points of departure in mind. It starts with a case study on a multinational which, together with the following two chapters on the world economy and balance of payments, deals with the traditional distinction between the world of finance and that of (international) trade. In addition, the case study raises several questions with respect to the international environment of a multinational. These questions introduce the themes discussed in the rest of the volume, and show students why these themes are relevant in the reality of today's business world.

Bearing the target group in mind, the use of mathematics was avoided. However, particularly in Chapters 3–11, this volume contains a wealth of supporting figures, serving to clarify the text; in most cases, these figures are presented in separate boxes. While the case studies in the textbook aim to give an introduction to – or an application of – the theory, the boxes are meant to develop further or supplement the theories.

We hope we have succeeded in writing an introductory textbook to International Economics which is attractive not only to economists, but also to businessmen or students having a background other than in the field of economics.

We gratefully acknowledge the valuable suggestions and extensive commentary made by the external referee, Walter Vanthielen, as well as the comments on the didactics of Anja Lkoundi and the support of Wytze van der Gaast and Alexander Mollerus.

Heerlen, 3 November 1995

On behalf of the writing team
Catrinus J. Jepma
Professor of International Economics and
coordinator International Business Programme

Introduction:
Miscellaneous international economic questions: an illustration based on a case study

0.1 Introduction

Why does virtually every businessman need to keep informed of developments in international economic relations? The answer is that he needs to know what effect the internationalisation of economic activities might have on his business. Over the years, economic ties between regions, countries and companies have become ever closer. This internationalisation is taking place both in the real world (e.g. on the international commodity markets or the international markets in technology or factors of production) and in the financial world (on the international money and capital market). Since the Second World War, internationalisation has taken place mainly by the progressive elimination of all kinds of barriers to trade in goods and services, and later financial transactions, between countries. Internationalisation may also come about because entrepreneurs themselves are increasingly operating beyond their national borders, e.g. owing to ever improving transport facilities or the constant expansion of information and communication networks between the various market operators. Internationalisation also takes place when companies can only survive by operating on a larger scale, for instance via international alliances, joint ventures, the establishment of foreign subsidiaries or other forms of cooperation.

In this Introduction we shall first use a detailed case study to show the various ways in which international economic relations can affect a company (section 0.2). Next we shall give a brief account of the different questions which arise from the case study (section 0.3). These points illustrate the type of question central to this book. In the different chapters which follow, we therefore examine these various questions successively in greater depth.

0.2 The company in its international environment

Every entrepreneur has direct or indirect dealings with international trade as a result of internationalisation. If he himself is involved in international trade, that is obvious. But even if he is not, the running of his business is nevertheless

1

influenced by it. Even a businessman who concentrates all his purchases and sales on the home market has to take account of potential foreign competition, or the fact that his domestic competitors can strengthen their market position by internationalisation. The following example taken from real life illustrates that a business can benefit from international trade but that, on the other hand, internationalisation can also pose a threat.

The case study analyses the global interaction between a company operating internationally and its environment. It deals with all kinds of aspects of internationalisation which a company may encounter and forms an introduction both to Chapter 1 and to the whole book. The purpose of the case study is to arouse the interest of the reader. It is not intended to provide a full answer immediately to any questions which may arise in going over the case study; that is done in the text of subsequent chapters. After studying all the material you are advised to re-read the case study to establish whether you have a better understanding of the problems presented and can combine that with your existing knowledge.

The company chosen as the focus of the case study is the chemical group DSM, which – like the Netherlands' Open University itself – is located in Heerlen, Netherlands. The case study shows that DSM owes its existence to internationalisation, but that – at the same time – internationalisation also represents a threat. When the study was being prepared, people at DSM believed that the economic focus was shifting towards East or South-East Asia. DSM has been exporting to such countries as Taiwan and Korea for many years, and the Far East accounts for some 10 per cent of its turnover. The shifting economic focus will therefore presumably have less effect on DSM than on many other companies. At the time of writing (1993), the threats posed by internationalisation come mainly from Eastern Europe.[1] Low wages, the lack of environmental regulations, or failure to comply with such regulations, and cheap sources of energy currently mean that East European businesses can supply more cheaply, making them formidable competitors for DSM. However, in the longer term DSM envisages a new market for sales in Eastern Europe. [The case study was compiled on the basis of annual reports and interviews with the head of the Corporate Strategic Planning department, M. Jansen, and the senior business analyst, F.W.H. Aerts.]

---

1. The case study relates to 1992 and 1993. However, the pressure from Eastern Europe declined significantly in 1994 because Eastern Europe had to contend with infrastructure problems; energy prices increased and local economies began to recover.

Case study 0.1: DSM, a company operating internationally

Characteristics of DSM

The State set up DSM as a mining company in 1902. In 1920 DSM started producing coke and coke oven gas. Ten years later DSM switched from coke to artificial fertilizer production. In 1950 it added caprolactam production followed by ethylene and plastics in 1960. After closure of the Zuid-Limburg coal mines in 1965–73, DSM substantially expanded its chemical activities.

DSM focused on markets outside the Netherlands right from the start. For one thing, it was forced to do so because there was already sufficient basic material processing capacity in the Netherlands. Economies of scale played a major role here as well. DSM's international outlook is also due to the internationalisation of economies, which is engendering an ever more uniform world market. Thus, technological know-how and the level of education of employees in different countries are converging. Workers who trained in the US, for example, can be found throughout the world. Internationalisation also has a positive effect on the import and export of goods because import barriers have been dismantled, transport has become cheaper and logistical facilities have improved. Internationalisation has also led to the liberalisation of capital markets, making it easier to finance foreign investments. Finally, market philosophies are becoming increasingly uniform throughout the world – particularly since the collapse of the communist regimes and their ideology. Thanks to internationalisation, DSM has gained ever increasing scope both for exporting, and for setting up production facilities and financing investments abroad.

Thus, DSM has now developed into a highly integrated international chemical group with annual sales totalling approx. NLG 10 billion in the first half of the 1990s. The areas in which the business is concentrated are: basic materials (hydrocarbons and basic polymers), performance materials (engineering plastics, synthetic rubbers and structural resins), materials processing (engineering plastic products, plastic consumer products, plastic packaging and compounds and mouldings), basic chemicals (fibrous raw materials, melamine and fertilizers), fine chemicals, coating resins and energy. DSM is also active in oil and natural gas exploration and extraction. The group has a strong technological base and is a world market leader in a number of products. DSM mainly produces materials which industrial customers process into end products, such as cars, computers, electrical and electronic appliances, packaging, synthetic fibres and dyes. DSM also supplies fine chemicals for medicines and food and beverages. The group comprises a large number of companies, mostly located in Europe and the United States. The head office is in Heerlen, Netherlands. DSM's activities are divided into 25 strategic business units (SBUs) grouped into 9 divisions. In principle, the SBUs operate independently, but large investment projects have to be approved by the Managing Board. SBUs are sometimes organised geographically (as in the case of elastomers) and sometimes by product (e.g. resins).

In 1992 the group had around 22,000 employees, 40 per cent of whom worked at locations outside the Netherlands. Of these, 70 per cent worked in Europe and 30 per cent outside Europe. DSM's international character is also seen in the

Table 0.1 Composition of DSM's long-term
liabilities, by currency (1992, NLG million)

Currency	1992
Dutch guilders	1,109
American dollars	631
German marks	216
Other currencies	92
Total	2,048

method of financing. Almost half of DSM's long-term liabilities are in foreign currencies, predominantly the dollar (see Table 0.1).

If we read the 1992 annual report, we see immediately that DSM is an international operation:

- In 1992 the international chemical industry faced persistently low economic growth of 1 per cent. The European chemical industry's production in 1992 was 2 per cent up on 1991. This led to lower demand for chemicals and lower margins.
- Economic growth continued to slow down in the European countries, in particular. In the Far East, growth was somewhat down on 1991 and only in the US was a slight recovery evident at the end of the year.
- In Europe the supply of plastics and raw materials exceeded demand, leading to worldwide surplus capacity. Market conditions in Europe were also influenced by increasing competition from the US and Eastern Europe. For DSM – with its relatively high proportion of production in the Netherlands (see Figure 0.1a) – this was compounded by the effects of the appreciation of the guilder against most European currencies.
- The world market for caprolactam is even now being influenced by very cheap imports from Central and Eastern Europe.
- The market for fertilizers in North-West Europe is in structural decline as a result of EC policy aimed at reducing agricultural surpluses, and also as a result of a stricter environment policy in the agricultural sector. In addition, there is still pressure from imports, including from Eastern Europe. As a result, in 1992 prices fell by around 15 per cent against 1991.
- These negative factors severely depressed DSM's results. Turnover fell by 5 per cent. The volume of sales increased by 2 per cent but the average prices made were 9 per cent down. On balance, the impact of acquisitions and deconsolidations on the result was +3 per cent. The lower average dollar rate had a 1 per cent negative effect.
- One positive factor was that Curver Rubbermaid Group (60 per cent DSM) further strengthened its European market position, particularly in the United Kingdom and Southern Europe.

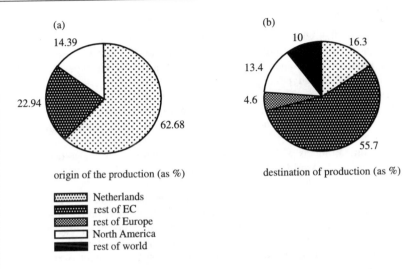

(a)

14.39

22.94

62.68

origin of the production (as %)

(b)

10   16.3

13.4

4.6

55.7

destination of production (as %)

▨ Netherlands
▨ rest of EC
▨ rest of Europe
☐ North America
■ rest of world

Figure 0.1a and b Origin and destination of DSM's production (1992, %)

In 1990 DSM completed a study of developments and trends relevant to industry in general and to DSM in particular as a medium-sized chemical group.

This caused DSM to opt for a strategy of largely concentrating its activities on a number of key areas where the group holds or can attain a leading international position. It is evident from the 1992 annual report that DSM is strengthening its strategic position, partly by means of international acquisitions and alliances, and partly by selling off a number of operations and subsidiaries.

Internationalisation

It is now clear that DSM is a company which operates internationally. But what does DSM itself understand by internationalisation? For DSM, internationalisation takes place only if sales outside Europe increase. DSM sees Europe as the home market. Figure 0.1b shows turnover broken down geographically.

It is evident from Figure 0.1a and b that some 86 per cent of DSM's total production takes place in Europe and 72 per cent is sold there. Since most of DSM's customers are industrial enterprises which can be regarded as a homogeneous target group, and since the products are simple, DSM can tackle the European market as a single market. Another reason why DSM regards Europe as the home market is that transport costs in Europe are low. The only difference between the European and the national market is the presence of foreign currencies; this inherently means foreign exchange risks in transactions with other countries.

Globalisation

DSM prefers the term 'globalisation' to 'internationalisation', referring to globalisation if worldwide production and sales (outside Europe) increase.

The producer determines the form of globalisation by the types of goods offered. The following types of goods can be identified:

First, commodities. These are goods with a high raw material content. In locating the production of these goods, it will generally be necessary to weigh up the location of the raw materials against transport costs from that location to the market.

Next come products with a high value added. These goods are produced and sold throughout the world and necessitate close customer relations, which is why they are produced near the customers.

There are also new products. In most cases they have short life cycles with heavy investment in research and development. It is therefore important to achieve maximum sales of these products as rapidly as possible. For this purpose, other countries will be targeted at an early stage, because in practice it is harder to gain a large share of the home market than smaller market shares scattered over various continents.

However, the form of globalisation is not only determined by the producer but also depends partly on the consumer. A feature of the industrial market where DSM operates is that the consumer can be of the same type all over the world: we talk about the 'global customer'. This means that DSM does not need to consider specifically producing different types of product for different regions, and the products can be made anywhere. DSM also develops products necessitating close relations with the customer. These are normally produced close to the customer. In only the engineering plastics products and elastomers (synthetic rubbers, thermoplastic rubbers and high-grade fibres) divisions, does product development specifically take account of customer requirements. Example: since Japanese companies require their rubber supplies to meet specific requirements, it is not sufficient for DSM to recommend products to potential customers. In order to meet the Japanese requirements, DSM has an office in Japan which acquires specific knowledge of Japanese rubber and the requirements relating to it. Once the product has been made with the aid of that knowledge, DSM arranges for it to be tested in Japan. After many tests and experiments, DSM can eventually obtain approval for supplying the rubber to the Japanese car industry. The final phase then consists in selling the rubber to Japanese car manufacturers in Europe (the UK) and the US. This method is very laborious because the requirements imposed by Japan on its suppliers are often very exacting and specific. But once the Japanese requirements have been met, there is a good chance of the product being a selling point for European customers, too: 'When you make it in Japan, you make it everywhere.'

Another way of gaining access to Japanese transplants in Europe and the US is to enter into alliances or joint ventures with Japanese companies.

Location factors

Some production is 'footloose' and can thus be set up anywhere. One location factor here may be the level and variability of the exchange rate. Countries with unstable exchange rates are generally not attractive locations for investment. Wage costs may be another factor. Most of DSM's products are capital intensive and raw material intensive, so that wages represent only a small proportion of the total costs. Thus, wage differences are not a primary factor in DSM's location policy, although they do have an indirect influence. Part of the textile industry has moved from Western Europe to the low wage countries of Asia. As DSM supplies raw materials for the textile industry, it is natural for DSM to follow the textile processing industry. Moreover, internationalisation means that production processes are becoming more alike and prices of capital and raw materials are becoming standardised. As a result, wage differences will play an increasing role in competition.

The production of Curver Rubbermaid Group (60 per cent DSM) is concentrated mainly in Germany and the Netherlands. These are both countries with high wages and a strong currency, factors which push up the costs; yet production has not been relocated. Labour productivity and government measures such as subsidies and tax rules can also affect the decision whether or not to relocate production internationally. However, most of DSM's production is not 'footloose', and in 1993 the bulk of it was still located in the Netherlands. The reason was simple: when considering whether or not to move the production abroad, the additional costs often appear to be greater than the local advantages.

Export or set up production facilities abroad?

From Figure 0.1 we see that DSM is a net exporter (i.e. it exports more than it imports). In 1992 most of its production took place in the Netherlands while only a small percentage was sold there. DSM sold most of its production abroad, while only about 40 per cent was produced in other countries. This means that more than a third of DSM's turnover is produced by its direct foreign investments. Table 0.2 gives more detail on the geographical distribution of investments.

Table 0.2 Breakdown of DSM's investments and book value of tangible assets by geographical area (1992, NLG million)

	Investments	Book value fixed assets
Netherlands	889	4,178
Other EC-countries	88	670
Sub-total	977	4,848
Other European countries	4	27
Northern-America	56	427
Other continents	3	13
Total	1,040	5,315

We see from the table that foreign investments totalled NLG 151 million in 1992: that is 15 per cent of total investments. The book value of foreign tangible assets was NLG 1,137 million, almost a quarter of the total.

It is not so surprising that DSM is a net exporter, since the company usually reconnoitres the market via exports before proceeding with foreign production. If exports go well, DSM considers the possibility of setting up a production plant elsewhere. In the first instance, the decision to continue exporting or to set up production facilities abroad depends on the target market and the type of product. Products can be developed in two ways: In the case of a small-scale production process, the group first builds a pilot plant. If the product is successful, the market is gradually expanded and the necessary production facilities are added. In the case of a large-scale production process, DSM opts to take advantage of economies of scale by building a large factory straightaway and exporting. The choice of method affects the scope for and timing of international production.

Sales are organised according to geographical distance and product complexity. On its home market, DSM sells the products mainly through sales offices. For more distant exports, DSM uses agents (intermediaries) or traders. The agents seek customers for DSM and sell the products on commission. Traders are totally independent dealers who resell the products at their own risk. Once sales are going well, the establishment of a sales office is considered.

Influence on government policy

Lobbying is an activity in which DSM is not greatly involved, nor are any lobbyists employed in the US or Europe. DSM prefers to leave lobbying to organised pressure groups. However, as we shall see, DSM does try to influence European industrial policy in certain cases.

An example: caprolactam suffered severely from the intense competition from Central and Eastern Europe. The 1992 and 1993 annual reports state that cheap imports from Eastern Europe continued to have a negative impact, especially on the world market in caprolactam, which is important to DSM. It is not only because of low wages, the absence of environmental regulations and low energy prices that East European companies are able to supply these products so cheaply; according to DSM, unrealistic pricing is also a major factor. Companies in Central and Eastern Europe operate at a loss but nevertheless continue producing. Worse still, according to DSM, Polish factories exported so much that the permitted quantities of duty-free imports of caprolactam from Eastern Europe exceeded the EU import ceiling by a factor of 10. DSM wanted the arrangement agreed in the EU to be applied, whereby the excess would be subject to import duty.

DSM is trying to influence competition from Central and Eastern Europe by convincing the Commission that the textile processing industries in those areas ought to be supported. Before the wall came down, Central and East European chemical firms produced caprolactam for the textile processing industries in Central and Eastern Europe. Since the collapse of the wall, Central and East European producers have needed hard currency, and to earn it they export their products to the EU. The result is that the textile processing industries in Central and Eastern Europe are being made idle because they can no longer obtain any raw materials from their suppliers and do not have the hard currency to import them. Since the textile processing industries are labour intensive, there has been a huge increase in unemployment in Central and Eastern Europe caused by the closure of these plants. That is the argument used by DSM to convince the European Commission that the textile processing industries should be supported. In the present situation – they argue – from the macro-economic point of view, production is being transferred from clean, environment-conscious, profitable producers to polluting, obsolete and unprofitable raw material processors. The situation that DSM wants to see means a shift from competition between raw material producers in East and West to competition between textile processing industries in East and West.

Exchange rate risks

The difference between sales on the national market and international sales is the exchange rate risk incurred in international transactions. DSM pursues a conservative exchange rate risk reduction policy, using traditional instruments to hedge against exchange rate risks. DSM's treasury department is responsible for covering exchange rate positions. Before doing so, they cancel out the exchange rate risks on the various international transactions as far as possible against one another (matching).

For long-term planning, DSM uses a consultant to predict exchange rates. Exchange rate predictions are still only forecasts, so that they cannot form the basis of any strategic decisions. Exchange rate changes can alter the value of the assets when subsidiaries are established, and this is taken into account to some extent when setting up abroad.

Finally, exchange rates influence a country's competitive position. A country whose currency is increasing in value can suffer a competitive disadvantage as a result. When setting up establishments in such countries, DSM makes extra provision if the value of the currency concerned is expected to change. The price of the important raw material, naphtha, affects DSM's competitive position. Naphtha is derived from crude oil, and crude oil is priced in dollars. Fluctuations in the value of the dollar have therefore less impact on DSM's competitiveness with respect to American companies. Say the dollar depreciates: this causes a deterioration in the competitive position in relation to American companies on foreign markets. However, naphtha compensates for this deterioration because its purchase price becomes more favourable owing to the cheaper dollar. In the case of products not priced in dollars, depreciation of the dollar can be a reason for making them on the American sales market. This happened, for example, when the dollar depreciated against the yen. This caused many Japanese to invest in the US. Conversely, investors in Japan were at a disadvantage because of the expensive yen. This was one reason why a joint venture by DSM in Japan produced a loss in 1993. The 1993 annual report states that the depreciation of various European currencies against the guilder, which occurred primarily in September 1992, depressed prices of many products and hence DSM's gross margins, in spite of the relatively low oil and gas prices. Later it was acknowledged that the detrimental effect of the ERM crisis for DSM had been exaggerated at the time, as most of the exchange rates subsequently recovered.

0.3   Questions relating to the case study

The case study shows that even a company operating on the international market right from the start can be confronted by developments which could not be foreseen. In 1992 DSM had to contend with low economic growth worldwide, a falling dollar, the ERM crisis, increasing competition from East European countries following the revolutions there, and the agricultural and environmental policy developments in Europe. In order to operate successfully on the international market, a company must be able to respond quickly to such developments. DSM covers exchange rate risks; when investing in countries with fluctuating rates, provision is made. DSM is trying to tackle the competition from Eastern Europe by influencing European policy. For Japanese customers, DSM meets specific requirements, which also makes the product more attractive to customers in other countries, etc.

Like the choice between exporting goods or setting up production facilities abroad, such responses demand a thorough knowledge of how the international economy works. This book offers an insight into international economic relations which is as essential to the operation of a multinational like DSM as to a small export company or a national company facing foreign competition. But also for anyone wanting to follow world economic trends, the more general questions raised by this case study and discussed in the rest of this book are important; for example:

1. What are the different types of international transaction (Chapter 2)?
2. Why does international trade take place and who gains by it (Chapter 3)?
3. Why do multinationals exist (Chapter 5)?
4. What is an anti-dumping levy and why is it introduced; what other protective measures can be applied to deal with foreign competition (Chapters 6, 7 and 10)?
5. What is the connection between trade barriers and lobby groups (Chapter 11)?
6. How can international transactions be financed (Chapter 12)?
7. What determines the level of an exchange rate and how can exchange rates be predicted (Chapter 13)?
8. What risks are associated with international transactions (Chapter 15)?
9. What is the effect on businesses of all kinds of international economic agreements and forms of integration, such as the EU (Chapter 16)?
10. What is the role of government in exchange rate uncertainty (Chapter 14)?
11. How can one safeguard against uncertainty caused by exchange rate instability (Chapter 15)?

However, the first question to arise from the case study is perhaps this: what can we say, more generally, about the increasing internationalisation of the business environment? The next chapter will begin to answer this question.

1 The world economy: key data and central concepts

1.1 Introduction

This chapter gives an outline of the international environment in which businesses operate, as in the case of DSM described above, on the basis of the global nature and scale of the various types of international economic transactions. First we consider the volume, characteristics and direction of international trade flows (sections 1.2 and 1.3) and international capital flows (section 1.4). Since almost all international transactions generate a transaction on the foreign exchange markets, regardless of whether they take place in the real world (trade flows) or in the financial world (capital flows), section 1.5 gives a general account of the nature and volume of activities on these markets. We also look briefly at the resulting price, the exchange rate. Thus, this chapter gives a general picture of the principal components of international economic relations.

1.2 Volume and direction of international trade flows

In the post-war period, international trade expanded enormously. In fact, the growth in the volume of world trade in this period exceeded that of world production almost every year. This was even true in the early 1970s when governments introduced numerous new forms of trade restrictions (see also Chapters 7 and 10). Since the mid 1980s, the volume of world trade has grown in real terms by over 5 per cent per annum, while growth in world production has been below 3 per cent.

Figure 1.1 illustrates for various sub-periods how international trade has developed in relation to world Gross National Product (GNP) over the same period.

International trade did indeed expand strongly in the post-war period, as we can see from the figure; however, we can also see that the opposite pattern applied during the first half of this century – a period when there were all kinds of barriers to trade. Not only was growth in world GNP at a low level then – around 2 per cent – but growth in the volume of international trade was even lower at about 1 per cent. Figure 1.1 also shows that at the beginning of the 1990s, growth in world trade clearly exceeded growth in world production. This indicates continuing integration of the world economy.

Figure 1.1 raises the question whether and to what extent trade expansion and

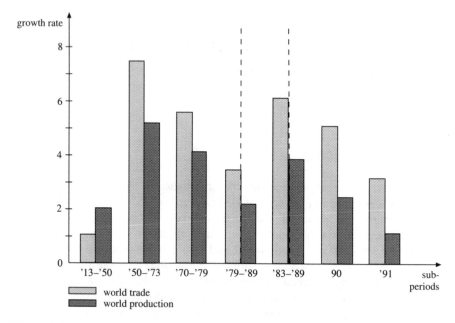

Figure 1.1 Annual average aggregate growth rates for world GNP and world trade in real terms: various sub-periods, 1913–91 (%)

Source: Figures for 1913–50 and 1950–73, Maddison (1989); other figures taken from GATT statistics.

economic growth have influenced one another. This book will discuss that question in more detail. It is noticeable that most trade theories concentrate on the effect of trade liberalisation on economic growth and its distribution (Chapter 3); the opposite question, i.e. the extent to which economic growth influences the opening up of the economy, has received far less attention in the formulation of theories and belongs more to the sphere of political economy (Chapter 11). In practice, the post-war development meant that foreign goods and services became increasingly important not only in the consumption package, but also in processing by industry. This was another factor leading to the extremely rapid internationalisation of trade and industry.

In order to provide more detail on trade flows, Figures 1.2 and 1.3 respectively show the growth rates of world trade and world production broken down by the main types of goods. The decline in the growth of world trade and world production is naturally reflected in the growth rates of the different types of goods. Only export growth and volume growth of agricultural products did not fall but increased slightly. In Figure 1.2 we notice that, in spite of the fall, the volume growth of manufactures still far exceeded that of other product groups from 1983 onwards. From both graphs we again see that the growth of trade exceeds that of production, except for agricultural products, up to 1990. We can draw the cautious conclusion that increasing economic integration in the world

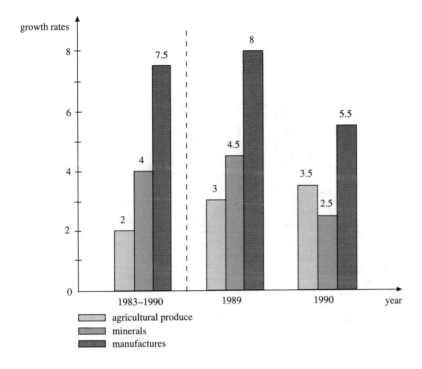

Figure 1.2 Average annual growth of world exports of the principal types of goods from 1983 to 1990 (% change)
Source: GATT, 1991, vol. I, p. 6.

economy has taken place mainly in the industrial sector and to a far lesser extent in agriculture and minerals.

A closer look at international trade patterns prompts a number of striking observations. First, the bulk of international trade takes place between industrialised countries; in fact, in the post-war period the volume of this type of trade flow actually increased faster than that of other trade (as shown for the period 1980–9 in Figure 1.4a and b). This is a refined pattern of specialisation which has developed in the industrialised world. Figure 1.4a and b illustrates the structure of international trade flows in 1980 and 1989. The graphs show the export flows for the main economic regions of the world as percentages of total world trade.

The first point which we notice from the graphs is that, in the 1980s, both export flows within the regions and from one region to another increased, particularly trade between North America and Asia and between the European Community and Asia. It is noticeable that, compared with the other two regions, the European Community exports a relatively large amount to the rest of the world, mainly to developing countries and the former centrally planned economies.

13

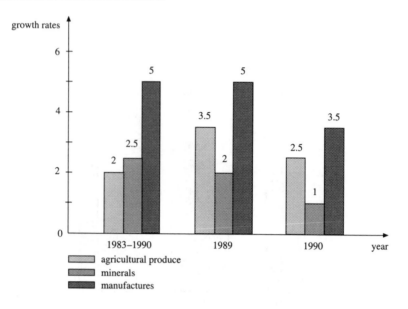

Figure 1.3 Average annual growth of world production of the principal types of goods from 1983 to 1990 (%)
Source: See Figure 1.2.

We also notice that the countries of the European Community (the European Union, EU, since November 1993 when the Treaty of Maastricht came into force) export mainly to one another. This is due in part to the fact that the EU consists of a large number of countries. During the 1980s this tendency was actually intensified, as illustrated by Figure 1.4c, which was compiled from

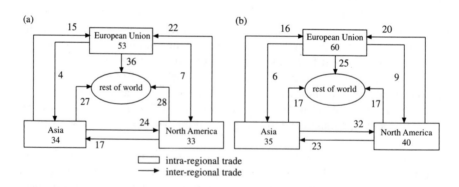

Figure 1.4a and b Regional structure of world trade in (a) 1980 and (b) 1989 (% of total exports/imports per region)
Source: International Monetary Fund, *Direction of Trade Statistics, Yearbook*, 1990; GATT, *International Trade*, volumes I and II, various years.

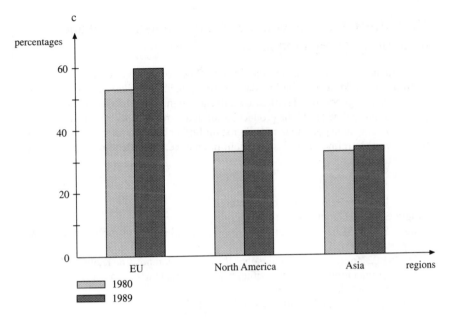

Figure 1.4c Export flows within the regional blocs as a percentage of total trade of countries in those blocs (1980 and 1989)
Source: Own calculations based on data in Figure 1.4a and b.

Figure 1.4a and b. It shows the extent to which trade took place within the region for the EU, North America and Asia. By comparing the 1980 figures with those for 1989 we find that in all three different regions, but particularly in the EC and North America, there is a trend towards further trade regionalisation.

A second important trend evident in the pattern of international trade concerns the enormous growth which has taken place in *intra-industry trade*, particularly between the industrialised countries. This type of trade occurs if a country both imports and exports products in a particular category of goods, and reflects the increasingly refined pattern of specialisation among Western companies. In practice, this usually concerns variants of the same type of product. For example, France exports Peugeots but imports Toyotas, Opels, Fiats, etc.

At this point we should acknowledge that the volume of intra-industry trade shown in the statistics depends very much on the degree of refinement in the records of goods and services. It is easy to see that as this refinement increases, the recorded volume of intra-industry trade falls (see Case study 1.1). However, even if a high level of disaggregation is applied (this is the degree of refinement with which trade statistics are defined), a substantial proportion of trade for most countries can still be called intra-industry trade. The relatively large increase in the volume of intra-industry trade over the years is therefore generally regarded as typical of modern trade flows.

Case study 1.1 The volume of intra-industry trade and the trade flow aggregation level

In international trade statistics, the various flows of goods are classified by a uniform system known as the Standard International Trade Classification (SITC). In this system, goods are classified by a decimal numbering (digit) system which is increasingly refined until the product has been described in maximum detail. The international system goes up to nine digits; for further disaggregation, the countries themselves can refine their classification. In practice, it is often only seven digits that are used.

An example:

1 digit SITC 8 'miscellaneous manufactured articles'
3 digits SITC 851 'footwear'
5 digits SITC 851.01 'footwear with outer soles and uppers of rubber or artificial plastic material'
SITC 851.02 'footwear with outer soles of leather or composition leather; footwear (other than footwear falling within heading 851.01) with outer soles of rubber or artificial plastic material'
7 digits SITC 851.02.07 'sand shoes, rubber soled'.

In the literature, various indices are used to express the level of intra-industry trade. Normally this means checking to what extent there are both imports and exports of each different category of goods for a particular country (sometimes with adjustment for the effect of any balance of payments imbalances). Using a particular formula, one can now calculate the volume of intra-industry trade for each aggregation level. The chance that precisely defined products are both imported and exported by a country is then naturally less than for global categories of goods. Thus, in a calculation of British intra-industry trade for 1982, for example, Greenaway and Milner found a figure of 97 per cent for SITC 751 (office machines), 41 per cent for SITC 7511 (typewriters) and 10 per cent for SITC 75112 (mechanical typewriters).

The third point we notice is that certain countries have managed to enhance their position considerably on the international market, while the relative importance of other countries has declined. Table 1.1 illustrates this: it shows the shares in industrial product exports for a few dozen of the countries most involved in trade for 1965–90. Countries producing strong growth are, for example, West Germany (alternating with the US as the leading world exporter in recent years), Japan and the 'NICs' (Newly Industrialising Countries such as Taiwan, South Korea, Hong Kong and Singapore; later, various other countries were also given that title) and more recently China; the relative importance of countries such as the US, the UK and various developing countries in world trade has declined in recent decades. However, we should point out that the table must not be interpreted as if growth in one country's share of trade automatically means less scope for trade by another country. Trade is not a *zero-sum game* (i.e.

Table 1.1 Shares in exports of industrial products, 1965–90 (%)

Country	Rank							Shares in exports of industrial production					
	1965	1973	1979	1980	1986	1989	1990	1965	1973	1980	1986	1989	1990
West Germany	2	1	2	1	1	2	1	13.8	15.9	13.9	14.8	11.0	11.4
Japan	4	3	3	3	2	3	3	6.8	9.3	10.4	13.6	8.9	8.3
US	1	2	1	2	3	1	2	15.4	12.4	12.2	11.1	11.8	11.3
France	5	4	4	5	4	4	4	6.4	6.9	7.0	6.1	5.8	6.2
Italy	6	6	6	6	5	6		5.0	4.9	5.5	5.7	4.6	
UK	3	5	5	4	6	5	5	9.9	6.9	7.2	5.5	4.9	5.3
Canada	9	9	10	9	7	7	8	3.4	3.6	2.8	3.9	3.9	3.8
Belgium	7	7	11	7	8	10	9	4.6	4.9	4.1	3.8	3.2	3.4
Netherlands	10	8	8	8	9	9	7	3.2	3.6	3.2	3.1	3.5	3.8
Taiwan	40	18	22	15	10	12	12	0.1	0.9	1.4	2.4	2.1	1.9
Switzerland	13	12	13	11	11	16	14	2.3	2.3	2.3	2.4	1.7	1.8
Soviet Union	8	10	7	10	12	18	10	4.4	3.3	2.3	2.4	3.5	3.0
Sweden	12	11	12	12	13	15	16	2.4	2.5	2.1	2.1	1.7	1.7
Korea	47	25	29	18	14	13	13	0.1	0.7	1.3	2.1	2.0	1.9
East Germany	11	13	28	17	15	23	32	2.5	1.8	1.3	1.5	0.9	0.7
Australia	16	17	17	19	16	19	20	1.1	1.2	1.2	1.3	1.2	1.2
Spain	30	22	19	16	17	18	17	0.4	0.9	1.3	1.3	1.4	1.6
China	25	27	34	24	18	14	15	0.6	0.6	0.8	1.3	1.7	1.7
Hong Kong	19	15	27	14	19	11	11	0.9	1.3	1.5	1.3	2.4	2.4
Czechoslovakia	14	14		21	20			2.1	1.4	1.0	1.2		
Singapore	33	31	32	22	21	17	18	0.3	0.5	0.9	1.0	1.4	1.5
Finland	23	24		23	22		27	0.7	0.7	0.9	0.9		0.8
Denmark	20	20	30	26	23	25	23	0.9	0.9	0.8	0.8	0.9	1.0
Brazil	39	33		28	24		25	0.2	0.4	0.7	0.7	1.1	0.9
Bulgaria	27	30		29	25			0.5	0.5	0.6	0.7		
Total								88.0	88.3	86.7	90.0		

Source: Figures for 1965–86, *United States, Yearbook of Trade Statistics*, various volumes, 1989; figures for 1979 and 1989, GATT, 1990, Vol. 1, p. 30; figures for 1990, GATT, 1991, vol. II, p. 31.

an activity in which one player's gain is always equal to other players' losses), as will be explained in more detail in Chapter 3. The percentage distribution in the table came about in a general climate of very strong growth in the volume of international trade with annual average growth rates of 5.5 per cent in the 1970s and 3.5 per cent in the 1980s, with average growth of world production over one percentage point lower.

1.3   The importance of international trade for a country

Table 1.2 provides a summary giving some idea of the importance of international trade for a number of countries; this concerns both industrialised countries and countries which are in the industrialisation phase.

The table suggests that countries with a relatively small population import more per capita than countries with a relatively large population and that, in economic terms, large countries generally export less per capita than small countries. (Thus, for example, US exports total $1,461 per head of population and Dutch exports $7,200.) This is actually logical because large countries can usually meet many of their own needs (thus, they are largely self-sufficient); small countries will much more readily be forced to obtain products elsewhere. Large countries also have a larger home sales market than small countries, and therefore need to sell less abroad.

Table 1.2 Some key data on the importance of international trade in goods and services*

Country	Population (m)	GNP ($ bn)	Imports ($ bn)	Exports ($ bn)	Imports/ capital ($)	Imports % GNP	Exports % GNP
US	249	5,200	493	364	1,980	9	7
West Germany	62	941	270	341	4,355	29	36
Japan	123	2,834	210	274	1,707	7	10
UK	57	839	198	152	3,474	24	18
Netherlands	15	223	104	108	6,933	47	48
China	1,111	422	58	52	52	14	12
Singapore	3	29	50	45	16,667	172	155
Brazil	144	338	20	34	139	6	10
South Africa	23	87	18	22	783	21	25

*The figures relate to 1989 except in the case of Brazil (1988)
Source: IMF, International Financial Statistics 1990.

1.3.1 Comments on ascertaining the openness of an economy

Export shares as shown in the last column of Table 1.2 are often taken as one of the most obvious indications of a country's economic openness. But some comments are called for here. First, a substantial proportion of the value of imports and exports is often not produced in the country from which the product (or service) is supplied. Estimates of the exports of a medium-sized, open economy like that of the Netherlands have shown that only around one third of the value of Dutch exports is added in the Netherlands. The domestic component is particularly unimportant in the case of trade which is largely transit trade: the exporting country has then added hardly any value apart from transshipment and transport activities, and in fact often functions as a port for the hinterland (only in the case of pure transit is the transaction not recorded in the trade statistics of the country of transit). Since not all the value added to the goods and services traded takes place domestically, the *export ratio* (exports/GNP) can actually be over 100 per cent as Table 1.2 shows for Singapore. This also means that countries which have similarly open economies can still be subject to foreign influence in widely differing degrees.

A second factor which can distort the picture of the openness of a country, as already noted in connection with Table 1.2, is geographical size. Compare the Netherlands and Germany, for example. If every business in the two countries were to sell its products within a 200 km radius of the production site, the Netherlands would have a much higher export ratio than Germany, in spite of the 'identical' sales pattern.[1] If we go one step further by assuming that the goods from both countries are sold throughout the world and that the sales pattern between producers in the two countries is again identical as regards distance, then we also find that remote exports represent a smaller share of Dutch than of German exports; because of its smaller geographical size, the Netherlands will export within Europe sooner than Germany, so that – by definition – the share of non-European exports is reduced. This can give the false impression that small countries neglect remote markets.

Even if we nevertheless want to illustrate the openness of a country on the basis of the ratio between imports or exports and total economic activity, there is still the question whether we should look at average or marginal entities. These can also yield a varying picture. In some countries, for example, the import sector is relatively small, but economic growth demands the use of a relatively large volume of foreign goods. In that case, the *marginal import ratio* (the change in imports per unit of increase in national product) is high, but the *average import ratio* (a country's total imports in relation to total national product) is not; the opposite can of course occur.

---

1. In practice, of course, geographical distance and 'economic' distance (in the sense of trade barriers) do not coincide, partly owing to differences in language, culture, institutions, currency and the like.

1.3.2 Structure of world trade in goods

Finally, when using export shares as a measure of the openness of an economy, one should bear in mind that it makes quite a difference to a country whether the imports consist primarily of essential raw materials and energy or whether they consist to a large extent of end products competing with goods produced at home. In the first case, imports are clearly essential to domestic production; in the second, they compete with domestic products. The latter case can cause domestic producers to increase their efficiency or to lobby the government to protect the home market against foreign competition. One important factor for exports is whether they are diversified (i.e. spread over various types of goods and/or services) or whether they are concentrated mainly on primary products. In the latter case, the exporting country is highly susceptible to changes in price and quantity on the world market (this is explained by Case study 1.2).

Case study 1.2 Illustration of exports and production structure

Export structure does vary somewhat among Western countries. Table 1.3 illustrates this: it shows export shares for a number of industrial countries broken down by category of goods.

Table 1.3 Exports by category of goods, 1988 (% of total exports)

	Agriculture*	Energy**	Other
Australia	34	18	48
Canada	19	9	72
France	17	2	81
Germany	6	1	93
Italy	7	2	91
Japan	1	–	99
New Zealand	61	1	38
UK	8	7	85
US	16	3	82

*Food, drinks, tobacco; agricultural non-food
**Mineral fuels, etc.
Source: IMF, June 1992, p. 46.

A country's export structure is of course closely linked to its production structure. In most industrial countries, one fifth to one third of production consists of manufactures.

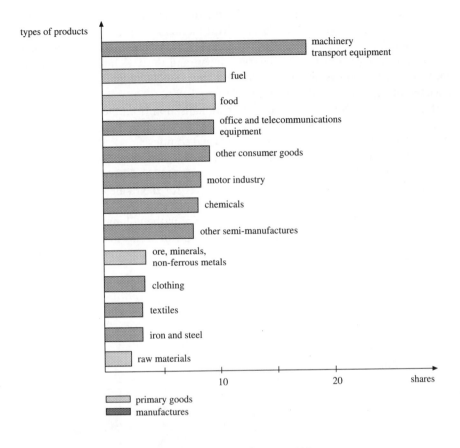

types of products

Figure 1.5 Shares of types of products in world trade, 1990
Source: GATT, *International Trade 90–91*, vol. II, p. 35.

The fact that most world trade consists primarily of manufactures is evident from Figure 1.5, showing world trade shares by product group. Figure 1.5 also shows that the largest component relates to trade in machines and transport equipment.

We see from this that, in order to judge the openness of different economies, the analysis must take account not only of the import and export shares but also other indicators such as the value added component, geographical size, marginal and average import and export ratio and the nature of import and export products.

1.4 Volume and direction of international capital flows

Among other things, *international capital flows* cover direct investment, international transactions in securities, credit and loans or gifts. With the elimination of the principal barriers to international capital movements in major Western countries such as the US and West Germany, a process of increasing internationalisation of the various financial markets emerged from the mid 1970s, particularly in OECD countries. Japan and the UK introduced similar measures at the end of the 1970s, followed by the Netherlands, Italy, France, Switzerland, Australia and New Zealand in the 1980s.

Figure 1.6 shows the increasing internationalisation from the mid 1970s and indicates gross international capital flows for the leading industrial countries broken down into direct investments, bonds and equities.

The internationalisation of the financial markets cannot be viewed in total isolation from the internationalisation of trade and industry. If companies increasingly operate on the international market for their sales, purchases and production, it is logical that the corresponding financing should also acquire an international dimension. This leads to a sharp rise in the volume of activities on the international financial markets; the operation of these markets forms the

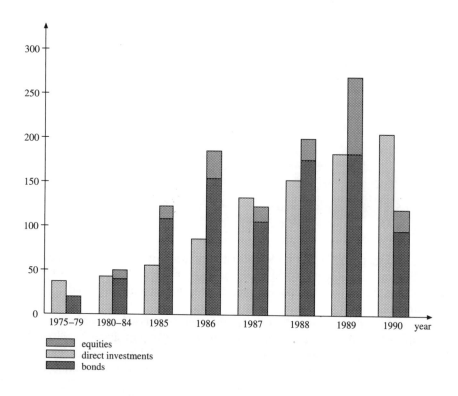

Figure 1.6 Gross capital outflows of Group of Ten and Australia, Austria and Spain (annual averages, $ billion)

Source: IMF Balance of Payments Statistics.

From: P. Turner, *Capital Flows in the 1980s: A Survey of Major Trends*, BIS Economic Papers, no. 30, April 1991, p. 23.

subject of Chapters 12 to 15. The volume of and change in international capital flows give an indication of this internationalisation of financial activities. However, in view of the problems in obtaining an accurate record of the volume of capital flows, it is difficult to say anything definite on this. (In the next Chapter and in Chapter 12 we shall go into the question of records in greater depth). Nevertheless, we can distinguish a number of medium-term trends in international capital movements, and we shall discuss these briefly below: (a) the sharp increase in direct investment; (b) the explosive increase in the volume of international investment transactions; (c) the decline in capital flows to developing countries, particularly in the 1980s; and (d) the increase in macroeconomic imbalances and their influence on capital movements.

1.4.1 Direct investments

A special category of international capital movements consists of direct investments: these are international capital transfers for the purpose of acquiring a significant degree of control over a foreign company in which capital is invested. An example might be the establishment of a foreign subsidiary by a multinational. This form of international capital movements expanded sharply in the 1980s, to a much greater extent than international trade flows. This is clearly illustrated by Figure 1.7, which uses index data on trade and direct investments.

Table 1.4 sets out the annual average value of direct investment flows from and

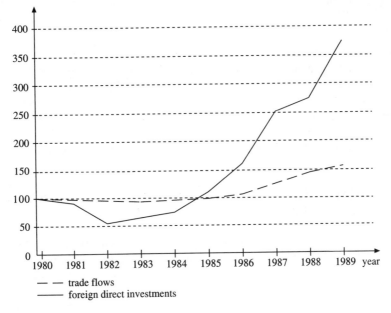

Figure 1.7 Trends in world direct investment flows and trade in goods, 1980–9
(1980 = 100)
Source: GATT, 1990, p. 41.

Table 1.4 Pattern of direct foreign investment, annual averages ($ billion)

	1976–80	1981–5	1986–90	1990	1991	1992*
Total outflow	39.8	43.6	165.9	226.0	182.2	158.5
Industrial countries	39.2	42.1	157.4	213.0	171.1	147.1
US	16.9	8.4	24.6	32.7	27.1	35.3
Japan	2.3	5.1	32.1	48.0	30.7	17.2
EU	16.9	20.8	74.4	99.4	90.9	82.5
Developing countries	0.6	1.5	8.5	13.0	11.1	11.4
Asia	0.1	1.1	7.5	11.4	9.5	10.4
Latin America	0.2	0.2	0.6	1.0	0.8	1.0
Total inflow	31.8	52.5	145.6	186.0	143.3	133.6
Industrial countries	25.2	34.9	122.6	156.2	101.8	83.9
US	9.0	19.1	52.5	45.1	11.5	−3.9
Japan	0.1	0.3	0.3	1.8	1.4	2.7
EU	13.5	12.8	54.5	86.0	68.6	70.3
Developing countries	6.6	17.6	23.0	29.8	41.5	49.7
Asia	2.1	4.9	13.3	18.6	24.0	28.0
Eastern Europe	0.0	0.0	0.1	0.3	2.4	3.3
Latin America	4.1	5.0	6.3	7.3	12.0	13.0

*Partly based on estimates
Source: IMF, Balance of Payments Statistics, miscellaneous national data; Bank for International Settlements, 63rd Annual Report, p. 90.

to industrial countries and developing countries for the period 1976–92. Up to 1990 there was a huge increase in direct investment by industrial countries. From 1991 onwards, a decline set in, due mainly to the sharp fall in foreign direct investment by Japan; this was connected with domestic financial adjustments in Japan.[2] Direct investment in the US, in particular, produced a loss (around $2 billion). The position of the US as the largest annual investor recovered in 1991. In relative terms, the US has recently been investing most heavily in Latin America.[3]

Case study 1.3 An impression of the pattern of direct investment flows

Of late, the pattern of direct investment flows into the US has been rather different from that of the direct investment outflow. Owing to liquidation of earlier

---

2. At the beginning of the 1990s, cumulative direct investment by Japan totalled over $175 billion; the total return on this was $7.7 billion in 1992.

3. In 1992, direct investment by the US in Latin America totalled over $11 billion, while the US invested $8.5 billion in the EC.

investments, this flow was actually negative in 1992. The flow of direct investment in the rest of the world remained largely steady, in spite of the recession. The bulk of this went to the EC. Mergers within Europe and the increasing presence of non-EC companies in the EC played an important part here. The UK accounted for the largest share of direct investment in Europe ($19 billion), followed by France ($16 billion); relatively little was invested in Germany and Italy ($3–4 billion each year). The high levels of 1980s direct investment in Spain and Portugal also declined. In Asia there was a shift in direct investment from South-East Asia to China, where the inflow of investment went up from $4.4 billion in 1991 to $7 billion in 1992. Direct investment in both Latin America and Eastern Europe increased sharply.

Chapter 5 goes into more detail on direct investment and the principal player concerned, the multinational corporation.

1.4.2 International portfolio investments

An investment property means an item or a right which is expected to produce a return in the future. An investor can choose from various investments such as equities, bonds, private loans, deposits, property, precious metals and works of art. In contrast to direct investment, this type of investment is not aimed at acquiring control over the property purchased: the expected return is the primary consideration. The substantial growth in the volume of international trade in recent years is vastly overshadowed by the huge growth in the volume of international portfolio investment transactions occurring mainly since the mid 1980s, as we see from Table 1.5.

Table 1.5 shows international portfolio investment transactions over a number of years. The table gives the annual average investment flows from and to

Table 1.5 Portfolio capital movements in industrial countries, annual averages ($ billion)

	1976–80	1981–5	1986–90	1990	1991	1992*
Total outflow	15.0	60.6	185.0	152.8	274.0	238.0
US	5.3	6.5	13.6	28.8	45.0	48.6
Japan	3.4	25.0	85.9	39.7	74.3	34.4
UK	2.3	13.6	26.1	29.2	51.6	47.3
Other EU-countries	3.8	10.4	44.4	47.2	69.2	92.3
Total inflow	31.9	77.8	184.6	154.9	374.6	308.5
US	5.2	9.4	44.7	–0.9	51.2	65.0
Japan	5.1	12.6	26.9	34.7	115.3	8.2
UK	2.3	3.5	22.1	9.4	28.7	29.6
Other EU-countries	9.7	18.5	57.3	85.0	123.6	168.9

*Partly based on estimates
Source: IMF, Balance of Payments Statistics; miscellaneous national data; Bank for International Settlements, 1993b, p. 91.

industrial countries for the period 1976–92. The first point we notice is that growth in the volume of the inflow and outflow of indirect investment has been all but explosive, particularly since the beginning of the 1980s, and particularly from and to the 'other countries' category. The second obvious point is that the figures can vary quite significantly from year to year; Japan's position is particularly striking here: in 1991 it still had large inflows and outflows while a year later, according to the table, they had largely dried up.

Detailed information not apparent from the table further reinforces the picture of sharp fluctuations in international portfolio investment transactions. This is illustrated by some figures which became available in the early 1990s. In this period the continent of Europe accounted for over half the total inflow of indirect investments; bond transactions predominated, while net investments in securities fell sharply. Portfolio investments in Germany and France increased, in contrast to Italy, Spain and Sweden. On balance non-residents sold Japanese bonds because of the low rate of interest on them, while uncertainty about the Japanese equities market impeded net share purchases. These two factors together led to the virtual disappearance of the inflow of indirect investment capital into Japan. Although the figures on developing countries are incomplete, there are clear signs that portfolio investments in those countries, and particularly in South-East Asia and Latin America, remained substantial.

One effect of the increasing investment in foreign securities and the frequently high level of trading in international securities is that transactions relating to investments sometimes greatly exceed those relating to trade. As we can see from Figure 1.8, this was already true for the US, Japan and the UK in the mid 1980s, and subsequently for continental Europe.

1.4.3 Declining capital flows to developing countries

A feature of international capital flows in recent years has been that, owing to the debt problems of the developing countries, the supply of capital to those countries stagnated from the beginning of the 1980s. In the middle of the 1970s there had been a sharp increase in the gross supply of capital via a process of channelling balance of payments surpluses, primarily from OPEC countries. This took place in the form of loans to developing countries. When a world economic recession set in soon afterwards, combined with a sharp increase in interest rates, these countries were faced with financial problems as export earnings fell and the interest burden increased, laying the foundation for the subsequent debt problem. This occurred in the 1980s when a large number of mainly Latin American developing countries were confronted by a situation in which they could no longer meet their interest and redemption obligations. The ensuing shock to the financial world led to great caution in private international lending to developing countries. Figures 1.9 and 1.10 show the trend in total gross and net capital flows to developing countries during the 1980s. We see that, particularly during the first half of the 1980s, there was a decline in the total capital flow to these countries, a trend which was even stronger if we confine

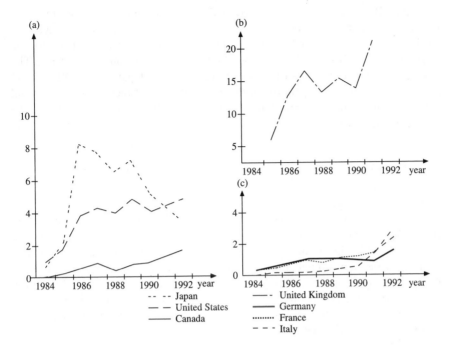

Figure 1.8 Gross international portfolio transactions many times as high as trade transactions
Source: IMF, Balance of Payments Statistics, national figures (BIS), various volumes.

ourselves to the real, net flow. In 1984–5 there was actually a net outflow of funds. Without the contribution from the official financial institutions and governments, this decline would have been even more dramatic. In the latter half of the 1980s there was a degree of consolidation, due mainly to a revival in direct investment and an increase in development aid and official loans to these countries.

1.4.4 Macro-economic imbalances

One explanation for the very sharp increase in the volume of international capital movements between the industrialised countries lies in the increasing macro-economic imbalances between the main economic blocs in the 1980s. Thus, the US faced persistent, substantial deficits on the balance of payments current account. These contrasted with equally persistent surpluses for Japan and Germany (until reunification in 1989). Since a current account deficit occurs if, in total, the country in question spends more than it produces – the opposite situation producing a surplus – then, if the balances are persistent and large, we can rightly refer to an imbalance. The effect of this on international capital movements is that deficits must, by definition, be financed by attracting capital

27

from abroad (see also Chapter 2); by definition, surpluses are offset by a net outflow of capital to other countries. The Japanese balance of payments surpluses of the 1980s show the extent to which these can lead to the establishment of historically enormous capital assets in other countries. The cumulative total net outflow of long-term capital from Japan from 1981 to 1991 was at least $550 to 600 billion! (In the first half of 1991 there was a net capital inflow again for the first time, totalling about $10 billion, as a result of the Japanese stock market crisis.)

1.5   Foreign exchange markets and exchange rates

All foreign exchange transactions resulting from international trade in goods and services and international demand for and supply of financial assets converge on the *foreign exchange market*, where national currencies are exchanged for one another. Since banks conduct the foreign exchange conversions associated with the said transactions on behalf of domestic and foreign customers, the banks are the main players on the foreign exchange market (Chapter 13 has more information on the operation of the foreign exchange markets and the role of the various market players). The volume of actual foreign exchange transactions is dominated by those between the banks themselves, so that the greater part of the

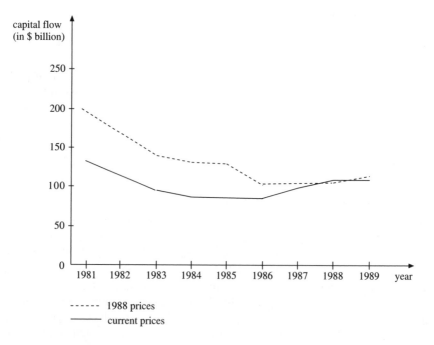

Figure 1.9 Total gross capital flows to developing countries
Source: OECD, 1990a, 1990b.

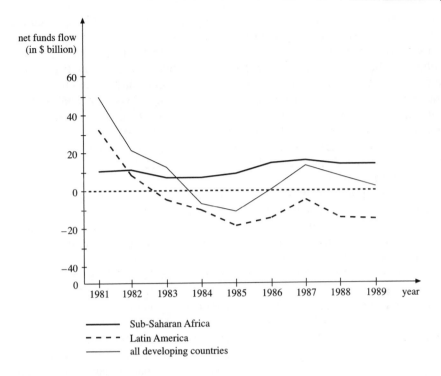

Figure 1.10 Net capital flows to developing countries
Source: OECD, 1990b.

foreign exchange market is an interbank market. The leading foreign exchange markets are London, New York and Tokyo. The foreign exchange departments of banks maintain continuous contact with one another and with these foreign exchange markets.

The price at which one currency is exchanged for another is called the *exchange rate*. This is the ratio (relative price) which indicates how much domestic currency has to be paid for one unit of foreign currency, e.g. the value to a Dutch person of a dollar expressed in guilders is the current exchange rate of the dollar. International trade in goods and services and financial transactions are shown on the balance of payments of the countries in question. The way in which the transactions are recorded, classified and defined will be discussed in detail in the next chapter; the relevant question here is: what is the quantitative importance of the various types of international transactions for the foreign exchange markets. Although the balance of payments entries (see also Chapter 2) can give an indication of this, they cannot provide the definitive answer. One reason why this is so is that transactions in which the foreign exchange acquired is replaced by a different foreign currency are not entered on the final balance of payments summary because equal debit and credit items cancel one another out.

Moreover, the speed of dealing and the large number of operators on the

29

foreign exchange markets make it virtually impossible to keep an accurate record. That is why monetary authorities use occasional surveys of international banks involved in foreign exchange transactions to try to ascertain the total volume of business on international foreign exchange markets. In 1992, 1989 and at the end of 1986, central banks and other monetary authorities checked the transactions of foreign exchange market operators. In 1986 only 4 countries took part in this survey; in 1989 it included 21. Some countries of economic importance were not covered. However, in 1992 all countries with important foreign exchange markets – 26 in total – did take part in the survey. Table 1.6 gives the estimated daily turnover in billion dollars for the largest foreign exchange markets.

The table shows how massive is the scale and the growth of turnover on the foreign exchange markets (particularly the growth of the Tokyo foreign exchange market up to 1992). The Bank for International Settlements (BIS: this is the central banks' umbrella organisation, located in Basle) estimated the total daily turnover on all foreign exchange markets together at $620 billion in April 1989 and $967 billion in April 1992. Thus, in three years, the volume of business on the international exchange markets expanded by over 40 per cent. Although the growth percentage is high, it is slightly lower than in the period from March 1986 to April 1989, when growth doubled. If we convert daily turnover into annual turnover on the foreign exchange markets, it comes to roughly 75 times as much as the total volume of world trade (around $7,090 billion in 1990). International capital transactions obviously dominate the international exchange markets; in comparison, trade transactions play a minor role.

The figures in Table 1.7 give the total volume of foreign exchange transactions per currency in 1989 and 1992, in absolute terms and in percentages.

Table 1.6 Daily turnover on the principal foreign exchange markets ($ billion)

Country	March 1986	April 1989	April 1992
UK	90	187	300
US	59	129	192
Japan	48	115	128
Singapore	–	55	74
Switzerland	–	57	68
Hong Kong	–	49	61
Germany	–	–	57
France	–	26	35
Australia	–	30	30
Canada	9	15	22
Total			967

Source: Group of Thirty (1985, p. 11); *Financial Times*, 14 September 1989; BIS, March 1993.

Table 1.7 Gross daily turnover on the foreign exchange markets in a number of selected currencies ($ billion, %)

Currency	April 1989		April 1992		
	Daily volume	Share	Daily volume	Share	Change
US dollar	838	90	1,114	83	−7
Deutschmark	247	27	544	38	11
Yen	253	27	313	24	−3
Sterling	138	15	185	14	−1
Swiss franc	na	na	116	9	na
French franc	na	na	51	4	na
Canadian dollar	na	na	44	3	na
ECU	8	1	40	3	2
Australian dollar	na	na	32	2	na
Remainder	380	40	269	19	−21
Total	1,864	200	2,707	200	0

Source: Bank for International Settlements (BIS), February 1990 and March 1993.

Any foreign exchange transaction in one currency implies a corresponding transaction in another currency. The total daily volume of all transactions in the individual currencies ($2,707 billion in April 1992) is therefore double the gross daily turnover on the foreign exchange markets ($1,354 billion in April 1992).

Table 1.7 shows that the dollar has remained by far the most important currency for foreign exchange market transactions, in spite of the 7 per cent decline over the past three years. Although the dollar is still the leading currency in foreign exchange transactions, its position varies from one market to another. Thus, in 1992, 98 per cent of foreign exchange transactions in Canadian dollars involved the US dollar, while the figure was 93 per cent in the case of Australian dollars and 87 per cent in the case of the Japanese yen. The dollar holds a less prominent position in exchange transactions with European currencies. Thus, it accounted for 70 per cent of transactions with sterling, 64 per cent with the German mark and 60 per cent with the French franc. Table 1.7 shows that the German mark has confirmed its position as the second most important currency. The strong position of the mark has clearly been at the expense of the dollar, and to a lesser extent the yen.

The figures on the currencies in which international invoicing takes place present a rather different picture. Figure 1.11 shows the proportion of the various currencies in export invoices in 1987–8. During this period, the US, Germany, Japan, the UK and France together generated 54 per cent of total exports. As we can see from the graph, over 45 per cent of these total exports was denominated in dollars, almost 25 per cent in marks, and about 10 per cent in French francs and sterling, while under 7 per cent were invoiced in Japanese yen. These figures reflect the differences in the degree to which a country's international trade is invoiced in its own currency. The graph also gives the share of the national currency in national import and export invoices. Exports amounted to 96 per cent for the US, over 80 per cent for Germany, almost 60 per cent for France and the United Kingdom and around 35 per cent for Japan. Only 13 per cent of Japanese imports were invoiced in the country's own currency. The other extreme is the 0.5 per cent of US imports denominated in dollars.

Thus, the yen is used far less for international invoicing than one might expect on the basis of the volume of business on international exchange markets. The reasons are: Japan exports a relatively large amount to the US, a country where a relatively high proportion of imports are traditionally invoiced in its own currency; Japanese banks charge relatively high transaction costs for export financing; as part of their marketing strategy, Japanese exporters prefer to fix the price of goods in the currency of the importing country. In addition, over half of Japan's imports consist of primary products and semi-manufactures, goods whose value is traditionally expressed in dollars and sterling.

Nevertheless, international use of currencies other than the dollar has been constantly increasing in recent years. The German mark, in particular, and to a lesser extent the Japanese yen, are playing an ever more important part in international payments. We saw from Table 1.1 that the economic positions of

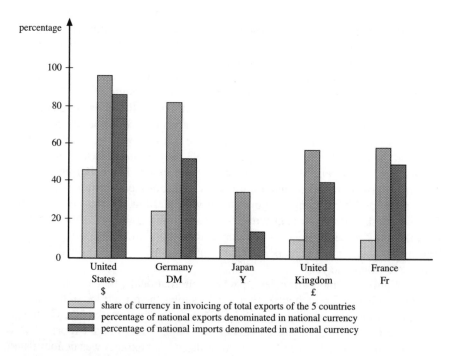

Figure 1.11 International use of currencies in invoicing, 1987–8 (%)
Source: Tavlas, 1991, Table 8.2; Tavlas and Ozeki, 1992, Table 17.

countries in industrial exports have shifted; similar shifts are taking place on the foreign exchange markets. This means that responsibility for world monetary stability is increasingly being transferred away from the US. The scope for risk-spreading by both official bodies and private investors has also increased. In addition, the existence of several competing international currencies can undermine monetary policy discipline because portfolio holders can more readily sell off the currencies of countries with bad economic policies. However, the other side of the coin is that the substitution of international currencies demands more coordination between the countries of the currencies concerned, and can lead to unexpected adjustment burdens for those countries.

Thus, the internationalisation of the markets in goods and services as well as financial transactions is very important for a better understanding of the factors which determine exchange rate fluctuations (we shall go into this in more detail in Chapter 13). It seems plausible that, in a world with such extensive international capital mobility, it is becoming ever more difficult to stabilise exchange rates by policy measures, especially if we compare total activity on the foreign exchange markets with the size of the central banks' monetary reserves, the buffer stocks which can be used to influence exchange rate movements. To give some idea, the total stock of monetary reserves (excluding gold) was $982.5 billion at the end of 1992, roughly equal to *one day's* turnover on the various foreign exchange markets in 1992.

In the post-war period it was possible for a world monetary system with more or less fixed exchange rates to be successfully maintained until the early 1970s, when international capital movements were far less extensive than now (see Chapter 13). At that time, most countries were willing and able to gear their policy to the maintenance of fixed (but adjustable) exchange rates and the monetary authorities supported that aim, e.g. by actively intervening on the foreign exchange markets themselves, if necessary. That policy has now been abandoned and replaced by the maintenance of fixed exchange rates on a limited, regional scale (e.g. between countries in the European Union, EU; see Chapter 18) with no more than a certain degree of strategic intervention by the central banks beyond those areas. This intervention is aimed, to some extent, at stabilising exchange rates, a policy often referred to as 'leaning against the wind' or 'managed floating'; see also Chapter 16).

1.6 Summary

This chapter outlined the increasing internationalisation of the business environment using a variety of statistical material. This shows that the international commodity and capital markets have become an important factor in the world economy, and thus also for the entrepreneur.

The first point to emerge from the figures is that the volume of world trade grew faster than that of world GNP in the post-war period. The growth of international flows of goods, which have more and more the character of intra-industry trade, is in turn lagging behind the expansion of direct investment and pales into insignificance compared to the growth in the volume of business on foreign exchange markets. As regards trade patterns, we also notice that most trade takes place between the industrialised countries themselves.

In the case of capital flows, a number of different trends can be identified in the 1980s. First, strong growth of capital flows, due partly to tendencies towards liberalisation and deregulation in international capital movements. There was an explosive increase from the beginning of the 1980s in both international portfolio investment and direct investment. This period also saw major external imbalances between the principal trade blocs. Finally, a striking feature was that private capital flows to developing countries slumped in the 1980s as a result of the debt crisis, in spite of an increase in official flows to these countries. Last, there was a general tendency for the dollar to lose its former dominant role on the foreign exchange markets. As economic positions of power shifted, so the international use of other currencies such as the yen and the DM increased.

This chapter has focused on the globalisation of economies. Chapter 2 will discuss the recording and definition of the various types of transaction; subsequent chapters will consider why countries are opening their borders and why businesses are operating on an increasingly international basis.

Bibliography

Bank for International Settlements (1993a), *Central Bank Survey of Foreign Exchange Market Activity in April 1992*, Basle, March.

Bank for International Settlements (1993b), *63rd Annual Report, 1st April 1992–31st March 1993*, Basle, 14th June.

GATT, General Agreement on Tariffs and Trade (1990), *International Trade 89–90*, vol. I, Geneva.

GATT, General Agreement on Tariffs and Trade (1991), *International Trade 90–91*, vol. II, Geneva.

Goldstein, M., P. Isard, P.R. Masson, and M.P. Taylor (1992), *Policy Issues in the Evolving International Monetary System*, International Monetary Fund, Occasional Paper 96, June.

Greenaway, D. and C. Miller (1986), *The Economics of Intra-industry Trade*, Basil Blackwell.

Grilli, E. and E. Sassoon (1990), *The New Protectionist Wave*, Macmillan.

Hermes, C.L.M. (1992), *De internationale schuldencrisis* [The international debt crisis], Wolters-Noordhoff.

International Monetary Fund (1990), *Direction of Trade Statistics, Yearbook*, Washington DC.

International Monetary Fund (1991), *Determinants and Systemic Consequences of International Capital Flows, A Study by the Research Department of the International Monetary Fund*, Occasional Paper 77, Washington DC, March.

Maddison, A. (1989), *The World Economy in the Twentieth Century*, Paris, OECD.

OECD (1990a), *Development Co-operation, 1990 Report*, Paris, OECD, December.

OECD (1990b), *Financing and External Debt of Developing Countries, 1989 Survey*, Paris, OECD.

Tavlas, G.S. (1991), *On the International Use of Currencies: The Case of the Deutsche Mark*, Princeton Essays in International Finance, no. 181, Princeton, New Jersey: International Finance Section, Department of Economics, Princeton University, March.

Tavlas, G.S. and Y. Ozeki (1992), *The Internationalization of Currencies: An Appraisal of the Japanese Yen*, International Monetary Fund, Occasional Paper 90, Washington DC: International Monetary Fund, January.

Turner, P. (1991), *Capital Flows in the 1980s: A Survey of Major Trends*, BIS Economic Papers, no. 30, April.

2 The balance of payments

2.1 Introduction

In Chapter 1 we saw that national economies are becoming increasingly intertwined. For the purpose of statistical processing, all economic transactions between residents in a particular country and the rest of the world – and thus international transactions as described in Chapter 1 – are systematically recorded on the balance of payments. Thus, analysis of the balance of payments can provide information on an economy's relations with other countries and hence an impression of a country's economic position. The balance of payments is a summary of all international transactions by a country over a particular period, usually one year, the various transactions being classified according to a logical system. The balance of payments falls broadly into two sub-balance sheets: the current account recording mainly transactions associated with international trade in goods and services, and the capital account showing international financial transactions. Economic activities relevant to the current accounts form the focus of Chapters 3 to 11; transactions relating to the capital account (with the exception of direct investments) form the subject of the second part of the book, Chapters 12 to 18.

For a proper balance of payments analysis, it is necessary to know how transactions are recorded on the balance of payments and what system is used. This chapter is concerned mainly with the method of recording, the balance of payments classification and the definition of the transactions. In spite of the uniform definitions and recording systems, it is in practice quite tricky to interpret the information supplied by the balance of payments. Balance of payments comparisons between different countries and the aggregation of balance of payments figures on several countries should therefore be treated with caution.

It is evident from Case study 2.1 that the balance of payments tells us more than just the figures. The case study analyses the trend in Japan's balance of payments over the decade 1981–91. We shall see that a country's balance of payments position does not exist in isolation but can prompt reactions by other countries. A balance of payments also provides an indication of the economic position of the country concerned. The case study deals with the current account balance on the balance of payments and how this relates to long-term capital flows from or to a country. A number of new concepts (which are printed in italics at first mention) are introduced in the case study and will be dealt with in this chapter.

Case study 2.1 The trend in Japan's balance of payments, 1981–91

Figure 2.1 shows the current account balance and the net capital outflow from Japan for the years 1981–91. The balance of these two quantities together is also given, and indicated as the *basic balance*.

What does the figure tell us? First, it is evident that the Japanese balance of payments produced a rapidly increasing *current account surplus* during 1981–7. This means that Japan was exporting increasingly more goods and services than it imported. In the latter half of the 1980s this surplus did decline somewhat, but was restored in the early 1990s. It will be no surprise that this systematic surplus gave rise to some criticism, particularly from countries with lasting deficits such as the US. Japan was accused, rightly or wrongly, of aggressive export competition and the systematic exclusion of competing imports. Here it should be borne in mind that, as we shall explain in more detail, a surplus for one country in the

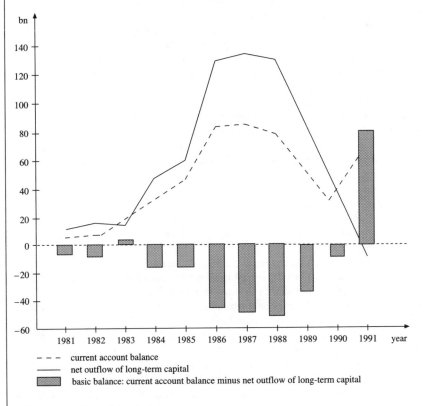

- - - current account balance
——— net outflow of long-term capital
▨ basic balance: current account balance minus net outflow of long-term capital

Figure 2.1 Japan's basic balance
Source: Nomura, Bank of Japan.

world balance of payments figures means, by definition, a corresponding deficit for the rest of the world. Thus, on that basis one could state that a country with systematic current account surpluses is condemning the rest of the world to equally large systematic deficits; and the converse is equally valid.

Second, the graph shows that the current account surplus was associated with a net outflow of capital resulting from the acquisition of long-term foreign assets by Japan. This means that the current account surplus during the 1980s led to a historically massive volume of assets being built up abroad. Over the entire period from 1981 to 1991, the net outflow of Japanese capital resulting from long-term capital transactions was all of $550 to $600 billion!

If we combine the above two trends, we immediately see one of the characteristics of the balance of payments system, namely that current account surpluses, by definition, lead to an equivalent net accumulation of assets in the form of claims on other countries. This can be expressed, for example, by banks increasing their net *foreign assets* (see also below) or by the central bank increasing its holdings of foreign exchange reserves. If we confine ourselves to long-term capital transactions, the discrepancy between the current account balance and the net inflow and outflow of monetary capital from or to other countries is shown by the basic balance sheet. For Japan, the net outflow of capital in terms of long-term capital transactions was, roughly speaking, actually larger than the current account surplus, giving rise to deficits on the basic balance. The principal reason was that Japanese investors were increasingly investing their money abroad, owing to the liberalisation of Japanese capital exports and the extremely low interest rate in Japan.

Third, the graph shows that in the late 1980s and early 1990s a change took place in various respects: the net outflow of capital to other countries abruptly disappeared and actually turned into a substantial inflow in 1991. An important factor here was that the interest rate in Japan had risen sharply, owing to a drastic revision of monetary policy in 1987. The aim of this revision was to burst the bubbles which had been caused by the previously low interest rate and to try to bring about a reduction in Japanese investment abroad aimed at strengthening domestic investment capacity. This was done by a *tighter monetary policy* resulting in a higher domestic interest rate. The effects were dramatic. The very high share prices slumped by over 70 per cent at the end of 1992. Much the same happened on the property market, too.

Naturally, this also affected Japan's foreign investments; they declined because Japanese banks and businesses needed to strengthen their liquidity position, which had been impaired by the share and property crisis. The Japanese banks also had to prepare for the new international regulations on *solvency standards*. As a result of all these developments, Japan ceased to be a net capital exporter.

Since economic growth also stagnated in Japan at the end of the 1980s, certainly in comparison with previous years, the expansion of imports remained limited so that the current account balance improved again significantly in 1991 (and in subsequent years as well). This combined with the end of the acquisition of foreign long-term capital led to a major change in the basic balance, which suddenly showed a considerable surplus in 1991.

The basic balance has a major influence on the exchange rate of the country in question, the idea being that if the balance is negative, as was the case in Japan in the 1980s, the country is a net purchaser of foreign currency in exchange for its own currency on account of its investments (capital export). This depresses its own exchange rate. When the basic balance was reversed in 1991, various experts therefore expected this to lead to the eventual appreciation of the yen. And they were right.

The first point to emerge from this case study is that international transactions and the domestic economy are indissolubly linked. For instance, interest rate policy affects exchange rates; excessive foreign direct and portfolio investment can influence the domestic economic situation. It is also clear that a country's international transactions can have international repercussions. In the case study, we saw that the Japanese current account surplus automatically means a current account deficit for the rest of the world. The US, in particular, had a current account deficit during the 1980s. Moreover, Japan's current account surplus was accompanied by a negative basic balance (for a definition, see the first paragraph of Case study 2.1). It appears that the US current account deficit was (in part) financed by Japanese capital.

We must exercise caution in general in interpreting the current account balance on the balance of payments. A current account surplus is sometimes taken as evidence of a strong competitive position, but it may also imply trade restrictions or low growth of imports due to a sluggish domestic economy. Conversely, a deficit is often seen as a sign that a country is living beyond its means; but it can also mean that there is strong growth potential, so that other countries are glad to grant net credit. In the end, this produces a current account deficit and a capital account surplus. Finally, it should be remembered that governments often try to influence international trade and financial flows.

The case study prompts a number of questions, such as:

1. How are the various economic activities leading to transactions with other countries recorded on the balance of payments?
2. What is the system of the balance of payments and how are the various transactions arranged?
3. When can we say that the balance of payments is in equilibrium or in disequilibrium?
4. How is a balance of payments deficit financed?
5. How can one interpret the various sub-balances on the balance of payments?

We shall consider these questions in this chapter.

2.2 Balance of payments accounting

The *balance of payments* collates all international transactions between persons, businesses and institutions in one country with those outside by type and size (we refer here to 'residents' and 'non-residents'). The figures are normally recorded quarterly and annually. The term 'balance of payments' can be confusing because it is not an account of liabilities and assets (i.e. stocks) at a given time, as in the case of a company balance sheet, but a record of international flows during a particular period based on payments for trade and goods and services provided, and international capital movements.

The basic philosophy in balance of payments accounting is that a distinction is made between current or income transactions and capital or asset transactions. Although the dividing line between the two categories is not always equally clear, it is perhaps possible to visualise it as follows: any monthly income which you receive and your rental payment can be regarded as current activity; any balance on current income and expenditure can contribute to a change in the level of your assets. On the other hand, purchase of a house or sale of your securities must be seen as an activity aimed at changing the composition of your assets. Thus, in the first case there is a flow which may contribute to a change in the level of your assets; in the second case, the composition of your assets is changed.

This distinction also applies to the classification of international transactions on the balance of payments. International trade in goods and services is treated as an income activity; this also applies to payment for factors of production made available (labour and capital).[1] These are called current transactions. Such transactions are recorded on the balance of payments *current account*. They are transactions concerned with the day-to-day (hence 'current') formation, distribution and spending of the national income, in contrast to all international capital transactions in the sphere of capital investment, which are also known as capital transactions. Obviously, such transactions are recorded on the balance of payments, *capital account*.

An economic transaction normally entails a two-sided obligation, except in the case of unilateral income or capital transfers (these concepts will be discussed below). One party supplies the product, service or financial assets;[2] the other party provides the sum of money to be paid. The corollary is that there are two rights: the right to supply of the product, etc. on the one hand and the right to payment on the other. For balance of payments accounting, this means that – in principle – each transaction is recorded twice.

---

1. Regular, unilateral income transfers form an exception. Although these take place under the heading of income, they only influence the level of available national income, not the national income earned.

2. A financial asset confers the right to a future payment. Examples are: bonds, equities, treasury certificates or loans.

Say a Dutch company sells computer parts worth $10,000 to a company in the US; the US pays in dollars. In that case the export of computer parts is entered on the credit side of the Dutch current account; the payment is shown on the debit side of the Dutch balance of payments capital account.

What do we mean by credit or debit items and what do these items imply for the current and capital accounts? In the case of the current account, each transaction which contributes to domestic income is entered as a credit and each transaction leading to an increase in foreign income is shown as a debit. In the first case, domestic claims on other countries increase: a credit entry (+). In the second case, foreigners claims on the domestic economy increase: a debit entry (–). The sale of computer parts means that the Netherlands acquires a claim on the US and national income increases; thus, there is a credit entry. In the case of the capital balance, the opposite applies, namely credit items (capital imports)[3] relate either to an increase in foreign claims on the domestic economy or a reduction in domestic claims on other countries. In the case of debit items (capital exports), there is a decline in foreign claims on the domestic economy or an increase in domestic claims on other countries. The payment for the computer parts means an increase in foreign exchange and thus an increase in claims on other countries (–).

The system of capital account entries is particularly liable to cause confusion. A simple rule in recording transactions on both the current and the capital account is that *inflows* are recorded as debits ('–') regardless of whether they consist of goods, services or asset titles, and *outflows* are shown as credits ('+'). The export of computer parts is an outflow of goods; the payment for those parts is an inflow of foreign currency. A second rule for distinguishing between debit and credit entries is to look at the effects of a transaction on the foreign exchange market. Any transaction (outflow) which creates demand for the country's own currency on the foreign exchange market and a supply of foreign exchange (another country's currency) means a '+' item on the balance of payments. Any transaction (inflow) which creates a supply of the country's own currency on the foreign exchange market and demand for foreign currency leads to a '–' item. In order to cash the payment for the computer parts, which was in dollars, the Dutch company will probably want to exchange the dollars received against guilders. This generates demand for domestic currency and a supply of foreign currency.

A second example: say a German citizen buys bonds in the US. This is shown on the German balance of payments as an increase in foreign assets owned by a resident (capital export).[4] This acquisition of the bond (an asset) is entered as a debit (–) on the German capital balance under (long-term) international investment transactions. The payment is recorded as a credit.

---

3. Capital imports exist because the credit items on the capital account mean that there is an inflow of liquid assets from abroad.

4. Purchase of the bond means an inflow of foreign assets. The term *capital export* refers to the monetary capital that the other country receives as a result of the sale of assets.

The heading of the German balance of payments under which the said payment is shown depends on the method of payment. The German can pay for the bonds by reducing his dollar credit balance at an American bank or by buying dollars from a German bank (the bank's dollar credit balance then declines). In both cases, the dollar credit balances (claims on other countries) are reduced and the payment leads to the supply of foreign currency. This gives rise to a '+' on the balance of payments. If the German finances the transaction with a foreign loan, then the loan is entered as a credit (+) under long-term capital transactions. As a general rule, except where otherwise stated, the contra entry is always shown under changes in foreign currency reserves held by banks. Thus, in this case it is a credit entry (+) of these foreign currencies into a dollar *supply* on the foreign exchange markets.

Depending on the nature of the international transaction, it is recorded either by customs, by the private banking system or by the central bank. The latter is also responsible for overall supervision. The records naturally contain errors and omissions because of the varying sources of the underlying figures. This explains why the book-keeping system which the balance of payments in fact constitutes has to be corrected in places with the help of the 'balance of statistical variations', indicated in international publications as 'errors and omissions'. In addition, people sometimes succeed in preventing certain transactions from being recorded by the aforesaid bodies. This seems to occur mainly in the case of international capital transactions and the ensuing flow of revenue from such investments (e.g. for the purpose of tax evasion or avoidance).

As we have said, the good thing about balance of payments accounting is that it offers a periodical summary which is as complete as possible on the broad range of international economic transactions. It will also be clear that, with the exception of exchanges in kind, for instance, every transaction shown on the balance of payments corresponds, in principle, to a transaction on the foreign exchange market: once a product or asset is traded with another country, sooner or later one will have to exchange one's own currency for foreign currency, or vice versa. This implies a transaction on the foreign exchange market, i.e. foreign currency is bought or sold. Thus, over time, the balance of payments also offers information, albeit indirectly, on developments on the foreign exchange markets.

It would be a misconception to think that both parties involved in an international transaction have to conduct a corresponding foreign exchange transaction. In principle, only one of the two parties needs to do so. Which of the parties takes charge of that foreign exchange transaction is naturally a matter for mutual agreement. For example, if a German businessman sells a machine to a French businessman, they may agree that the Frenchman pays in francs; the German then has to exchange the francs for German marks. The parties may equally agree that the Frenchman pays in German marks, in which case the Frenchman has to conduct the foreign exchange transaction. Both conversions have the same effect on the foreign exchange market, which is a genuine world market. The situation is different if, as often happens, settlement takes place in a third currency such as the dollar. Both parties then have to conduct a foreign exchange market transaction, unless they both hold a dollar account, in which case neither of the parties need conduct a foreign exchange transaction.

Obviously, the significance of the balance of payments for economic analysis depends on the way in which the vast maze of international transactions taking place every year is classified and recorded. Apart from that, the timing of the entries can also differ in two ways, namely: on a *cash basis* (transactions are recorded at the time of payment); on a *transactions basis* (transactions are recorded when the product in question is transferred to the new owner abroad; in the case of a service, this means the time of performance). The commonest system is recording on a transactions basis. The International Monetary Fund (IMF) has published a *Balance of Payments Manual* containing recommended concepts, definitions and rules. Western countries generally keep to these guidelines, and non-Western countries are increasingly adhering to them when classifying international transactions.

2.3 The balance of payments classification

An outline of the balance of payments classification is shown in Figure 2.2 on page 46; an example of a balance of payments layout is given in Table 2.1 on page 47. Both give an idea of how the balance of payments is actually drawn up. Before discussing the balance of payments system, we shall first briefly examine the various sub-balances and items.

2.3.1 The current account

In the balance of payments, current transactions are generally divided into categories according to the nature of what is supplied, distinguishing first of all between trade in goods and trade in services. In 1990 the value of goods exported worldwide was $3,485 billion and services $810 billion. Trade in services includes, for example, travel, transport, technical services, works contracts, telecommunications, financial services such as banking and insurance, building, business services (advertising, accountancy, etc). From the economic point of view, there is no essential difference between services and goods, but in practice it is harder to keep a proper record of international services than of trade in goods. One reason is that, in contrast to physical goods, services are intangible and therefore cannot be observed crossing the frontier. That is one reason why it is still usual when ascertaining the various balance of payments balances to include the *trade balance* as well. This relates only to trade in goods. When ascertaining the balance of trade in goods and services, we refer to the *goods and services balance*.

Apart from this breakdown, an income account is often distinguished in current account transactions, with a further division into factor or investment income and unilateral transfer income. The *factor income account* records remuneration for imported and exported factors of production, labour and capital (e.g. *investment income* or personal earned income). Interest and dividend appear on the investment income account because they are considered payments for the services of capital that is 'working' abroad. It is important to distinguish these payments from the original investment itself, which appears in the capital account. The *unilateral transfer account* shows the international transfer of income not earmarked for any direct, identifiable purpose, such as gifts or contributions to international organisations. This covers income transfers in the form of development aid, gifts or transfers by foreign workers to their family, and so on.[5] Sometimes the difference between supplies of goods and the rest of the current account items is known as the difference between *visible* (goods) and *invisible transactions*. Thus, the latter covers not only services but also international transfers of factor or investment income and unilateral transfer income.

2.3.2 The capital account

The first distinction in relation to the capital account is between changes in the composition of capital in the *non-monetary* sector, items 5 and 6a in Figure 2.2, and the *monetary sector*, items 6b and official reserves in the figure. The monetary sector means banks, including the central bank. Capital in the non-monetary sector is owned by the government and the private sector (pension funds, institutional investors and other private individuals).

Another distinction relating to the capital account is that between long-term and short-term capital transactions.

2.3.3 Long-term capital transactions

Long-term capital transactions in the private sector cover international transactions in securities, for example, and long-term loans (this usually means transactions relating to financial assets with an original contractual maturity of more than one year). Direct investment is also included. This last category of long-term capital transactions is usually expressly distinguished from other long-term international capital transactions in the private sector, which are referred to in general as *portfolio investments*.[6] We refer to such investments in securities (equities and bonds) if the investor is interested only in the expected return. Such investments are made not only by the private and public sector, but also by banks. In contrast, *direct investment* takes place where the transaction with

---

5. In so far as unilateral transfers constitute an investment, they come under the capital account and are then called *unilateral capital transfers*. However, the distinction between unilateral capital transfers and unilateral income transfers is vague. Examples of unilateral capital transfers are non-consumer development aid or war damage compensation.

6. As already mentioned in connection with the current account, capital account transactions also include unilateral capital transfers.

another country is intended to confer control over the enterprise in which one has invested. For that purpose, the foreign acquisition must concern a substantial proportion of the capital in the company in which one is investing. Thus, foreign direct investment mainly means situations in which firms with an international outlook take over a large part of a foreign company (e.g. by buying a substantial proportion of the shares) or set up a foreign branch. It is not always easy to distinguish between the two types of international capital transactions on the basis of the available data. Sometimes, substantial blocks of shares in foreign companies are bought for portfolio investment reasons, i.e. without the investor having any ambition to become involved in the internal management of the business. Another time, a company might acquire only a small stake in a foreign business, so that statistically there is no question of any direct investment (the border line is normally defined as ownership of at least a quarter of the share capital). Yet the investing company may in fact intend in that case to take over the management of the company, e.g. by sending in managers on secondment or by other business arrangements. The central bank usually tries to find out, by means of interviews, if and when any direct investment is involved.

2.3.4 Short-term capital transactions

Short term capital includes investments in treasury bills, commercial paper, bank deposits, and commercial credits. The (private) banking system has a special position in capital transactions because it holds the private foreign exchange reserves. Changes in the level of these reserves can *affect the money supply*, as we shall see later, and are thus relevant to monetary policy. All banking transactions which affect the level of *foreign exchange* held are generally recorded as short-term capital transactions by banks. Foreign exchange consists of foreign bank notes, demand deposits with foreign banks and other claims on foreign countries which can readily be converted into foreign bank demand deposits. The banks will always keep a reserve of such liquid assets so that they can conduct the desired international transactions at any time. The foreign exchange reserves held by commercial banks (the money-creating banks) are also known as *net foreign assets*. Since the banks are also businesses just like other enterprises, securities transactions and direct investments by the banks themselves are shown on the balance of payments in accordance with the IMF rules just as if they were conducted by private companies. Such transactions are recorded under long-term and short-term capital transactions. Long-term capital transactions include, for instance, bank loans to governments in developing countries while short-term capital transactions cover loans to foreign businesses and deposits held by foreigners in the banking system.

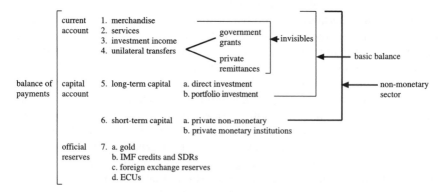

Figure 2.2 The balance of payments in outline

2.3.5   *The official reserves*

The liquid assets of the central banks available for international payments are known as *international liquidity*, usually referred to as the *official reserves* (or also monetary or international monetary reserves). These reserves relate to liquid claims on non-residents and debts to non-residents, both in foreign currency. They include all liquid resources of central banks accepted internationally to cover balance of payments deficits. The central banks can, of course, change the composition of their official reserves, e.g. for the purpose of the intended monetary policy, including exchange rate policy which they are traditionally responsible for implementing. Normally it is only the level of reserves that matters to the domestic impact of exchange rate policy. The official reserves consist of the central bank holding: gold stocks, IMF (International Monetary Fund) special drawing rights (SDRs), the IMF reserve position, ECUs (European Currency Unit, reserves in the European monetary system) and foreign exchange reserves (we shall come back to these concepts later on in the book).

2.4   The balance of payments system

The arrangement of the above categories of international economic transactions on the balance of payments creates a system which lends itself to analysis. Figure 2.2 outlines the way in which the balance of payments is usually divided into sub-balance sheets and items. It is also clear from the diagram that the balance of payments as a whole is first built up from a current account and a capital account. The two accounts are further sub-divided. This division will be briefly explained below for both the current and the capital account; we shall also take a look at a special capital accounts category: change in official reserves.

Examples of the way in which the system is applied in practice in accordance with the above outline is given in Tables 2.1 and 2.2. These show, respectively,

Table 2.1 The balance of payments of Finland, 1993 ($ million)

Current account	
1 Merchandise exports	23,098
2 Trade balance	6,383
3 Services net	–6,798
4 Travel	–368
5 Investment income	–4,984
6 Other services	–1,446
7 Transfers net	–551
8 Private	–99
9 Current balance	–966

Capital account	
10 Long-term capital, net	6,995
11 Private, direct	–1,238
12 Private, portfolio	5,748
13 Public	805
14 Short-term capital, net	–6,358
15 Private non-monetary	332
16 Private monetary institutions	–6,690
17 Miscellaneous official accounts	–329
18 Allocation of SDRs	0
19 Errors and omissions	955
20 Change in official reserves	626

Balance non-monetary sector (9 + 10 + 15 + 19)	7,316
Change in official reserves (balance non-monetary sector + 16)	626

Source: OECD 1995, p. 120.

the balance of payments summaries of Finland and Australia for 1993 as presented by the OECD.

The following points emerge from the figures in Table 2.1: current account balance (9) + long term capital (10) + non-monetary short-term capital (15) + correction factor (19) = balance of non-monetary sector, and balance of non-monetary sector + net short-term capital balance of private monetary institutions (16) = change in official reserves.

The figures in Table 2.2 show the following points: current balance (5) + long term capital (6) = basic balance (9); basic balance + non-monetary short-term capital (10) + errors and omissions (11) = balance of non-monetary transactions (12); and balance of non-monetary sectors (12) + banks' short-term capital balance (13) = balance on official settlements or official reserve transaction balance.

Table 2.2 The balance of payments of Australia, 1993
($ million)

1	Exports, f.o.b.[1]	42,179
2	Imports, f.o.b.	42,327
3	Trade balance	−148
4	Invisibles, net	−10,627
5	Current balance	−10,775
6	Long-term capital	9,081
7	Private	1,232
8	Official	7,849
9	Basic balance	−1,694
10	Non-monetary short-term capital	376
11	Errors and omissions	1,361
12	Balance on non-monetary transactions	43
13	Private monetary institutions' short-term capital	−53
14	assets	−931
15	liabilities	878
16	Balance on official settlements	−10
17	Use of IMF credit	0
18	Special transactions	0
19	Miscellaneous official accounts	−19
20	Allocation of SDRs	0
21	Change in reserves	−29
22	Gold	−13
23	Current assets	24
24	Reserve position in IMF	−26
25	SDRs	−14

Basic balance (5 + 6)	−1,694
Balance on non-monetary transactions (9 + 10 + 11)	43
Balance on official settlements (12 + 13)	−10
Change in official reserves (16 + 19)	−29

[1] f.o.b. = free on board. This means that the price includes all charges associated with transporting the merchandise until it is put on board the ship.
Source: OECD 1995, p. 154.

2.4.1 Balance of payments equilibrium

Use of the double entry system means that the balance sheet as a whole always balances in *formal*, i.e. book-keeping terms: the sum of the credit items is equal to that of the debit items. If we now ascertain the balance for all current transactions, this has to be equal to the corresponding balance of all other items. In practice, this means that if, for example, a country has a deficit of $2 billion on the basis of current transactions (imports exceed exports), there must be a corresponding capital account surplus of $2 billion: essentially, the deficit is financed by a foreign loan. The only possible exception to this is where the country itself uses up part of its supply of foreign exchange, e.g. by reducing the official reserves (in formal terms, the balance of payments remains in equilibrium). However, since these reserves act more or less as working reserves, this effect will, on average, be limited in the long term. If the *current account balance* is negative, this therefore means that, on balance, the country borrows from other countries so that the country's *net savings* figure (the difference between national savings and investments) is also negative.

Thus, a positive *current account balance* means that, on balance, credit has been provided for other countries during the reporting period. This was possible because the country's *net savings* figure (the difference between national savings and investments) was positive.

2.5 The economic interpretation of the balance of payments

2.5.1 *Ascertaining the net balance of payments figures*

By adding together certain items on the balance of payments we obtain specific balances, such as the trade balance, the balance of goods and services, the current account balance or the capital account balance. If we combine them in other ways we obtain other balances, such as the balance of invisible transactions or the balance of non-monetary sectors. These balances are not an exhaustive list of possibilities for aggregating the basic material: the literature distinguishes various other balances as well (see below).

Depending on the purpose for which the balance of payments is to be analysed, items are thus added together on the basis of different criteria in order to ascertain a particular balance. The current account balance and the capital transactions balance of non-monetary sectors together form the *balance of non-monetary sectors* (numbers 1 to 6a in Figure 2.2). This balance is regarded as very important for exchange rate movements and indicates the difference between total receipts from and total payments to other countries by the non-monetary sectors.[7] If the balance of non-monetary sectors is not equal to zero, this means that demand for foreign currency by non-monetary sectors does not equal the supply of foreign currency by non-monetary sectors. A positive balance means that, overall, more revenue is flowing into the country than out of it, and this creates a net demand for domestic currency so that its value on the foreign exchange market tends to increase. A negative balance means that payments to other countries exceed revenue from other countries, exerting upward pressure on the exchange rate (and thus reducing the external value of the country's own currency).

---

7. Transactions by non-monetary sectors are also known as autonomous transactions, since they are conducted regardless of the balance of payments position.

Since the balance of monetary sectors is entered as a balancing item, the balance of non-monetary sectors is always equal to (but the opposite of) the balance of monetary sectors (net private banking transactions and net official reserves). As a result, the balance of payments *formally balances*. A deficit or surplus on the balance of non-monetary sectors will thus be offset by the net change in foreign assets of the banking sector or of the central bank's official reserves.[8] An economy cannot permit itself a structural deficit on the balance of non-monetary sectors without this affecting the exchange rate and foreign confidence, because the stock of bankers' foreign exchange and official reserves is not infinite.

Without central bank intervention in the foreign exchange market, the balance of banking transactions is the exact mirror image of the non-monetary balance: in the case of a surplus there is a net outflow of bank capital – and thus an increase in the banks' net foreign assets (the banks' foreign claims increase) – and in the case of a deficit in banking transactions there is an inflow of capital from abroad and thus a decline in the banks' net foreign assets. *Intervention on the foreign exchange market* means that the monetary authorities act as sellers or buyers of foreign currency on the foreign exchange market. The purpose of such intervention is to influence the exchange rate or to moderate sharp fluctuations.

Table 2.2 shows that, in Australia in 1993, the balance of banking transactions (item 13) is negative and more than compensates for the surplus on non-monetary transactions (item 12). This means that the central bank's official reserves decrease (item 21), in spite of a surplus on the balance for non-monetary transactions.

A balance mentioned earlier that is also considered important for exchange rate movements is the *basic balance*. This combines the current account balance with the long-term capital transactions balance[9] and its purpose is to show the longer-term trend in the balance of payments. It provides an indication of longer-term demand and supply for the currency in question. The current account balance usually follows the opposite trend to the balance of long-term capital transactions, partly under the influence of monetary policy: the net inflow of liquid assets generated by capital transactions is 'drained off', and vice versa. This means that policy measures are used to try to prevent excessive fluctuation in the basic balance. As a result, the effect which economic transactions with other countries have on the money supply and thus on the exchange rate remains limited (see also the following section).

Under certain special economic conditions, the sub-balances may produce a parallel trend so that the basic balance may vary sharply. A typical case was the trend in Japan in the early 1990s, as illustrated in Case study 2.1. As a result of the rise in Japanese interest rates since 1987, the virtual halving of stock market

---

8. The financing transactions conducted to offset a deficit or surplus for the non-monetary sector are known as balancing or accommodating transactions.

9. This does not include the long-term capital transactions of the banks.

prices that followed and the greatly reduced solvency of Japanese banks,[10] the net outflow of capital to other countries ceased. Since the current account improved at the same time, this caused the annual basic balance to change from –$40 billion in 1986–8 to +$80 billion in 1990–1! It was therefore not surprising that the yen appreciated in the latter period.

2.5.2   The money supply

At this point it is important to note that if there is a change in the level of net foreign exchange held by the banks or in the official reserves, e.g. because the private sector offers foreign currency in exchange for national currency, this affects the level of the *money supply*. The money supply consists of notes and coin plus deposits on transfer accounts not held by the private non-bank sector; stocks of national currency held by commercial banks or the central bank are not traditionally counted as part of the money supply. Thus, if the balance of non-monetary sectors is not in equilibrium, the level of the money supply changes. If there is a deficit on the balance of non-monetary sectors, there is net conversion of national currency into foreign currency by the public, so that the money supply falls; if the central bank sells the foreign currency, then this potentially restricts the money supply. Sales of foreign currency to the central bank increase the banks' liquid assets and (possibly) domestic credit, and hence the money supply. The importance of this link between the level of official reserves and stocks of foreign currency held by commercial banks and the level of the money supply is that international transactions and the quantity of money in circulation are known to be closely connected. You can therefore imagine that the trend in the balance of payments has an effect on macro-economic policy or its effectiveness via the influence on the money supply. Later in this book, when we discuss a country's macro-economic policy, we shall come back to this in detail (see Chapter 14).

2.5.3   The reliability of the balance of payments figures

Case study 2.2 The mystery of the missing surplus

An open economy may well have a deficit on current account but for a closed economy, like the global economy, the current and capital accounts must balance, because exports by one country mean equivalent imports for other countries. According to Table 2.3 there was an average world deficit of SDR 53 billion per annum from 1982 to 1988 on current account. How can such a deficit arise? Apart from statistical defects, the difference might be explained by the time factor: if a product is sold to another country at the end of the year and recorded immediately,

---

10. Bank solvency refers to the capacity to cover any losses in the exercise of banking business out of asset components which are permanently available and together constitute the equity capital.

Table 2.3 World balance of payments balances for 1982–8 (SDR billion)

	1982	1983	1984	1985	1986	1987	1988
1 Current account	−85.9	−64.1	−69.5	−62.9	−36.1	−12.2	−41.3
2 Capital account	56.7	63.8	47.6	38.2	7.2	4.9	27.3
3 Statistical differences	29.1	0.1	21.5	23.9	28.3	6.9	13.8

Source: International Monetary Fund, Balance of Payments Statistics, Part 40, 2nd half.

it may not arrive in the country of destination until the next year, owing to the transport time. However, such factors are insufficient to explain why the global current account balance in the 1980s showed a deficit for years in a row, never alternating with a surplus. One reason for the systematic deficit might be that certain services are under-recorded owing to defective accounting. Thus, for example, a high proportion of merchant shipping is recorded in countries which do not report their earnings from seaborne freight to the IMF for lack of accounts or smuggling. On the other hand, the countries which use these services (imports) do report to the IMF. This will cause exports of services to be undervalued on a global scale in the statistics.

A more plausible explanation lies in systematic incomplete accounting of interest payments. Interest payments from other countries are often not declared to the authorities of the recipient country. In most cases, such interest payments are credited direct to a foreign bank account, so that they do not even cross the border into the country of residence of the person receiving the interest. This probably causes world international interest flows to show a negative balance overall. According to the IMF, interest payments explain most of the discrepancies on current account.

In Chapter 1 we tried to describe internationalisation on the basis of flows of goods and capital. These flows are recorded on the balance of payments of every country. Individual countries may have current account or capital account deficits or surpluses, but if all reported inflows and outflows of goods, services and capital are added together for all countries by type of flow, this must ultimately produce a balance of zero, provided that all countries use the same recording method and provided the method is complete and reliable. As we can see from Table 2.3 and Case study 2.2, that is certainly not the case for either the capital account or the current account.

The case study specifically examines two reasons why the world current account is structurally in deficit. In recent years, international capital movements have played an ever greater part in the measurement problems relating to balance of payments accounting, as reflected in the discrepancy on the world capital account (see second row of Table 2.3). During 1982–8 the discrepancy averaged SDR 35 billion per annum.

In 1989 (not included in the table) the statistical difference for international capital flows was at least $65.8 billion. IMF researchers could only trace half of this amount, so that a large discrepancy remained. According to the IMF, the amount draining away each year through institutions other than banks (stock brokers, insurance and finance companies) could be $50 billion more than shown by the figures.

Such discrepancies can arise first of all if certain transactions are not reported or if there is asymmetrical reporting. That can easily happen with transactions entailing an exchange of money for financial assets or vice versa. For example, if a foreign investor in Canada reinvests the return on his investment in Canada, there is no actual payment from a foreign country to Canada, but the foreign assets owned in Canada do increase. This can easily cause confusion in the records.

Second: how do we record changes in the value of foreign financial assets which do not result from transactions with non-residents? A special case here relates to changes in value due to fluctuations in the exchange rate or in the value of the asset. It is customary for capital gains or losses to be recorded on the balance of payments only if they are expressed in connection with a change of ownership. This, too, can easily cause confusion.

Finally, new financial instruments and the existence of offshore financial centres (these are countries offering highly favourable tax facilities, etc., so that it may be attractive to channel financial flows through these centres for accounting purposes) are factors in the above measuring problems. For new instruments such as interest rate and exchange rate swaps (see also Chapter 15), new accounting systems need to be developed. Their development often lags behind reality. More generally, changes in computer and telecommunications technologies have widened the scope for domestic institutions to engage in transactions with non-residents without meeting the requirements of the existing domestic reporting systems. The extent to which these structural changes have led to under-reporting of capital flows is unknown.

Case study 2.3 Crisis in statistics

Since the liberalisation of capital movements has led to an unknown increase in the volume and complexity of international financial transactions, the statistics on international capital flows are becoming increasingly unreliable. According to the IMF, this has actually caused a crisis in statistical methods. The result is that governments can receive the wrong signals when mapping out their monetary and budgetary policy. According to the IMF, better information on capital flows can be useful to governments in deciding their policy on foreign exchange transactions because capital flows have the most significant effect there. The amounts that central banks can spend in support buying of currencies bear no relation to the financial flows that can be mobilised by the private market. Turnover on the foreign exchange markets now (in the first half of the 1990s) totals roughly $1,000 billion gross a day, about double the combined currency reserves of the industrial countries. In order to reduce the statistical defects in the recording of capital flows, individual countries would need to adapt their data collection systems.

According to the IMF, that is what is wrong with the recording of international capital flows. This does not imply that individual balance of payments figures have become worthless. However, one should be cautious in comparing balances of payments and in aggregating balance of payments figures, in particular. Case study 2.1 showed that various balances on the balance of payments produce economic consequences which can have repercussions on international relations, because policy-makers and politicians go by these figures. But not only policy-makers and politicians: businessmen planning to invest abroad may take the balance of payments position into account in their decision, in order to obtain an impression of the economic situation.

In spite of the problems surrounding the balance of payments, particularly in the case of aggregation, we have to work with these figures for lack of anything better. The accounting problems are all connected with the internationalisation and liberalisation of the world economy. The figures in the various graphs and tables in Chapter 1 may thus at most underestimate the degree of internationalisation.

2.6 Summary

International transactions in goods and services are recorded together with factor or investment income and requited transfers on the balance of payments current account. Capital transactions (including international portfolio investments and direct investments) are recorded on the capital account. The monetary sectors comprise the central bank and commercial banks. A deficit or surplus on the balance of the non-monetary sectors is offset by changes in the stocks of foreign currency held by banks or changes in the central bank's official reserves. This means that disequilibrium in the non-monetary sector balance affects a country's money supply. Since a balance of payments always formally balances, the balance of monetary sectors must always be offset by the balance of non-monetary sectors.

On the basis of the balances of payments, we can obtain an idea of the scale of international trade and capital flows concerning a particular country for the accounting period. In practice, flows of goods, services and capital are not perfectly recorded. The liberalisation of capital movements, in particular, seems to be causing considerable measurement problems in the aggregation of international capital flows. For economic analyses, the various balance of payments balances are taken as ratios. The ratio between the money supply and the balance of non-monetary sectors is regarded as particularly important for policy. Chapter 14 goes into this ratio in more detail. Another balance often considered in practice is the current account balance, because this can give some indication of the trend in the competitive ability of the country in question.

Bibliography

De Nederlandsche Bank (Central Bank of the Netherlands) (1992), *Annual Report.*

International Monetary Fund (1991), *Determinants and Systemic Consequences of International Capital Flows, A Study by the Research Department of the International Monetary Fund*, Occasional paper 77, March 1991.

OECD (1995) *Australia*, Economic Survey, Paris.

OECD (1995) *Finland*, Economic Survey, Paris.

3 International trade theory

3.1 Introduction

As we saw in Chapter 1, residents in different countries are linked by a network of trade relations. We also saw that since the Second World War global international trade generally expanded faster than total world GNP. This prompts the question: Why 'trade' and 'who gains by it'?

Traditional trade theories focused on why countries trade with one another and the pattern of trade flows. Both the regional pattern and the composition can be explained. However, these theories are based on abstract undertakings or industries and thus overlook the specific characteristics of individual producers. As well as answering the question why certain industries are competitive, more modern trade theories mainly stress the characteristics of those industries or companies rather than national characteristics. This means such factors as economies of scale, restricted competition or simply random and/or historical circumstances. The theories discussed in this chapter attempt primarily to explain why countries trade with one another. Chapter 5 tries to find the reason for international trade from the point of view of the (multinational) entrepreneur. This chapter begins with a case study concerning emerging industrial countries in East Asia. These countries, known as NICs (Newly Industrialising Countries) produced rapid economic growth from the early 1970s. This case study provides a starting point both for the free trade theories in this chapter and for the theories in Chapters 6 to 9 which examine free trade regulation or restriction and its effects. The case study shows that international competition between regions can change greatly over time, and also examines the export success of this type of country and the question: who benefits from trade?

After this introductory case study, we shall first consider the traditional trade theories based on the concept of comparative costs. These theories form, as it were, the traditional foundation of trade theory and are based on the idea that circumstances specific to certain locations determine international competitive relationships and therefore the pattern of trade flows. *Locational factors* include such variables as: level of technological development, availability of factors of production, structure of domestic demand and prevailing standards, values and culture. Next we consider the fact that international specialisation may also be based on the existence of economies of scale. This means that producing on a larger scale cuts the average unit cost of production. Here we shall see that economies of scale can explain the existence of international trade even in the absence of comparative cost advantages. The chapter ends with the 'Porter approach' which combines elements of traditional trade theories (why do countries trade certain goods with one another?) with those of modern trade theories (why can some industries compete internationally but not others?). This makes the explanation for international trade more precise but less uniform. The multiplicity of potential causative factors means that the explanation has to be tailor-made: different trade flows all require their own explanation.

3.2 The emerging industrial countries: a case study

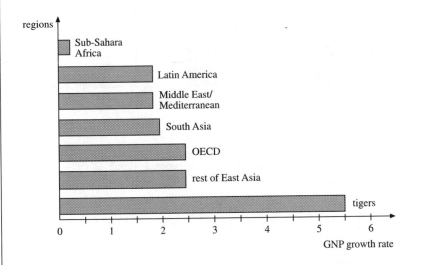

Case study 3.1 The importance of East and South-East Asia for the world economy

Figure 3.1 Growth in per capita GNP (annual average increase in %, 1965–90)

Since the early 1970s East and South-East Asia have represented a fast growing part of the world economy. For several decades, growth of *trade and production* in this region has far outstripped that in the rest of the world. Over the past 25 years, Hong Kong, Indonesia, Japan, Malaysia, Singapore, South Korea, Taiwan and Thailand have achieved average annual growth in per capita GNP (gross national product) of 5.5 per cent. This growth rate is twice that of the rest of East Asia and three times that of Latin America. In 1965 the South and South-East Asian countries could still be called 'poor', but within a single generation the situation changed so that some of their industries were among the best in the world. Figure 3.1 shows the difference between the growth rates of these South and South-East

Asian economies and those of other groups of countries over the period 1965–90; this makes it obvious why these Asian economies are called 'tigers' on the basis of their growth figures.

The 'tigers' include: Hong Kong, Indonesia, Japan, Malaysia, Singapore, South Korea, Taiwan and Thailand. These countries' exports have grown particularly rapidly, increasing their share of world trade in industrial products from 9 per cent in 1965 to 21 per cent in 1990 (see Figure 3.2).

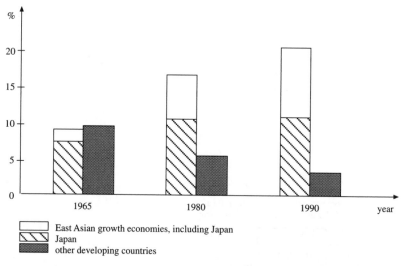

Figure 3.2 Share of world exports of industrial products (1965–90)
Source: World Bank, 1993.

From the mid 1960s, Japan headed the list of fast-growing Asian economies, initially followed by South Korea, Taiwan, Singapore and Hong Kong. These last countries are known as the Asian NICs (Newly Industrialising Countries). Later, Indonesia, Malaysia and Thailand followed. These *NECs*[1] (*Newly Exporting Countries*) located mainly in South-East Asia still export a significant volume of *primary products* (for agricultural products, see Table 3.2), but at the same time their exports of *industrial products* (Table 3.1) are growing at an amazing rate. This means that they are potential NICs.

According to Table 3.1, the NECs' industrial exports expanded even faster than those of the NICs from the beginning of the 1970s. The primary reason for this was that it is easier to achieve high growth rates from a low starting level (NECs) than if there is already a substantial industrial base, as in the case of the NICs. Second,

---

1 The Philippines are usually included among the NECs as well as Thailand, Malaysia and Indonesia. However, the Philippines cannot be counted as one of the eight fastest growing economies (Hong Kong, Indonesia, Japan, Malaysia, Singapore, South Korea, Taiwan and Thailand).

Table 3.1 Growth rates of real industrial exports (% per annum)

	1965–70	1970–3	1973–7	1977–80	1980–3	1980–90
NICs	21.1	· 25.6	9.9	12.5	12.7	15.0
NECs	6.0	36.6	12.9	21.1	18.0	26.7*

*Excluding Philippines
Source: G.A. Hughes and D.M.G. Newbery, April 1986, p. 428; GATT, *International Trade 90–91*, vol. II.

the industrial countries, fearing serious competition from the NICs, protected their markets against exports from them. The products exported by NECs are generally less affected by protectionist measures since they were seen as less of a threat by the industrial countries. As a result, *multinationals* transferred part of their production from the NICs, the launching point for exports to the west, to the NECs in order to circumvent the import restrictions. The NICs reacted in turn to the trade barriers set up against them by upgrading their range of products (i.e. trying to increase the local value added per unit of product by switching to more advanced, higher quality types of product) and by turning to new markets, particularly in the Middle East. Finally, the economic successes in the NICs reduced the surplus of cheap local labour so that real wages increased. As a result, the NICs lost some of their *competitiveness* in typical, labour-intensive production activities to the NECs. We can deduce from Table 3.2 that the fast-growing exports of industrial products were probably at the expense of the export position of agricultural products.

One explanation for the growth achieved by the Asian NICs lies in the high level of domestic saving; on the one hand, this is attributed to cultural factors, but a number of institutional factors – e.g. relating to pension provision and home ownership – also seem to play a part. Be that as it may, with the aid of capital imports this enabled the NICs to finance the rapid accumulation of domestic capital. In 1986 the national savings ratio (national savings as a percentage of GNP) in Taiwan, Hong Kong and Singapore was over 30 per cent. Another factor

Table 3.2 Share of exports of agricultural products in relation to merchandise (%)

Country	1980	1990
Thailand	57	24.5
Malaysia	46	31
Indonesia	22	16
Hong Kong	5	5.5
Singapore	18.5	8
Taiwan	10	5.5
South Korea	9	4.5

Source: GATT, *International Trade 90–91*, vol. II.

Table 3.3 Productivity and real wages (average annual change in %)

Country	Productivity		Real wages	
	1975–9	1980–5	1975–9	1980–5
Taiwan	11.5	4.0	10.8	4.6
South Korea	6.2	5.6	12.9	4.0
Hong Kong	7.9	7.2	5.3	1.7
Singapore	4.0	3.0	5.8	6.8

Source: World Financial Markets, January 1987, p. 5.

which contributed to the *export success* of the Asian NICs in comparison with other countries was the favourable combination of *productivity of labour, wages* (see Table 3.3) and *exchange rate* (the currencies of the NICs were not generally overvalued, in contrast to those of many typical developing countries).

Trade relations

Trade relations between Japan, the Asian NICs and the NECs now consist of a complex structure in which both competing and complementary goods are traded. Initially, Japan was the only industrialised country in the region. This meant that the structure of trade between the three regions represented a simple, complementary exchange of industrial products from Japan for primary products from the other two regions. From the 1950s, the NICs stopped their traditional *import substitution policy* and began to export light industrial products to the US and Europe in the 1960s. This gave rise to an element of competition in trade relations between the NICs and Japan and at the same time a complementary relationship with the NECs. In the 1970s competing light industries were also set up in the NECs, thus launching competition with the NICs. The NICs proceeded with heavy industrialisation and continued to compete with Japan on certain products.

According to the World Bank, the explanation for the growth achieved by the Asian tigers lies mainly in their economic base, which features high domestic savings, low inflation, a sound government financial policy, substantial investment in education and, finally, greater willingness to accept foreign investment and technology than other comparable countries. Over the past 30 years, inflation has averaged 8 per cent in the East Asian tigers, against 18 per cent in other developing countries. Although education spending was not significantly higher than in other similar countries, the resources were allocated in a different way: in contrast to other developing countries, the bulk of the education budget was spent on primary and secondary education, not university education. For example, in the mid 1980s Thailand, Indonesia and South Korea spent over 80 per cent of their education budget on primary education. By way of comparison, the figure was less than 50 per cent in Argentina and Venezuela. Moreover, partly thanks to the stable macro-economic climate, private investment as a percentage of GNP was twice as high as in other comparable countries.

Apart from these economies' huge export achievements, they were also successful in distributing the benefits. In South Korea, for example, the income of the wealthiest 20 per cent of households is eight times higher than the poorest 20 per cent. In contrast, in Brazil and Mexico the wealthiest 5 per cent of households are now 20 times richer than the poorest 5 per cent. In Malaysia the percentage of the population living below the poverty line fell from 37 per cent in 1960 to less than 5 per cent in 1990. Compare that with Brazil, where the proportion of the population living in poverty fell from 50 per cent to 21 per cent, so that a fifth of the population is still below the poverty line.

Table 3.4 Exports and imports by Asian NICs ($ billion)

	1980	1986
Aggregate exports (f.o.b.[1]) to:	76.4	131.2
US	19.0	49.1
Japan	7.7	13.1
EC	12.7	17.3
Aggregate imports (c.i.f.[2]) from:	88.5	116.1
US	15.6	18.6
Japan	20.7	30.9
EC	8.8	14.1
Net balance of trade with:	−12.1	15.1
US	3.4	30.3
Japan	−13.0	−17.8
EC	3.9	3.2
Balance on current account NICs	9.0	22.3

[1]f.o.b. = free on board. This means that the price includes all charges associated with transporting the merchandise until it is put on board the ship.
[2]c.i.f. = cost, insurance, freight. This means that the price of the goods bought or sold is increased because of the cost of freight and insurance being included in costing.
Source: World Financial Markets, January 1987, p. 2.

This case study prompts a number of questions which will be discussed mainly in this chapter, but also in the next one.

1. Why does Japan export industrial products and import primary products?
2. Why are and were the NICs so successful in exporting industrial products?
3. What is the connection between productivity of labour, wages and export performance?

4. Why did real wages rise in the NICs?
5. How is it that trade between Japan, the NICs and the NECs was initially complementary but later became competitive?
6. Does international trade promote welfare?
7. What can be said about the distribution of the welfare generated by international trade?

3.3 Traditional trade theories

The theory concerning the causes behind international trade and whether international trade increases welfare dates from a period when international trade relations were far less intensive than now. In the late eighteenth and early nineteenth centuries, in particular, there was much debate over whether governments should regulate international trade, and what effect free international trade would have on the distribution of welfare between countries and between groups within a country. As we shall see, the central assumption in the development of this theory lay in the competitive conditions which depend on circumstances at a particular location. There are still traces of this idea in trade theory today, although it is gradually becoming increasingly disputed.

3.3.1 Mercantilism

In the seventeenth century the ideas of the Mercantilists predominated in Europe. Their philosophy was that international trade is a *zero sum game*, i.e. that the benefit which one country gains from international trade means a corresponding detriment to another country. This view arose because people focused very much on the international payments resulting from international trade transactions; for at that time (in the days of the gold standard, see Chapter 16), if a country imported more than it exported, there was a net outflow of gold to other countries. This was seen as weakening national power and hence wealth, so that people were inclined to control international trade flows and arrange things so that there would preferably be a net inflow of gold from abroad.

This idea was severely criticised in around 1800 by British economists such as Hume, Smith and Ricardo. They stressed that international trade is a *positive sum game* and that the Mercantilists were thus fundamentally wrong. Their criticism focused on two points: first, the heavy emphasis placed by the Mercantilists on the accumulation of gold, the legal tender of the time. Hume, in particular, drew attention to the illusion that one could build up a substantial lead in prosperity by accumulating gold. He argued that if economic activity does not increase, the extra stock of gold is mainly inflationary in its effects. This followed from the general assumption prevailing at the time that, although flows of goods and money were in principle equivalent to one another, what happened in the sphere of money could not influence developments in the sphere of goods. More gold would not then lead to more economic activity but to an increase in prices (the quantity of gold available per product). However, such an inflationary trend weakens the ability to export and it becomes attractive not to buy goods from domestic suppliers but to obtain them by importing from other countries where they are relatively cheap. Both effects, fewer exports and more imports, contribute to the automatic outflow of the accumulated gold to other countries. This was in fact experienced by countries such as Spain and Portugal after they had plundered huge quantities of gold and silver from Latin America. The Mercantilists expected the extra gold to depress interest rates while demand for money remained the same. But inflation prevented this, because investors do not only want payment for postponing their consumption, they also want compensation for the effect of that same inflation on their capital. This Mercantilist argument was therefore also destroyed.

The second criticism of the Mercantilist view originated from Smith and Ricardo, among others. They advocated free international trade and thus the abolition of government interference. Smith stressed in particular that free international trade created the opportunity for the optimum international division of labour, from which everyone could benefit. In his view, this situation was like the case in which an individual country has an optimum division of labour so that prosperity increases. In Smith's view each country ought to specialise in the product in which it has an *absolute cost and hence price advantage* over its trading partners. He also stated that international trade can help to break down national monopolies, generating sounder competitive relationships. 'Excess' labour resulting from concealed unemployment or unexploited mineral resources could also be activated by new sales opportunities on the international market.

Box 3.1 Absolute cost model

In an absolute cost model, a country has the lowest production costs and supplies foreign markets, too, as a result. Example: say Turkey and Greece have the same average wage level. Turkey has higher productivity of labour than Greece in producing leather clothing, while Greece's productivity of labour is higher in wine production (the value of the goods is deemed to depend only on labour costs). If Turkey concentrates on producing and exporting leather clothing, while Greece specialises in producing and exporting wine, consumers in both countries will have access to more of both goods under free trade than without free trade.

Although Smith's arguments combined with those of Hume looked fairly convincing, quite a few people remained sceptical, fearing that if international trade were left to the free market, some countries would in fact gain but at the same time the economic development of other countries might be nipped in the bud by international competition. This fear primarily concerned countries with an economic advantage trading with less industrialised countries. In that case, the first type of country would have an absolute cost advantage over the other type in all products.

A second objection to free international trade was that, even if a country as a whole could benefit by the opportunities for trade, that need not mean that all groups within the country would do better. There was also fear that, in practice, free international trade would be beneficial to some groups in a country but detrimental to others.

3.3.2 The comparative cost model

Ricardo's contribution lay in destroying the first of the above objections. In his opinion, all countries can benefit by international trade, even if their economy is less developed. He demonstrated this by using an extremely simple model known as the *comparative cost model*. The Ricardo model is still relevant to some extent even today.

First, the model links the trend in wages and productivity with the international competitiveness of a country (see question 3 following Case study 3.1 on p. 62). This indicates that it does not really matter if a country's productivity of labour is lower than that of the foreign competitor across the board, so long as that is offset by a correspondingly lower wage cost level.

Case study 3.2 Productivity of labour and wage trends in industrialised countries

Table 3.5 Growth of productivity (average annual change in GDP per worker,[2] %, 1973–89)

Country	1973–9	1979–89
Belgium	2.7	1.6
Netherlands	2.3	1.4
Germany	2.8	1.4
France	2.5	2.1
UK	1.3	1.7
US	0.0	0.9

Source: OECD, *Employment Outlook 1991*, OECD, Paris, 1991, p. 37.

---

2 Gross Domestic Product per worker is only a rough measure of the productivity of labour, as it takes no account of the time worked by each worker. According to Maddison's figures (1991), the annual working hours per worker were the same for all countries in the table in 1987, except for the Netherlands. In the Netherlands the average worker worked roughly 240 hours per annum less than in Belgium. The productivity of labour is therefore much higher in the Netherlands than in other countries, except the US.

Table 3.5 shows that trends in rising productivity of labour can actually differ between industrialised countries.

If the trend in wages does not correspond to this, imbalances arise; the large external deficit of the US and the surpluses of Germany and the Netherlands in the 1980s might perhaps be seen as an illustration of this.

A complication concerning the relationship between wage and productivity trends is that while high wages do compel businesses to rationalise, so that the productivity of labour increases, this can also lead to lay-offs and thus increasing costs on account of higher tax payments and social security contributions. High gross wages are then associated with high payroll deductions, so that net wages are much lower. As a result, the nature of the relationship between wages and productivity of labour depends very much on whether one considers gross or net wages.

Second, the model shows that if wages in the various sectors are the same throughout the country, ranking the sectors by productivity of labour must also roughly imply their ranking in terms of international competitiveness; because if productivity is lower than the wage level a country can justify, there is a comparative disadvantage in production costs compared to other countries; if it is higher than the wage level would suggest, then there is a comparative advantage. If the relative wage level moves in relation to the relative level of productivity, then this borderline also shifts.

Box 3.2 The comparative cost model

The comparative cost model is based on two countries, two products and one factor of production: labour. Technical know-how or the state of technology is different in the two countries. There are also constant returns to scale and perfect competition.

Let us call the two countries 1 and 2 and say that, in principle, they each produce two products x and y using their available quantity of labour. Since we assume that there is perfect competition everywhere and that labour moves freely from one sector to another within a country (but does not move abroad), in the absence of international trade we have a certain production and price relationship between the two goods with domestic demand and supply equal to one another. However, if a different pattern of demand emerges under international trade, the economy will adapt to that. It is important to know here what combinations of goods a country is technically capable of producing with the given labour potential. In the absence of economies of scale, this can be depicted as a straight line *production possibilities frontier* (in the following indicated as pp curve); the pp curve gives the various combinations of goods which a country can produce, given its technology and quantity of factors of production. In Figure 3.3 on page 67, lines aa and bb indicate the pp curves of country 1 and country 2. Production combinations above or to the right of the pp curve are not possible; below or to the left of the line are production combinations which are feasible but not optimum. The slope of the pp curve indicates how many units of product y have to be sacrificed to produce an extra unit of product x using the labour thus released. We call this the *opportunity cost* of producing product x. The slope of the pp curve thus changes if the exchange ratio between x and y changes for one reason or another.

It is pure chance if the opportunity costs are the same in both countries, because they depend on local production conditions and the available technical know-how, which were assumed to differ between the countries.

An arithmetical example

For example, let us take Indonesia and Japan as countries 1 and 2, and electronics and rice as products x and y. It takes Japan 2 hours of labour to produce one unit of electronics and 6 hours to produce one sack of rice. It takes Indonesia 4 hours of labour to produce one unit of electronics and 8 hours to produce one sack of rice. Since the productivity of labour depends on production per hour worked, this means that the greater the number of working hours needed to produce one unit of the product, the lower the productivity of labour.

Table 3.6 Number of hours' labour needed to produce one unit of a product

Country	Electronics	Rice
Japan	2	6
Indonesia	4	8

If Japan produces one unit less of electronics, then it can produce $\frac{1}{3}$ of a unit more rice; in Japan the opportunity cost of electronics is $\frac{1}{3}$ of a unit of rice. In Indonesia the opportunity cost of electronics is $\frac{1}{2}$ a unit of rice. Since the local cost ratios (= comparative costs) differ between the two countries, the slope of the pp curve is also different. This is usually also the case if the absolute production costs (in hours of labour) are lower in both sectors in one country than in the other. In our example, the absolute production costs of both rice and electronics are lower in Japan. However, since the opportunity cost of electronics is lower in Japan than in Indonesia, Japan has a *comparative cost advantage* in producing electronics and Indonesia has a comparative cost advantage in producing rice. If countries whose pp curves have different slopes engage in free trade in the product in which they have a comparative advantage, they can both benefit, as we shall see if we extend the arithmetical example. This provides an answer to question 1 following Case study 3.1: since Japan has a comparative advantage in producing electronics and Indonesia has an advantage in rice, if international trade takes place, Indonesia will export rice and Japan electronics.

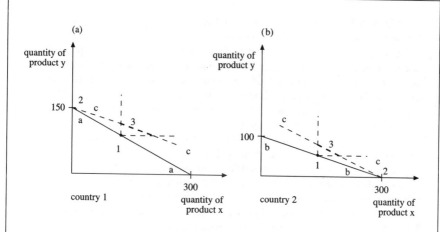

1 = level of consumption and production before free trade
2 = level of production under free trade
section 3 of line (bold section of line cc) = consumption possibilities under free trade
aa = pp curve of country 1; the slope indicates the opportunity cost of product x in country 1
bb = pp curve of country 2; slope indicates the opportunity cost of product x in country 2
cc = international exchange ratio; the slope is between the slopes of aa and bb and is the same for both countries.

Figure 3.3 Illustration of differences in comparative cost

Let us also assume that the available quantity of labour in Japan is 600 and in Indonesia 1,200. aa is now the pp curve for Indonesia; its slope is equal to the opportunity cost of electronics expressed as units of rice. As already calculated, that is $\frac{1}{2}$. In the absence of international trade this is equal to the relative domestic price of electronics. If Indonesia specialises totally in rice, it can produce $\frac{1200}{8} = 150$ units of rice. In Figure 3.3a this is shown by the point of intersection between the pp curve and the y axis.

If Indonesia specialises totally in electronics, it can produce $\frac{1200}{4} = 300$ units. In the case of autarky, Indonesia produces both goods. Autarky means that a country provides for all its own needs and has no contact with other countries. Given a domestic price ratio of $\frac{1}{2}$, and depending on demand factors, Indonesia produces 150 units of electronics and 75 units of rice (point 1 in Figure 3.3a).

bb is now the pp curve for Japan; the slope is equal to the opportunity cost of electronics expressed as units of rice. The opportunity cost of electronics in units of rice is $\frac{1}{3}$. In the absence of international trade, this is the same as the relative domestic price of electronics. If Japan specialises totally in rice, it can produce $\frac{600}{6} = 100$ units of rice. If it specialises totally in electronics, Japan can produce $\frac{600}{2} = 300$ units of electronics. Like Indonesia, Japan will produce both goods if it is autarkic. Depending on the demand factors, and given an exchange ratio of $\frac{1}{3}$, this might mean 50 units of rice, for example, and 150 units of electronics (point

67

1 in Figure 3.3b). If they are autarkic, Indonesia and Japan will together produce 125 units of rice and 300 units of electronics.

Let us assume that international trade takes place. If Indonesia specialises in rice and Japan in electronics, a total of 150 units of rice and 300 units of electronics can be produced. Thus, total production has increased by 25 units of rice. The quantity of both goods actually imported and exported depends on demand for the two products. In any case, it is clear from the example that both countries can improve their consumption possibilities.

The reason why both countries benefit from free trade is that, once the borders have been opened up, a price ratio will be established which depends on the original cost ratios in the two countries combined with aggregate demand. This means that the international price ratio will logically lie between these original national cost ratios (in specific cases the demand structure can cause the new price ratio to correspond to the original price ratio in one of the countries; we shall ignore that special case here). As we can see from Figure 3.3, specialisation combined with the opportunity for exchange on the international market according to the international price ratio means that both countries can have combinations of the two products (section 3 of line) such that they have more of both than before.

3.3.3   Criticism

The second objection to the free trade philosophy – some groups in a country will suffer if a country permits free international trade – was not conclusively refuted by Ricardo. Essentially, Ricardo actually believed that a redistribution of income ought to take place in his country, the UK, from the landowners to the rising industrialist class. During the Napoleonic wars, food prices in Britain went up. The British landed gentry benefited from this price rise and tried to safeguard the high food prices after the wars by advocating protectionism. This damaged the interests of the industrialists, because protectionism hinders not only imports but also exports. Presumably because Ricardo wanted to disguise the internal conflict of interests as much as possible, he assumed in his writings, for the sake of convenience, that those whose prosperity increased, the industrialists, would be prepared to compensate the losers, the landowners. However, this assumption was not sufficiently convincing, so people continued to try to find out what shifts take place within an economy if it opens its borders to international trade.

3.3.4   The Heckscher-Ohlin-Samuelson (HOS) model

This search eventually led over 100 years later to a simple theoretical model that was developed at the beginning of this century by the Swedes, Eli Heckscher and Bertil Ohlin. It was in particular the American economist, Paul Samuelson, who further refined and developed the theoretical model. This model was also based on the comparative cost concept and the idea that competitive positions depend on the supply conditions in specific locations and are therefore linked to countries (rather than companies). On this basis an attempt was made to describe in all their simplicity the principal adjustment processes which occur if two countries decide to open their borders to one another's products. This model is based far more explicitly than the Ricardo model on the idea that a general equilibrium is established in the economies, in which the equilibria in the various sub-markets are, in principle, inter-related: if the balance shifts in one sub-market, this affects the balance in other sub-markets.

Box 3.3 The HOS model

The HOS model distinguishes two countries, two products and two factors of production. In the HOS model, just as in the Ricardo model, it is assumed that returns to scale are constant and there is perfect competition. In contrast to the Ricardo model, the production structure (i.e. technical know-how) is assumed to be the same in both countries in this model, with fixed technical coefficients (i.e. it is only ever possible to achieve optimum production with one specific combination of capital and labour which is the same in both countries). It is also assumed that consumer preferences are the same in the two countries. However, the available quantities of the factors of production are not the same. One country has a relatively large amount of capital while the other has a relatively large amount of labour. It is assumed that one product is always, by nature, relatively labour-intensive to make, and the other relatively capital-intensive. Also, the productivity of the factors of production, labour and capital, falls the more they are used in the production process. From this one can deduce that the production possibility frontier will be concave or bowed out from the origin.

Thus, in the HOS model there is declining marginal productivity. This determines the level of remuneration (wages and interest). In that case, wages in the country well-endowed with labour will be relatively low so that the country has a comparative cost advantage in the labour-intensive product; the converse is true of the other country. Finally, according to the HOS model (just as in the Ricardo model), end products can be freely traded internationally, but factors of production cannot cross national borders.

As an example let us again take Japan and Indonesia. Japan now has 600 units of labour and Indonesia 1,200. In addition, the available capital is 400 units in both Japan and Indonesia. Both countries produce both rice and electronics when autarkic. Production of one unit of electronics takes 4 units of labour and 12 units of capital in both countries. Production of one unit of rice costs 20 units of labour and 10 of capital. The amount of labour relative to capital needed for one unit of electronics is $\frac{1}{3}$ and 2 for a unit of rice. Thus, rice production is labour-intensive and electronics production is capital-intensive. The relative amount of units of labour available in terms of units of capital is $\frac{3}{2}$ in Japan and 3 in Indonesia. Thus, Indonesia has relatively more labour and Japan relatively more capital. Since labour is relatively scarce in Japan, the level of remuneration will be higher for labour in relation to capital in Japan than in Indonesia. This therefore means that rice is more expensive in Japan in comparison with Indonesia and that Japan has a comparative advantage in producing electronics and Indonesia has an advantage in rice production.

Just as in the Ricardo model, international trade will establish a single world price ratio between the products somewhere between the original national cost ratios (= price ratios). This generates patterns of specialisation in the product in which one has a comparative advantage. (It is possible to prove that as a result of the concave shape of the pp curve, international trade need not lead to total specialisation, in contrast to the outcome of the Ricardo model). Japan will specialise in producing the capital-intensive product, electronics, and Indonesia will specialise in the labour-intensive product, rice. This then determines the export pattern. The export of capital-intensive electronics means that Japan *indirectly exports* capital; importation of labour-intensive rice means indirect importation of the factor labour. This reduces the relative surplus of capital (and the relative scarcity of labour). Thus, the level of remuneration for capital in Japan will increase and that of labour will fall. As capital becomes relatively more expensive in Japan, the production process in both sectors becomes more labour-intensive. This raises the marginal productivity of capital and reduces that of labour, which implies an increase in the return on capital and a fall in wages in Japan. In Indonesia the opposite happens: the level of remuneration of labour increases and that of capital falls. Thus, according to the HOS model, the remuneration of the factor of production in relative surplus increases and that of the factor which is relatively scarce declines.

Since production technology is in principle the same in the two countries, this means that as the prices of the goods become the same in both, the production processes also tend to converge. Thus, if a product was originally produced on a more labour-intensive basis in one country than in the other, free trade will cause this difference to tend to disappear. Since the difference in the relative remuneration of labour and capital between the two countries also disappears, a situation arises in which the original differences between the countries in the level of wages and interest rates disappear with specialisation in accordance with the original comparative cost differences. This is called *factor price equalisation*. It may perhaps explain the way that wages in the NICs are rising towards western levels (question 4 following Case study 3.1).

If factor price equalisation has come about, the comparative cost differences will have disappeared and a new balance is thus established in which the capital-intensity of production has adapted to the new cost ratios (in the labour-rich country, production has become more capital-intensive, and vice versa). Since it is assumed that the available quantities of factors of production have remained the same, the change in the level of wages and interest *must* have caused a change in the way in which total income is distributed between the two factors of production. In the labour-rich country, the purchasing power of the owners of the labour has risen and that of the owners of the capital has fallen; the reverse is true in the capital-rich country (check this for yourself taking the example of Japan).

The HOS model can now also be summarised simply with the aid of symbols. Let us call the two products x and y and their prices p_x and p_y; we call Japan and Indonesia J and I, capital and labour C and L and wages and interest w and i. In that case, the starting position for the HOS model (no international trade) is as follows:

$$(L/C)_J < (L/C)_I \qquad\qquad\qquad\qquad\qquad (a)$$

$$(L/C)_x < (L/C)_y \qquad\qquad\qquad\qquad\qquad (b)$$

this applies in both countries; also, $(L/C)_x$ and $(L/C)_y$ are the same in both countries.

It follows from (a) that:

$$(w/i)_J > (w/i)_I \qquad\qquad\qquad\qquad\qquad (c)$$

It follows from (b) and (c) that:

$$(p_x/p_y)_J < (p_x/p_y)_I \qquad\qquad\qquad\qquad\qquad (d)$$

or Japan has a comparative advantage in producing x and Indonesia in producing y.

With totally free trade, eventual equality arises:

- as regards (d): this is the international terms of trade
- as regards (c): this is called factor price equalisation.

As shown in Box 3.3, an important mechanism in the HOS model as in the Ricardo model is that free international trade influences the prices of goods; for while they were originally established on the national markets on the basis of national demand and supply, with international free trade the international market situation determines the value of the goods. However, if product prices change, adjustment processes take place in the economy: the sectors with a strong competitive position on the international market will expand under free trade, while others must shrink under the impact of foreign competition. However, in contrast to Ricardo's model, there are simultaneous changes on the markets in the factors of production as a result of the emphasis on general equilibrium. Since the only distinction is between labour and capital, these changes are expressed in different wage and interest rates in the two countries. This in turn leads to a change in the intensity of factors in production, which means a change in the ratio between capital and other factors of production in the production process. (More generally, *factor intensity* means the extent to which a particular factor of production is used in the production process.) The change in wage and interest levels also means that a shift will take place in the distribution of income. From the model in Box 3.3 we can infer that the owners of the country's surplus factor of production will see their purchasing power increase as a result of free trade; however, the owners of the other, scarce factor of production will be worse off. Overall, the country as a whole will benefit but whether that will apply to all owners of factors of production depends on willingness to compensate the losers.

3.3.5 The Leontief paradox

However elegant the HOS model may be in its simplicity, it did not mark the end of the development of international trade theory. First, empirical research conducted by Leontief quite soon after the Second World War showed that the specialisation process in the US, for example, did not correspond to what HOS predicted (and this was repeatedly found in later research). Where free trade ought to have caused the Americans to concentrate increasingly on producing relatively capital-intensive goods – the goods in which the US had a comparative advantage – this did not appear to be what happened in practice; the US imported relatively capital-intensive goods instead of exporting them. From that time on, people talked of the *Leontief paradox*. A paradox is an apparent contradiction, so use of this term indicated that it ought to be possible to reconcile the outcome of the model with reality. Thus, for example, it was pointed out that three factors of production needed to be distinguished: human capital as well as labour and capital. Human capital means investment in labour via education, thus changing the quality of the labour. The fact that the US exported relatively labour-intensive goods can be explained by the fact that it was mainly human capital that was concerned. It was also stated that part of international trade results from the fact that people cannot have access to certain goods themselves (e.g. oil and other raw materials). Since raw materials are often capital-intensive to produce, the necessary imports of such materials into the US could also be a factor in the capital-intensive character of US imports.

3.3.6 Factor reversal

A fundamental criticism of the HOS model was that it assumes that the sectors can be arranged in order of capital-intensity and that this arrangement is universal, i.e. the same in all countries. This does not appear to be so in reality: for example, where the agricultural sector in the industrialised countries often has above average capital-intensity, in the developing countries it is often highly labour-intensive in comparison with other sectors in those countries. Such a phenomenon is known in theory as *factor reversal*. In that case it is not possible to draw a strict dividing line between goods which are relatively labour-intensive and those which are relatively capital-intensive to produce, but that is a central assumption in the HOS model. (In the example given in Box 3.3 there is factor reversal if, for instance, the substitution of labour for capital in the capital-intensive sector, electronics, in Japan takes place to a greater extent than in the labour-intensive sector, rice; check this for yourself.) It should be clear that if, as some people think, factor reversal is fairly widespread, there is essentially no foundation for the idea that hitherto prevailed in trade theory, namely that countries have a comparative cost advantage 'by nature', i.e. because of prevailing conditions of supply, in a range of goods and services which can be specifically and objectively specified in a universal manner.

As there was ever increasing doubt about whether there is in fact any systematic pattern in the specialisation processes of countries, so the need arose for new trade theories. For how could traditional theory explain why Canada, which is well-endowed with capital, is just as important a net exporter of agricultural products as Thailand, for example, which is far richer in labour? How could one explain why trade between Japan and the Asian NICs was initially complementary and later competitive? Or why France, for example, both exports and imports cars? This last case is known as *intra-industry trade* (trade within an industry), as opposed to *inter-industry trade* (trade between industries) which is predicted by traditional theory. Finally, how was it possible that, as stated in Chapter 1, the greatest growth in international trade after the Second World War took the form of more intensive mutual trade between countries with fairly similar supply structures (e.g. in the European Union) and not between countries with very different supply characteristics, as in the case of North-South trade?

3.4   Modern trade theories

The new trade theories therefore focused increasingly on the question: what can we say about the business characteristics of exporting companies as opposed to companies which do not or cannot export? The idea is that it is not so much national factors – or, if you like, locational factors – that explain in which goods a strong competitive position can be developed, but rather factors relating to specific sectors or companies. Another important difference in relation to traditional trade theories is that modern theories abandon the assumption of constant returns to scale and replace it with the concept of economies of scale in production. For example, this may mean that as a company produces on a larger scale, average costs fall (*internal economies of scale*), but also that costs will decline if numerous other businesses are established in the vicinity (*external economies of scale*), or both. In the first case, namely internal economies of scale, average costs fall because an individual company can produce more efficiently by expanding the scale of its production. In this case, the company's earnings increase disproportionately to the increase in use of all factors of production. The company then gains an ever-increasing advantage over other firms in its sector, thus ending perfect competition. Economies of scale are external if an individual company cannot itself influence its average costs by expanding production, but the average costs depend on the scale and structure of surrounding industry. This is the case if the industry reaches a size where all kinds of facilities which reduce production costs become viable; for instance, education, infrastructure or component suppliers. Thus, internal economies of scale arise at company level, and external economies of scale at industry level, often by chance. Where internal economies of scale occur, this also demolishes another important assumption of classic trade theories, namely perfect competition. Because economies of scale favour scaling up and concentration a company which, for whatever reason, succeeds in expanding its sales and hence its production will then be able to eliminate its competitors by lower costs.

3.4.1   *Internal economies of scale and the pattern of specialisation in free trade*

It should be clear that if economies of scale, regardless of their precise basis, largely determine international competitiveness, it is mainly incidental factors or even chance that will decide why one country, for example, has a strong aircraft industry as a result of internal economies of scale and another country has acquired an electronics industry, say, as a result of external economies of scale. A second implication of economies of scale is that even if countries have comparable supply structures (so that there are no comparative cost advantages and, according to traditional theory, no reason for specialisation either), there are still reasons why one country specialises in one product and another in something else. If they do so, production costs can be reduced in both countries by economies of scale, and everyone involved in international trade can benefit (Box 3.4).

Box 3.4 International trade and internal economies of scale

Let us again take two countries, two products and two factors of production. There are now internal economies of scale in production in both sectors. The pp curves of the two countries, which are identical because we assume that there is no difference at all in the supply situation in both countries, have a convex shape as indicated in the graph in Figure 3.4. The reason is that if we move along a curve to one of the turning points, the cost of producing the product which we are making in larger quantities will fall, while for the other product they increase. As a result, the opportunity costs are not constant as in Box 3.2 but variable. Since the slope of the pp curve indicates the opportunity costs, the two curves take on the shape shown. The curve towards the origin can be explained as follows. Starting at point 2 of Figure 3.4a, country 1 specialises in producing product y. If country 1 wishes to produce one unit of product x, country 1 will have to sacrifice a relatively large number of units of product y, owing to the economies of scale inherent in the production of y (check for yourself why the curve is flat in the vicinity of the intersection with the x axis).

1 = level of production/consumption under autarky
2 = level of production with international specialisation
3 = possible level of consumption with international specialisation
slope aa = domestic price ratio before international trade
slope bb = international price ratio

Slopes aa and bb are chosen in such a way that they are identical; thus, in the first instance there are no comparative cost advantages. In reality, that would be pure chance, even if the demand and supply situation were totally identical in the two

---

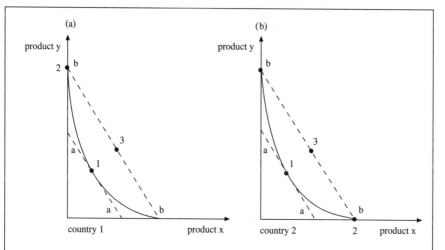

Figure 3.4 Production, consumption and trade with internal economies of scale

countries. This is because the domestic price ratio can also deviate from the international price ratio as a result of all kinds of factors, such as trade restrictions or differences in tax rules.

If, in the case of autarky, production and consumption are at level 1, both countries' welfare can increase if each country concentrates on one of the two products and part of the output is then exchanged for the other product via international trade. The graph shows that in that case, even if the international price ratio is totally the same as the original national price ratio, consumption levels are attainable in both countries (e.g. level 3) such that people in both countries have more of both products than before.

An example

Let us call the two countries in Figure 3.4 Spain and Portugal. The two countries are identical and produce wine using labour as shown in Table 3.7. We see from

Table 3.7 Number of hours of labour needed to produce one litre of wine

Litres of wine	Hours of labour	Units of labour per litre of wine
10	80	8
20	120	6
30	150	5
40	160	4
50	200	4

the table that internal economies of scale exist. Let us say that both countries have 160 hours of labour available for wine production. In the case of autarky, both countries can either produce 40 litres of one type of wine or 10 litres of red and 10 litres of white wine. If consumers in both countries want to consume both red and white wine, the second case applies. If both countries then trade with one another, wine producers in Portugal can concentrate totally on red wine and those in Spain on white wine. Both countries can now produce 40 litres of wine and exchange say half of it for another type. Thus, the consumers can now have 20 litres of red and 20 litres of white wine instead of 10 litres of each.

It is conceivable that subsequent developments may cause producers to diversify their production, with Portugal, for example, proceeding to produce both dry and sweet red wine (10 litres of each); wine producers in Spain could similarly specialise further in white wine. In this case, free trade means that consumers do not only have more litres of wine, but also four types instead of two. The conclusion is the one that, given economies of scale, international trade increases welfare, either because more goods are available, or because there is a greater choice based on greater product differentiation.

Economies of scale need not extend to the overall costs of producing a product: they may actually be important at the sub-process stage of production, because production can be considered as a series of sub-activities ranging from design to assembly and perhaps marketing. Under certain circumstances, a company can create economies of scale by concentrating on a few sub-activities such as design and production of certain components or assembly. Other sub-activities then take place elsewhere, perhaps abroad. The amusing thing is that when it comes to explaining the location of these sub-activities, one often resorts to the familiar concept of comparative costs: labour-intensive assembly takes place where labour is cheap, i.e. in the developing countries, and the design phase takes place where there is plenty of technological know-how, while the production phase, for example, can be located where the raw materials are readily obtainable. The product life cycle theory presented in Chapter 4 develops this idea further.

Market forms

Apart from the criticism of traditional trade theory based on the argument that comparative cost advantages are often less important than economies of scale in determining patterns of specialisation, a second major stream of publications emerged on the subject of the characteristics of international trade which also threatened the basis of traditional trade theory. These pointed out that a substantial part of production for the international market does not take place in a market with perfect competition, as assumed by traditional trade theory. Attention was drawn to the fact that many sub-markets are controlled by international oligopolies in which a small number of companies, often multinationals, operate on the various sub-markets. As we have already seen, even increasing economies of scale are enough to lead to market forms which deviate from perfect competition. But they also drew attention to factors such as technological advantage, price leadership and market entry barriers. All of these factors lead to a complex analysis of how and why international trade exists. We shall go into this in greater depth in subsequent chapters.

It was also pointed out that even if the number of suppliers on the international market is fairly large, e.g. as in the cosmetics industry or beer production, the producers will try to convince the consumer that their product is unique. This form of market is known as monopolistic competition: consumers regard products from the different countries as comparable but not the same. Since the individual consumer's taste as expressed in demand behaviour is increasingly personal, there is more and more scope for firms to specialise and export variants of a particular product. Moreover, the producer can choose from a wide range of instruments to try and strengthen his international market position. It was not until the 1970s, when researchers also began to develop more and more models from the point of view of 'industrial organisation', with imperfect competition, that a great deal of attention focused on the effect of this market form in trade theories.

Monopolistic competition

Attention concentrated particularly on the market form with monopolistic competition: this type of competition exists if many suppliers have access to the market (competition), but every supplier creates his own sub-market by product variety (monopolistic). In this situation the presence of internal economies of scale is generally assumed, so that average costs per unit of product will fall and an entrepreneur can make a profit. But as soon as other entrepreneurs find out, they will also enter the market and profits will drop back to stabilise at a certain level. However, they will not market exactly the same product but a slightly different one. This makes every entrepreneur see himself as a monopolist on his own sub-market. The monopolist assumes that there are so many suppliers that his prices do not influence those of the competitors (although the competitors' prices do, of course, influence the price-sales curve relevant to our supplier). If such a market form exists and if international trade then takes place, the advantages of larger-scale production and product differentiation increase as a result of market expansion; if the same quantity of production resources is used, consumers will have greater choice while at the same time the average cost per unit of product has fallen.

The monopolistic competition model not only answers question 4 following Case study 3.1 and explains the regional structure of world trade as we saw in Chapter 1 (Figure 1.2), but also indicates how important it is for exporters to obtain information on sales opportunities in the various sub-markets. This point will also be examined later in greater depth in Chapter 8.

Oligopoly

A market form such as monopolistic competition hardly ever occurs in reality, as almost every entrepreneur who does not have a total monopoly takes some account of the conduct of his competitors. A market form in which the number of suppliers is small enough that they are noticeably influenced by one another's actions and reactions is known as *oligopoly*. This market form is closer to reality than the monopolistic competition form mentioned earlier. The markets in beer production, detergents, cars, etc. are already moving close to monopolistic competition, but the competition almost always receives serious attention and we can call this an oligopoly situation.

The application of oligopoly models in international trade is a highly complex matter, because oligopolists react to one another and we therefore need to know what competitive behaviour is expected of the oligopolists in order to determine their price-sales behaviour. The reactions of competing companies can be so different that almost any form of price-sales ratio is possible. Moreover, oligopolists may or may not collaborate with one another; this collaboration may be formal (cartel) or informal. For example, informal agreement may take the form of price leadership, open price systems and market information systems or market division agreements. All kinds of cartel are also possible, such as price cartels, profit division cartels or market division cartels. Cartels are often prohibited, but in the case of informal collaboration, in particular, proof is very hard to find. As a result, it is often difficult for the authorities to control cartels. Free trade may then offer a solution if it leads to pressure on the collaboration between oligopolists, breaking their de facto monopoly. Chapters 8 and 9 which examine the implications of trade policy will pay more explicit attention to the oligopolistic market form.

3.4.2 External economies of scale

External economies of scale arise if a company gains a cost advantage from the nature and size of its immediate industrial environment. Thus, these advantages are nothing to do with the scale of its own production. If a large number of firms are geographically concentrated, for example, they can generate economies of scale: the establishment of a good infrastructure, the presence of well-trained employees, access to component suppliers and all kinds of other services. It is difficult to predict the occurrence of situations comprising external economies of scale. For example, why is a watch industry located in Switzerland and why are semi-conductor industries found in Silicon Valley, California? It seems that the country or region where the industry first happens to be established develops an advantage over other countries or regions. External economies of scale then cause this advantage to become so great that it is very difficult for other areas to catch up (see Box 3.5).

Box 3.5 An example of external economies of scale

Table 3.8 Economies of scale in Japan and Thailand, an example

Japan			Thailand		
Number (× 1,000)	Average costs = price	Global demand (× 1,000)	Number (× 1,000)	Average costs = price	Global demand (× 1,000)
1	10,000	1.5	1	6,000	3
2	5,000	4	2	3,000	6
400	1,000	700	600	250	875
875	250	875	1,000	100	1,000

Both Japan and Thailand can produce calculators. Let us assume that external economies of scale apply to calculator production and this production takes place under perfect competition so that the price is equal to the average cost. The economies of scale cause the aggregate average cost curve to fall. Japan is the first to set up a calculator industry. Initially, the calculators cost an average of 10,000 units. Since demand exceeds supply (see Table 3.8), the supply will be increased. This may lead to each company producing more (internal economies of scale) but it may also cause more and more such firms to be set up in the neighbourhood of the company that had begun producing calculators (external economies of scale). This causes average costs to fall. The process continues so long as there is excess demand on the market and, according to the table, will result in a situation in which 875,000 calculators are produced in Japan at an average cost of 250 units each. If at that stage another supplier, say Thailand, wants to penetrate the market, the only way to achieve it is by launching production in that country straight away on a massive scale of at least 600,000 units because, according to the table, it is only if production exceeds 600,000 units that Thailand can undercut Japan's unit production costs for 875,000 calculators (we assume that the average cost curve in both countries is constantly falling). Obviously, such a huge, abrupt expansion will be far riskier in practice, so that the chance of anyone venturing such a switch is small. If the industry were nevertheless to be transferred in this way, then in view of the size of the market it is clear that Japan will also lose the remaining production to Thailand, which produces more cheaply and will eventually be producing 1,000,000 units.

The multinational company

The rise of the multinational has contributed to the realisation that adjustments are needed not only in the theory of entrepreneurial behaviour but also in trade theory. Traditional theory was based on the concept of comparative costs, the philosophy being that characteristics of a particular location mean that certain goods and services can be produced there on internationally competitive terms. These characteristics may relate to physical circumstances or, as assumed in the HOS model, the availability and hence the cost of factors of production. Thus, the comparative cost concept is essentially based on the existence of locational advantages. Chapter 5 sheds some light on the rise of the multinational, concentrating on entrepreneurial factors which are deemed to determine competitiveness. In the literature, changing ideas on the background to competitive relationships have prompted discussion on the degree to which locational or company characteristics decide the competitiveness of businesses in Western countries. Some writers go so far as to say that competitive production depends almost entirely on factors specific to the company; they therefore refer to arbitrary comparative advantages and make the point that the substantial intra-industry trade between industrialised countries is incompatible with the idea of locational advantages. In their opinion, one should analyse the specific characteristics of companies, the degree to which there are economies of scale, technological advantages and the position of the company in relation to supply and sales markets and competitors, etc., in order to offer a satisfactory explanation for the relative export successes observed.

In contrast, other writers keep to the idea that locational characteristics still count for quite a lot in explaining international competitiveness. For example, this idea forms the basis of the World Competitiveness Report, published annually by the IMEDE management institute in Geneva and World Economic Forum. On the basis of some 300 indicators (derived partly from business surveys) grouped into 10 main determinants, this report ascertains the competitiveness by country of over 30 industrial and industrialising countries.

Another example of analysis of international competitiveness published by the German weekly *Wirtschaftswoche*, is taken as an illustration here (Table 3.9). This analysis looks at how various countries score in terms of labour, technology, capital and government. Those aspects are then subdivided into four components each. The highest score in any component is 100 points. The country with the most points in all components together is proclaimed the most competitive country.

3.4.3   The Porter analysis

The idea that the combination of production location and business organisation determines whether the product is internationally competitive is also found, for example, in the Porter approach, named after its originator, Michael E. Porter. Using a large team he examined for ten industrial countries (Denmark, Germany, Italy, Japan, Korea, Singapore, Sweden, Switzerland, the UK and the US) which industries were internationally successful in exports or foreign investment activities during 1971–85. He then examined the circumstances and factors that lay behind these successes. The most significant result of this fairly comprehensive, realistic approach was that, although competition is becoming increas-

Table 3.9 International competitiveness of the nine leading industrial countries

	Labour				Technology				Capital				Government				Total
	Wages	Labour productivity	Training	Product quality	Information technology	Inventions	Training & research expenditure	Use of technology	Interest	Inflation	Creditworthiness	Banking system	Education	Tax burden	Infrastructure	Political system	
Japan	24	90	98	100	100	86	100	100	100	100	100	96	63	42	93	39	1,331
Germany	18	98	100	86	87	100	95	82	62	38	99	100	89	38	93	100	1,285
Netherlands	23	100	80	74	80	47	73	73	61	47	97	93	48	71	90	77	1,134
United States	28	82	37	54	83	48	93	73	61	44	96	74	64	55	94	63	1,049
Great Britain	32	72	43	52	64	50	76	62	52	39	93	63	100	76	75	67	1,016
France	27	80	45	58	61	49	81	69	56	56	94	76	79	48	89	37	1,005
Canada	24	94	60	53	78	11	46	54	53	88	90	93	49	56	100	46	995
Korea	100	27	84	46	76	6	61	52	27	26	74	73	77	100	76	40	945
Spain	32	74	52	42	51	5	29	39	36	27	83	61	80	71	57	73	812
Italy	22	96	51	61	59	24	45	56	39	29	84	58	36	52	55	8	775

Source: Wirtschaftswoche.

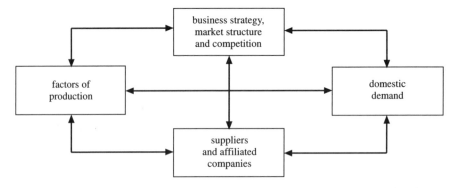

Figure 3.5 The Porter diamond

ingly international, the role of locations is ever more decisive for competitiveness. In addition, a country's competitiveness depends on scope for innovation and constant modernisation of production facilities. Every country has specific characteristics and structures making it better suited to one type of production than another. However, according to Porter this suitability is based on a much more complex set of determinants than factor costs as suggested by traditional trade theory. In Porter's view, the system of factors determining a country's competitiveness can be depicted as a diamond shape (the *Porter diamond*). The idea is that the cluster of companies whose production ties in with the specific characteristics and structures of the country of location will not only enjoy international success but will also usually continue to innovate and thus remain a strong competitor on the international market.

The national economic environment for the entrepreneur is determined separately and jointly by the four national characteristics given in Figure 3.5: availability and quality of the factors of production; the dynamism and quality, and to a lesser extent the level, of domestic demand; the presence of related or supporting industries which are also internationally competitive; the circumstances in the country which influence the establishment, organisation and management of businesses; and the nature of domestic conditions of competition. These four characteristics were present in varying degrees in the theories discussed previously. In both the HOS model and the Ricardo model, the available factors of production played a part in explaining international trade. The presence of suppliers and related industries is the most important factor in external economies of scale. The nature of demand plays a central role in theories concerning economies of scale and market forms. The theory on market structures is linked to business strategies, the structure of the sector and domestic conditions of competition.

The availability and quality of factors of production

Porter divides the factors of production into two groups: first there are the natural or 'inherited' factors such as labour, land, capital, infrastructure and natural resources. In advanced economies there are also 'created' factors of production such as human capital, infrastructure and research institutes. According to him, successful industries are not those that make intensive use of surplus natural factors of production (as in the HOS model) but those using mainly created factors of production. If industries benefit from natural factors of production, that is probably favourable to costs but in the long term the incentive to innovate may be lost, so that a comparative advantage becomes a disadvantage. Conversely, a comparative disadvantage can eventually be turned into an advantage if industries are forced to invest in created factors of production and to innovate and improve their quality in order to catch up. Japan is a clear example.

Consumer preferences

Consumer demand is important in forcing businesses to innovate and to obtain advanced knowledge and competitive advantages. In contrast to traditional trade theories, the level of demand is less important here than its nature. Demand factors have an important positive influence on competitiveness particularly if: consumer requirements are made plain to the industry, consumers are critical and constantly force entrepreneurs to innovate and make quality adjustments, and above all if the consumers' requirements anticipate demand. In this last case, the export of goods and services sometimes also leads to the 'export' of national values and consumer preferences.

Suppliers and related industries

If a country has an extensive network of internationally competitive suppliers and related sectors, this can confer major competitive advantages. The suppliers can readily give their domestic customers access to new information, new ideas, new understanding and innovations. In short, external economies of scale occur. Here it is important that the suppliers are also internationally competitive and use short lines of communication.

Business strategy, structure and competition

National habits, standards and values largely determine the way in which businesses are established, organised and managed. Countries also differ in the objectives which businesses and individuals set themselves. For example, these objectives are important in motivating talented people to make an effort at work, in the level and nature of the education chosen by employees, willingness to travel, etc. The objectives set by employees and businesses together with the prestige attached by a country to certain industries partly determine the direction of capital flows and human capital, which in turn influence the competitiveness of industries.

The presence of local competition is the last and also the most important factor in the diamond. One example is Switzerland, where competition between pharmaceutical companies such as Hoffmann-La Roche, Ciba-Geigy and Sandoz has resulted in a leading world market position in spite of the small home market. To quote another example, in Japan there are 112 companies competing in machine tools, 34 in semi-conductors, 25 in car parts and 15 in cameras. Often it is domestic competition that in the end explains why businesses turn to foreign markets. In the case of economies of scale, in particular, local competitors force one another to tackle the foreign market.

The diamond as a system

The greater the stimulus provided by the various facets of this national environment, including the stimulus on one another, the more this will contribute to the success of the clusters of companies located there. Porter regards two factors as being the most important in the integration of all four characteristics to give a system which, overall, provides a good business climate: the presence of active economic rivalry at home and the concentration of economic activities in a particular area. In practice, these two factors seem to act as a strong catalyst on the vitality of businesses.

One of the consequences of the above approach as far as policy is concerned is that there is, in fact, a role for national government as regards the national business climate. The situation in Japan is often quoted as an example of the optimum performance of that role, partly because it is assumed that the time horizons of government and businesses coincide better there than in other industrial countries. Although direct government involvement in the business world is inappropriate in this approach (except perhaps in the case of countries at an early stage of development), total withdrawal is also wrong. The government can perform an important function in stimulating innovation and should create a climate that challenges entrepreneurs to improve their performance. This means a policy of actively creating conditions, e.g. in the form of promoting educational activities, imposing uniform rules and standards, preventing all kinds of distortion of competition, stimulating investment in depth, etc.; the government should also promote flexibility on the labour and capital market.

An application of the Porter approach

The Porter approach can be used to analyse the strengths and weaknesses of a country. For example, it was used in this way in the Netherlands in the second half of the 1980s. Here, 11 sectors representing 15 per cent of exports were selected on the basis of their international competitiveness. They belong to four clusters:

- the agriculture and food cluster: cut flowers, cocoa powder and butter, dairy products and dairy industry machinery;
- the chemical cluster: plastics and polymers, industrial textiles;
- the electrical engineering cluster: recorded sound media, copying machines;
- the transport cluster: road haulage, lorries, yacht building.

It seemed that the reason for the success of these sectors should be sought mainly in the presence of the research and knowledge infrastructure and keen mutual rivalry which does not preclude cooperation in order to achieve certain effects of scale. It also emerged that the success of certain sectors could be explained principally by the combination of small scale (business acumen, improvisational talent and service), a traditional approach, the existence of a national network and a high level of technological development. Thus, the result was broadly in line with Porter's more general findings.

3.5 Summary

This chapter focused on how and why trade between countries exists. According to the traditional explanations, international trade is based on comparative cost advantages. Here, theories are usually based on the assumption of constant economies of scale and a market form where there is perfect competition. Ricardo laid the foundation for these theories, as can be illustrated by using a model comprising two countries, two products and one factor of production (labour). If both countries concentrate on exporting the product in which they have a comparative cost advantage (i.e. that is cheaper for them to make than the other product), both countries will benefit from trade. Hecksher and Ohlin then extended the Ricardo model by adding the factor of production: capital. They also imposed an additional limitation by assuming that technology is internationally the same. They conclude that a country has a comparative advantage in the product that makes intensive use of the factor of production which is in relative surplus in that country. The purchasing power of the income that the owners of these factors of production obtain will increase as a result of international trade, while the incomes of the owners of the relatively scarce factor of production will decline. Overall, however, the national welfare of each country still increases in this model through specialisation and exchange; but the phenomenon of factor reversal, in particular, undermined the theoretical basis of this model.

Modern trade theories are no longer based on the idea that a country's exports and imports are determined mainly by circumstances specific to the country. In these theories it tends to be factors specific to certain sectors or companies that decide the country's export structure. Economies of scale, market forms and chance can play a major role here.

The Porter analysis is a modern 'theory' but it does partly resort to the concept of comparative cost advantages between countries. Although local conditions are combined with the characteristics that a business must satisfy in order to compete internationally, national circumstances are still considered decisive.

Finally, the rise of multinationals has also necessitated adjustments to trade theory. International trade then takes place not only via the export and import of goods but also by the transfer of factors of production across borders. In the next two chapters we shall no longer focus on why countries export certain goods, but why entrepreneurs operate internationally.

Bibliography

Bhagwati, J.N. (1989), Is free trade passé after all?, *Weltwirtschaftliches Archiv*, vol. 125, no. 1, pp. 17–44.

Helpman, E. and P.R. Krugman (1985), *Market Structure and Foreign Trade*, MIT Press.

Hughes, G.A. and D.M.G. Newbery (1968), 'Protection and Developing Countries, Exports of Manufactures', in *Economic Policy*, April.

Krugman, P.R. (1987), Is free trade passé?, *Economic Perspectives*, vol. 1, no. 2, Fall, pp. 131–44.

Krugman, P.R. and M. Obstfeld (1989), *International Economics, Theory and Policy*, Scott, Foresman and Company.

OECD (1991), *Employment Outlook*, Paris.

Porter, M.E. (1990), *The Competitive Advantage of Nations*, Free Press.

Williamson, J. and C. Milner (1991), *The World Economy*, Harvester Wheatsheaf.

World Bank, *East Asian Miracle*, 1993.

4　International production factors

4.1　Introduction

The literature often distinguishes between the international transfer of goods and services and that of factors of production. One of the essential assumptions in the comparative cost theories discussed earlier, for example, was that factors of production present in a country could move freely between companies and sectors within that country but could not cross national borders. However, if the international mobility of goods affects the economic growth and welfare of countries, we can expect the same to be true for the international mobility of factors of production.

The international mobility of labour and capital has become an important subject in the study of international economic relations. As we can see from the statistical material in Chapter 1 and in this chapter, it is now clear that the international mobility of factors of production can no longer be ignored in the formulation of theories. That mobility applies not only to the factors of labour and entrepreneurship, but also and increasingly to monetary capital. So far as long-term capital transactions are concerned, the international transfer of monetary capital takes place mainly as investment. The international mobility of monetary capital permits international lending which, as we shall see later, can be regarded as inter-temporal trade. Monetary capital is also used to finance foreign direct investment (FDI). This last type of international capital flow is the focal point of the next chapter.

Chapter 3 showed that the sharp increase in the mobility of factors of production necessitates amendments to trade theories. While the theories discussed earlier focused on the question of why do countries exchange certain goods and what are the effects of this on wealth, in this chapter and the next the question will be: why are factors of production transferred internationally and what are the effects on welfare?

4.2　The motor vehicle sector: a case study

The following case study concerns a sector where business management is very internationally oriented and competition is fierce, namely the motor vehicle sector. Until recently, this competition was reflected mainly in a strong increase in the supply of Japanese cars on the European and American markets. However, exports of Japanese cars to the US and Europe are increasingly being replaced by the establishment of Japanese car production facilities in Europe and the US, from which the cars are then distributed to other places.

Case study 4.1 From car export to the export of production facilities

In the motor vehicle sector there is fierce competition, partly because the European and American markets have long been under threat from the *competitiveness* of Japanese cars.

Figure 4.1 shows the breakdown of the American car market by suppliers for 1980, 1985 and 1990. The table indicates that the share of the American market held by Honda and Toyota increased in the 1980s at the expense of GM and Chrysler. In 1990 alone, the Japanese share of the American market rose by 2.6 per cent to 22.5 per cent, while at the same time the share of American passenger cars fell by 2.2 per cent to 66.8 per cent. Moreover, GM ended the last quarter of 1990 with a loss, and production was cut back. Ford also anticipated a loss in the last quarter and Chrysler suffered a loss of $240 million on car production in 1990. Although the situation has turned in favour of the American car makers during the 1990s, the case study is still important for an understanding of changing competitive relationships in industry.

In the first half of the 1980s the American car industry went into recession. This plus the competition from Japan led to substantial protectionist measures, mainly in the form of quantitative restrictions. From 1981 onwards this took the form of 'voluntary' export restrictions by Japan under pressure from the US (in fact, the 'voluntary' export restriction was preceded by an American appeal to the GATT safeguard clause, Art. XIX, presumably to exert pressure on Japan to limit exports). As a result of this voluntary export restriction, the Japanese share of the American market fell from 22.6 per cent in 1982 to 18.3 per cent in 1984. From 1983 to 1985, demand for passenger cars increased and the financial situation of the US car sector

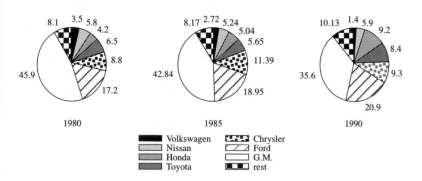

Figure 4.1 The breakdown of the American car market by suppliers in 1980, 1985 and 1990 (%)

Source: Ward's Automotive Yearbook, 1991.

---

improved. The US first planned to abolish the 'voluntary' export restrictions on Japanese cars in 1985, but reconsidered them later. The Japanese government then decided to raise the ceiling on the number of cars for export by 24 per cent. This caused the Japanese share of the market to increase to 20.1 per cent in 1985 and 20.7 per cent in 1986. Partly in response to maintenance of the 'voluntary' export restriction on Japanese cars and the depreciation of the dollar, Japanese car exports increasingly began to be replaced by the establishment of Japanese production facilities in the US, mainly on a joint venture basis. The same trend emerged in the EU.

Thus, more and more Japanese car plants were set up in the US (via FDI). While Ford, Chrysler and GM were closing plants in the US, Toyota, Nissan and Mitsubishi decided to set up new operations there. In 1986, Japanese production facilities represented 5 per cent of US passenger car output. In 1984 the figure was only 2.4 per cent. Japanese production on the American market was expected to exceed 10 per cent in 1989, with capacity of 1.4 million units per annum. In 1993 this figure had already been surpassed, with Japanese car production totalling 1.65 million. In early 1994 Honda decided to expand overseas production by almost 20 per cent, mainly in the US. This would reduce exports by some 15 per cent. A week later Nissan decided to produce the Sentra model in the US from 1995, owing to the expensive yen.

In response to the rise of the Japanese cars, the American car industry took various initiatives over the years in an attempt to turn the tide. Thus, in the 1980s GM decided to enter the market with a totally new make of car. This make, the Saturn, is like a Japanese car not only in size but also in price (around $8,000). According to some people, the Ford Taurus produced in the US is also comparable to the Honda Accord in terms of price and quality, mainly because the latter is larger and has a six-cylinder engine. These producers face little serious competition from Japan in the traditional, powerful American cars.

Since the early 1990s the US seems to have recovered some of its competitiveness, partly thanks to the sharp depreciation of the dollar. This is also expressed in higher quality. While GM was still receiving 740 complaints per 100 cars in 1981, this figure had been cut to 168 by 1989. By way of comparison: the number of complaints concerning Japanese cars fell from 188 to 121 over the same period.

In spite of the improvement in the quality of American cars, US producers find it difficult to push their Japanese competitors out of the market. In the period 1989 to 1990, the J.D. Power Customer Satisfaction Survey listed only two American makes among the top ten: Cadillac and Buick of Lincoln. According to a similar survey, the Japanese Toyota Camry, Corolla and Cressida have for years been the best cars in their class; for two years in a row, the Honda Accord was the top selling car in the US. Moreover, all new Ford and GM models were traditional 'gas-guzzlers' using at least a litre of petrol every ten kilometres.

Although the Americans are producing more efficiently, they have been slow to catch up with the Japanese in terms of competitiveness in the 1990s. At the beginning of the 1990s, Japanese plants in the US took 13 to 27 man-hours to produce a car, GM 25 to 30, Ford an average of 20 hours and Chrysler 25. As a result, and in spite of the excess capacity on this market – the market capacity being estimated at 10 million cars per annum – the Japanese managed to build capacity totalling 3.1 million cars in 1993, securing a market share of 23 per cent of production.

Nevertheless, American car makers were optimistic at the beginning of 1994. Although 3.1 million Japanese cars were sold in the US in 1993, that was still not enough to maintain Japan's market position in the US. Thanks to close cooperation with the Japanese production facilities, the Big Three of Detroit (General Motors, Chrysler and Ford) were able to learn a great deal from the Japanese production method and are now producing much more efficiently. As a result, the Ford Taurus was the top selling car in the US in 1993, displacing the Honda Accord which had held that position for a decade.

The case study illustrates that internationalisation can also take place via the international mobility of factors of production, in this case entrepreneurship and capital. According to the case study, the export of Japanese cars is based partly on the comparative advantage of the higher productivity of labour. In addition, there were differences in the quality and speed of innovation of Japanese and American production. In short, a number of elements from the theories described in preceding chapters offer partial explanations for the situation in the motor vehicle sector: comparative advantages and productivity of labour (Ricardo), innovation, demand and market structure (Porter) and the theory of internal economies of scale. However, the case study also raises a number of questions which will be discussed in this chapter and the next. These questions include:

- Why are more and more Japanese car makers setting up production facilities in the US and the EC?
- To what extent is the international mobility of Japanese car makers a unique phenomenon?
- To what extent are the production facilities a substitute for or an extension of car exports?
- Are the Japanese car manufacturers multinational enterprises?
- Are there also reasons other than increasing their market share which prompt companies to invest abroad?
- What are the consequences of the international mobility of the factors of production for the national welfare of the countries concerned?
- How can the above elements be combined with the various trade theories?

4.3   International mobility of factors of production

Case study 4.2 International mobility of goods in relation to factors of production

The international mobility of factors of production has increased considerably in recent years, not only in absolute terms but also in comparison with the growth in world trade. The following figures illustrate this:

- in 1980 the total volume of world trade was around $2,000 billion and around $3,500 billion in 1990: ignoring the change in the value of the dollar this meant that it increased by a factor of 1.75;
- the total annual volume of outward direct investment was about $36 billion in 1981–4 and about $142 billion in 1988–9, i.e. it increased by a factor of 4;
- the daily volume of trading on the leading foreign exchange markets, London, New York and Tokyo, was estimated at $44 billion in 1979 and around $430 billion in 1989, approximately ten times as much. Recent estimates relating to 1992 put the volume of foreign exchange dealing at an average in excess of $1,000 billion per day!
- In 1980, long-term international capital transactions totalled around $300 billion per annum, while the estimated figure for 1989 was $5,500 billion, eighteen times the level of less than ten years earlier.

Finally, a few figures on the scale of the international mobility of labour: in the first half of the 1980s, the number of immigrants into the US averaged roughly 600,000 per annum and annual immigration into Germany from Eastern Europe exceeded 400,000 persons.

Obviously, we should first compare the international mobility of factors of production with international trade in goods and services. In practice, the strict distinction between the international transfer of goods and services and that of factors of production is looking increasingly artificial:

(a) A large part of international trade consists of primary commodities and semi-manufactures; these goods can be seen both as intermediate products made with the aid of factors of production, and as goods which themselves serve as inputs in making the end product.
(b) International trade is increasingly dominated by trade in services. It is not always easy to draw a dividing line here between the transfer of human capital and the provision of final services.
(c) International transfers of technology are taking place on a large scale, with know-how being made available by licensing contracts granted to other countries; this is really neither international trade nor the international transfer of factors of production, but it does offer an intended advantage for those concerned.

Theoretically, there are also a number of analogies regarding the impact on welfare, on rates of pay for factors of production and on problems of distinguishing between the international mobility of goods and services (international trade) on the one hand and the international mobility of factors of production (international factor mobility) on the other.

In the first place, both movements contribute towards increased wealth. As far as international trade is concerned, we refer you to the preceding chapter. It is easy to see that the international movement of factors of production also increases welfare if we assume that payment for the use of labour or capital depends on the production achieved; because in principle, factors of production do not move to other countries unless there is the incentive of higher pay. Since higher pay represents a reward for higher productivity, this automatically means that more productive performance can be achieved, so that total welfare can increase.

Second, the international transfer of labour and capital encourages a tendency towards international equality in rates of pay for factors of production. The idea behind this is based on the theory that where availability of the factor of production declines, its rate of pay will increase because of the greater scarcity, while elsewhere it will fall for the opposite reason. Here, too, we have an analogy with international trade. In this connection the reader will remember one of the curious points to emerge from the HOS model in the preceding chapter, namely that in the eventual equilibrium situation for the model, payment rates of factors of production are internationally equal, even if these factors are not internationally mobile. According to this model, international trade has just the same levelling effect on rates of pay for the factors of production as if they were internationally mobile and thus constantly seeking the location with the highest pay.

Third, just as in the case of international trade there is the issue of income distribution in the case of international factor mobility, too. Which groups will be better off when capital and labour leave or enter a country, and can we also say something about the consequences for the distribution of welfare between the countries concerned? Public debate focuses closely on this type of question. To illustrate, let us assume that Japanese capital flows to the US and Japanese firms buy American companies and property: is that then favourable or threatening to the US? Let us assume an increase in the flow of immigrant workers and asylum-seekers from Africa and Asia to the EU: is that a threat to other people's European jobs and how does it affect wage costs and profits? What factors decide whether the home country from which the migrants originate is better off or not, in the end? These distribution aspects will be briefly discussed in the next section.

4.4 International factor mobility and the distribution question

It is not easy, generally speaking, to make unambiguous statements about the distribution aspects of international factor mobility. A first complication is how this mobility can be reduced to the underlying variables. If an untrained Kenyan worker and a Vietnamese computer expert emigrate to France simultaneously, can they be compared with one another in economic terms? The answer is 'yes' only if labour is assumed to be homogeneous, but the answer is 'no' if we also wish to consider the human capital elements. Let us take a second example: a

Canadian investor buys Belgian treasury certificates worth $1 million and at the same time a Canadian company makes a direct investment in Belgium to the same value, very successfully taking a new technique developed in Canada and applying it in Belgium. In both cases the financial flow is the same but the effect in terms of technology transfer is totally different. In short, it is not easy to find a good basis for comparing different flows of factors of production.

A second complication is that changes which take place on one sub-market always have repercussions on the situation in other sub-markets because of the economic interrelationships. Thus, if the quantity of available labour in one country suddenly declines as a result of emigration, the organisation of the production process will adapt and so will production, prices of goods and services, rates of pay of other factors of production, etc. This was one of the central elements of the HOS model, for example, namely that internationalisation of an economy eventually works through into all markets. Thus, we need to know about all connections within the economy in order to state the effect of the said emigration. Such knowledge is often lacking.

A third complication is that much will depend on the question of the destination of the pay for the performance of the internationally transferred factors of production. What proportion of it is channelled back to the home country as income transfer? Sometimes a high proportion, as is frequently the case with migrant workers, who commonly send at least 10 to 15 per cent of their earnings back to their country of origin. And sometimes there is no transfer to the home country. This question arises in a similar way in the case of international investments. For the host country, it makes quite a difference whether the profit made there with the help of foreign capital is reinvested in the host country or returned to the home country.

A fourth complication concerns the effect of international labour and capital movements on the country of destination. Questions which arise here include the extent to which these international flows can be controlled, e.g. in view of the economic situation in a country. Let us assume that a country is enjoying rapid economic growth but growth is liable to be held back by a shortage of available labour and capital. In such a case an influx of factors of production can have a beneficial effect, so long as not too much of the additional growth leaches back out to other countries or leads to inflation. But let us assume that, a few years later, this same country faces precisely the opposite situation: unemployment, heavy reliance on welfare provision and under-utilisation of production facilities. In this situation it can be economically desirable to achieve the opposite process, i.e. to get immigrant workers to leave the country.

A typical example of a favourable case occurs if foreign capital, and perhaps labour, can be used to cushion temporary shocks in the domestic economy. International capital flows or migration can also promote the transfer of technology, and this can produce a highly profitable mix of transfers for the recipient country.

An example of an unfavourable case arises if labour and/or monetary capital or even entrepreneurship leave a given country en masse at an inopportune moment, e.g. in the case of a capital exodus or large-scale emigration. This can have substantial economic repercussions, as various developing countries have found over the years. A long-term outflow of labour, in particular, can weaken the economy; for instance, highly trained workers who leave developing countries for the higher income countries: the 'brain drain'.

Case study 4.3 The significance of international migration in population scenarios

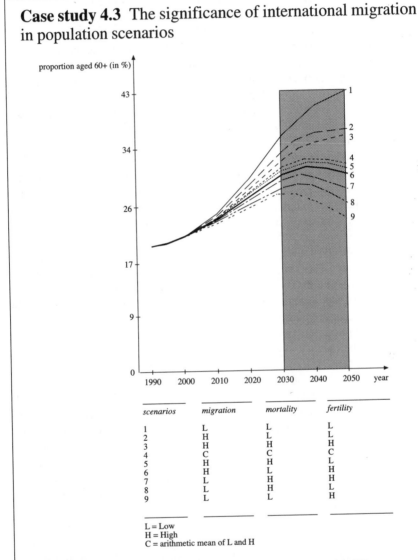

scenarios	migration	mortality	fertility
1	L	L	L
2	H	L	L
3	H	H	H
4	C	C	C
5	H	H	L
6	H	L	H
7	L	H	H
8	L	H	L
9	L	L	H

L = Low
H = High
C = arithmetic mean of L and H

Figure 4.2 Proportion of elderly population (aged 60 and over) in Western Europe
Source: IIASA, 1994, p. 7.

As part of the Population Project of IIASA (International Institute of Applied Systems Analysis), a seven-year study was conducted on the link between population, development and environment. One section comprised generation of a number of world population scenarios. These scenarios combined assumptions regarding mortality, fertility and international migration. One of the resulting sets of scenarios, namely the one relating to the ageing in Western Europe to around the year 2040, is shown in the graph in Figure 4.2. For the purposes of this chapter, the principal points are the extent to which ageing – measured here by the proportion of the population over age sixty – is determined by the assumption adopted for international migration. The graph makes this clear if we compare the top two curves. According to the projection, within a few decades the proportion of over sixties will already be approaching 40 per cent (currently over 20 per cent) given low net immigration, and will actually increase slightly after that; in contrast, with high net immigration, the ageing rate will be 'only' 36 per cent.

4.5   Inter-temporal trade

If we talk about the international mobility of capital, we usually do not mean physical capital or capital goods (moreover, capital goods are often difficult to transport), but the international mobility of monetary capital. Monetary capital is not in itself a factor of production; only if it is used to finance investment does it function as an instrument contributing to the creation of (additional) production capacity. It should be no surprise that monetary capital, being anonymous, is much easier than labour to transfer internationally. The economic consequence of the international mobility of monetary capital is that it exercises an indirect influence over the ability of a country to build up its own stock of capital goods (or to demolish it, as in the case of refugee capital). In addition, the international transfer of monetary capital often has a crucial influence on the national capital market conditions, such as the various interest rates and other terms on which loans are available.

Since there is only a vague connection between the availability of foreign capital and the establishment of national stocks of capital goods, the information given in Chapter 1 on the mobility of foreign direct investment, credit, loans and gifts can provide no more than a very indirect indication of the effect on stocks of capital goods. In any case, it is clear that financial flows are very mobile. However, there remains the central question whether it is the international flow of capital that causes the build-up of capital goods or vice versa.

International mobility of (monetary) capital in the form of *international credit* means that an exchange takes place between countries in which the possibility of immediate consumption is exchanged for the possibility of more consumption in the future, and vice versa. The phenomenon in which one country is a net lender to another is therefore interpreted as *inter-temporal trade*; because if country A lends money to country B, country B can use that money to buy consumer goods. Country A has postponed present consumption for the moment

Table 4.1 Current account balance for Japan, US and the developing countries 1985–94 ($ billion)

	1985	1986	1987	1988	1989	1990	1991	1992	1993	1994
Japan	49.2	85.5	87.0	79.6	57.2	35.8	72.9	117.6	137.2	141.3
US	−123.9	−150.2	−167.3	−127.2	−101.6	−91.9	−8.3	−66.4	−111.6	−130.0
Developing countries	−27.5	−48.4	−6.4	−24.9	−16.2	−12.1	−82.2	−62.4	−80.1	−84.6

Source: International Monetary Fund, 1993.

and will not be able to use this money for consumption until country B repays the loan (with interest). As far as the inter-temporal aspect is concerned, the international credit situation is comparable with individual saving; because if a person puts money in the bank as savings, that person sacrifices consumption today in order to be able to consume more tomorrow. The reward that a saver requires for postponing consumption in this way is expressed in the interest paid to him or her. For a country which is a net borrower, future obligations are entered into and the country thus has to use the credit in such a way that, in future, it is indeed able to meet the interest and redemption commitments. If it is not, then the country loses creditworthiness and situations such as the debt crisis of the early 1980s can arise (see also Chapter 17).

Chapter 2 explained that if a country is a net borrower from other countries over a given period, the current account balance for that period is negative. Table 4.1 shows the current account balance for the US, Japan and the developing countries (DCs) for 1985–94. It is noticeable that both the US and the developing countries were constantly in deficit during this period, and Japan had a surplus. When deficits persist for a long time, a country becomes a *debtor country*. This is the case if, when all current account balances over the years are added together, there is still a cumulative negative balance. In the opposite case we refer to a *creditor country*. However, the question is how to explain in economic terms why one country eventually adopts a debtor position and another a creditor position. Or, in other words, why one country has systematic current account deficits and another surpluses.

One way of explaining this might lie in differences in time preference between countries. *Time preference* means preferring immediate consumption rather than deferred consumption. The degree to which this applies may differ between countries. In places such as the OPEC countries where, certainly in the 1970s, large amounts of money were relatively easy to come by and the population was small, the time preference was generally low: people had no difficulty in postponing consumption; the same trend is generally found in the ageing industrialised countries. In contrast, developing countries will have a high time preference because they cannot afford the luxury of postponed consumption and have a young, dynamic population which would like to consume as soon as possible. A high time preference can, of course, be caused by the government's propensity to spend or by cultural factors. The large-scale use of consumer credit in the US might cause us to conclude that there is a relatively high time preference there.

Since interest represents payment for postponing consumption, in the absence of international trade, in countries with a high time preference interest rates will be high, and in countries with a low time preference the rates will be low. For as people in the country with the high time preference want to spend quickly, their demand for consumer goods is high; they are only prepared to save if the interest rate is high, so that only the more profitable investments can be financed; in the country with a low time preference the opposite applies: people are already willing to save at a low interest rate, so that less profitable investment projects also become easy to finance.

We can put this another way: countries with a low interest rate have a comparative advantage in current consumption and, given international trade, they will export current consumption by granting loans to countries with a comparative advantage in future consumption and hence a high interest rate. If it becomes possible to grant international credit, the capital will flow from countries with a low initial interest rate to those with a high interest rate, so that the return on capital in the different countries tends to converge. If the US has a high time preference and Japan a low preference, then – according to this theory – capital will systematically flow from Japan to the US. This will equalise any interest rate differentials.

4.6 Summary

The assumption that factors of production do not cross borders is contrary to reality. International differences in income and severe economic decline have always encouraged international mobility of labour. Regional alliances such as the EU have also promoted the mobility of labour as a factor of production.

The liberalisation of international capital movements and the rise of the multinationals have greatly increased the international mobility of capital as a factor of production. This raises the question: who can benefit from capital mobility and who may suffer? The analysis showed that there are many analogies with the theory of international trade. Thus, the international transfer of factors of production is not a zero sum game either; at the same time, the analysis still seemed to concentrate on the distribution aspects, both within the country and between countries. However, analysis of the distribution problem is complicated. First, factors of production are not homogeneous. Second, all economic markets have to be included in the analysis. Third, we need to know where the payment for the factor of production ends up; and finally, the effect of factor mobility depends on government control. A special aspect of international capital movements is that they in fact facilitate international credit between countries. The degree to which this takes place each year may be deduced from the balance of payments current account balance. If it is persistently negative, then adjustment will have to take place sooner or later. One of the questions which this prompted was: how can it be that certain countries are fairly systematically in deficit and others in surplus. In so far as this occurs between the major industrialised blocs, as in the 1980s, in particular, it can be regarded as macro-economic imbalances presenting a potential threat to the stability of the world economy in the long term. In theory, this type of imbalance is attributed to such factors as differing time preferences which are known to exist between different countries.

Bibliography

IISA (1994), *World Population, 'Options'*, Laxenburg, Austria, autumn.
International Monetary Fund (1993), *World Economic Outlook*, Washington DC, October 1993.

5 Direct investment and multinational enterprises

5.1 Introduction

By direct investment, a national company can set up production facilities abroad, thus developing into a multinational enterprise (MNE). This chapter will first examine what direct investments mean and how this type of capital flow has developed (section 5.2). Since it is typically MNEs that account for the bulk of foreign direct investment activities, section 5.3 specifically discusses the MNE phenomenon.

However, if a company engages in direct foreign investment, the question is: why does it not use the alternative, namely international trade, or international licensing agreements if an invention is to be exploited? Some theories which specifically focus on these selection processes, such as the product life cycle theory and the so-called eclectic theory of international entrepreneurial behaviour are therefore considered in section 5.4 of this chapter.

5.2 Foreign direct investment

The possibility of transferring capital across borders not only exists for the investor or speculator interested solely in return and risk, but also enables businesses to pursue their activities beyond national frontiers. This option is usually of interest if a high proportion of sales are destined for other countries (see the DSM case, for example, or the car market case study). If the investment crosses the border of goods or services instead, and the capital provider also gains a degree of influence or control over the foreign activities (e.g. by acquiring ownership of at least 25 per cent of the business), we call this *foreign direct investment* (FDI). The control associated with FDI can be acquired in practice by setting up foreign subsidiaries or branches, or by purchasing a substantial proportion of the share capital in the foreign company. The investment activities of multinationals through their foreign subsidiaries are one of the clearest examples of FDI. Traditionally, it was principally entrepreneurs in the mining and energy sector who engaged in FDI; later the emphasis shifted more towards the industrial sector, while nowadays there is more and more FDI in the services sector.

The term FDI causes some confusion because people mix up stocks and flows. If we refer to FDI as flows, we usually mean the volume of the capital flows to be classed as direct investment, transferred from or to a particular country in one year. We can consider either gross flows or net flows by balancing inward and outward flows against one another. If we concentrate on stocks of FDI, then we have to add up the total of all annual flows during the preceding periods. Here, too, it is very important to state whether we are ultimately referring to gross or net stocks.

Apart from the need for a precise definition of the FDI concepts, it is equally important to be as accurate as possible in valuing FDI. In practice, various complications arise in determining the precise value of FDI, the lack of reliable statistics being just one of them. Thus, it is often difficult to ascertain how much of the profit reinvested in the subsidiary in fact constitutes direct investment. If the profit were first paid out to the parent company and subsequently reinvested in the subsidiary as FDI, the volume of FDI would be fairly transparent; however, if the profit remains in the subsidiary and is used direct to finance new investments, the position is often far less clear. Another problem is the basis of valuation. Let us assume that a parent company invests $20 million in a Brazilian subsidiary, but the latter has already been running at a loss for several years; in that case, how should we value the direct investment (as a stock variable) if it is clear that this cannot be done by adding up past flows? This is not the place for closer investigation of these technical questions; however, it is important to point out that statistics on FDI must always be used with great caution.

FDI is playing an ever greater role in internationalisation. We can illustrate this with some figures. Over the period 1984/5 to 1989/90, direct investment flows grew by 33 per cent while world GNP expanded by only 12 per cent and exports of goods and services by 13 per cent. If the trend represented by these figures continues, FDI will hold an increasingly important position in the future, in relation to the traditional forms of trade. Table 5.1 sets out the volume of inward and outward FDI broken down by countries for 1980, 1985 and 1990. We see from the table that the total world volume of net FDI flows was around $1,500 billion in 1990 (the fact that the inward and outward flows for the world as a whole are not exactly identical is presumably due to shortcomings in the records). This is three times the value of the FDI flows in 1980.

In order to provide a further illustration of the growing importance of FDI in the international economic process, Table 5.2 relates both inward and outward FDI flows to the GNP of the countries concerned. From this we see that the volume of FDI flows represented 5 per cent of GNP in 1980, and that this figure had already risen to 8 per cent by 1990.

Tables 5.1 and 5.2 show that internationalisation via FDI takes place mainly between companies in industrial countries. In 1980, one quarter of FDI went to developing countries; however, the pattern is rather variable: in 1985 the figure was 27 per cent, in 1987 (not in the table) it was 12 per cent and in 1990 18 per cent. It is only recently that companies from developing countries have also been active themselves in outward FDI, and these are almost exclusively from the Asian growth economies; however, their share in outward global FDI was less than 4 per cent in 1990.

Table 5.1 Value of inward and outward FDI flows broken down by countries for 1980, 1985 and 1990 ($ billion)

Country	Outward			Inward		
	1980	1985	1990	1980	1985	1990
US	220	251	423	83	185	404
Canada	23	36	73	52	59	109
Germany	43	60	155	37	37	94
UK	79	107	249	63	63	206
Netherlands	40	50	105	20	25	66
France	45	19	100	16	20	78
Italy	7	18	64	9	19	61
Switzerland	22	24	66	9	11	18
Japan	20	44	202	3	5	15
Total	499	609	1,437	292	424	1,051
Other industrial countries	25	40	140	70	90	200
Developing countries	8	20	60	120	185	270
World	532	669	1,637	482	699	1,521

Source: Jungnickel, 1993, p. 120.

Inward FDI can be particularly important to developing countries in providing the necessary capital to achieve satisfactory economic growth and the transfer of technology and employment. That is why many of these countries are willing to offer major tax concessions and other favourable arrangements for setting up businesses in order to succeed in attracting foreign investment and retain that already acquired. At the same time, however, it is specifically in developing countries that we find some opposition to the introduction and presence of FDI. First, the opponents claim that there is often no effective transfer of technology. Second, they point out that foreign companies take advantage of the low wages and other favourable production conditions, but often channel much of the resulting profit back to their home country. Finally, a common criticism is that the national authorities have hardly any control or influence over foreign companies because they can easily threaten to leave the country, owing to the *footloose* character of their international activities (i.e. they are not tied to production in a particular location). As a result, it is alleged that foreign companies are not much bothered about national regulations.

5.3 The multinational enterprise

Decisions which lead to international transactions are usually made in the company. It is therefore important to examine the factors which cause individual

Table 5.2 Inward and outward FDI flows as a percentage of the GNP of the country concerned for 1980, 1985 and 1990

Country	Outward			Inward		
	1980	1985	1990	1980	1985	1990
US	8	6	8	3	5	7
Canada	8	10	13	20	17	19
Germany	5	10	10	5	6	6
UK	15	24	26	12	13	21
Netherlands	24	39	37	12	20	24
France	2	4	9	2	4	7
Italy	2	4	6	2	5	6
Switzerland	22	26	29	9	12	8
Japan	2	3	7	–	–	1
Total (weighted average of percentage)	7	8	10	4	5	7
Other industrial countries	3	5	7	8	10	10
Developing countries	–	1	2	5	9	8
World	5	6	8	5	6	8

Source: Jungnickel, 1993.

companies to adopt an increasingly international approach as time goes by. In the initial phase of their development, most companies focus on the home market; in fact, this type of business predominates in most countries. If expansion is held back by the limitations of the home market, the company in question may be inclined to try selling abroad. Chapter 3 sought reasons why certain companies in a country export certain goods. In the first instance, the company need not always organise these exports itself. For example, it is possible to export via another domestic company (indirect export) or even by selling licences to other countries for the production method or the specific characteristics of the production process. However, export activities usually start by first making use of foreign sales agents; if exports go well, businesses then often set up their own foreign sales offices or take one over. Thus, the latter case can be the start of a process towards FDI.

Taking this a step further, the company may then consider making an actual foreign investment, e.g. in the form of a *joint venture*. In this case, the company together with one or more foreign companies participates in some way in a joint foreign subsidiary. For example, the joint venture may then be aimed at joint production activities, or it may be set up for the purpose of jointly organising foreign sales, etc. Particularly where there are still many legal uncertainties on the foreign market (consider the situation in Eastern Europe or in various developing countries), a joint venture may be an attractive interim solution in the process towards setting up independent subsidiaries abroad. It is also common for the host country's government policy to be aimed at restricting the influence of foreign companies set up in its territory by deliberately requiring a certain national share in the management of those companies.

Continuing the progressive transfer of a company's activities to foreign countries, we automatically arrive at the final stage in which the company relocates a part of its production activities abroad. In such cases the company develops into a *trans-national enterprise*. If it then wants to become a true multinational, then the whole management of the business needs to be based on an internationally oriented strategy.

A diagram showing the successive stages which may lead to the point where we can refer to an MNE is given in Figure 5.1. This illustrates how companies might develop into an MNE by various channels and successive intermediate stages.

5.3.1 *Definition of the term MNE*

If a company owns production facilities in several countries and the business management comprises an internationally oriented strategy, that company is called a *multinational* or *multinational enterprise* (MNE). Obviously, this constitutes a very diverse category of businesses, ranging from groups with annual sales in excess of the GNP of a medium-sized industrial country to companies with a turnover of just a few million dollars but a very strong international orientation. Thus, not all MNEs are massive. That is why attempts have been made to devise a typology of the MNE so that various sub-categories of MNEs can be meaningfully distinguished. Although any typology contains arbitrary elements, it can be useful to classify MNEs on the basis of criteria such

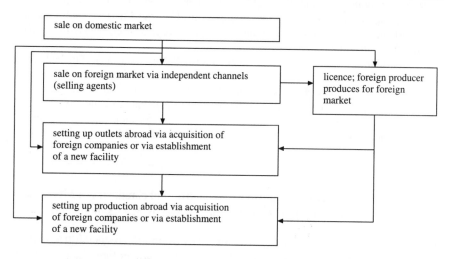

Figure 5.1 Possible process of development into a multinational enterprise
Source: P. Dicken, 1986, p. 129.

103

as: turnover, the number of countries where a processing activity takes place and its regional distribution, the share of foreign activities in overall operations, and the degree to which the organisational structure is internationally oriented. The typological classification to be built up on this basis may be important, for example, in determining the degree to which the conduct of a particular MNE can be controlled by the local government; because the larger the MNE, the wider its international distribution, the greater its dominance of the various markets and the more *footloose* it is, the weaker the national government's negotiating position in relation to the MNE (see also Case study 5.1).

Case study 5.1 Hoover relocation not contrary to EC rules

In February 1993 the American vacuum cleaner manufacturer, Hoover, decided to transfer production from France to Scotland, partly because workers there had made major concessions regarding conditions of employment. This caused uproar in France, one reason being the more or less simultaneous decision by the management of a Grundig television factory in Creutzwald (France) to transfer production to Austria. Almost a thousand French workers went to Brussels to protest against this form of what they called 'social dumping'. However, the European Commission could do little for the protestors, even if it had wanted to, because the relocation of the vacuum cleaner factory was not contrary to EC rules.

This case was also influenced by the fact that Britain had not committed itself to the social chapter of the Treaty of Maastricht. Nor had Britain signed the Social Charter (a political declaration of intent to lay down European rules on social matters) at the end of 1989. Some of the basic social rights endorsed by the Social Charter are: improvement in living conditions and terms of employment, the right to social protection and the right to freedom of association and collective bargaining; since Britain had not committed itself to the Charter, conditions of employment which deviate in a number of respects from those elsewhere in the EU are permissible in the UK.

Apart from that, in the EU negotiations Britain had also blocked the introduction of a directive obliging large multinationals to set up a European staff council and to supply that body with information. If such a directive had been adopted in the EU, then in any case the Hoover management would have had to consult the workers in France and Scotland on the relocation plans at an early stage. (Of course, this need not mean that the relocation would not then have gone through.)

In spite of the need to distinguish between different categories of MNEs, there are still a number of common characteristics shared by MNEs in general:

- companies in the group are legally linked by a common ownership structure;
- member companies have economic links with one another since they have access in varying degrees to a common source of resources, information and control instruments; this concerns not only common access to financial

resources, but also common participation in information and information systems, organisational structures, marketing strategies, patents, brand names, etc.
- the various companies are all subject to a common overall management philosophy and group strategy, and each one usually has an international orientation.

The above implies that subsidiaries of MNEs have not only financial obligations towards the parent company as a result of the control and/or shareholding relationship, but also have to accept the organisational structure of the parent company. These characteristics mean that financial relations between the parent company and the subsidiaries are greatly complicated by the fact that there is often two-way traffic: the parent company may finance new activities in the subsidiary while the subsidiary may transfer profits to the parent company. Since the various international financial dealings offset one another to some extent, there is often some scope in practice for exploiting an ever-existing certain amount of freedom in accounting, e.g. in order to minimise the group's total tax burden. This aspect of the multinational may be further reinforced if there is internal trade, e.g. in components or semi-manufactures, between the parent company and the subsidiary or between subsidiaries themselves; it is estimated that this type of transaction accounts for a quarter of world trade. In such cases, in particular, there is a degree of freedom within the enterprise as regards the valuation of these transactions, so that an attempt can be made to transfer the profit internationally to the country with the most favourable tax rules.

The policy on valuing transactions within the MNE is known as *transfer pricing*. The possibility of making use of this is a typical example of the relatively independent position of the MNE in relation to local and/or national government policy. This independence is sometimes translated into a strong negotiating position vis-à-vis the local government, especially in countries where foreign investors are also regarded as the driving force of the local and/or national economy.

5.3.2. The relative importance of MNEs

The first point which we notice on examining the social importance of the MNE phenomenon is the huge growth in their numbers and in their share of the world economy and world trade. United Nations (UN) researchers have calculated that there were at least 35,000 MNEs at the beginning of the 1990s, controlling 170,000 subsidiaries. According to the same source, the 100 largest MNEs owned \$3,100 billion of the world's assets in 1990; \$1,200 billion of this related to assets outside the MNE's home country. According to a rough estimate by *The Economist*, the total assets of businesses worldwide in 1990 came to approximately \$20,000 billion altogether.[1] This would mean that the top 100 MNEs

---

1. For the basis of this estimate, see *The Economist*, 27 March 1993, p. 6.

owned roughly a sixth of the total assets in 1990; at that time the top 300 MNEs held perhaps a quarter of the world's assets. The importance of MNEs for the world economy is even greater if we remember that an estimated 40 to 50 per cent of the international transfer of assets takes place via the same 100 leading MNEs. This means that MNEs in fact play a very dominant role in international economic relations.

The enormous quantitative significance of MNEs in the world economy is a fairly recent phenomenon in historical terms, which is typical of this century and has surged ahead mainly in the past few decades. Essentially, this strong growth mostly began after the Second World War. The volume and quality of the statistical information on direct investment made it impossible to give any accurate idea of the international activities of MNEs during the period up to 1970. At the end of the 1960s, with the exception of the US and the UK, most countries did not have sufficient data to determine the cumulative value of FDI, so that they had to confine themselves to estimates, based on annual flow figures which were difficult to compare with one another.

Thus, businesses are unmistakably becoming ever more international. In 1970 the UN identified 7,000 MNEs, more than half of them from the US and the UK. Today, almost half of the 35,000 MNEs identified as such by the UN come from the US, Japan, Germany and Switzerland. The UK has now slipped to seventh place in the list of home countries. As already mentioned, FDI by businesses from new industrial countries such as Taiwan and South Korea is evidently also on the increase.

It is estimated that about half of all industrial production now takes place in MNEs or similar organisational structures, at least if we leave aside businesses in the former planned economies. As already remarked, trade within multi-national groups can be estimated as representing around a quarter of world trade in goods. Figures for the latter half of the 1980s indicate that the share of foreign-owned companies in the total national volume of business fluctuates around 20 per cent in Europe, 10 per cent in the US and 1 per cent in Japan. The corresponding share of foreign companies in national employment is usually somewhat lower.

Just as the distance factor is very important in explaining the regional pattern of trade, so distance is equally important in the choice of region for direct investments. As we can see from Figure 5.2, there are clusters of countries around Japan, the US and the EU receiving FDI from the three respective blocs.

5.4 The international relocation of production activities: some theories

The enormous growth in the importance, number and size of MNEs after the Second World War prompted ever increasing interest in the reasons why businesses develop into multinationals. To begin with, the literature was dominated by the simple, neo-classical idea that international investment flows

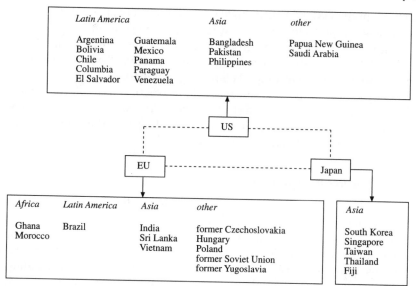

Figure 5.2 Principal countries of destination for foreign investment flows from the US, the EU and Japan, 1986–9
Source: UN

come from countries with low productivity of capital and are directed towards countries with high productivity of capital, thus enabling businesses investing internationally to achieve the maximum return. When the late 1950s brought an increase in FDI from the US to Europe, this theory actually appeared to be correct. At that time, the return achieved after tax by American subsidiaries in Europe was higher than that made by American industry. In the 1960s the return achieved by American subsidiaries in Europe generally dropped below the level of returns in the US; however, the net flow of direct investment from the US to Europe continued to increase.

In the face of trends such as this, the simple neo-classical theory therefore came to be seen as increasingly unsatisfactory. First, it was difficult to explain the normal two-way traffic in FDI, and also the fact that FDI takes place mainly between fairly similar industrial countries. Second, if companies were principally interested in the return, it was not entirely clear why they should want to retain control over the business use of the financial transfer (see also the eclectic approach in sub-section 5.4.2). Third, there was growing doubt about the neo-classical explanation for FDI as it became increasingly apparent that the return on foreign investments could hardly be estimated in many cases, owing to risks and institutional obstacles. This led to the subsequent search for new explanations for the MNE phenomenon.

Initially, the emphasis was mainly on partial explanations, often based on case histories. Thus, for example, in the case of MNEs in the mining and energy sector, people referred to such factors as securing lines of supply from other countries; in the case of FDI in highly protectionist countries, they referred to the evasion of protective trade restrictions; as regards the wave of direct investment flowing at that time from the US to the newly-established EC, they mentioned the exploitation of economies of scale; and in other cases they pointed to factors such as risk spreading, tax advantages or market strategy.

Although all this type of arguments will, in practice, have played some part in decisions about FDI – in most cases there was some empirical evidence supporting these arguments – they do not offer a sufficiently systematic explanation for the multinational phenomenon.

5.4.1 Product life cycle theory

One of the first ideas to incorporate a number of the above elements in a theory was the Vernon product life cycle theory of the mid 1960s, applied mainly to the rise of the American MNEs. On the basis of this theory, people tried to explain the start and subsequent decline of US production of such goods as radios, televisions, plastics, transistors, simple electronic products, etc. According to this theory, which was particularly popular in the 1960s and 1970s, the MNE phenomenon is attributable to the recognition of various phases in the life cycle of a product. Table 5.3 summarises the features of the product life cycle theory.

While the HOS model was based on stable, identical production functions for certain goods, the production functions in the Vernon model depend on the current phase in the production process. In the initial phase, many alterations and adjustments are made to the product design, so that the production process necessitates non-standard work, much use of special skills and a short time-scale. When a new product is introduced, it is difficult for consumers to compare it with those made by other producers. Total demand for the product therefore has a low price elasticity in the initial phase. (This means that the volume of demand is fairly insensitive to price changes. In this case, the rise in demand is disproportionately small if the producer cuts the price of the product, so that turnover declines. A price reduction of 15 per cent, for example, generates an increase in demand of less than 15 per cent, say 5 per cent. This is therefore called inelastic demand.)

If, as time goes by, the producer has gained an understanding of what the consumer wants, the product and the production process can be standardised. In this growth phase, the production process is characterised by internal economies of scale while the consumer has become more familiar with the product and can compare prices. This causes price elasticity to increase, and the producer will begin to compete on the basis of price. (High price elasticity means that the increase in demand for a given product is disproportionately great if the price falls. This is known as elastic demand.)

In the maturity and saturation phase, the production process is totally standardised and the level of education of the workers is no longer important. Competition then takes place via price or product differentiation. Businesses which do not produce efficiently enough price themselves out of the market;

Table 5.3 The product life cycle

	Stages Launch	Growth	Maturity
Demand structure	– low price elasticity of aggregate demand – nature of demand not quite known	– growing price elasticity of demand – start of price competition	– manipulating demand via marketing techniques, product or price differentation
Production	– short processes – rapid technological changes depending on degree of training – capital intensity low	– mass production methods	– long processing using stable techniques – degree of training irrelevant – capital intensive
Industrial structure	– small number of companies	– large number of companies, associated with losses and merges	– number of companies declines

those which are efficient, e.g. because they have better access to particular factors of production, can hold their own. It is particularly in this final phase that traditional comparative cost differences regain their importance.

Assumptions

From this we see that Vernon assumes that products are subject to predictable technological changes and marketing methods, and that the production process may vary between countries. In addition, consumer incomes and their associated preferences may also differ from country to country. Another important assumption incorporated in other models but dropped by Vernon is the free availability of information. According to Vernon, this is mainly true within national borders, but even then there are costs associated with the transfer of knowledge from the market to the company. This leads to the following three conclusions:

(a) if there is strong consumer demand in a given country for product and process innovation, the chance of innovation is greater than in countries where consumer demand is more conservative;

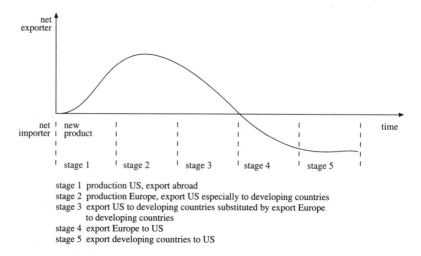

stage 1 production US, export abroad
stage 2 production Europe, export US especially to developing countries
stage 3 export US to developing countries substituted by export Europe
to developing countries
stage 4 export Europe to US
stage 5 export developing countries to US

Figure 5.3 Patterns of trade for a product introduced in the US during the stages in the product's life

(b) an entrepreneur generally prefers to invest in innovations for the home market rather than those for the foreign market;
(c) the closer the producer is to the market, the lower the costs associated with the transfer of market knowledge.

The Vernon model explains the MNE phenomenon as follows. From the assumption that information is not freely available, it follows that during the introduction phase it is mainly local producers who are aware of the possibilities of introducing a new product on to a specific market. This causes the new products to have special characteristics for the home market. In the case of the US, for example, the high incomes and high labour costs are reflected in strong domestic demand for expensive, high-technology products, and the corresponding high level of domestic supply. During the introduction phase (stage 1 in Figure 5.3), the non-standardised character of the production process means that direct communication between consumer and producer is essential for further product development. In this phase, production takes place on the local market, which means that any foreign demand is supplied by exports (see also Figure 5.3).

If the product is so standardised that direct communication between producer and consumer becomes relatively less important than production costs, production starts up in other countries: the growth phase, as it is called. The timing of this depends on economies of scale, duties, transport costs, income elasticity of demand and the level of incomes and market size in other countries. According to Vernon, in the first instance the company mainly sets up production facilities abroad to reduce production and distribution costs or because of the potential threat to its market position. The nature of the production cycle means that foreign production will first take place in high-income countries. Thus, US companies, for example, will start by setting up their subsidiaries in Canada or

Western Europe. In the beginning, foreign production will also be limited by the fact that the products are only sold on the local market in the foreign country (stage 2).

As a result of cost advantages, exports (stage 3) from the foreign subsidiaries will gradually increase until, in our example, the US imports the product altogether (stage 4); meanwhile, new products are naturally introduced in the US and go through the same phases. In the end, the production process is totally standardised so that there is scope for economies of scale and mass production, and the product can actually be made at low-cost locations in developing countries (stage 5); this is called the saturation phase. Thus, as the product life cycle progresses, so the optimum production location also changes.

Companies which, in our example, continue to concentrate on traditional production of goods in the saturation phase will, according to this theory, be confronted by stagnant and declining demand and keen competitors who have often also set up their production facilities in low-wage countries. This causes the 'traditional' businesses to lose their profit potential and they will generally have to cut back their production, eventually diversifying or turning to other products.

Comments

Although the product life cycle theory abandons a number of assumptions of the HOS model, the basis for them still exists in the familiar comparative cost concept, albeit in a dynamic context: labour-intensive assembly is located where labour is cheap, e.g. in developing countries; the design phase takes place where there is plenty of technological know-how, while the production phase, for example, can be sited where raw materials are readily available.

However, in the course of the 1970s the product life cycle theory was considered increasingly unsatisfactory, e.g. to explain the rise of the American MNEs. It began to seem less and less necessary for a product to be developed on the home market first, before export and FDI can be considered, since the MNEs were acquiring ever greater knowledge of markets and technological developments outs' le the US. (In this connection, Vernon himself referred as long ago as 1979 to the ever increasing 'global scanning capabilities' of the MNEs.) Moreover, the technological and income differential between the US and other industrial countries has declined over the years, so that the locational characteristics of the US became increasingly unimportant in explaining the optimum production location. As a result, the theory lost its attraction. One might argue that the theory is now mainly relevant in explaining FDI by small firms or certain FDI in developing countries.

5.4.2   The eclectic theory of the MNE

Apart from the fact that the product life cycle theory was constantly superseded by reality, some fundamental questions concerning the MNE phenomenon still remained unanswered. For example, it was unclear why certain companies in a country develop into multinationals while others do not; because any company in a country can take advantage of the special characteristics of the home market. It is also unclear why MNEs wish to retain control over the production process. If a company has developed a particular product and this product can be produced more cheaply abroad, then the argument is that the company can easily sell the product via a licence for the know-how or export it to other countries. Why should anyone transfer the production to another country and yet want to retain control over it?

In other words, to explain the existence of MNEs, we need a theory which provides a satisfactory answer to all these questions. This is so in the case of Dunning's *eclectic approach*, for example (i.e. an approach which combines elements of various theories). This states the conditions for the creation of an MNE as the presence of advantages dependent on ownership, the presence of locational advantages and arguments for internalisation.

The first condition, the presence of an *ownership advantage*, means that a given company enjoys specific, unique production conditions enabling it to generate a future flow of income and profits. Thus, these unique production conditions are reserved for the company in question, but can be combined with other production resources, both in the home country and outside it. These unique characteristics may relate to tangible goods, such as exclusive access to certain natural resources, manpower or capital. They may also relate to intangible production conditions such as specific technical knowledge, including market knowledge, more advanced information, specific organisational and entrepreneurial qualities or market access. There are, of course, many conceivable combinations of circumstances which create advantages. The condition concerning ownership advantage will always have to be fulfilled to some degree if investment is to be successful.

The second condition is the existence of *locational advantages* relating to production in the host country. The production conditions responsible for the additional profitability of the investment are then not linked to ownership of a particular business but to a specific production location. These advantages are therefore available to any company investing in production in that location. *Export processing free zones* are extreme examples of measures creating locational advantages. These are special zones, often situated in emerging industrial countries, with many special facilities for the foreign companies being set up there as regards tax rules, available infrastructure, an adequate supply of very cheap labour, subsidies, etc. But of course, many more general factors, such as a low wage level, low levels of taxation or a high standard of education, can also be important positive factors for a location.

An ownership advantage for a national company combined with a locational advantage on a foreign market appears to provide an explanation for direct foreign direct investment, because the company will be keen to invest and will choose the most appropriate location for the purpose: another country. Examples of this are legion. They include the subcontracting of manual assembly work to firms in developing countries or production on sales markets because of the shorter lines of communication between producer and customer. However, there is also a third requirement.

This third factor is the existence of arguments for *internalisation*: exploiting ownership advantages by not contracting out the associated activity but deliberately pursuing it and retaining control over it oneself. Generally speaking, there are arguments for internalising economic activities if there is an advantage in the certainty created by incorporating part of the company's economic environment in one's own business. This is the case, for example, where people want to be more certain about market events connected with the technology process, which is known as the *technology transfer* problem. In the case which we are discussing here, this means that the option of selling a licence for the said advantage is not appropriate. There may be various reasons for this. Let us assume that the ownership advantage is based on the combination of a unique set of workers, their unique organisational structure and their unique use of equipment. We can see that logistical reasons might prevent this advantage from being sold to another company by licensing (unless part of the business is transferred complete). Also, any negotiations on the transfer of licences are hampered by the fact that both parties can initially conclude only a rather general agreement, because too much detailed information passed to the purchaser in the pre-contract phase would often essentially mean the transfer of the licence. This hinders the process of reaching agreement on (the price of) the licence. Finally, the seller is often worried that if other people use his specific knowledge, that information may either be liable to leak out or it may be used so inexpertly as to damage the reputation of the original owner.

Finally, parts of the production process may be internalised, e.g. with a view to reliable supplies or sales. This constitutes *vertical integration*. It should be clear that in this type of case, too, licences cannot be granted for the ownership advantages. Thus, in practice there are countless arguments which explain why companies need to keep control over the exploitation of the exclusive right to use innovations, ideas, organisational characteristics, etc.

The three factors mentioned in this section together explain the existence of FDI and thus MNEs as follows. Assume that a company has an ownership advantage. There are then three options: invest internally in the company, invest abroad, and finally, sell a licence for the advantage and thus leave the investment to others. It is easy to see that if there is a simultaneous locational advantage in foreign production and advantages in internalisation, the first and last options automatically cease to apply, leaving the direct investment option.

5.5 Summary

Since the 1980s in particular, flows of foreign direct investment (FDI) have increased very rapidly in relation to flows of goods and services. FDI means that an entrepreneur invests in foreign activities and also acquires a certain degree of influence or control over them. If a company has acquired several production facilities in various countries via direct investments, we can call it a multi-national enterprise (MNE).

Vernon's product life cycle theory tries to explain the MNE phenomenon on the basis of the different phases in the life of a product. Dunning's eclectic approach combines a number of conditions for the existence of MNEs into a single theory. That theory is based on the following elements: locational advantages, ownership advantages and markets which function imperfectly, so that internalisation is the best option.

It should be clear that the policy of national governments influences all three of the above elements in the eclectic theory explaining the conduct of MNEs. That relationship between companies operating internationally and government policy will be examined in more detail in the next chapters.

Bibliography

Dicken, P. (1986) *Global Shift, Industrial Change in a Turbulent World*, Harper & Row, London, p. 129.

Dunning, J.H. (1993), *Multinational Enterprises and the Global Economy*, Addison-Wesley.

The Economist, Multinationals, 27 March 1993, pp. 5–28.

International Monetary Fund (1991), *Determinants and Systematic Consequences of International Capital Flows*, Washington DC, March.

Jungnickel, R. (1993), Recent trends in foreign direct investment, *Intereconomics*, May–June, pp. 118–25.

Vernon, R. (1979), The product cycle hypothesis in a new international environment, *Oxford Bulletin of Economics and Statistics*, vol. 41, pp. 255–67.

Wells, L.T. (ed.) (1972), *The Product Life Cycle and International Trade*, Harvard University.

6 Trade policy: a classic welfare theory analysis

6.1 Introduction

Discussion of the advantages and disadvantages of international free trade for national welfare (see Chapter 3) is of direct relevance to the question whether one should attempt to influence international trade directly or indirectly via government intervention. For a long time, traditional trade theory held that free trade maximised overall welfare for all those concerned (jointly). There was fairly general recognition that two important assumptions of this theory, namely perfectly efficient markets and constant economies of scale, did not hold true in practice. The modern trade theories which form the focus of Chapters 7 to 11 also initially supported and reinforced the impression that free trade can produce the best result in the end for all parties. This automatically means that the objections to protectionism prevailed in the theoretical literature. This idea was likely to be further reinforced by the tendency illustrated in Chapter 1 for national economies to become more closely interlinked and for businesses to operate increasingly internationally.

Against this background, we may express surprise that in current trade policy practice very divergent trends are observed, ranging from escalating protectionism to countries being systematically opened up to international competition. This chapter gives an example of both using an introductory case study. One of these case studies illustrates a sector in which protectionism is greatly increasing and the other a country which is reversing the direction of its trade policy, trying to switch from a strongly protectionist tradition to a policy oriented more towards free trade.

The ambivalence evident from these examples can be partly explained by the considerations taken into account in applying protectionism. These vary according to the viewpoint from which protectionism is considered: that of the world as a whole, that of national welfare or that of specific interest groups. In general, the advantages of free trade become clearer the higher the level of aggregation applied. At national and international level, the advantages of free trade outweigh the disadvantages; at branch or sector level this need not be so, certainly not if a sector is liable to be driven out of business as a result of free trade. In trade policy practice, a combination of different considerations is often applied, based partly on international and national interests and partly on those of specific interest groups. This often makes the discussion of trade policy rather confusing.

Different starting points are also used in theory. Traditional theory was based mainly on the criterion of national welfare. Recently, however, there has been increasing recognition that, in order to represent behaviour with respect to trade policy, it is equally necessary to use models which concentrate on particular aspects, such as micro-economic considerations at the level of the individual company (Chapters 8 and 9), the effect of specific interest groups and lobbying and political influence (Chapters 10 and 11).

In this chapter we set out arguments why governments may or may not protect their economies against foreign competition. The starting point and hence the limitation of this analysis is always in the first instance that of the optimal welfare implications for the country as a whole. Although the literature also contains arguments which defend protectionism from that perspective, the objections to protectionism still prevail. In contrast, in Chapters 8 to 11 we tackle protectionism from the point of view of the specific interests of individual companies, or groups within those companies.

6.2 Protectionism

Case study 6.1 illustrates how easily protectionism can escalate further even under today's conditions.[1]

Case study 6.1 The American steel industry

On 5 October 1992 top managers in the steel industry from all over the world assembled in Tokyo at the annual meeting of the International Iron and Steel Institute (IISI). The meeting took place at a time when many steel companies were hit by recession. In spite of drastic rationalisation, heavy investment and substantial government aid, most steel producers were worse off than ten years previously. This once again brought the steel industry to the brink of a trade war.

American steel companies had filed many dumping complaints with their government. This irritated steel producers outside the US, particularly in Japan, because they had taken part in modernising American steel plants via joint ventures with American companies. What fundamental factors lay behind this situation?

---

1. There are some terms which need explaining here, namely dumping complaint and voluntary export restraint (VER). Both terms refer to an action by a firm or government aimed at influencing trade. Although mainly Chapter 11 concentrates on these types of restriction, we give a brief explanation here for the purpose of Case study 6.1. A dumping complaint is made where a firm accuses a foreign firm of selling its products on the domestic market at less than the price in the country of origin and/or less than cost (dumping). The accuser's government may then impose levies on the foreign firm's products to make them more expensive. Dumping complaints are often intended to restrict foreign competition. On paper, VERs are voluntary actions by the exporter to set a particular maximum limit on annual exports of a particular product to a particular country; in reality, these restrictions are often extracted by the importer in a negotiating situation.

After the Second World War the American steel producers were the symbol of US industrial power. In the early 1980s, however, the American steel industry showed symptoms of chronic industrial decline. The once mighty companies were struggling to survive. Up-and-coming foreign competitors (whose costs were only a fraction of those of the American companies) conquered an ever larger share of the market.

Ten years later, in the early 1990s, the situation looked different again. Thanks to substantial investment, the American industry was operating much more efficiently than before. By 1992, the American steel producers had halved the number of man hours needed to produce a tonne of steel, compared with 1980 (3.5 man hours). This doubling of productivity meant that parts of the American steel industry were again up to the world standard.

The basis of this improvement in efficiency was controversial, as the industry was protected against foreign competition in the 1980s. In 1982, after a series of allegations of dumping by American steel producers against foreign rivals, the American government negotiated voluntary export restraints (VERs) with the EU, Japan and South Korea, for instance. The ensuing agreements restricted the share of foreign firms on the American steel market, in order to give American producers the chance to restructure. When American businesses were once again deemed to be internationally competitive, the VERs were abolished on 31 March 1992.

The question is whether the American steel industry did in fact regain its competitiveness thanks to the VERs. This will require further analysis.

The American steel industry's problems began back in the 1950s. After the Second World War demand for steel initially continued to rise. The American industry expanded its capacity in an ad hoc manner: a new smelting works was added at one factory, a new finishing plant at another, etc. After a while, Japanese and European producers took over the leading position from the American production plants. These producers were highly competitive because after the war they were forced to build new factories from scratch.

In the 1960s Japan produced steel in new factories with furnaces where casting could take place continuously (continuous production); in contrast, American rolling mills were saddled with old technology. As well as that, inflation in the US caused wage costs in that country to be almost double those in Japan and West Germany.

The result was that American producers complained of unfair competition to their government, leading to the said VERs which were to limit steel imports to about 20 per cent of the American market from 1984 onwards. The American producers were to have five years in which to restructure their industry. In 1988, however, the steel producers successfully argued for an extension of the VERs.

Initially, the VERs had the desired effect: the share of imports in steel consumption fell from 26.4 per cent to 25.2 per cent within one year, and the proportion of imports continued to decline after that. By limiting the supply of steel on the American market, producers could demand higher prices and thus, so they argued, create a surplus to finance the necessary investments.

However, other factors were probably at least equally significant. First, the value of the dollar fell very sharply after 1985, reducing the profit margins of producers exporting to the US and increasing the competitiveness of the American producers.

The average domestic price of steel rose by about 3 per cent between 1984 and 1990. Expressed in dollars, steel prices outside the US went up by an average of 25 per cent.

The result was that sales on the American market became less important, as did the VERs. After 1985, foreigners who had agreed to the VERs were no longer even able to fill their quota. After 1987, imports declined to 21 million tonnes below the agreed quota. This in itself indicates that the decline in imports was caused by the cheaper dollar rather than the protectionist policy.

A second factor which played a major part in the rationalisation of the American steel industry was domestic competition. Producers exploiting in mini-mills on US soil proved to be stronger competitors for the large American steel producers than the foreign producers. These mini-mills, such as Nucor Corporation and Birmingham Steel, had a 21 per cent share of the American market in 1992, while foreigners held only 18 per cent. The six largest American steel producers claimed that in 1991 they made a loss of $27 on every tonne of steel sold; in contrast, the mini-mills made a profit of $10 per tonne of steel.

According to an estimate made in the mid 1980s by the Institute for International Economics, the VERs cost consumers $7 billion per annum in respect of steel. In future, most of the cost of the VERs will come from the resulting dependence on government protection for economically weaker plants. In anticipation of the end of the VERs, such firms filed a string of dumping complaints against foreign producers. In February 1992, in a decision against six accused countries, the American Commerce Department expressed the intention to ensure strict application of the anti-dumping laws since the American steel industry was no longer protected.

So long as the anti-dumping instrument remains that easy to use, the steel industry still has a long way to go before free trade, in spite of the abolition of the VERs.

Case study 6.2 concerns India which, after a period of strict government control over foreign trade, is trying to switch to a policy oriented more towards free trade.

Case study 6.2 India awakes and discovers the world around it

India persisted for a long time with the ideology of self-reliance. The country was not open to foreign investors. However, in 1991 Premier Narasumha Rao tried to implement a radical change of direction.

In 1990 the popular newspaper *India Today* printed a political cartoon showing the then premier Chandra Shekhar standing in a paper boat with a placard in his hand reading 'clear off!' That message was aimed at huge freighters which were going by far out at sea, marked EU, Japan and USA. The cartoon was an accurate description of India's situation: in world trade, India is no more than a paper boat compared with the world's economic giants. The tragi-comic point made by the cartoon was that the premier was chasing away the passing ships of the large trade blocs. The message was clear: while the world economy ignored India, the government persisted in its ideology of self-reliance and turned away foreign investors and traders which had long since found other partners, such as Indonesia, Malaysia and Thailand. However, a great deal changed within a year. If such a cartoon had been drawn in 1991, we would have seen Narasumha Rao, Chandra Shekhar's successor, paddling furiously across the ocean in the hope of attracting the attention of the great ships.

What happened in India in that single year? First the financial indicators in the economy continued their slide towards bankruptcy. At the end of 1990, after rising by $6 billion in one year, foreign debt was over $70 billion. Interest and repayments on that debt were costing India $7 billion, almost 30 per cent of India's exports and thus 30 per cent of its foreign exchange revenue. In addition, the domestic debt had reached a level where the finance minister could only meet his interest obligations by allowing a constant increase in the budget deficit. That deficit totalled 8.6 per cent of GDP and thus fuelled inflation. In the meantime, the deficit had gone into double figures and was 14 per cent in 1991.

Although industry and the agrarian sector continued to do well, with growth rates of 8.4 per cent and 4.5 per cent respectively, the creditworthiness of India was reduced to the lowest investment class or even the 'credit watch' category by the international credit institutions. This made it difficult if not impossible for the country to borrow money on the international markets, so that there was a danger that the inflow of capital for private domestic banks would abruptly cease. In May 1991 the country actually had to sell small quantities of its gold reserves, and if the IMF had not offered short-term credit, India would have faced financial collapse.

Within a week of Rao taking office, the rupee was devalued twice and a trade policy plan was put forward, followed by an industry plan. These plans had three features in common. First, they indicated that India could no longer live in a fantasy world of economic isolation. Second, the plans assumed that the country did not have the resources to achieve the required economic growth and must therefore call on the investment potential of the private sector at home and abroad. Finally, it was realised that India must cut back its profligate public expenditure.

The new trade policy made a clean sweep through the complex web of regulations which successive cabinets had introduced to restrict imports. Various 'channelling bureaus', a number of import procedures and an inefficient financial sector delayed goods traffic and created a fertile breeding ground for corruption. In combination with the world's highest import duty (weighted average: 112 per cent), they also formed a barrier behind which domestic businesses could shelter from foreign competition. Instead of making the competitive position the cornerstone of its export policy, the government had in the past often opted for *export subsidies*. At a stroke, the trade minister Chidambaran abolished the most complicated import rules and some of the export subsidies by introducing a financial instrument called the *Exim certificate*. Exim certificates are licences which entitle exporters to import goods corresponding to the value of their earnings in foreign currency. The certificates are freely negotiable and firms can save them up in order to buy goods abroad.

The object was to get the economy to earn the vital foreign currency by its own efforts. At one time the certificates were fetching 40 per cent more than their face value. They thus formed a powerful export incentive and curbed imports which wasted foreign exchange.

An important element of India's new industry plan was that foreign companies could acquire a majority stake in certain branches of industry, such as the manufacture of metal-working machinery, energy generation and distribution, electrical and electronic machinery, telecommunications, machine tools, agricultural machinery and chemicals. In order to compete better at international level, companies were free to conclude agreements on imports of technology for which they obtained 'automatic licences'. In India's traditional way of life these measures represented a radical step towards a market economy.

Whether all these measures went far enough is another question. One problem here was the huge army of officials who had to implement the policy, even though at the same time it undermined their own jobs. It was also likely that traditionally protected domestic businesses would strongly oppose the new plans. The problem was not so much a lack of willingness on the government's part to send the Indian boat across the ocean of international economic relations, but rather the fact that it was overloaded with bureaucrats and industrialists who wished to hinder its progress.

These case studies prompt a number of questions, such as:

1. In what form can protectionism occur and what are its effects, including the effects on welfare?
2. What arguments were previously put forward in favour of self-reliance and protectionist measures?
3. What caused India to change its mind?

Finally, there is the question: to what extent can specific interest groups in a country influence the outcome of policy changes as described in the above case study, and what arguments can be expected from the groups let down by free trade?

In connection with trade theory, we have already seen that, within a country, free trade can create losers who are afraid they will not receive any compensation. Everyone knows of companies or lines of business which lose out or even disappear because they cannot stand up to international competition. The interest of those directly concerned in such companies in strongly lobbying their government for protection is greater than the interest of consumers in resisting the possibility of protection which might affect them. (The subject of protection on the basis of safeguarding the interests of individual entrepreneurs or other specific interest groups comes up in Chapters 10 and 11.)

Before discussing the arguments for and against trade policy intervention, it is important to make a few more general comments first. First, protectionism can restrict trade – take import duties or export levies, for instance – but they can equally stimulate trade, e.g. in the case of export subsidies or soft export credit terms or export credit guarantee conditions.[2]

Second, we only refer to protectionism if the government takes measures which are intended to exert a direct influence over international trade, or which have that effect. If a country tries to stimulate exports and restrict imports by changing its exchange rate or via a low wage policy, this is not usually classed as protectionist behaviour because the influence on trade is only generic and indirect. However, Case study 6.3 indicates that, in such a situation, a country is also open to criticism.

Third, protectionism usually refers to government policy, but it is obvious that the behaviour of businesses can also influence trade. For example, if a number of companies operating internationally conclude a deal which restricts competition, or if they actually form a cartel, this can lead to a restriction on international trade (and can drive up prices). However, this is not usually referred to as protectionism because the players belong to the private sector.

Fourth, it is important to realise that protectionism can occur in numerous forms. Some examples: if a government customarily places its orders only with national companies, if development aid is tied to national tenders, or if customs formalities, environmental standards, health regulations or product characteristics are unjustly made more stringent for imports, it is usual to speak of protectionism.

Case study 6.3 The IMF criticises wage moderation in the Netherlands

On Friday, 22 February 1991 the International Monetary Fund (IMF) Board of Governors discussed the Dutch economy, criticising wage moderation in the Netherlands. It was evident from the rapidly growing current account surplus on the balance of payments that the Netherlands was earning increasingly more than it was spending in economic relations with other countries. This process was reinforced by the policy of wage moderation, which kept down the price of Dutch exports, so that the growth required to create jobs and generate tax revenue was based on competitive advantages over other countries. In 1990 the current account surplus was NLG 19.5 billion, and was expected to increase to over NLG 26 billion in 1991. An IMF expert judged that: 'The Netherlands is not at all short of competitiveness.' He went on: 'The problem is that demand on the home market is being held back by government policy. In the Netherlands, wage moderation is regarded as a calvinist virtue; but if this policy continues for a few more years, the Netherlands will become a European low-wage country comparable with the

---

2. We refer to *protection* when speaking of actual trade protection; *protectionism* means the degree to which a government is generally inclined to grant protection. *Protectionist measures* are measures to protect one's own industry.

developing countries. In the long term, that will not do the economic structure any good. A technologically advanced economy requires internationally competitive net salaries.' In short, the IMF was increasingly critical of the exceptionally high Dutch balance of payments surplus which according to the IMF was partly due to the low wage policy pursued by the Dutch government.

6.3 The optimum tariff theory

6.3.1 *Protection and welfare*

On the basis of traditional trade theory, the conclusion is that free trade is generally preferable to protection according to the criterion of national welfare. But at the same time, and from the same point of view, two arguments in favour of protection are traditionally recognised as theoretically valid. The first is based on the *optimum* tariff theory. In essence, this argument, which will be developed below, means one can use import protection to force foreign suppliers to make price concessions, so that a country can maximise its wealth by setting a particular level of tariffs, so long as other countries do not retaliate. The second argument, which will be explained in section 6.5 below, is that protectionism can sometimes increase a country's wealth if there is a market distortion or market failure in that country. *Market failure* means that market prices sometimes do not accurately reflect the cost pattern. In that case, demand and supply react to the wrong signal so that too much or too little is sold. In welfare terms this can result in a loss. According to the second argument, one can try to limit this loss by trade policy measures. In the case of this argument, too, it is very important to note that it holds true only if there is justification for assuming that the other party, the country hit by protection, does not retaliate. Thus, both arguments assume a rather asymmetrical situation between trading partners.

In practice, of course, many other arguments are also put forward in defence of protectionism – some connected with national welfare and some not actually to do with economics at all. For example, non-economic arguments include the effort to achieve independence from other countries in building up basic industries or self-sufficiency in food supplies. This last argument was a factor in the European agricultural policy, for instance (Case study 6.5).

Other arguments for protection are based on: a country's economic situation, expansion of employment or the balance of payments position. In most of these situations, an attempt is made to transfer national problems to other countries via protection; there is therefore a high risk of escalation, because if a number of closely connected economies are all suffering recession simultaneously, as is usually the case, and one country decides to restrict imports, this can only cause further deterioration in the economic situation in neighbouring countries. It is only in the exceptional case of countries in which one group is confronted by under-utilisation of capacity and the other group is simultaneously overspending that protection by the first group does not necessarily conflict with the macro-economic objectives of the other group of countries. Trade restrictions by the first group can then moderate the overheating of the economy in the second group. Cutting imports from that group of countries reduces their spending, and exporting more to that group of countries spares part of the production capacity.

A protectionist climate often causes people to seek a scapegoat for domestic problems outside their own economy. In such cases, people sometimes actually look not just at the overall trend in the balance of payments but also at the trend in relation to one or more specific trading partners (e.g. the US current account deficit in trade with Japan or the European Union; see also Case study 6.4).

Case study 6.4 The trade negotiations between the US and Japan

Under President Clinton (and under Reagan and Bush before him) the US attitude towards trade policy in particular is moving in the direction of judging the fairness of the policy of trading partners. This means that a country is judged by the degree to which its market is opened up to American products. In order to reinforce this policy, under the Omnibus Trade and Competitiveness Act, Congress extended Article 301 of the American Trade Law by adding a new provision, Super 301. Under this provision the American president is obliged to take trade policy action against trading partners unilaterally designated by the US as 'unfair', i.e. partners who hinder American exports. This provision applied between 1988 and 1990. Its use was considered once again in 1994, in order to put trade policy pressure on Japan.

The object of this rather aggressive attitude by the US is partly to try to reach agreement between the US and Japan, for example, on how much each will buy from the other in a particular product group. This gives rise to a bilateral 'tit for tat' trading situation, euphemistically known as 'managed trade'. Although Japan has always formally rejected such an approach, an informal bilateral agreement was nevertheless concluded in this atmosphere in 1986, with the Japanese promising to reserve 20 per cent of the Japanese market in semi-conductors for American products with effect from 1 January 1993. In mid 1993 a broader agreement was reached, known as the *'Sushi agreement'* between the American President Clinton and the Japanese Premier Myazawa, under which numerous global trade policy arrangements were made providing for better access for the Americans to the Japanese market, economic cooperation and a gradual reduction in the Japanese trade surplus with the US (1993: approx. $60 billion). Although on paper this settlement aims at a general improvement in access to the Japanese market – i.e. to the advantage of all trading partners – one can assume that it is primarily intended to benefit American exporters.

6.3.2 *The optimum tariff*

The starting point of the optimum tariff theory is the attempt to maximise a country's total welfare. This theory is based on the idea that in certain situations a country can exert so much pressure on the foreign supplier by protectionist measures, e.g. in the form of import levies,[3] that the supplier is prepared to cut the price at which he offers the imported goods to preserve his market situation. If this is done systematically, the importing country *improves its terms of trade*. The terms of trade indicate the ratio between export and import prices. If the terms of trade improve, import prices fall without any need for export prices to be reduced as well, so that a country's national income increases. As remarked earlier, all this applies only if the other country is not in a position to take protectionist counter-measures.

It is also important to make the point here that the following argument forming the basis of the optimum tariff (Box 6.2) assumes that economies rapidly adapt to new market conditions. To give an example, if certain sectors can expand under the influence of trade policy measures while other sectors have to shrink, this will in practice entail adjustment costs for society, e.g. in the form of accelerated depreciation or costs in connection with retraining and unemployment. These costs are disregarded by the analysis in Box 6.2.

To return to the terms of trade effect, it should be clear that an improvement in the terms of trade in fact means nothing more than an improvement in the terms on which exports are exchanged for imports on the international market, or the purchasing power of exports. Because falling import prices mean that a given quantity of exports can buy more imports. It is equally logical that an improvement in the terms of trade brings positive welfare effects. In Box 6.1, two examples are used to illustrate how an improvement in the terms of trade is reflected in the welfare of a country.

Box 6.1 Welfare effect of an improvement in the terms of trade

The degree to which a given change in the terms of trade affects a country's welfare depends on:

- the volume of exports and
- the extent to which the export sector generates value added.

This can be illustrated by an example. Say a country like the Netherlands records a 1 per cent deterioration in the terms of trade in a given year; this was the case in 1991, for example. It means that the same quantity of exports can be exchanged for 1 per cent fewer imports than before on the international market. Since the

---

3. As we shall see later, a similar idea can be developed regarding the application of export subsidies.

124

average export ratio of the Netherlands, the value of exports in relation to GNP, was about 60 per cent in that year and the value added domestically per unit of exports could be estimated at one third, the total welfare of the Netherlands declined by $-1 \times 0.6 \times 0.33 \times 100\% = -0.2\%$ as a result of the 1 per cent deterioration in the terms of trade; because that 1 per cent deterioration only influences Dutch GNP via the export ratio (0.6), and then only in so far as these exports relate to the value added in the Netherlands (one third of the exports). Although the result in the example means only a slight reduction in GNP, the Netherlands still has to maintain the same level of production as before.

A rather more extreme example which also contains an element of reality can be based on the position of the OPEC countries at the time of the two oil shocks in the 1970s. The abrupt jump in oil prices brought a dramatic improvement in the terms of trade for these countries, totalling all of 400 per cent. At the time, the OPEC countries had export ratios of approximately 80 per cent; assuming that the domestic value added component of the oil produced was very high, say 90 per cent, this meant that, for these countries, the terms of trade effects resulted in an increase in GNP of $400 \times 0.8 \times 0.9 \times 100\% = 288\%$!

Sometimes the change in a country's terms of trade is not just a fact but is influenced by the country's own technological development. For example, let us assume that a 3 per cent improvement in productivity is achieved in the export sector. Let us also assume that, owing to the world market situation, this advantage is reflected in a corresponding reduction in the price of the export product (or a quality improvement) for foreign customers. If the contribution of the export sector to the economy is 25 per cent, the increase in welfare due to the greater productivity will thus be $0.25 \times 3\% = 0.75\%$. However, this is offset by a 3 per cent deterioration in the terms of trade, so that the gain in welfare drops back by $0.25 \times 3\% = 0.75\%$. There is thus no net change in welfare in spite of the increase in productivity! (On the basis of this example, it is easy to see that, given a slightly different combination of figures, a situation can actually arise in which the negative terms of trade effect is greater than the other possibly positive effects. In that case we have a situation in which growth leads to impoverishment!) It is easy to deduce that if, in contrast to the above case, the productivity increase had taken place in the sector competing with imports and had therefore led to a decline in import prices, the two effects would have enhanced one another in a positive sense.

If protectionism yields an improvement in the terms of trade, this effect therefore increases the welfare of the country applying the protectionism. However, other welfare effects also occur at the same time, which have to be offset against the terms of trade effect. Let us assume that protectionism takes the form of an import tariff: in that case prices of the product are also likely to rise within the country. Unless the price reduction at the border is greater than the tariff per unit of actual product, the price will go up in the importing country, where the tariff will of course be passed on in the price. If we confine the analysis to the changes in the section of the market where protection applies, we can identify three effects:

(a) Some domestic producers of the product can now produce profitably at this higher price, and for the original producers the higher price may increase profits. This positive effect is reflected in an increase in the producers' surplus as a result of protectionism (area a in Figure 6.1, Box 6.2).

(b) Consumers in the country see that the 'protected' product has become more expensive, so that some purchasers will drop out and those that remain will pay more. This negative effect is reflected in a decline in the consumer surplus as a result of protectionism (areas a + b + c + d in Figure 6.1, Box 6.2).

(c) The government receives tariff revenue on the quantity imported and can then transfer that to its citizens by cutting taxes or in other ways. This positive effect is called the tariff effect of protectionism (c + e in Figure 6.1, Box 6.2).

Clearly, the balance of the three effects, e − (b + d), determines whether a country would be wise to adopt a protectionist attitude. We can also infer (Box 6.2, last paragraph) that a given tariff is optimum from the country's point of view, because the positive and negative effects do not change to the same extent as a result of a small change in the tariff.

Box 6.2 The optimum tariff

Figure 6.1 shows the domestic supply and demand curve of the EU for citrus fruits. The *consumer surplus* is the positive difference between the selling price of a product and the price which individual consumers would have been prepared to pay for the same product, aggregated for all consumers. Thus, the consumer surplus under free trade (at P_w) consists of the area above P_w up to the demand curve. The *producer's surplus* is the positive difference between the selling price of the product and the minimum price which the individual domestic entrepreneurs wish to receive on account of their cost structure, aggregated for all producers. Under free trade, this producer's surplus is shown by the area below P_w down to the supply curve. In this case that corresponds to the marginal cost curve.

If the EU introduces a tariff on citrus fruits, this will be reflected in the producer's surplus and the consumer surplus. Say the tariff causes the price of citrus fruits in the EU to increase to P_t. Consumers now have to pay a higher price than under free trade, so that the consumer surplus falls by a + b + c + d. In contrast, producers receive a higher price for their products, so that the producer's surplus increases by a. As a result of the higher price, consumption of citrus fruits in the EU falls from O_{d2} to O_{d1} and EU production increases from O_{s1} to O_{s2}. This means that the government's tariff revenue relates to the volume of imports $O_{d1} - O_{s2}$. Since the difference $P_t - P^*$ gives the level of tariff per unit of product, c + e represents the tariff revenue for the government.

The net welfare effects can now be divided into two components. On the one hand, there is the efficiency loss shown by triangles b + d. This loss will always

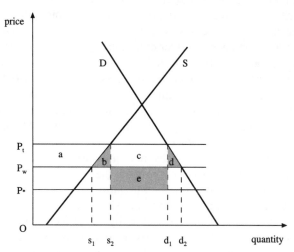

D = domestic demand curve
S = domestic supply curve
P_t = domestic price after the imposition of the tariff
P_w = world market price under free trade
P* = price charged by the foreign country after imposition of the tariff
$P_t - P^*$ = tariff per unit of product

Figure 6.1 The optimum tariff

occur when a tariff is imposed: b and d indicate the losses caused to society by the distortion of the price signals for consumers and producers as a result of the imposition of a tariff. On the other hand, there is the gain in welfare based on the terms of trade effect of the imposition of a tariff on citrus fruit imports by the EU, because the tariff led to a fall in the export prices of foreign citrus fruits. This means a positive welfare effect for the EU totalling e. Thus, the ultimate net wealth effect is the balance of the negative effects, b + d, and the positive effect e. Figure 6.1 provides a graphic illustration that this net effect may be positive.

Since a change in the level of the tariff does not cause areas b and d to change to the same extent as e, it is intuitively obvious that there is a certain tariff level at which the positive net welfare effect is maximised. That level is called the optimum tariff.

Using a similar analysis we can also show that if the country is small, so that it cannot influence the world market price (in Figure 6.1 P* = P_w), no improvement in the terms of trade is possible, so that a tariff will always reduce the welfare of the protectionist country: the optimum tariff is then zero. This is also an important point to understand; in the first place because many countries are unable, on account of their economic size, to influence relative prices on the international market by means of protectionist behaviour: thus, it is certainly not always possible to force an improvement in one's terms of trade. In the second place, because in these cases a country can gain by scrapping its own protectionist measures even if other countries do not. It is a common belief that other countries can only be expected to make trade concessions if one offers something in return (see also Chapter 10); this philosophy also dominated ideas on trade policy during the last century. However, the above theoretical model shows that unilateral trade concessions can also increase domestic welfare, and this was the argument that largely determined the British attitude to trade policy in the latter half of the last century.

The optimum tariff theory does not only apply to those imports which represent a threat to an industry belonging to the country in question. It is equally applicable if protectionism is oriented towards exports, in that the government decides to tax exports and not imports. This seems paradoxical: how can a government increase the country's welfare by taxing its own exports? One would expect it to have to subsidise its exports for that purpose. But it is easy to show that, apart from exceptional cases, there are in fact more reasons for the government to tax exports than to subsidise them.

6.3.3 An export tax

Let us assume that a country exports a large number of units of a product at NLG 10 each and the government imposes a tax of NLG 2 each. If nothing else happened, the exporter would get NLG 10, the foreign customer would now suddenly have to pay NLG 12 and the government would collect NLG 2 per product. However, foreign demand can be expected to fall at a price of NLG 12, and this would force domestic suppliers to cut their price until their supply was absorbed by the other country. Exactly how the new market equilibrium looks naturally depends on how rapidly demand and supply adjust to the change in prices. We can expect that if the exporter has some influence in the market, the eventual situation will be that illustrated in Box 6.3: the price received by the

---

Box 6.3 The effects of an export levy

Figure 6.2 shows the demand and supply curves for bicycles in the UK. Under free trade the quantity $O_{s2} - O_{d1}$ of bicycles is exported at price P_w. The British government decides to tax bicycle exports. This will cause bicycle manufacturers in Britain to cut their selling price in order to remain competitive on the world market. It is assumed that the British suppliers do not apply any price discrimination on market segments, so that their price also falls on the British market to level P. The price at which bicycles from the foreign market are offered on the British market now also falls to level P.

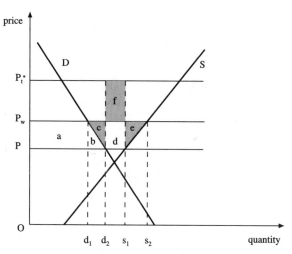

price

D   S

P_t^*

f

P_w

a   c   e

P   b   d

O

d_1 d_2 s_1 s_2 quantity

D = domestic demand curve
S = domestic supply curve
P = domestic price after imposition of the export tax
P_w = world market price under free trade
P_t^* = price charged on the export market after imposition of the export tax
$P_t^* - P$ = export tax per unit of product

Figure 6.2 The optimum export levy

The price at which the bicycles are exported from the UK is now P_t^*, i.e. P plus the export tax. The reduction in the price of bicycles on the home market has caused the consumer surplus to increase by area a + b. The producer's surplus has fallen by area a + b + c + d + e. At the new price, exports are $O_{s1} - O_{d2}$. When multiplied by the export tax per unit of product, $P_t^* - P$, this yields tax revenue for the government totalling d + f. The net welfare effect is the balance of c + d + e (negative) and d + f (positive), or c + e − f. The triangles c + e can again be regarded as efficiency losses due to distortion in consumption and production decisions; f can be attributed to the improvement in the terms of trade resulting from the higher price of export products.

Whether or not the improvement in the terms of trade will exceed the efficiency loss so that any positive net effect can be maximised will depend on the level of the export tax, demand and supply elasticities for the product concerned on the home market and the elasticity of foreign demand. The smaller or more inelastic the foreign demand for the product, the greater the chance of a net positive welfare effect for the country imposing the export tax. This is because, if foreign demand is inelastic, the other country will continue to want the product even if the price goes up.

One last question: what effect does the export tax have on the welfare of the two countries together? Figure 6.3 shows a foreign demand curve; for convenience, it is assumed that the other country does not actually make any of these products, so that domestic demand and demand for imports coincide.

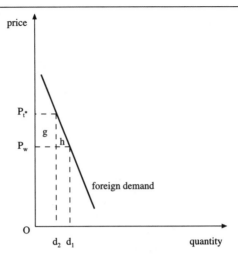

Figure 6.3 Effects of an export tax on the other country

The demand curve in Figure 6.3 indicates the quantity imported by the foreign country at a given price. Before the export tax, the foreign country imports O_{d1}. If the export tax is imposed, the price rise causes foreign demand to fall to O_{d2}. The consumer surplus has then dropped by g + h. g indicates the terms of trade effect and thus reflects the transfer to the UK, but h is the additional loss of welfare for the foreign country caused by distortion of consumption decisions. The net welfare in both countries together is, of course, unaffected by the transfer because that just means shifting funds from one place to another. This only leaves the efficiency losses. In the UK these were c + e in Figure 6.2; we now add h from Figure 6.3. Thus, there has been a net decline in total welfare (by c + e + h): the welfare gained by one country is thus insufficient to compensate for the welfare lost by the other country.

exporter has fallen, but foreign customers are forced to pay a higher price overall, because of the export levy.

For the country as a whole, this means an improvement in the terms of trade at the expense of the other country, just as could result from an import levy. This produces two effects which have to be taken together to determine the overall welfare effect: (a) the producer's surplus and the consumer surplus. The former has fallen because some exporters have dropped out at the lower price; moreover, the rest receive a lower price than previously. In contrast, the latter has risen as a result of the price cut on the home market; and (b) the government's tariff revenue generated by exports. Some of this can be used, for example, to compensate the producers in one way or another. The point is that foreign customers can be made to pay part of this compensation because they are 'forced' to pay a higher price for our exports (the positive terms of trade effect). This means that there is a good chance that domestic exporters can readily be compensated in full by using the tariff revenue, and in the end there will still be a net gain in welfare for the country. This is strange because, in this model, domestic production has declined as a result of the export tax, and exports have also fallen from $O_{s2} - O_{d1}$ to $O_{s1} - O_{d2}$. However, the dominant, positive terms of trade effect ensures that there is nevertheless a net increase in national welfare. This illustrates that the arguments for an optimum import tariff are evidently applicable in a symmetrical manner to the optimum export tariff situation. This is known as *Lerner's symmetry theorem*.

6.3.4 *An export subsidy*

However, if instead of an export tax there is an export subsidy, the opposite situation arises. Let us once again assume the same case as before in which a country exports a large quantity of a product at NLG 10 each. The government now grants an export subsidy of NLG 2 each. In the first instance, the exporter is still satisfied with NLG 10 and can thus charge the foreign customer a price of NLG 8. We therefore initially base our argument on the assumption that the exporter passes on the subsidy in full in the selling price. This will cause an increase in foreign demand so that there will be more scope to sell our export products. As a result, new exporters will appear on the market, but we can expect them to be less efficient than the existing ones. This may lead to a new equilibrium situation in which the price for customers rises to say NLG 9 and the exporter thus receives NLG 11 per unit.

Two welfare effects now occur: the producer's surplus increases, because a greater quantity is exported at a higher price. However, this costs the government a substantial amount in export subsidies. There is also a deterioration in the terms of trade, so that part of the subsidy essentially ends up with the foreign customers: the taxpayer is then subsidising the foreign customer. It is precisely because part of the subsidy is lost in this way that the overall costs of the export subsidy often, if not always, exceed the increase in the producer's surplus gained by the exporters. This benefits the individual interests of the country's own exporters but damages the interests of the country as a whole.

Box 6.4 The effects of an export subsidy

We now see that the export subsidy confronts other countries with an export curve which has shifted downwards by the amount of the subsidy per unit of exports (Ex'). This shift is logical because the exporter's conduct is unchanged: if he

---

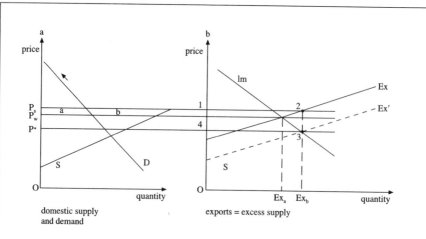

S = domestic supply curve
D = domestic demand curve
Ex = export curve before subsidy
Ex' = export curve after subsidy
Im = import curve
P_w = price before subsidy
P* = price on the international market after subsidy
P_s = price on the home market (= exports) after subsidy
P_s – P* = subsidy per unit of product
Ex_b – Ex_a = increase in exports as a result of the export subsidy

Figure 6.4 The wealth effect of an export subsidy

receives export price x, he still offers the same quantity y as he did before the subsidy was granted; however, the foreign customer now benefits from the subsidy and sees the export supply as being based on a supply curve which has fallen by the amount of the subsidy per unit. Thus, Ex' is the relevant curve for the foreign customer; Ex is the relevant curve for the exporter. The price on the international market is now P* (demand and supply are equal on the international market), which implies a deterioration in the terms of trade for the exporter.

On the exporter's home market there is now a higher price level P* + export subsidy = P_s. This is the price that the exporter receives: he receives P* from the foreign customer and the rest is added by the government. If there is a competing supply in the foreign country, we can assume that its price will settle at the level received for exports, so that the overall domestic price level for this product rises to level P_s.

So what can we conclude about the net welfare effect for the exporting country? It is negative. First, the producer's surplus increases by a + b, but that is offset by a decline of a in the consumer surplus, leaving a balance b. However, in order to arrive at this balance – which corresponds roughly to the area above P_w bounded by 1 and 2 in (b) – an export subsidy is granted totalling 1234. Since 1234 > b, there is a net loss of welfare. As a result of the deterioration in the terms of trade, part of the subsidy is 'lost' to the other country.

For the two countries together the export subsidy in this model produces a net loss of welfare. The effect of the change in the terms of trade is again just a transfer of funds, and hence neutral. This leaves the negative effects as a result of efficiency losses through distorted allocation.

Governments often argue that export subsidies are not only granted in the interests of exporters but are also in the interests of employment. As we can see from Box 6.4, exports increase as a result of the subsidy, so that – all other things being equal – national production and employment expand. However, the point is that the subsidies have to come from somewhere and that the hidden costs of the subsidy must therefore also be taken into account. If this is done, it will often be apparent that there are plenty of more cost-effective options for creating jobs. We shall return to this in section 6.5.

Research which attempts to analyse the actual costs of an export subsidy policy in fact points in the direction suggested by the theory. The fact that, in practice, export subsidies are far more common than export taxes therefore demonstrates that, in the application of trade policy measures, governments are often persuaded more by specific interests of producers or spurious arguments concerning employment, rather than by arguments based on the total welfare of a country. Case study 6.5 illustrates this by describing the costs of the EU export subsidy policy for agricultural products.

Case study 6.5 Costs of the EU agricultural policy

A favourite sector for government protection is agriculture. In the EU, for example, this protection is granted partly via measures aimed at the home market, such as production subsidies, guaranteed prices and income supplements, and partly via measures aimed at international trade such as import levies and export subsidies. These measures form a single cohesive package, because the intended higher price level in the EU must not be undermined by cheaper imports from outside the area. That is why internal price guarantees have to be accompanied by import restrictions, to correct any price difference between the international and the internal market. One effect of such a policy is that the area's own farmers cannot sell outside the protected market except at prices which are lower than those guaranteed on the home market. That is why export subsidies are regarded as a logical complement to the guaranteed price system.

The above account roughly describes the EU agricultural policy on several leading products. One of the principal objections to this system is that it encourages excess production, because if the price is set above the level at which demand and supply are in equilibrium, then under normal circumstances there will be surplus supply. Owing to the system, this can only be exported with the aid of

Table 6.1 Annual domestic costs as a result of government intervention in agriculture ($ billion)

Region	Year	Consumer's costs (1)	Taxpayer's costs (2)	Producers' benefits (3)	Total domestic costs (1 + 2 − 3)
European Union	1980	34.6	11.5	30.7	15.4
Japan	1976	7.1	−0.4	2.6	4.1
United States	1985	5.7	10.3	11.6	4.4

Source: Johnsen, Hemmi, and Lardinois, 1985.

export subsidies, which is an expensive policy option. The agricultural rationalisation process – which was started in the EU back in the 1960s in order to prevent the surpluses – did lead to a gradual exodus from farming, but production did not decline owing to the huge increase in agricultural productivity. Furthermore, the agricultural land which became available was mostly put to use again, so that the costs of the European agricultural policy continued to impose a heavy burden on the EU budget and hence on taxpayers over the years.

In order to arrive at an overall assessment of the welfare effects of the support policy described above we must, according to the theory, take account of the lower consumer surplus and the higher producer's surplus as well as the costs to the taxpayer. By way of illustration, Table 6.1 shows such calculations for agricultural protection in the leading western blocs, the EU, Japan and the US.

Finally, there is also the terms of trade effect of protection, because the agricultural policy influences the world market situation via the export subsidies. The result is that world market prices are lower than they would have been under free trade. The policy also causes the world market to develop increasingly into an unstable surplus market. From this point of view, the taxpayers are thus not only supporting their own agricultural sector, they are also subsidising foreign consumption. On the other hand, however, the industrial countries' agricultural policy will in the long term damage the competitive position of exporters in other countries, including the developing countries.

Research in fact shows that world market prices of agricultural products can be expected to rise if agricultural protection declines. Valdés and Zietz (1980), for example, concluded that a tariff reduction in the OECD countries would cause agricultural prices to increase, thus raising the agricultural export earnings of the developing countries. This would be favourable to developing countries which were net exporters. In developing countries which were net importers, however, welfare would decline as a result of the deterioration in the terms of trade. In a report for the World Bank in 1986, Tyers and Anderson actually concluded that unilateral liberalisation of agriculture by the industrial countries and/or by the developing countries would yield great advantages for the initiating bloc at the

Table 6.2 Gain in welfare as a result of the liberalisation of agriculture ($ billion)

Region	Unilateral liberalisation industrial countries	Unilateral liberalisation developing countries	Global (multilateral) liberalisation
Developing countries	−11.8	28.2	18.3
Industrial market economics	48.5	−10.2	45.9
European planned economics	−11.1	−13.1	−23.1
World	25.6	4.9	41.1

expense of the other blocs. As we can see from Table 6.2, multilateral liberalisation of agriculture could also produce advantages for other blocs.

6.4 Volume restrictions on trade and the effect on welfare

Section 6.3 focused on the welfare effect for those cases in which attempts are made to influence international trade by means of taxes or subsidies, in a market-conforming manner. In this connection, 'market-conforming' means that, apart from the tax or subsidy, the market mechanism is left intact. This is not the case with non market-conforming intervention: here, an upper limit (or in some cases a lower limit) is set in advance for the volume or value of international trade: no more than a particular quantity or value of a given product may be imported each year, or the customers have to buy a given minimum quantity or value of that product each year.

Developments since the war have shown how, in practice, non market-conforming measures are playing an ever increasing role in trade policy. As we shall see in Chapter 10, some people considered that one of the reasons for the expansion of non market-conforming instruments was that, under the GATT rules, market-conforming instruments were being increasingly driven out so that governments looked for other instruments to influence trade. A very common variant is the voluntary export restraint (VER): an example of this was also given in Case study 6.1. What are the welfare effects of the introduction of a VER in the importing country? Are they comparable with the effects of market-conforming trade policy?

6.4.1 Voluntary export restraint

In any case, it should be clear that the application of a VER, as in the example given in Case study 6.1, will not be neutral in its effects on welfare. As a result of the restriction on imports of foreign goods, the market price will be higher than if there were no VER. This leads to a transfer of income from the consumers (they pay a higher price for cars) to the domestic and foreign producers (they make higher profits as a result of the higher price). To that extent, the effect is comparable with that of an import tariff. However, there is a difference in that, in the case of an import tariff, the government of the importing country receives import duties. That is not now the case (unless we are talking about the theoretical situation in which the government of the importing country is able to auction the right to the VER in some way). If the price on the sales market is driven up by the trade restriction while the production costs remain constant, a kind of excess profit is produced. This excess profit normally goes to the foreign producers who manage to secure a position in the limited market. It is also possible for this excess profit to go to the intermediaries who benefit from the higher margins. Thus, in any case it is not certain whether this excess profit will eventually go to the importing country; it is more likely to end up somewhere abroad. In that case, the welfare effect of the VER for the importing country is less favourable than if imports were restricted by a market-conforming instrument.

6.4.2 Import quota

While the VER limits imports because the exporting country imposes volume restrictions itself, in the case of an *import quota* imports are restricted by the measure introduced in the importing country. The effect of an import quota is therefore the same as that of a VER, and at first sight it is also the same as the effect of an import levy. Here, too, a transfer of welfare takes place from the domestic consumer to the domestic and foreign producers via higher prices. A fundamental difference between an import quota or VER and a tariff is that the difference between the international market price and the domestic market price in the importing country is not certain to go to the importing country, because whether trade is limited by an import tariff or by a volume restriction, this always creates a scarcity situation in the imported product in the importing country, so that the price which people are prepared to pay differs from that at which the exporter would be willing to sell. In the case of an import tariff, this price difference goes to the government of the importing country, which then passes that sum on to its own society. However, if there is any kind of volume restriction on imports, then it is unclear which party will succeed in collecting the artificially created trade margin. The trader who manages to buy the product from the exporter at the export price and sell it at the higher price in the importing country can gain this excess profit. If the exporter wants to gain this excess profit, then he has to make certain that he can supply within the quota limits. The government of the importing country can only gain the excess profit by auctioning export licences for foreign suppliers.

Another objection to volume restrictions on the international markets is that they rule out competition and give the foreign supplier no chance to respond by offering keener terms.

Case study 6.6 illustrates the welfare effects of the application of a trade restriction on Japanese cars by the EU.

Case study 6.6 Welfare effects of trade restrictions

A study by Smith and Venables (1991) on the trade restrictions applied by various EU countries to exports of Japanese cars to the EU includes three estimates of the welfare effects of:

1. the abolition of the trade restriction by the individual EU members;
2. the replacement of the individual trade restrictions of each member by a 'comparable' import tariff for each member; and
3. the replacement of the individual trade restrictions of each member by a common EU trade restriction.

Ad 1

As already stated, a trade restriction transfers income from consumers to producers. As a result of the restriction on foreign competition, the supply of cars on the EU market will be less than under free competition with the Japanese producers. This increases car prices, so that part of the consumer surplus is converted into a producer's surplus. According to Smith and Venables, abolition of the French trade restriction on Japanese cars, for example, will cause the consumer surplus in France to increase by ECU 1,543 million per annum, while the profit for French car manufacturers falls by ECU 940 million per annum and the French government's tax revenue increases by ECU 168 million per annum. This estimate is based on the assumption that, as a result of abolition of the import restriction on Japanese cars, a (standard) common EU import tariff of 10.3 per cent is levied; this yields ECU 177 million in import duties; the other welfare effects were not computed here.

Italy also records a substantial annual gain in welfare in a comparable situation: an additional ECU 2,736 in consumer surplus, while the loss to the Italian car makers is estimated at ECU 966 million per annum. Similar welfare effects were found for other countries which also apply a trade restriction on Japanese cars (such as the UK, Spain and Portugal).

If all EU member states were to abandon trade restrictions on Japanese cars, this would increase the consumer surplus in the EU by ECU 6,349 million. The profits of all EU car manufacturers together would fall by ECU 2,701 million.

Ad 2

France which, together with Italy, applies the most stringent trade restrictions on Japanese cars, was the only country for which the researchers produced an estimate of the effect on national welfare of replacing the trade restriction by a 'comparable'

---

tariff (they assumed a level of 34.9 per cent, which is the tariff at which the production level of EU manufacturers remains constant). In comparison with the above case, it is mainly the decline in the profits for French producers that is smaller ('only' ECU 215 million). In this case the increase in the consumer surplus is ECU 738 million, roughly half the increase found under Ad 1 above. Finally, the French government obtains additional tariff revenue totalling ECU 354 million.

Ad 3

In a third exercise the researchers examined the welfare effects which occur if each member's trade restriction is replaced by a common trade restriction which maintains a constant share of the EU market for Japanese producers. This exercise is of great practical significance because, in the long term, the establishment of the single market in the EU will mean that national import quotas can no longer be effectively applied. The result of the introduction of a common VER is that the welfare effects are much smaller than if the individual trade restrictions were totally abolished (case 1). In this case, the consumer surplus in France and Italy increases by ECU 520 million and ECU 1,327 million respectively, according to the calculations, while the car makers' profits fall by ECU 251 million and ECU 481 million respectively in these countries. It is noticeable, that in this case, a country such as Germany which does not impose any trade restrictions on Japanese cars is confronted by a substantial loss of welfare: here, the consumer surplus falls by ECU 1,098 million while the German car makers' profits increase by only ECU 77 million. For the EU as a whole, introduction of a common trade restriction instead of individual trade restrictions by member states yields only a small increase in the consumer surplus: ECU 197 million, while there is a decline of ECU 405 million in the profits of the EU motor vehicle sector.

From the case study we can conclude that the protection of the EU producers by a trade restriction leads to loss of welfare for the EU member states. This loss is greatest if each member imposes its own trade restriction: the loss of welfare to consumers is considerable as a result of the higher EU market price, while the higher price also transfers part of the welfare to the Japanese producers. In the case of a common trade restriction, the welfare losses in the EU are smaller, but this measure will also lead to a higher EU car market price, so that there is again a transfer of welfare to Japan at the expense of the consumers.

6.5 Trade policy and market failures

The government's objectives are not always the same as those of a company's managers. As in the case of the optimum tariff, the government can be expected to consider the welfare of the country as a whole; in principle, the company considers only its own profit and survival. In practice, the distinction is not so clear-cut: driven by political opportunism, governments often allow themselves to be persuaded by lobbies and thus specific interest groups; companies sometimes feel a social responsibility, expressed in sponsoring of sport and the arts, for example. In principle, however, the said difference in objectives is a correct assumption.

6.5.1 External effects

A government may believe that a certain economic activity, such as the establishment of a multinational subsidiary, must go ahead while after weighing up the risk and the expected return, the company – possibly together with the potential financier – concludes that the investment is not justified. For example, such a difference of views can occur if the business generates positive spin-off, e.g. improving the conditions for setting up other businesses by creating infrastructure and training facilities. (Here the reader will recognise the elements of the concept of external economies of scale, as explained in Chapter 3.) Often the company cannot itself take advantage of this type of advantages for others, because the legal framework is lacking or because the spin-off cannot be individually attributed. In that case the firm generates positive *external effects*: these are not counted in the commercial calculations and are not expressed in the price, but they are important in the government's welfare estimate. When a young industry is just getting off the ground so that there are still only a few general facilities, the government's view is particularly likely to differ from that of the business community. In all the cases mentioned, the individual cost-benefit calculation differs from a calculation which takes account of all welfare effects, and we speak of a market failure. (External effects can equally be negative: think of environmental pollution, noise, etc. In that case the opposite difference of opinion between business and government may result: the firm considers the investment to be profitable, but the government considers it socially undesirable, unless there is compensation for the external effects.)

Where market failures occur, a government can, in principle, eliminate the effects quite easily by subsidising the company in the case of positive external effects and imposing additional taxes on it in the case of negative external effects. The advantage of such a policy is that there are no longer any additional efficiency losses due to distortion in consumption or production decisions, as there would be if the effects of the market failure were tackled by a tariff or export subsidy (because in that case one is always left with triangles b and d or c and e in Figures 6.1 and 6.2 respectively). In the case of domestic market failures, it is therefore more efficient to eliminate them by appropriate domestic policy instruments rather than using the external trade instrument to deal with the symptoms. That is why the 'solution' of domestic market failures by means of trade policy is classed as *second best*.

Earlier in Europe, and in more recent times mainly in developing countries, however, the attempt to use subsidies to help launch infant industries with positive external effects often encountered the practical obstacle of an inade-quate and incomplete domestic tax basis. That is why in Europe in the last century, and in many developing countries from the 1930s onwards, industrial-isation – which was expected to produce clearly positive external effects – was stimulated mainly by protectionist measures at the border instead of a system of domestic levies and subsidies. Because it is much easier and cheaper for the tax authorities if the country's industry is protected against foreign competition rather than subsidised with its own hard-won tax revenue. In fact, protection is an attempt to make other countries pay the bill for industrial development (and/ or, if that fails, to make the domestic consumer pay by driving up prices). Since this usually concerns building up young industries, the literature refers to the *infant industry argument* of protection.[4]

Use of trade protection as an instrument for building up an industry is often central to an *import substitution policy* pursued by many developing countries in the past. This is a systematic attempt to replace imports by domestic production. History has taught us that such a policy often backfires in the long term (in this connection, cf. Case study 6.2). This can be explained with the aid of the theory discussed above, because import tariffs can increase a country's welfare if two conditions are met: namely, if the country can exert substantial influence over world market prices and if other countries do not retaliate. In that case, the negative effects of a tariff, the production and consumption costs, can be eliminated by an improvement in the terms of trade. Since neither of these conditions was normally met in the case of developing countries, the tariffs reduced welfare to such an extent that the additional, positive external effects were overshadowed. Moreover, the substantial import protection destroyed the dynamic effect of international competition on domestic industry. This also meant that companies became increasingly bureaucratic and inefficient. Fur-thermore, such a policy was often associated with foreign exchange rationing, so that the allocation of foreign currency took place via inefficient (and corrupt) bureaucratic channels instead of via the market. As time went by, more and more developing countries therefore began to realise that protective measures at the border were not ultimately appropriate for eliminating domestic market failures and establishing a healthy, competitive industry. As a result, the import substitution policy has been abandoned on a fairly massive scale in the past few decades.

Although trade policy can neutralise certain effects of domestic market failures, and although import and export levies can improve the terms of trade, it cannot be emphasised enough that retaliation by other countries can destroy these advantages. In more general terms, it is also true that the support given to certain sectors via protection is almost always accompanied by a negative effect on the unsupported sectors because it is seldom possible to pass on the whole cost of protection to other countries; as a result, the unsupported sectors

---

4. However, over the years protectionist measures have increasingly been used to delay or halt the decline of obsolete industries; for those cases the concept of the senile industry argument has become popular more recently.

automatically pay part of the cost. In that sense, protection almost always means giving an advantage to one at the expense of another, even within countries.

6.6 Summary

This chapter takes up the traditional trade theories discussed in Chapter 3 which, on the basis of perfectly efficient markets, conclude that free trade is in the interests of national welfare. Levying a tariff or granting a subsidy always distorts the decisions made by consumers and producers. In principle, traditional trade theories state two exceptional situations in which the above conclusion does not hold true, at least in theory. First, if a country is large enough to influence the world market situation and hence the terms of trade, national welfare can be increased by means of certain import or export tariffs (but not by export subsidies). Here it is usually possible, at least in theory, to determine an optimum tariff. This gives the maximum positive balance of the producers' gain, the consumers' loss and the improvement in the terms of trade.

Second, trade policy intervention is sometimes regarded as defensible in the case of domestic market failures. Particularly in the case of emerging industries (think of the infant industry argument) and more generally in the case of external effects of production, trade policy can at least partly eliminate the effects of market failures. Such a solution is called 'second best' because, from the welfare point of view, domestic taxes and subsidies are the optimum – and hence 'first best' – policy for eliminating the distortion. It was recognised at an early stage that both arguments assume that other countries do not retaliate with their trade policy; because this could ultimately reverse the effects of a country's own trade protection.

Bibliography

Hoekman, B.M. (1988), *Agriculture and the Uruguay Round*, IPPS Discussion Paper no. 292, University of Michigan.

Johnsen, D.G., K. Hemmi, and P. Lardinois (1985), *Agricultural Policy and Trade: Adjusting Domestic Programs in an International Framework*, Task Force Report to the Trilateral Commission.

Smith, A. and A. Venables (1991), 'Counting the Cost of Voluntary Export Restraints in the European Car Market' in: E. Helpman and A. Razin (ed.), *International Trade and Trade Policy*, MIT Press, pp. 187–220.

Tyers, R. and K. Anderson (1986) in: World Bank (1986), *Distortions in World Food Markets: A quantitative assessment.* Background paper for the World Development Report, 1986.

Valdés, A. and J. Zietz (1980), Agricultural protection in OECD countries: its costs to less developed countries. *IFPRI*, Res. Rep., 21 December.

7 Modern arguments relating to protection

7.1 Introduction

In the preceding chapter we discussed the reasons why governments influence international trade. These reasons were based on the traditional trade theories examined in Chapter 3. However, that chapter also considered modern trade theories. We can expect that the insights offered by these trade theories will also influence ideas on the application of trade measures. In the 1980s, in particular, trade policy theories underwent a wave of revisions, the common feature being that they took much more account than before of the reactions which trade policy can provoke in other countries. Thus the question is not so much whether, in a static environment, trade policy is favourable or unfavourable from a wealth point of view; instead, what counts is the process of action and reaction unleashed among the various parties concerned once politicians intervene in international trade.

Two insights played an important part in the theory revisions. First, people were increasingly aware of the importance of the presence of certain (strategic) sectors for the rest of the economy and for the international competitive position. Strategic sectors are those deemed to be vital to a country on such grounds as employment, value added, advanced technology, defence, expected future growth potential or positive external effects. It had become increasingly clear that while competitiveness depends on the performance of businesses, it is also determined by the environment in which they operate. It can therefore be important to encourage certain activities because of their catalyst effect on the rest of the economy. This view, based very much on the concept of internal and external economies of scale, is discussed in the next section of this chapter.

Second, there was growing awareness that, in its increasingly international context, trade policy can be regarded as a game of negotiation in which both enterprises and governments of different countries are, in principle, involved. Various tactics or strategies can be used in this 'game', ranging from threatened action to the formation of coalitions. Obviously, the description of this type of process demands a fundamentally different approach from the comparative-static approach used for the classical arguments. We shall consider this approach in section 7.3 of this chapter.

As in the previous chapter, strategic behaviour and economies of scale emerge as a result of market failure or domestic distortions. Domestic *market distortions* involve any deviation from the conditions necessary for perfect competition.

Specially Chapters 8 and 9 consider the relationship between domestic market distortions and trade policy. Thus, in this chapter and in Chapters 8 and 9 as in the previous chapter, too, trade policy intervention is not the 'first best' instrument.

7.2   External economies of scale and the competitive position

The development of modern trade theories sheds new light on the traditional argument for protecting industries with important positive external effects; because, as we saw in Chapter 3, there was a growing conviction that comparative advantages were largely determined by random factors and also that patterns of specialisation could depend very much on the existence of external economies of scale. On that basis, people realised that, as regards industrialisation, if a certain 'critical mass' is attained at a particular location, further development often takes place of its own accord. The combination of sufficient production capacity, a sufficiently large sales market in the vicinity, a well-developed network of businesses supplying one another and a healthy competitive climate (e.g. a combination such as that given in the Porter diamond), can ensure that an 'endogenous' development process takes place, aided by a sound international competitive position.

If we translate the concept of positive external effects into modern trade policy theory, then this means, for example, that protection of certain industries, especially if there are mutually beneficial influences owing to a combination of positive external effects and external economies of scale, can sometimes be extremely effective in improving the overall welfare of a country. In practice, this combination of external economies of scale and positive external effects generated by surrounding enterprises occurs mainly in the case of technologically advanced industries. Here, the investment costs as regards knowledge and development are relatively high. The companies concerned cannot generally capitalise on the whole of the return on that investment themselves, so that there are positive external effects for other businesses in the surrounding area; moreover, the success of this type of business is often heavily dependent on a dynamic environment, e.g. because of the possibility of attracting trained staff or the proximity of service companies as suppliers or customers: thus, there are also external economies of scale.

In the above case, trade policy can help to foster the development of the advanced technology industry in the home country, thus ultimately creating a comparative advantage. Here we can once again use the example given in Chapter 3 in which the production of calculators is accompanied by (external) economies of scale because enterprises in that sector have a positive influence on one another. This causes production to be concentrated at one location. Here, again, we assume that Japan happens to be the first to produce calculators, so that production in Thailand, which would actually be cheaper, is virtually impossible.

143

Table 7.1 Calculators: supply, costs and demand

Japan Supply (× 1,000)	Average cost = price	Global demand (× 1,000)	Thailand Supply (× 1,000)	Average cost	Global demand (× 1,000)	Domestic demand (× 1,000)
1	10,000	1.5	1	6,000	3	1
2	5,000	4	2	3,000	6	3
400	1,000	700	600	250	875	600
875	250	875	1,000	100	1,000	700

However, in relation to the previous case the difference now is that demand from Thailand represents a large proportion of international demand, as we can see from the final column added to Table 7.1.

Let us assume that in Thailand people are worried that they will never manage to produce calculators even though production would potentially be cheaper than in Japan, because Japan happened to start production sooner. Let us assume that Thailand then prohibits the import of calculators from Japan on these grounds. In that case, equilibrium will initially be established on the home market in Thailand, which is now self-sufficient, so that domestic demand equals domestic supply. According to the table, this occurs at a volume of 600,000 and a price of 250. The remaining world demand at this price is 875,000 – 600,000 = 275,000, so that there is insufficient demand left for Japan to produce at a competitive price. As a result, all world demand will then switch to Thailand! This will cause a further decline in production costs. In a possible new equilibrium, the traded volume will be 1,000,000 at a price of 100.

Thus, thanks to its own protection, Thailand has become the world supplier of calculators. Paradoxically, it no longer needs the protection once the industry is operational. A temporary import ban is evidently sufficient to bring about the switch in production location: an aggressive export promotion policy is not necessary. Moreover, on balance the consumer is also better off worldwide, seeing the price of calculators drop from 250 to 100.

The figures given in Table 7.1 relate to price/sales combinations over a given period. Although it is not explicitly stated in the table, the demand figures could apply per one year period. In other words, at a price of 250, annual sales total 875,000. However, this is a static picture, because the implicit assumption is that the production costs will not change if that is the annual volume of sales. In practice, however, a learning process often takes place whereby unit production costs are gradually cut further and further by means of improved efficiency. In this situation the average costs decline not only in relation to the annual volume of sales but also in relation to cumulative production over the years. Where this effect occurs, it can be shown in the graph by a 'learning curve'. In terms of the above table, this learning process would mean that production costs in the country where production takes place could decline still further as time goes by. Clearly, learning effects can only increase the effectiveness of protection as an instrument for shifting the location of production, especially if internal and external economies of scale on the one hand, and learning effects on the other, influence one another positively.

7.3 Strategic trade policy

Under certain circumstances, a situation can arise in which governments of different countries emerge as opponents, each wanting to protect a certain domestic sector which is regarded as vital. In this situation, protection can be understood as the move in a negotiating game in which, by trade policy or a trade policy threat, a country tries to influence foreign suppliers or their governments. In this situation we have *strategic trade policy*, because that is defined as forms of trade policy which take account of the expected reactions of the other party and aim to influence the behaviour of foreign suppliers.

A typical example which can be used to illustrate strategic trade policy is that in which two countries each have one enterprise in a particular sector but there is only scope for one supplier to sell on the combined markets. The classic example is that of aircraft manufacturers. On this market there are very high fixed costs owing to the start-up costs for developing a prototype. The break-even point cannot be achieved until the volume of sales is substantial. Let us assume that it is therefore essential to be able to count not only on domestic sales but also on sales on the foreign market in addition. Clearly, if this condition is true for both producers, there can be no situation in which both businesses are viable.

In this case the government may have a number of reasons for attempting to ensure that its own enterprise emerges as the victor of the battle, e.g. via trade policy. In the first place, because of the high fixed costs, we can expect the business profits to increase very rapidly once the break-even point is passed. The government will be able to cream part of this off via taxation. In the second place, exclusion of the foreign company means that the national company will be able to supply the whole world market, so that it in fact gains a world monopoly. As a result, the profit can be further increased via pricing. In this connection we refer to the opportunity for the company to acquire an excess profit or '*rent*'. This can create even more scope for the government to rake in taxes. In the third place, once the monopoly has been achieved, learning effects can be expected so that future profits may increase yet further, with even less chance for a foreign rival to penetrate the market. Finally, arguments in favour of the government offering trade policy support can be based on considerations relating to employment, national prestige, military/strategic interests, national security or other arguments of this type.

The situation in the above case features analogies with the duopoly situation, i.e. an oligopolistic market form in which two suppliers on a market both develop a strategy based on how they expect the other party to behave (see also Chapters 8 and 9). This means that tactics may emerge which attempt to influence the behaviour of the other party. However, the difference is that here, under free trade, there can be no market equilibrium in which there is room for both suppliers: if the national monopolies are maintained, only one can survive. The result is a strong incentive for strategic trade policy intervention because the survival of the domestic monopolist is at stake. The above case is illustrated in Box 7.1 using an example taken from Krugman (1989, pp. 12 and 13).

Box 7.1 Strategic trade policy

Two aircraft producers operate on the world market: Airbus in Europe and Boeing in the US. However, under free trade there is only room for one profitable producer: if both Airbus and Boeing produce aircraft, the profit for both will be negative. This is illustrated in Table 7.2.

Table 7.2 Profit in the case of competition

Boeing	**Airbus** producing	not producing
producing	**−5** −5	**0** 100
not producing	**100** 0	**0** 0

In Table 7.2 (as in Tables 7.3–7.5), four situations are distinguished, according to whether Airbus and Boeing both produce or not; for each situation the Airbus profit is shown at the top right and that of Boeing at the bottom left. The top left-hand cell shows the situation in which both manufacturers produce. This yields a loss of 5 for both Boeing and Airbus. The bottom right-hand cell shows the situation in which no one produces and so no one makes a profit or a loss. The top right-hand cell shows the situation in which Airbus does not produce but Boeing does. In this case, Airbus makes a profit of zero and Airbus makes a profit of 100. The bottom left-hand cell shows the opposite situation.

It is not possible to state in advance which of the two aircraft producers will enter the market first and make the profit of 100. Let us assume that we are in a situation where both companies are considering making the necessary investments to produce for the world market. Both know that the profit will be considerable if they ultimately gain the monopoly position, but also that they will suffer losses if they have to share the market with other suppliers. In these circumstances they will try in one way or another to discourage the other party from making the investment. We are assuming that the option of concluding a cartel agreement to apportion the market does not exist (see Chapter 9 on this subject). Regardless of the techniques used to discourage the other party, the action will always be rather unconvincing, because both know that the positions are symmetrical.

Table 7.3 Profit in the case of a subsidy to Airbus

Boeing	**Airbus** producing		not producing	
producing		**+5**		**0**
	−5		100	
not producing		**110**		**0**
	0		0	

Thus, in this case there is little chance that one supplier's threat to enter the market in any case will definitely discourage the other. This may change if one of the governments gets involved in the game. For example, say Airbus wins the support of the European government, which promises Airbus a subsidy of 10 units if it goes into production. The effect of this subsidy on the profits is shown in Table 7.3. Say the subsidy offer to Airbus was totally plausible and Boeing does not succeed in extracting a corresponding subsidy offer from its own government: we now have a fundamental change in the situation, because Boeing now realises that even if it is first to enter the market, it will still be profitable for Airbus to produce as well. However, this means that Boeing can be certain of operating at a loss. The expected effect of the subsidy of 10 to Airbus is therefore that, as a result of the 'game', airbus will produce and Boeing will not.

Part of the eventual profit for Airbus consists of the government subsidy totalling 10 units. However, in our example this small subsidy yields a profit of 110 for Airbus! Thus, the subsidy has generated much higher profits than the amount of the subsidy itself. This means that the European government can readily recoup the original subsidy out of taxes paid by Airbus. For example, if the tax on profits is 30 per cent, the European government will be left with a net balance of 33 − 10 = 23. The rest of the Airbus profits will also contribute in one way or another to European wealth. This means that Europe increases its wealth as a result of protection. It should also be clear that part of the profit is obtained at the expense of the US. Thus, strategic trade policy is an example of 'beggar thy neighbour policies'. The risk of retaliation by the other country is therefore normally high.

The case described in Box 7.1 thus indicates that a strategic subsidy by a government to a national company can, under certain circumstances, certainly increase the country's welfare. However, in practice these conditions are hardly ever satisfied.

First, neither government nor company can be totally sure about the business profits in the various production situations. In practice, they will have to make an estimate and arrive at forecasts with margins of uncertainty. The question is actually whether the information available at business level is complete and correct when it reaches the public authorities, because the business may have an interest in presenting the government with a distorted situation, showing it in a favourable or unfavourable light. This can be illustrated by the example in Box 7.2.

Box 7.2 A strategic subsidy with inaccurate information

Table 7.4 Profit in the real situation

Boeing	Airbus producing	not producing
producing	−5 5	0 *105*
not producing	**100** *0*	0 *0*

In this case, the initial situation of Boeing and Airbus differs somewhat in reality from that in Table 7.3, which related to the government's perception, given accurate information (see Table 7.4). The difference arises because, in this case, Boeing's position is actually more favourable than the European government thinks on the basis of whatever information it might have. As a result, even if Airbus is the first to start producing aircraft, Boeing will actually still be able to force Airbus out of the market. Since the European government is still working on the basis of the profit figures in Box 7.1, it nevertheless decides to promote production at Airbus with a subsidy of 10.

Table 7.5 Profit given inaccurate information in the case of a subsidy to Airbus

Boeing	Airbus producing	not producing
producing	**5** 5	0 *110*
not producing	**110** *0*	0 *0*

Table 7.5 shows the actual situation which ensues. In this case, the European subsidy proves to be too small to force Boeing out of the market. The result is that both Airbus and Boeing produce and each make a profit of only 5. Europe now suffers a net loss: the producer's profit of 5 is more than negated by the government's costs of 10.

In the second place, it is conceivable that positive international external effects could occur for the producing country in the case of production. It is quite possible that certain technical inventions on which aircraft production is based can easily be adopted abroad. In that case some of the positive external effects make themselves felt in other countries. If it is also true that any negative external effects of aircraft production, such as environmental pollution or excessive noise, are only felt at home, the impact on the picture may be decidedly unfavourable.

In the third place, the subsidising government will often be unsure about whether the other government will retaliate, because if it is so easy to recover the subsidy and increase national welfare, then given a symmetrical case, it is logical that both governments will see sufficient reason to grant the strategic subsidy. This means that a government which starts by granting a subsidy is liable to become entangled in an international subsidy race. As a result, a situation could arise in which, having once granted a subsidy, there is no going back and the circumstances necessitate the granting of higher and higher subsidies in order to avoid losing face because previous subsidies achieved nothing.

7.4 Summary

The more modern trade theories are not based on perfectly efficient markets or the absence of economies of scale and/or learning effects during production, nor do they assume that there is always perfect competition. On that basis, they recognise the possibility that the location of a given economic activity which competes successfully is often determined much more by chance than by comparative cost advantages which can be ascertained in advance. The primary factors are where certain activities are first started and whether there is the right combination of circumstances to produce a dynamic process culminating in a permanently strong competitive position. Since these circumstances are determined by chance and by external effects, a situation may arise in which emerging new production locations do not develop even though the production conditions are potentially very favourable. In that situation, (temporary) protection may be a way of successfully breaking the traditional location patterns. Thus, here we have the infant industry argument once again. It is all the more important in the case of industries which produce substantial positive external effects for the national economy.

Another aspect referred to in modern theories concerns the case in which an international market is shared among a few large producers. Large companies are often faced with the strategic question whether to invest heavily in a world market with few suppliers, thus conquering a significant segment of the international market. The main difficulty lies in guessing how rival suppliers will react. Their response often determines the eventual profitability of the investment. If it is not possible to conclude mutual market agreements in those circumstances, a game situation occurs with various possible outcomes. Here, a small trade policy measure on the part of one company's government can sometimes cause the various foreign market operators to make a fundamental change in their investment behaviour in favour of the domestic producer, so that the increased revenue for the latter exceeds the costs of the trade measure. That is an example of strategic trade policy.

Bibliography

Baldwin, R.E. (1992), Are economists' traditional trade policy views still valid? *Journal of Economic Literature*, vol. XXX, June, pp. 804–29.

Bhagwati, J.N. (1989), Is free trade passé after all?, *Weltwirtschaftliches Archiv*, vol. 125, no. 1, pp. 17–44.

Brander, J.A. and B.J. Spencer (1985), Export subsidies and international market share rivalry, *Journal of International Economics*, vol. 18, pp. 83–100.

Brander, J.A. and B.J. Spencer (1983), International R and D rivalry and industrial strategy, *Review of Economic Studies*, vol. 50, pp. 702–22.

Helpman, E. and Krugman, P.R. (1985), *Market Structure and Foreign Trade*, MIT Press.

Krugman, P.R. (1987), Is free trade passé?, *Economic Perspectives*, vol. 1, no. 2, pp. 131–44, autumn.

Krugman, P.R. (1989), Rethinking international trade, *Business Economist*, pp. 4–15, spring.

Krugman, P.R. and M. Obstfeld (1994), *International Economics, Theory and Policy*, 3rd edition, Harper Collins.

8 Trade policy and market forms: a micro-economic analysis

8.1 Introduction

Chapters 6 and 7 dealt with the welfare effects resulting from government trade policy measures. The unit on which the analysis was based was the country as a whole: the effects for the various market players were added together to decide whether or not trade policy was sensible. In practice, however, the application of trade policy is seldom assessed according to such an aggregate, or if you like elevated, welfare viewpoint. International trade takes place between or within companies, and companies have their own objectives such as increasing their profits and/or market share, continuity, etc. That is why there is growing interest in how businesses deal with trade policy from the point of view of their objectives and market behaviour. How do they react if faced with foreign restrictions on their exports, how do they play the game of securing market share, and how will they try to screen off certain sub-markets for themselves as far as possible? These are the kind of questions which form the focus of this chapter and Chapter 9. Businesses can, of course, also try to persuade governments to take measures which are in their interests, e.g. by lobbying the government for protection or subsidies. These forms of business behaviour and their consequences are the subject of Chapters 10 and 11.

8.2 The video recorder market: a case study

Case study 8.1 illustrates to what extent the effectiveness of a trade policy pursued by the government to protect its own domestic suppliers against foreign competition is influenced by: the existing form of the home market, the form of the exporting country's market, the competitive strategy of the foreign supplier and the trade policy of the latter's government. The case study concerns the agreements made by the European Commission in the early 1980s with the Japanese Ministry of Trade and Industry (MITI) on reducing exports of Japanese video recorders to the EC. An interesting aspect here is how, as an example of a reaction by a foreign supplier or foreign government to a domestic trade policy measure, the initiative in a creative approach to the trade restriction itself can shift completely from the domestic to the foreign supplier.

Case study 8.1 The battle for the video recorder market

In order to become the market leader on the video recorder market, it was important for the Japanese conglomerate, Matsushita, to introduce its own VHS system as standard. To do this, Matsushita had to compete with Philips and Sony, developers of the V2000 and Betamax systems respectively. The strategy adopted by Matsushita was two-pronged.

First, through its subsidiary JVC, the conglomerate sought cooperation with the British video hire group, Thorn EMI, which introduced the VHS system in Britain in return for technological support provided by Matsushita. This gave VHS-system recorders a 90 per cent share of the British market by 1982. For the record: the British market was at that time by far the largest video recorder market in the EC.

Second, Matsushita supplied VHS video recorders at very low prices on the American and European markets, using the brand names and distribution networks of American and European electronics producers. This was done on the basis of the '*original equipment manufacturing* (OEM)' concept whereby Matsushita supplied video recorders to an American or European producer under whose brand name the recorder was then marketed. The low prices of Japanese recorders (mostly made by Matsushita or JVC) prevented Americans and Europeans from competing by offering their own recorders.

In 1982, the fact that Matsushita was supplying video recorders on the EC market at very low prices gave rise to suspicions of *dumping*. Estimates made for 1982, such as those conducted by van Marion (1993, p. 189), yielded dumping rates of over 35 per cent. (Dumping was defined here as supplying the product on the export market at a price below that on the home market.) This caused a group of West European electronics producers to submit a dumping complaint to the European Commission, which thereupon started negotiations with the Japanese trade ministry, MITI, on restricting exports of video recorders to the EC by Japanese producers. Eventually, in February 1983, this led to an unofficial agreement which included the provision that Japan should set a minimum price for video recorders exported to the EC – depending on the type – and that the maximum number of Japanese video recorders exported to the EC should be 4.55 million in 1983 and 4.95 million in 1984. A striking feature of this 'agreement' was the inclusion of a quota for Japanese recorders assembled in Europe.

In spite of this 'agreement', suspicion persisted that some Japanese suppliers were maintaining their dumping policy. Since the agreement on the minimum price related to the 'free on board' price (the price of the product before transportation to the export market), Japanese producers had the opportunity to keep transport and distribution costs at a low level on the books. This was done in such a way that, depending on the type, the eventual selling prices of the recorders on the European market were between DM 123 and DM 170 lower than the European Commission had intended in the 'agreement'. Another Japanese producer, Sony, which – as we said – developed the Betamax system in competition with the VHS system, fell victim to this pricing policy. Sony normally offered its video recorders at a higher price than Matsushita and JVC, for example.

The way in which MITI implemented the 'agreement' with the European Commission in its own country aroused a strong impression that Japan aimed to gain a monopoly on the international market in video recorders for its market leader, Matsushita (and its subsidiaries, especially JVC), because MITI allocated export licences on the basis of export performance in previous years, and thus in fact on the basis of existing market shares. It is no surprise that this allocation and the possibility of recording a low figure for transport and distribution costs on the books enabled Matsushita to achieve a large increase in its share of the American and EC market and eliminate the competition from the Betamax and V2000 systems.

The example given in Case study 8.1 clearly indicates that, in pursuing trade policy in order to protect domestic suppliers, in this case the EC electronics producers, against competition from foreign suppliers, it is very important to understand the position held by the foreign suppliers on both the domestic market and their own market. It is also important to be able to assess how the government in the foreign supplier's country will react to domestic trade policy, because the example showed that the European Commission's measure imposing trade restrictions on Japanese video recorder producers – in this case via a voluntary export restraint – prompted the Japanese trade ministry to give preferential treatment to the largest Japanese electronics group, thus deliberately enabling it to secure a stronger position on the West European market.

On the basis of the foregoing, we can ask the following questions:

1. What are the criteria which determine the form of a market and what different market forms can be identified?
2. How can enterprises take advantage of the existence of various sub-markets, e.g. via pricing for each sub-market?
3. What decides the way suppliers behave when entering the market and how does this behaviour change if a market expands, e.g. in the case of access to an international market?
4. How do producers react to one another's behaviour on a market with few suppliers; what determines this reaction and in what way?
5. Under what circumstances can producers well make use of pricing or volume measures?
6. To what extent can national governments influence the competitive position of their national suppliers on the domestic or international market?
7. How can cooperation between producers influence the market form and competitive position of producers on that market?

These questions will be discussed mainly in the light of micro-economic theory in this chapter and the next.

8.3 Market forms

As is evident from the above case study, the form of market with which they are confronted is fairly important to the managers of a business; i.e., to what extent there is competition from other suppliers, what competitive strategies and instruments are used by others and to what extent competitive pressure can be mitigated by product differentiation or other means. The case study also revealed that the degree of openness in the trade system is also quite important, as this largely determines the market form which the entrepreneur faces in selling on the international market, and usually also affects the selling conditions on the national market. Thus, government policy on trade often has direct consequences not only for the enterprise concerned, but also indirectly changes the market form. In the case of serious national or international trade policy developments, this often engenders additional arguments why the companies concerned should reconsider their market strategies.

In identifying the various market forms, one generally looks first at criteria such as:

(a) the number of suppliers on the market and their mutual degree of organisation; and
(b) the degree of uniformity in the goods supplied.

By combining the two criteria, we arrive at a typology of market forms ranging from perfect competition to monopoly. More refined aspects which can then be taken into account to define the various market forms in more detail are:

(c) the extent to which suppliers can screen off sub-markets by design, marketing, etc;
(d) the freedom suppliers have of entering the market; and
(e) the level of uncertainty facing suppliers as regards rival suppliers' behaviour.

In the case of one extreme market form, perfect competition, the situation is clear: there are many, non-organised suppliers who cannot screen off any sub-markets, who are able to enter or leave at will and for whom supply conditions are dictated by the market. The position is equally clear in the case of a monopoly: the micro-economic analysis of the effects of a trade policy measure is given in this case in Box 8.1 (for a foreign monopolist selling on our market). Then there is only one supplier who can use his position on the market, or on the various sub-markets, if appropriate, purely to maximise his own profit. However, in the real world of international business, both extreme market forms are quite rare. In most cases, one encounters some intermediate form. In the rest of this chapter we shall concentrate on these intermediate forms, in trying to ascertain the advantages and disadvantages of trade policy.

Box 8.1 Confronting a foreign monopolist with import protection

Figure 8.1 shows the price-sales curve or the average revenue curve (AR), the marginal revenue curve (MR) and the marginal cost curve (MC) facing a foreign entrepreneur who, as an exporter, holds a monopoly position in exporting to our market. Thus, the price-sales curve corresponds to the domestic demand curve for imports; the MC curve corresponds to the average cost curve (AC curve) because it is assumed to be horizontal.

According to the usual assumptions, the monopolist follows the management rule: MR = MC. This optimum condition guarantees him maximum profit. On that basis, under free international trade he will thus set his price at P and will export volume O_y. Our country now imposes an import tariff of T, e.g. in order to cream off part of the profit which is going to the foreign monopolist. Imposition of the tariff can be depicted in the graph by an upward shift in the MC curve. Since he aims to make a profit, the monopolist will now supply less, namely O_x; the market price rises to P_t. Before the tariff was imposed, the monopolist's profit consisted of d + e + f + g (the difference between total revenue and total costs), and afterwards b + d. For convenience, let us assume that e and b are equal. (This is a simplification which is true only if the AR curve is at 135 degrees to the horizontal axis, as we can tell by geometry.) On the basis of this assumption, the monopolist's profit falls by f + g as a result of the tariff. Of this, f goes to our government and g represents the efficiency loss.

What has our country achieved? First, our government now has the said tariff revenue, f; on the other hand, the tariff has driven up the domestic price to P_t,

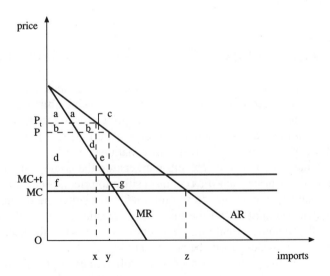

Figure 8.1 Rent snatching by the government

so that the consumer surplus falls by b + c. Our country makes a net gain from imposing the tariff on the foreign monopolist's imports if f is greater than b + c. If, for simplicity, we ignore the small triangle c + g, this means that the gain in welfare for our country depends on whether f is greater than b. Geometry tells us that this is in fact the case, since the MR curve, which is a median of the AR curve, is always steeper than the AR curve. Since area f results from a projection of xy on the MR curve and b from a projection of xy on the AR curve, it follows that f must always be greater than b. Thus, our country will always increase its welfare.

Paradoxically, it is thus relatively easy for our government to take trade policy measures against the foreign monopolist and achieve a net gain in welfare. Since the government creams off part of the monopolist's excess profit (rent), this special form of strategic trade policy is known as rent snatching. If there had been foreign supply under perfect competition, it would not have been possible for our country to increase its welfare by protection (check this for yourself). Finally, it should be noted that the Airbus subsidy in Box 7.1 was in fact the mirror image of rent snatching.

With regard to these intermediate forms, the characteristics of market forms mentioned earlier under (c) – (e) will be discussed in succession:

(a) the degree to which a supplier can take advantage of the existence of different national sub-markets (section 8.4);
(b) behaviour when entering international markets (section 8.5);
(c) market behaviour in relation to a small number of competing suppliers (sections 8.6 and 8.7).

8.4 Taking advantage of different national sub-markets

Let us assume that a firm has a monopoly on the national sales market but faces virtually perfect competition on the export market. Such a situation can occur, for example, if the firm's own government uses protection to safeguard the home market against foreign competition and foreign governments cannot or will not apply such a policy on their respective national markets. For such an entrepreneur, there are two separate sub-markets: on the home market, demand is presumably fairly price-inelastic (i.e. insensitive to price), because consumers have no alternative; in contrast, on the international market the demand which our entrepreneur encounters will be much more elastic, owing to the competition. Obviously, to some extent entrepreneurs will sometimes themselves try to create the situation described because, as we shall see, it offers good opportunities from the point of view of their profit. An example of how this can happen in practice is described in Case study 8.2a below. The fact that governments sometimes fully collaborate in this is illustrated by Case study 8.2b.

Case study 8.2a Price differences on the European car market

An example which illustrates how producers in different sub-markets can set different prices for their products can be found in the European car market. It is evident from Figure 8.2 that car manufacturers apply differential pricing on a large scale for each type of car on the different sections of the EU car market: this is a typical example of price differentiation.

The reason why car manufacturers can apply such price differentiation lies in the selective distribution system common in the European car industry. This means that the manufacturer sells his cars through a single dealer in each sales region (e.g. a country), and the dealer in turn confines his sales area to that region. This provides the car manufacturer with a network of dealers who only sell his cars in a specific part of the market. Depending on the actual price sales curve and hence also the price-elasticity of demand for cars in each sales region, the car manufacturer then sets the selling price for each region. This creates brand monopolies in each sales region, so that a particular type of car is available from only one dealer; thus, the only competition in the sales region is between the different brands.

In principle, such a form of artificial partitioning of geographical sub-markets

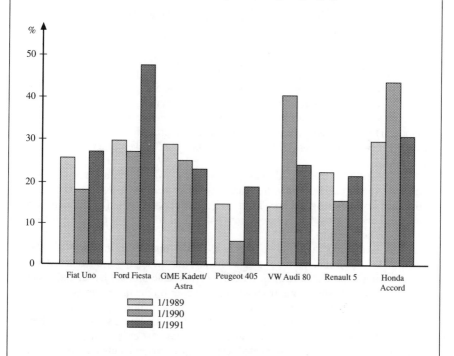

Figure 8.2 Price differentiation on the European car market
Source: European Commission, 1992.

is prohibited under EU law. Nevertheless, in 1985 the European Commission decided to permit an exception for the application of selective distribution by the motor vehicle sector (Regulation 123/85) on condition that the price differences between the sub-markets did not exceed 12 per cent over a certain period or 18 per cent at any one time. There were immediate protests from consumer organisations about the scale of the price differentiation thus allowed. In 1990 the European consumers' organisation submitted a complaint to the European Commission concerning the large price differential between various EU countries for the same type of car. According to the organisation, this was due mainly to the selective distribution policy. As we can see from Figure 8.2, in many cases the price differences for the seven brands shown (greatly) exceeded the 18 per cent maximum set by the Commission.

In spite of this criticism the European Commission did not decide to intervene direct. The stated view was that the price differences were largely due to exchange rate fluctuations and differences between EU member states as regards protectionist measures against cars from countries outside the EU, such as Japan. However, the European Commission has now announced measures to make car pricing in the EU more transparent.

Case study 8.2b Price differences on the European market in pharmaceutical products

An example of the existence of large price differences for products of a particular type, caused by government regulation and control, can be found in the EU market for pharmaceuticals. Trade in pharmaceuticals in the EU is hampered by a mass of legislation in the member states. Thus, the government of a member state has to grant a licence for each pharmaceutical product before it can be sold on the market. This entails an expensive, time-consuming procedure, which can also be used by producers to strengthen their market position or even to try to build up a monopoly.

If a producer has introduced a new product in his own country under a particular name, he can of course supply the product in other member states, too. If he does so – after first obtaining a licence from the government concerned – it is fairly easy to secure a strong market position there as well, if the market has not yet been entered by competitors.

If another producer wishes to supply a similar product in the same member state, under a different name, of course, he also has to apply for a licence. Thus, the licensing requirement applies even if a comparable product has already been available for quite some time from another supplier on the market in question. In fact, however, the expensive and time-consuming nature of the application procedure often forms a substantial barrier to competition on a sub-market where another monopolist is already established. This makes it easy for monopolies to continue once they have been created, especially if governments are prepared to lend a helping hand.

To give an example, the product Methorexate, sold in Italy as Methorexata, cannot be imported into Germany because, according to the Bundesverwaltungs-gericht (Federal Administrative Court), the difference in name suggests that the products are different. Clearly, in cases such as those described above, producers will endeavour to make optimum use of the stringent government regulations in order to strengthen or sustain their position on the various sections of the EU market. On the basis of the price-sales situation prevailing on the sub-markets, they will then try to maximise their profits via differential pricing (see also Box 8.2).

The existence of different, separate sub-markets can be depicted in graph form by the respective steepness and flatness of the two price-sales curves. The marginal revenues (MR curves) derived from these on the two markets will therefore show comparable differences in gradient (see Figure 8.3). For convenience, it is assumed that marginal costs are constant (see the horizontal dotted line of the MC curve in Figure 8.3).

The entrepreneur will now apply the combination p_1, q_1 and p_2, q_2 on the home market and the international market respectively in order to maximise his profit, because the theory tells us that in this case it is in the entrepreneur's interests to restrict the quantities supplied on the two sub-markets in such a way that marginal costs and marginal revenues are equal: for that is when he makes the maximum profit. In other words, if he is faced with different price-sales curves on the different, separate sub-markets, he adopts a position in which the marginal revenues on all sub-markets are the same (and thus also equal to the marginal costs). If he did not, he could increase his net revenues and thus his profit by switching from a market with lower marginal revenues to one with higher marginal revenues.

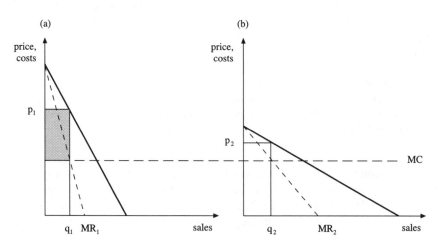

(a) Sub-market 1: the home market
Demand is inelastic

(b) Sub-market 2: the international market
Demand is elastic

Figure 8.3 Price discrimination

159

In practice, this might mean that, in order to achieve the maximum profit, he operates far more aggressively on one sub-market than on another, and also applies *price discrimination*. And that is what we often find in practice: the more competition a firm faces on the various sub-markets, the lower the price or the better the terms he will offer compared to a situation in which he has a monopoly on a sub-market.

If we go back to the situation in Figure 8.3, then we see that the entrepreneur adjusts his pricing behaviour to the market situation: his domestic price is higher than the price which he charges in the other country. If he knew the price-elasticity of demand relevant to him on the two sub-markets, e_1 and e_2, it would be easy for him to determine the optimum relationship between the prices which he charges, namely according to the formula derived in Box 8.2: $p_1/p_2 = (1 + \frac{1}{e_2})/(1 + \frac{1}{e_1})$.

Box 8.2 Pricing on separate sub-markets

The attempt to maximise profits by a firm which can sell on two separate sub-markets is based on the idea that the firm is confronted by a single cost function and two revenue functions. It can therefore maximise its profit if $MC = MR_1 = MR_2$. So long as the marginal revenue on the two sub-markets is not equal to the marginal costs, the entrepreneur can still increase his profit by transferring sales from one market to the other.

Let us first recall that marginal revenue in the general sense can be redefined as $MR = p + q \times dp/dq$ (on the basis of differentiating $p \times q$ (= TR) according to q by the product rule). Using this we can rewrite the equilibrium condition $MC = MR_1 = MR_2$ as $MC = p_1 + q_1 \times dp_1/dq_1 = p_2 + q_2 \times dp_2/dq_2$.

Since the price elasticity of demand in general can be stated as $dp/dq \times p/q$, $q_1 \times dp_1/dq_1$ and $q_2 \times dp_2/dq_2$ can be restated as p_1/e_1 and p_2/e_2 respectively. Thus: $MC = p_1 (1 + 1/e_1) = p_2 (1 + 1/e_2)$. Therefore, in equilibrium

$$p_1/p_2 = (1 + \tfrac{1}{e_2}) / (1 + \tfrac{1}{e_1}).$$

This can be illustrated by an example. If the elasticity of demand on the home market, market 1, is, for instance, –2 (a 5 per cent higher price causes demand to fall by 10 per cent) and –8 on the international market (a 10 per cent higher price causes an 80 per cent decline in volume), then it should be true that $p_1:p_2 = 7:4$. (Check this for yourself.)

The question is whether it is permissible to cream off profits in this way. The answer is negative: according to the definition used by the General Agreement on Tariffs and Trade (GATT, see Chapter 10),[1] and adopted by the World Trade Organisation, this constitutes dumping. (Dumping is the sale of products at a

---

1. See also the Open University 'International Economic Institutions' course as regards the formal GATT regime.

price below that in the country of origin and/or below the cost price. Foreign competitors can take formal action against dumping.)

A more pernicious form of dumping than the price discrimination just defined would occur if the supplier in our example were to use the profit made on the home market (the shaded area in Figure 8.3a) to try to destroy the competition on the home market in the long term. This could be achieved by supplying the product at less than cost and less than the competitors' cost price on the foreign market by using the profit buffer built up at home; for if the foreign suppliers do not have a comparable buffer, they are bound to lose the battle in the end. This is known as *predatory dumping*, because this form of dumping is intended to drive the foreign competitor out of the market. (cf. Case study 8.1.)

In the literature, part of the discussion on dumping has focused on the position of countries such as Japan on the world market. A number of anti-dumping procedures have also concerned supplies from that country. Some people claim that Japan's internal structure, in which producers cooperate in '*keiretsus*', in fact results in quite effective protection against rival supplies from abroad.

Box 8.3 The *keiretsu* as a specific market form

In a *keiretsu* the companies have a stake in one another's equity and regularly exchange top management. At the centre of a *keiretsu* is a bank around which entrepreneurs are grouped in clusters. Such an arrangement is called a *kinyu keiretsu*: a financially united group; if, instead of the bank, a large company forms the centre, then this is called a *sangyo keiretsu*: industrially united group. The *keiretsu* assigns a key function not just to the bank but also to the trading company, which supplies raw materials and the like to the companies and sells their end products. A *keiretsu* in fact excludes certain markets: the capital market is replaced by an internal financing system and the various commodity and intermediate markets are replaced by the trading company. In this way the trading company and the bank take over much of the market mechanism coordination.

Such an institutional structure makes it extremely difficult for foreign competitors to penetrate the protected market, break into domestic sales channels or secure any suppliers. Thus, from the point of view of a Japanese businessman, the situation would look roughly like that which could be described according to Figure 8.3. These cases can be said to represent *systematic dumping*. However, the extent to which this concept applies in certain sectors is the subject of debate. Although systematic dumping is seen as an unfair trade practice, and as such is covered by the trade regulations of most industrial countries, there are also good economic reasons why dumping should not be branded as damaging (except for predatory dumping), because the consumer benefits from the lower price of the foreign supply.

8.5 Behaviour on entering international markets under monopolistic competition

In practice, the size of the market limits the number of suppliers operating on it. There are almost always entry costs, and they are especially noticeable where there is some form of internal economies of scale, so that the average unit costs fall as production rises. In such a situation there are two opposing effects which apply as the number of suppliers on a market of a given size increases. On the one hand, it becomes ever less possible to benefit from economies of scale because the average size of business declines and average production costs therefore increase; on the other hand, the increase in the number of suppliers will stimulate competitive pressure, depressing market prices. Profit per product is reduced by these opposing trends as the number of suppliers increases, to the point where the last supplier to enter the market just fails to make a profit. According to the theory, once that point is reached there will be no more new suppliers entering the market.

In such a case, if there is a sudden opportunity to expand total sales on this market, e.g. as a result of international trade liberalisation, then not only will there be new chances of achieving economies of scale, but the sales prospects will also increase so that there will initially be more scope for suppliers to make a profit on the market. Since there is free access, the result of such a market expansion is that, in the next stage, more suppliers will arrive and if each one offers his own variety, type or brand of product, there will also be more consumer choice.

As we saw in Chapter 3, this form of market situation is known as *monopolistic competition*: in principle, there is free access, and there are many suppliers each unable to influence the market conditions himself, but each supplier does offer his own variety of product, so that his own sub-market is screened off to some extent. Thus, each entrepreneur feels that he has a monopoly in his own variety, but still experiences competition owing to the existence of many variants of his product.

Features of the behaviour described above in an expanding market were seen in the European Community in the 1960s, for example. The creation of the common market in the EC suddenly offered massive scope for businesses to benefit from the economies of scale provided by the enlarged EC market. From the consumers' point of view, this meant that there was now much more opportunity than before to buy unfamiliar European products. The expansion of the market – or if you like, the liberalisation of trade – increased competition, provided more scope for economies of scale and offered greater variety. In Case study 8.3 we see how the establishment of the EC in 1958 enabled the Italian refrigerator and washing machine manufacturers to take advantage of the resulting economies of scale, and how – as a result of the enlargement of the market – there was an increase in the variety of cars on the European market.

Case study 8.3 The market in domestic electrical appliances and the car market

The Italian manufacturers of refrigerators and washing machines (particularly Zanussi and Ignis) expanded their production on a large scale in the 1950s, hoping to take advantage of the economies of scale that the enlarged European market held in store. Although this substantial expansion of the scale of production did entail some risks – as it was not certain to what extent the proposed trade liberalisation in the EC would actually lead to rapid improvement in their access to the markets of other member states – the strategy adopted by the Italian producers proved successful in practice. Since refrigerators and washing machines developed into more or less standard products, the Italians – thanks to their large-scale production – were able to offer their products in other European countries at low prices. This subsequently enabled them to take maximum advantage of economic growth in the 1960s and the ensuing wave of mass consumption. In 1970 the Italian producers succeeded in supplying a quarter of the refrigerators and almost a fifth of the washing machines sold in Germany. In France, the Italians held almost half the market in refrigerators and about a fifth of the market in washing machines at that time. In response to the Italian success, producers in other member states showed a strong tendency towards concentration, e.g. by mergers and acquisitions.

A market where it is not so easy to achieve economies of scale but where the emphasis is more on competition by product differentiation is the car market. The creation of the EC did lead to an increase in trade in cars within the EC, but it was on a much smaller scale than on the domestic appliance market described above. Up to then, cars made in the various member states had been destined for the home market, the type of car depending very much on the population's per capita incomes and tastes. In so far as economies of scale were attainable, the main opportunities lay in production of parts. Establishment of the EC led to a sharp increase in trade in cars between member states, with a greater variety of cars available in the member states. Simple as it was for refrigerator and washing machine manufacturers in the first example to produce on a larger scale, this was much more difficult in the car industry owing to product differentiation. True, in the 1970s there was increasing cooperation between car producers, but the pace was generally slow.

The traditional product differentiation in the car industry did lead to greater variety of cars on the market after the creation of the EC, but placed restrictions on a rapid development towards larger-scale production. The 'problem' here was that, while competition in domestic electrical appliances takes place mainly on price, in the car industry it is mainly non-price instruments that are used, such as diversity of car types, after-sales service, reliability of servicing, durability (mainly the second-hand market price), style and design.

8.6 Oligopoly: analysis based on reaction curves

A market form often found in the international battle between competitors is the *oligopoly* (see also Chapter 3). This means that a few firms are active in one market and embroiled in competition with one another over the distribution of market shares. In most cases, all firms have developed their own brand or type of product, so that the products are competing but not identical. In the special case of only two competing producers we call this a *duopoly* (see section 8.7).

The question now is how these firms will behave in relation to one another on the market. If the home market enjoys quite a substantial level of protection against foreign competition, it seems obvious that the firms' strategy will be primarily geared to fighting off rival suppliers on the home market; only then will they turn to the export market. In any case, in the following analysis we initially adopt this assumption; after that we turn our attention to an international oligopoly.

If we look at the market behaviour of an oligopolist in the case of a closed economy, this means we can assume that the supplier will first try to guess how the other suppliers will behave on the home market. In other words, he will base his strategy on his assessment of how the other suppliers will respond to his market operations. The behaviour of the home market suppliers based on this concept can be shown in stylised form using what are called *reaction curves*. These are curves which show the market strategy which a firm believes will yield the maximum profit, assuming certain behaviour on the part of other (in this case domestic) suppliers on the market.

In order to understand the reaction curves it is best to assume that, in the first place, for whatever reason, the firm is a monopolist on its own market. Thus, in that case it supplies the quantity at which its own marginal revenue is equal to its marginal costs. The corresponding optimum sales are shown in Figure 8.4 by point M on the reaction curve MC*.

Let us assume that, in the next stage, the potential competitors see that they could probably make a profit by entering the same market. Taking account of the sales of our original monopolist and his expected reaction to the newcomers, they will determine, perhaps by experiments, how much they should sell on the market. Say the original monopolist continues to produce quantity OM in spite of the newcomers' supply. The total supply on the home market then increases by the quantity sold by the competitors. Depending on the elasticity of demand, this causes the price to fall, with a proportionate decline in profit for our entrepreneur. If, on the other hand, our entrepreneur were to cut back his own sales by precisely the same quantity as the volume of the new supplies from competitors, then the original market price could be maintained (as the total supply remains the same), but our entrepreneur's profit again falls, this time presumably in proportion to the decline in the volume of supply.

Thus, our entrepreneur now faces the classic dilemma: if he maintains his supply, the market price will fall and so will his profit; on the other hand, if he tries to keep the market price at the old level, he will have to cut back his supply

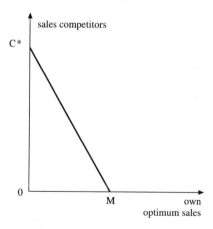

Figure 8.4 Reaction curve for domestic entrepreneur

so that his profit also falls. We now assume that our entrepreneur can minimise the decline in his profit by opting for an intermediate position. This means that he does reduce his supply, but by less than the quantity which the others are expected to offer. Although this will still cause a fall in market price – as the total market supply increases – the drop will be less than if our entrepreneur had maintained supplies at the original level. In fact, we now assume that the market situation is such that the combination of a small decline in sales and a small fall in price is more favourable for our supplier than the two extreme positions mentioned above.

As far as the reaction curve is concerned, this means that the greater the expected increase in the competitors' sales, the more our entrepreneur will withdraw from supplying the market, though not in the same proportion (shift from M to O projected at MC* in Figure 8.4). Finally, if the competitors end up supplying quantity OC*, then according to the graph our entrepreneur will cease supplying altogether. It is obvious that at point C* our entrepreneur can no longer make any profit on this market. Since this is theoretically the case under perfect competition, the total quantity sold by the other suppliers at C* corresponds to that for a market in which there is perfect competition. In other words, if in this case our entrepreneur still continued to supply the market, the market price would fall below the marginal cost level and a loss situation would result. The less than proportionate reduction in supplies by our entrepreneur, but also the fact that, under normal conditions, supplies are lower under monopoly than under perfect competition, makes it easy to see that in Figure 8.4 it must be true that: OM < OC*.[2]

---

2. This means that the tangent of the line MC* <– 1.

8.7 Duopoly: competitive behaviour on the international market

In the previous section we derived the reaction curve for an entrepreneur in a closed economy. We saw that its pattern is in fact based on the entrepreneur's profit maximising behaviour, if he is certain about his own cost function and price/sales opportunities but does not know how his competitors will behave. We now go a step further by also analysing the interaction between suppliers in rather more detail, on the basis of a *duopoly*. A duopoly is a special kind of oligopoly with two suppliers who are almost identical and challenge one another's sales on a particular market. To transfer to an international context, we assume that the competition consists of a single foreign entrepreneur.

Since this foreign entrepreneur's situation is virtually identical with that of our entrepreneur, he also acts, thinks and responds in the same way. This means that for the foreign entrepreneur more or less the same reaction curve can be deduced as for our own entrepreneur above, the only difference being that the coordinates are the mirror image of the position in the other reaction curve. So, in this case, we actually have a duopoly with two more or less equal opponents. (This model is based on a classic concept developed back in 1838 by the French economist, Augustin Cournot.) The model assumes that a duopolist seeking to maximise his profit thinks that his competitor will not respond to his decisions when determining the optimum sales volume. The duopolist is also deemed not to learn from his mistakes. Clearly, these assumptions do not normally hold true in practice.

Figure 8.5 shows two reaction curves relating to the sales of the two duopolists on a particular market, say our own domestic market. Thus, both suppliers are active in this market and our country also operates as an importer. The steep reaction curve, C*AM, relates to the market behaviour of the national producer on the market and shows how much the national producer sells, given the assumed sales by the foreign competitor. The flat reaction curve M*AC shows the market behaviour of the foreign supplier on the same market, given the assumed sales by our national entrepreneur.

The nice thing about the approach is that, since – according to our assumption – the two suppliers have an identical pattern of behaviour, the graph is, in principle, the same for the sales of both suppliers on the foreign market. In that situation the other country thus acts as an importer and our country as an exporter. Thus, owing to the identical behaviour we are, in principle, faced with simultaneous imports and exports of the product supplied and thus intra-industry trade (see also Chapter 3). However, since oligopolists from different countries do not, in practice, produce totally identical variants of the same product, that conclusion should not cause any surprise. Think of the market in passenger cars, cigarettes, computers or other markets controlled by oligopolies where each country engages simultaneously in importing and exporting.

Let us assume, on the basis of the situation in Figure 8.5, that the home market is initially protected against foreign competition. The national entrepreneur then

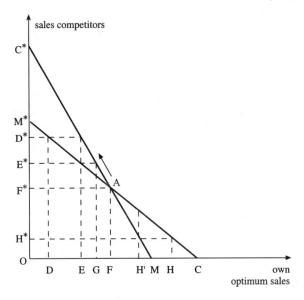

Figure 8.5 Reaction curves in a duopoly

sees himself as a monopolist and sells OM. Later, the market is opened up and a foreign producer enters. Let us assume that he starts by selling OH*. If the domestic firm cuts its sales by OH*, then the price is maintained. If the domestic entrepreneur maintains his sales, then the price falls. Here we recognise the dilemma outlined above and again assume that the reaction will lie between these two extremes. According to the reaction curve in Figure 8.5, the optimum reaction for the domestic entrepreneur is to supply OH′.

Market equilibrium will now come about where the two reaction curves intersect. This is point A in Figure 8.5, also known as Cournot's equilibrium; because if we move from point A to any point on one of the two reaction curves, then in the given situation one of the duopolists has maximised his profit but the other has not. For example, let us assume that the national producer sells the quantity OD. In this case, the optimum quantity sold by the foreign entrepreneur is OD*. If the quantity of imports is OD*, on the other hand, the optimum sales for the domestic producer will be OE. The foreign producer then supplies quantity OE*, the national producer OG, and so on. Given the same market shares, only A represents the maximum profit for both operators.

We can deduce that the total volume of supply (OF + OF* in Figure 8.5) lies between the total supply in the case of a single monopolistic supplier, OM (= OM*, given perfect symmetry) and the supply that would be available in perfect competition, OC (= OC* in perfect symmetry). Since it is easy to see from the graph that the quantity OF + OF* is between OM and OC, the volume of goods supplied has thus risen and the price has therefore fallen in relation to that in the assumed monopoly situation. (However, the reverse applies in the case of the assumption of perfect competition.) In other words, if as a result of trade liberalisation a foreign supplier is granted access to the originally monopoloid national market, then competition increases and so does the total volume of supply, and perhaps also the number of varieties, while the price comes under pressure. Thus, welfare has presumably increased.

An example of how an initial monopoly can, in practice, turn into a situation in which one suddenly faces foreign competition is the abolition of the *Reinheitsgebot* (purity law) on the German beer market. Case study 8.4 gives a brief outline of the abolition of the Reinheitsgebot. Although this example does not include any analysis of competition, it does indicate the context in which the reaction curve analysis described above might take place.

Case study 8.4 The Reinheitsgebot

A classic case of how a government can succeed in pursuing a protectionist policy on the basis of health requirements is the centuries-old Reinheitsgebot in Germany. This law enabled the German government to stipulate rules on the composition of both home-produced and imported beer. The law specified that a drink could only be sold as beer in Germany if it contained the ingredients hops, malted barley, yeast and pure water. If a brew contained other, additional ingredients, then according to the Reinheitsgebot it could not be called beer in Germany and thus could not be marketed as beer. This meant that the German market could be effectively protected against competition from foreign types of beer, because in practice they did not comply with the Reinheitsgebot.

In 1987 the European Court of Justice ruled that the Reinheitsgebot was contrary to the principle of mutual recognition of EC products and services. In general terms, this principle means that differences in national legislation cannot be used for the purpose of intra-European protection. This principle was first explicitly formulated by the European Court of Justice in the case commonly known as the Cassis de Dijon case, in which the Court condemned the German government for prohibiting a French liqueur, Cassis de Dijon, from being imported into Germany on the grounds that the alcohol percentage was too low (!) under German law. The Court of Justice decided that this ban was contrary to the EC rules and thus established a very important precedent for the functioning of the internal market, preventing the abuse of health regulations and the like for protectionist purposes. Similarly, the Court ruled that the Reinheitsgebot did not provide any grounds on which the German government could hinder the importing of beer from the rest of the EC.

To the former, the following can be added. An important study conducted in view of the creation of the internal market and known as the Cecchini report estimated the effect of the Court's judgment on the level of brewers' profits in other EU countries at ECU 105 million per annum. This figure consisted of: ECU 15 million due to elimination of the need to adjust the composition of the beer for sale on the German market, and ECU 90 million as a result of indirect effects, such as keener competition and economies of scale via expansion of trade.

8.8 Summary

This chapter discussed the competitive behaviour of producers on international markets, using micro-economic analysis. The subjects covered were: the degree to which producers can screen off sub-markets, the costs involved in entering a market, producers' uncertainty regarding the behaviour of their competitors, how and to what extent governments adopt protective measures, and the degree to which competitors are mutually organised.

Producers active on different sub-markets will fix their price for each sub-market on the basis of the price-elasticities of demand applicable to each one. Thus, a producer on a sub-market where he holds a monopoly will charge a higher price than on a market where he faces perfect competition. However, the higher price charged by a foreign monopolist on the home market can be creamed off by the national government in the form of an import levy. In that case, national welfare increases.

For example, sub-markets can arise through product differentiation in which suppliers market a variant or special type. The car market is a good example. In addition, as we saw in section 8.4, different sub-markets can arise because governments use regulations to protect national producers against foreign competitors. This was illustrated by the example of the pharmaceutical industry.

On the basis of an oligopoly, we worked out how competitors on the international market take account of the presumed behaviour of their competitors in developing their trade strategies. We said that if such a situation is analysed for two suppliers, the analysis can be made using reaction curves; by comparing the reaction curves of the two suppliers we can then ascertain the market equilibrium.

Bibliography

Pelkmans, J. (1984), *Market Integration in the European Community*, Studies in Industrial Organization, volume 5, Martinus Nijhoff.

van Marion, M.F. (1993), *Liberal Trade and Japan: The Incompatibility Issue*, Physica Verlag.

9 Trade policy and competitive behaviour: a micro-economic analysis

9.1 Introduction

In practice, the assumptions on which the reaction curves in the preceding chapter were based seldom apply. The entrepreneur does not, for instance, enjoy the certainty suggested by the reaction curves. First, he takes due account of the fact that his competitors respond to his decisions, but is not certain how the reaction curves of competing (foreign) suppliers will look; he can only estimate their market behaviour. Second, he cannot be certain about the customers' behaviour: how will they react to the supply conditions? This means he is also uncertain about the location of his own reaction curves. This chapter examines in more detail what that uncertainty may mean for the entrepreneur's behaviour. In particular, we consider whether it makes any difference if the entrepreneur tackles the competition via prices or quantities.

Depending on whether the situation is one of typical price competition or volume competition, we can then ask what are the effects of government trade policy measures.

Trade policy can readily escalate as governments attack one another, as it were, through the businesses which they support. If this type of process escalates, we have a tariff or subsidy war. This chapter will make a general analysis of what this may mean, not only for businesses but also for welfare.

Finally, we consider how firms can restrict mutual competition with the aid of cartel agreements, and why cartels easily collapse.

9.2 Uncertainty and competitive behaviour on the international market

Entrepreneurs frequently do not enjoy the certainty suggested by the theoretical reaction curves. They do not know for certain what the competing (foreign) suppliers' reaction might be, nor how customers will react to supply conditions. If we translate this into reaction curves, we can say that the entrepreneurs are also uncertain about the location of their own reaction curves.

Both the above uncertainties can complicate the outcome of the oligopoly case. For example, the entrepreneur could be inclined to underestimate the competitors' reactions as regards nature and size. In that case, for instance, he thinks that if he increases his supply the others will not notice and that the price will fall only for him. However, in reality the competitors certainly do notice the drop in price on the market, so that they will also increase their supply in an attempt to maximise profits and the overall market equilibrium will yield a net increase in volume (shown in Figure 8.5 by a shift from point A towards the top left, in the direction of the arrow; in analytical terms, both reaction curves have moved outwards a bit as a result of the distorted perspective described above). Thus, we are evidently in a situation in which the suppliers have been collectively pushed unawares in the direction of perfect competition. In practice, we do sometimes see this: initially, suppliers remain in equilibrium with one another, keeping to fairly cautious competitive behaviour, so that the supply remains limited and the price high. However, if a supplier surreptitiously conducts an aggressive competitive campaign and the others notice that on account of market signals, then all suppliers will become more aggressive so that the supply increases and the price falls. For example, see Case study 9.1 at the end of this chapter, which describes how the operation of the OPEC cartel came under stress because some suppliers increased their volumes.

Other forms of perspective distortion among suppliers like those above are equally possible, but it would take too long to go into them here.

Another complication occurs if people realise that none of the market operators is certain of the price/sales function appropriate to this market. Even if detailed, advanced market analyses are available, the assumed price/sales function will still be subject to uncertainty. People will therefore assume a particular price/sales pattern on the market and base their strategy on it, but it is still perfectly possible that they will subsequently have to acknowledge that they misjudged how the customers would behave. This uncertainty is inherent in any market situation and is therefore not a problem in itself. However, owing to this situation it is not clear in advance what is the optimum instrument for tackling competing suppliers: price or volume competition? (The reader should bear in mind that if the price/sales and cost function were totally definite, an optimum volume from the supplier's point of view automatically implies the optimum price, and vice versa; in other words, the outcome is then unaffected by whether one uses price or volume as an instrument of competition. On the other hand, if the price/sales function is uncertain, then this does matter.) So the problem of uncertainty over the price/sales function is that the choice of market instrument is of strategic importance for the profitability of production. This is more likely to be familiar to most firms from everyday practice, rather than the theoretical case in which it does not matter whether one competes on price or volume.

The conceptual framework is explained in Box 9.1.

Box 9.1 Volume or price competition?

In the situation below there is a difference between the ex ante and the ex post price/sales curve facing a supplier.

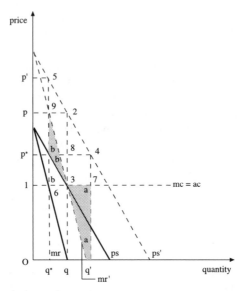

mr   = ex ante marginal revenue curve
mr′ = ex post marginal revenue curve
ps   = ex ante price/sales curve
ps′ = ex post price/sales curve
mc = marginal cost curve

Figure 9.1 Price and volume competition in the case of uncertainty

The ex ante curve gives the subjective advance impression of the producer, ps; the ex post curve shows how the price/sales curve actually looks afterwards, ps′. Thus, we assume that the sales possibilities (at a given price) subsequently exceed expectations, so that the (dotted) ex post price/sales curve lies to the right of the (solid line) ex ante price/sales curve. If the two curves coincide, as in the case of Figures 8.1 and 8.3, for example, it does not matter whether the supplier determines the point of his maximum profit on the basis of price or volume, because if the price/sales curve is totally certain, an optimum price clearly means one particular optimum volume and vice versa (namely where mr = mc). However, this changes if, as in Figure 9.1, the ex ante and ex post price/sales curves diverge. As we shall deduce below, in this situation it does make quite a difference whether the supplier opts for a *strategy of volume competition or price competition*.

Let us assume that the entrepreneur first determines the 'optimum' price/volume combination on the basis of the ex ante price/sales curve (p* and q*).

He can then either charge p* for his products and find out later what volume he can sell, or he supplies volume q* and ascertains subsequently what price he actually makes. For example, his choice of strategy will depend on the ease with which he can vary the volume which he supplies (e.g. on account of production and storage costs), or the importance which he attaches to fixed prices (e.g. on account of marketing and distribution costs). The services sector offers a good illustration of the variety of possible options: sometimes the hourly rate is fixed (fixed rate; variable volume) and sometimes, as in the case of contract work, the total price for the end result is fixed in advance (fixed volume, variable rate).

In this case, if the monopolist opts for p*, then he subsequently sees that his price was 'too low' because sales were underestimated; in retrospect, the price should ideally have been p. As a result, his sales volume, q', will subsequently be seen as 'too high' so that he makes losses on part of his sales. This loss is shown by the area a (triangle 37 q') in Figure 9.1, as this reflects the difference between mr and mc for the additional sales achieved. (The entrepreneur now has a profit totalling area p*174. In the ideal situation, the profit would total p231. Clearly, the area 8473 is smaller than pp*82, so that the monopolist makes less profit than in the optimum situation.)

If, on the other hand, the supplier opts for a volume policy based on q*, which is equally possible, then he will subsequently realise that he has passed over some profitable sales potential, thus forgoing profit totalling area b (triangle 639) in the graph. Area b is the profit on the sales not made, q – q*. (The entrepreneur now makes a profit totalling area 165p'. This area is clearly smaller than that of the profit in the ideal situation, p231, as 9263 is larger than p'59p. This means that here, too, the monopolist's profit is less than in the optimum situation.)

For the monopolist in the situation described above, the advance decision between applying p* and q* is important because, as we can see from the graph, area a is greater than area b.

The pattern of the cost function plays a significant part here. For example, if as a result of positive scale effects this had shown a strongly negative trend instead of being horizontal, then the opposite conclusion might have applied, as we can easily deduce from the graph; the same is true if the actual sales had been less than expected instead of more.

The main conclusion of Box 9.1 – in the case of uncertainty about the sales market, the choice of market instrument may be of strategic importance for the profitability of production – is relevant especially in the case of an entrepreneur operating internationally in an oligopoloid form of market, because in that case there is great uncertainty not just about the actions and reactions of foreign competitors but also about how the customers will behave. It is therefore very important for the entrepreneur to be aware of the circumstances which optimise his chances of making a profit. Should he aim at a high price and a small, preferably high quality and exclusive supply, or can he do better by competing on volume and trying to conquer the maximum market share at the expense of his competitors, even if this means a low price margin or perhaps even losses on some of the sales? This type of question will be examined in more detail below.

9.3 Trade policy and international duopoly

In principle, the situation described using reaction curves for the market behaviour of oligopolists on the home market applies in a similar way if sales take place on the international market. In that case one can also depict the competitive situation between suppliers from the different countries in stylised form, using two reaction curves and assuming that the competitors' behaviour can be represented by a single reaction curve.

However, there are also some differences between an oligopoly consisting of a few national firms and an oligopoly in which the competition is mainly between national and foreign suppliers. In the latter case the governments can initially try to influence the market outcome by government intervention on the basis of national considerations. Such intervention usually aims to improve the competitive position of the national firm. Possibilities include specifically targeted domestic subsidies and levies, but also trade policy measures (in this connection see also the earlier comments on this subject in Chapters 6 and 7).

Second, following such action, a situation may arise in which the battle between the firms actually shifts to their governments. This can cause protection to escalate and all kinds of transfer mechanisms to emerge, depending on the changes in the volumes and prices of international trade (section 9.4).

In the third place there will be a greater likelihood of (international) cartel agreements in relation to sales on the home market. Since the various suppliers know their own home market best, it is logical to come to an arrangement with the foreign competitors whereby each supplier has the chance to protect his own national market for the benefit of his own sales. This can lead to less rather than more competition, in spite of the apparent free trade (section 9.5).

Can governments influence the outcome of the market process as shown in Figure 8.5? The answer is that they can. This is easy to see if we remember that the position of the reaction curves is determined by the producers' assessment based on profit and thus on costs and revenues. If there is a change in a producer's costs or revenues, then the profit position and thus the pattern of the reaction curve and the market equilibrium will change.

Let us assume that there are two firms operating on the home market (which we can regard as an independent market): one foreign firm and one national firm, both making a substantial profit. The government wants to cream off part of the foreign firm's profit and decides to introduce an import tariff. This causes an increase in the foreign supplier's marginal costs; everything else remains the same. Under normal conditions, this firm will reduce its supplies since it aims to make the maximum profit; because the entrepreneur's profits were maximised when $MR = MC$. (For an explanation, see Figure 9.2. Here we see that an increase in the level of marginal costs, e.g. caused by the entrepreneur being forced to bear the costs of an import tariff himself, given the negative trend in the MR curve normal for oligopolists, leads to a decline in the volume supplied. In the graph, $MR = MC_2$ in the new situation; this causes supply to shift from q_1 to q_2.)

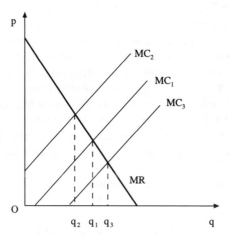

Figure 9.2 Effect on marginal costs of an export subsidy and a tariff

Thus, for the reaction curve for the entrepreneur affected by the import tariff, this means a shift to the left as illustrated in Figure 9.3. According to this same graph, in the new equilibrium the volume supplied by our national supplier increases by FG, at the expense of the competitor's market supply, which declines by F*G*. Since, in the new equilibrium situation, A', the total supply

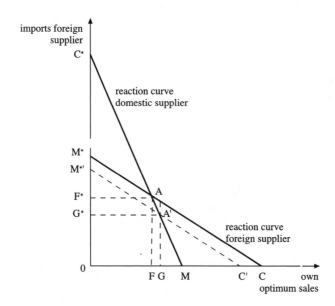

Figure 9.3 A duopoly in the case of an import tariff on goods supplied to the domestic market by a foreign supplier

has fallen (as $G*A' + A'G < F*A + AF$, because $FG < F*G*$), the price has risen. Thus, the tariff has caused both the price and the sales of the domestic supplier to increase. This situation is, of course, disadvantageous to the consumer.

If competition takes place on the foreign market, our government can also try to influence the outcome by means of an export subsidy. If the marginal cost curve in Figure 9.2 relates to the domestic entrepreneur, then it now shifts to a position to the right of MC_1. If we translate this trend into the reaction curves, we arrive at Figure 9.4. Figure 9.4 now shows the situation on the foreign market instead of that on the home market. The reaction curve of our national supplier shifts to the right on this market as a result of the export subsidy. The ensuing new equilibrium is A''.

In this situation, too, our national entrepreneur's market share has risen at the expense of the foreign supplier. The difference in relation to the previous situation is that the total supply has increased, as $G*A'' + A''G$ is larger than $F*A + AF$. Thus, the price will fall. For the foreign supplier this means a drop in profits. The impact on the domestic entrepreneur's profit is less clear and depends on which is stronger: the positive volume effect or the negative price effect. If we move along the foreign supplier's reaction curve (from $M*$ to C), then initially the domestic entrepreneur's profit will increase before it is actually decreasing. At $M*$ he still exports nothing. As soon as the domestic entrepreneur

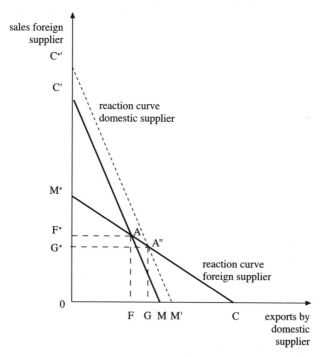

Figure 9.4 A duopoly in the case of an export subsidy by the national government (situation on the foreign market)

enters the market, the total volume of goods sold increases, as well as the profit for the domestic entrepreneur. At C his profit will be zero again.

As a final note with respect to the former it should be mentioned that for the international competitive position it need make no difference whether the government subsidises an export firm's production or any other activity (e.g. R & D) of an actual firm in so far as it exports. In both cases, their market share can be increased. This conclusion is important for policy. Thus, for example, in the Uruguay Round negotiations, the point was made that there should, of course, be no intention of replacing the EC export subsidies on agricultural products (which were to be abolished) by a system of income supplements and production-related subsidies with the same effect on the international competitive position.

9.4   Escalating protection and transfer mechanisms

Now that we have analysed two cases of trade policy effects under duopoly, we can easily draw a complete picture. The four basic cases of trade policy, import and export levies and import and export subsidies, and their effects on the market equilibrium are shown below in stylised form. For convenience, we assume that the duopoly is totally symmetrical (this means that the gradients of the reaction

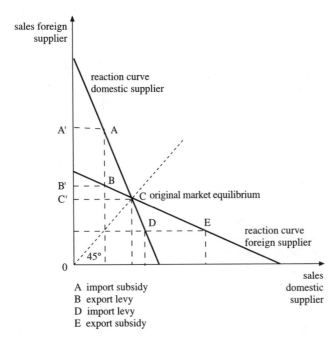

A   import subsidy
B   export levy
D   import levy
E   export subsidy

Figure 9.5 An international duopoly: equilibrium situations under various forms of national government trade policy

177

Table 9.1 Effects of trade instruments in a duopoly

	Foreign reaction curve	Domestic reaction curve	Volume traded	Prices
Import levy	inwards	–	falls	rise
Export subsidy	–	outwards	rises	fall
Export levy	–	inwards	falls	rise
Import subsidy	outwards	–	rises	fall

curves are reciprocal to one another, so that they intersect on an imaginary 45-degree line). The points are selected in such a way as to provide maximum comparability.

It is easy to deduce from Figure 9.5 that the total volume supplied to the market at points A and E is the same and also at points B and D, except that the supply at B and D is less than that at A and E. If we also take account of the total volume supplied before protection (corresponding to point C), then we can also deduce that B = D < C < A = E for the corresponding total volumes of trade. The conclusion is that subsidies on goods traded internationally cause the supply to be greater than if no subsidies were granted; the consumer will benefit via a lower price, at the expense of the suppliers. Import and export levies both have precisely the opposite effect: the volume supplied falls, driving up the price, so that we can expect the reverse transfer from the consumer to the producer. That the effects of an import and export tariff (subsidy) are symmetrical is called the Lerner symmetry theorem. See in this respect also Boxes 6.2 and 6.3.

The effects of import and export subsidies and import and export levies are summarised in Table 9.1.

We have already pointed out that trade policy measures can easily escalate: if one government uses instruments to enlarge the market share of the national company, why should the other government not do the same? This applies particularly where protection is the result of the combined action of the government machine and the business world, e.g. where it is a question of interpreting provisions implementing trade policy or dealing with complaint procedures. In fact, most of this type of administrative protection is beyond political control (see also Chapter 10).

Let us assume that a subsidy war breaks out between the two parties in a duopoly. What are the likely consequences? This is shown as simply as possible in Figure 9.6.

As a result of the escalating subsidies, the reaction curves of the two suppliers constantly move further outwards, as we have already seen, in the direction C → C″, etc. Both suppliers constantly expand the quantity offered so that the market becomes increasingly oversupplied, prices fall and a transfer from producers to consumers is initiated. Thus, the government subsidies are in fact passed on by the producers to the consumers (who have indirectly paid for these

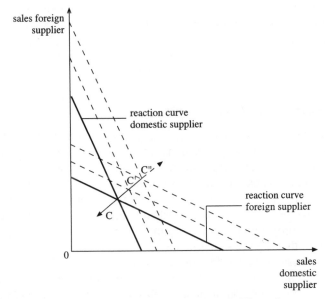

Figure 9.6 An international duopoly: a subsidy or tariff war between two countries

subsidies themselves through taxation); it is even conceivable that the fall in price might be so great that it is not offset by the subsidies, so that – paradoxically – the producers end up worse off than in the original situation C.

Similarly, we can deduce that an international escalation of import (or export) levies leads to a movement as shown by the arrow from C to the origin: international trade dries up; prices on the international market increase and a transfer takes place from consumers to producers (at least in this comparative-static context).

As regards world welfare, assuming that free trade is the most favourable regime and bearing in mind Chapters 3 and 6–7, the analysis illustrated with the aid of Figure 9.6 means that both a tariff war and a subsidy war reduce world welfare. Thus, in both cases there is no zero sum game in relation to the position without protection.

9.5 Other competitive strategies and international cartels

The above argument illustrates that entrepreneurs in a duopoly situation in fact face a dilemma: they can only increase their market share at their competitor's expense, and that means a battle. If they try to make it easier to increase their market share by expanding sales as a whole (e.g. by calling for export subsidies), they undermine the market price and also run the risk that the process of granting subsidies may escalate, so that prices fall still further. If, on the other hand, the government introduces trade restrictions, there is a risk of international trade drying up altogether. Thus there is a delicate interplay between suppliers, governments and customers/consumers with the suppliers in a vulnerable position. It is therefore logical for suppliers to seek other options. Here we shall concentrate on the conclusion of cartel agreements. Another case, the switch to price competition, is discussed in the Appendix to this chapter.

9.5.1 *International cartel agreements*

Let us assume that the producers actually face a scenario in which international competition and the actions and reactions of suppliers and governments eventually lead to a 'war' between suppliers from different countries. In this situation they can either oversupply the market in an attempt to secure their own market share, or they can attack one another with price competition, causing profit margins to dwindle away. The option taken may make a major difference to the entrepreneur's profit; an important argument for entrepreneurs always to think carefully about their choice of marketing strategy!

However, let us assume that international competition is so fierce that the various suppliers all end up in a loss situation but no one of them is prepared to be the first to reduce its supply on the market. What is the most obvious course of action in that case?

In such a case they could try to conclude a *cartel agreement*, e.g. by acting as a group in setting the optimum, joint volume of supply and then agreeing on a mutual apportionment formula, e.g. by partitioning sub-markets.

Similarly, they can also conclude mutual agreements on minimum prices, in order to prevent price competition; one could also think of many other forms of formal and informal agreements aimed at reducing mutual competition. In fact, all sorts of cartel agreements like this are used in an attempt to form groups which collectively behave more like a monopolist. The advantage of such a system of agreements is not only the increase in profit for each supplier but also the greater independence of government support, which is not always totally predictable, and less need to fear unpredictable behaviour on the part of other suppliers. Just as for a monopolist, the power of a cartel depends on the elasticity of demand. If demand is elastic, then every price increase by the cartel is punished by a relatively large fall in demand. If demand is rather inelastic, then a cartel can increase profits by raising prices because the fall in volume remains small. Figure 9.7 shows the difference between the excess profit under perfect competition (no excess profit) and under a cartel.

If the producers decide to form a cartel, then the group's marginal cost curve will act as the supply curve (comparable to a monopolist's supply curve). The demand curve naturally remains the same. The cartel now produces quantity q_k where MR = MC. The corresponding price is p_k. The quantity supplied under the cartel has declined but it is sold at a higher price. Each cartel member now produces a proportionate part of quantity q_k at the higher price p_k. The resulting joint profits are shown in Figure 9.7 by the shaded area.

The question therefore is why, in the case of market forms normally regarded

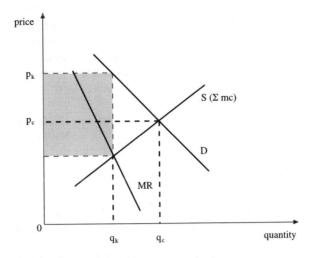

S = supply curve for all competitors together. This is obtained by adding together the producers'
    individual marginal cost curves[1]

D = demand curve

p_c = equilibrium price under perfect competition

q_c = equilibrium supply under perfect competition

Figure 9.7 Excess profit for a cartel compared with perfect competition

as imperfect competition – but where, in contrast to what the terminology
suggests, one in practice encounters the fiercest form of competition – the variant
of the international cartels is generally seldom seen. The answer is twofold.

First, the establishment of a cartel among suppliers from different countries
requires a high degree of organisation and – especially in the case of informal
agreements – trust. It often proves impossible to make all the arrangements,
simply because the transaction costs are prohibitive or in any case too high. The
cartel frequently takes the form of non-explicit, informal agreements in which
people's actual behaviour indicates that they are prepared more or less to
conform to the agreements.

Second, every cartel agreement carries the seed of its own destruction. This
is because, in a cartel, it is worthwhile cheating the group, and that is relatively
easy to do because of the difficulty of exercising control, particularly in the case
of international cartels. Since cartels seldom include all suppliers, it is often also
fairly easy to use anonymous outside sales channels to evade the cartel
discipline. Once again, the scope for evasion is presumably greater in an
international context than in a purely national cartel. In other words, if a cartel

---

1. In a market where there is perfect competition, the individual producer's supply curve is
formed by that part of the marginal cost curve which is above the average variable cost curve.

is successful then the collective volume of supply is restricted, driving up the price. By surreptitiously flouting the volume agreement, it is possible to gain a relatively large additional profit by selling a bit extra, on account of the high price. However, once a cartel begins to disintegrate, it ceases to be attractive to suppliers who do adhere to the agreements. The whole system then collapses and there is an automatic tendency to return to a market form with greater mutual competition.

An example of how a cartel could lose its cohesion and hence its effect at a given moment is the OPEC cartel during the 1970s and 1980s (see Case study 9.1).

Case study 9.1 The OPEC cartel

In the 1970s a number of oil-producing countries belonging to the OPEC cartel succeeded in increasing the price of crude oil almost tenfold in two stages (1973/1974 and 1978/1979) by specific mutual agreements on volume. This increased the OPEC countries' oil revenues in real terms (1989 prices) from about $50 billion in 1970 to over $400 billion in 1980 (Figure 9.8; see also Box 6.1, Chapter 6).

However, the spectacular success of this OPEC cartel simultaneously paved the way for its collapse. The high energy prices prompted adjustment processes aimed

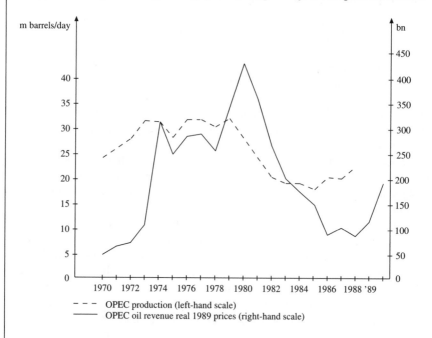

- - - OPEC production (left-hand scale)
——— OPEC oil revenue real 1989 prices (right-hand scale)

Figure 9.8 The OPEC cartel oil revenues ($ bn.)
Source: Cambridge Energy Research Associates (revenues adjusted by US consumer prices).

---

at saving energy on the demand side, and new sources of energy were tapped, causing tension on the energy market to decline. At the same time, the cohesion within the cartel came under pressure because some countries tried, openly or otherwise, to secure a greater share in deliveries in order to take advantage of the high prices. As a result, OPEC production declined during the 1980s, but the fall in prices caused an even greater decline in real revenues (Figure 9.8). Such developments meant that it was no longer possible to avoid the collapse of the once so successful OPEC cartel.

9.6 Summary

This chapter stated that if a producer cannot accurately determine the right price/sales curve, the optimum price/sales combination selected in advance does not always subsequently yield the maximum profit. The degree to which this causes an entrepreneur to forgo profit depends on whether he uses price or volume as an instrument of competition.

A national government can influence the competitive position of a domestic producer by a subsidy or tariff policy. We have seen that if the government grants an (import or export) subsidy, the total volume supplied to the international market by all producers together normally increases to a level which is higher than the original market equilibrium; in the case of an (import or export) levy, the market supply will normally fall to below the level of the original market equilibrium. Here it is assumed that the producers respond to one another's presumed behaviour by a volume policy; the market price adapts in this case to the volumes supplied.

If government intervention leads to counter-reactions by foreign governments, a process of escalation can easily ensue in the form of a tariff or subsidy war. In the first case, there will be a sharp decline in the volume of trade followed by a price rise. In the case of an escalating subsidy war, the volume of trade constantly increases, causing the price to fall and income to be transferred from producers to consumers. This implies that international welfare can be deemed to decline as a result of either an import levy war or a trade subsidy war.

Producers may also decide to compete via their pricing policy (see Appendix to this chapter). In that case an escalating subsidy process will lead to a fall in price on the international market so that the volume is likely to fall in relation to the original level. In contrast, in this case a tariff war causes prices to be constantly driven up, and as a result the volume of international trade can be expected to increase. Thus, the outcome of trade policy measures for the eventual market equilibrium in the case of price competition is the opposite of what we would expect in a situation where firms compete with one another on volume.

For instance if international competition is so fierce that a large group of producers makes a loss, they can form a cartel. In this form of market, producers can jointly determine the optimum price/sales combination and share the profit amongst themselves. If it is comprehensive, a cartel can actually gain a monopoly on the market. In practice, cartels are relatively uncommon because they require a high degree of organisation and are often associated with high transaction costs, while there is also the constant internal threat of participants not adhering to the agreements. Case study 9.1 showed that a cartel can also be threatened from outside, namely if substitutes for the product are supplied or if alternatives are sought.

The micro-economic analysis applied in this chapter demonstrated how a producer's competitive position is determined by: the form of market in which one is operating, government policy on influencing competitive relationships on the market and the way in which competitors respond to one another's behaviour (in an uncertain world). It is evident from case histories that many of the factors mentioned in this chapter come together in practice, in international trade. For decades now, the GATT has been endeavouring to foster transparency in international trade and eliminate the present forms of protection in international free trade. How the GATT works will be discussed in the next chapter. Then Chapter 11 will examine the way in which lobbying by businesses can cause an increase in protection.

9.7 Appendix: Competition on price

For producers, one solution to the dilemma in section 9.5 is to switch from competition on volume to other forms, e.g. price competition. In Box 9.1 we have already deduced that, where the market sales potential is uncertain, it can sometimes be more sensible to adopt a pricing strategy which risks forgoing some sales, rather than pursuing a policy aimed at volume objectives, with the danger that some of the sales may subsequently prove to have been unprofitable.

Let us assume that both firms therefore decide to compete with one another on price. The assumption is that their competitor will set a given price and they will then always try to set their own price at the corresponding optimum. Thus, we again arrive at two reaction curves and we can deduce that they will look like the ones in Figure 9.9. The basis of these curves is broadly similar to that in the case of volume competition, as stated in section 9.3. Thus, point A corresponding to the reaction curve of the national firm, indicates that if the competitor's price is set at level p_{for}, the national firm's profit will be maximised by setting a price of p_{dom}, etc. Under free trade the market equilibrium is at point C.

Once again, the government could intervene in the process of international trade with levies, subsidies or other measures. In the case of an escalating subsidy process, this will cause prices to fall, thus a movement CO, while an import tariff war constantly drives prices higher. The crucial difference in relation to volume competition, however, is that the effects on the volume of trade are not the same; because for an individual supplier a price rise means that the price/sales curve moves outwards and with it the derived MR curve (from mr

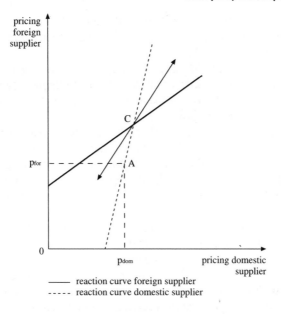

Figure 9.9 An international duopoly with price competition: a subsidy or tariff war between two countries

to mr' in Figure 9.10). This will cause supplies to increase; the opposite will occur if the price falls (from mr to mr" in Figure 9.10).

The conclusion is therefore that, in contrast to the case based on volume competition in section 9.4, although escalating government subsidies do cause

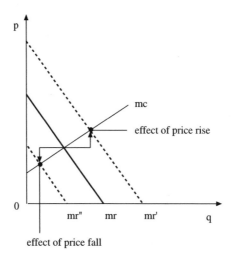

Figure 9.10 The impact of price competition on the marginal revenues

185

market prices to fall in a similar way in the present case, the volume supplied also falls. In the same way, escalating tariffs drive up both prices and the volume of international trade.

What does all this mean for the transfer process mentioned earlier? In the case of volume competition, tariff escalation leads to higher prices but smaller volumes of trade; thus, it is not clear in advance whether there will be a net transfer of welfare between producers and consumers; however, the government has more resources which it can apply at the expense of market players.

In the case of price competition, tariff escalation naturally also leads to higher prices in both countries and also to a shift to the right for the price/sales curves of both suppliers. This is because the similar price increases in the two countries in fact weaken mutual competition between the suppliers. All other things being equal, this means that both suppliers can sell on more favourable price terms than before, so that the volumes sold at the same price are higher than before. This effect makes it highly probable that there will be a transfer from consumers to producers, partly at the expense of the government.

In the case of escalating subsidies, the opposite is true. Here we may have the paradox in which the (production or export) subsidy war causes both prices and volumes of trade to fall, so that the producers in fact pass on the subsidy to those buying their products at home and abroad while trade declines. Table 9.2 summarises the effects of escalation (a trade war) on price, volume traded and producer's position in the case of competition on price and volume.

Table 9.2 The impact of a trade war in the case of competition on price and volume

	Escalation of	Volume traded	Prices	Likely consequence for producer
Volume competition	subsidies	rises	fall	producer's loss
	levies	falls	rise	producer's loss
Price competition	subsidies	falls	fall	producer's loss
	levies	rises	rise	producer's profit

10 The practice of protection

10.1 Introduction

In principle, businesses have two ways of trying to gain trade policy protection: either by exercising direct influence over the political decision-making process via lobbying, in order to change the regulations themselves, or by aiming to obtain administered protection, i.e. protection based on regulations and measures implemented by the executive machinery. The option selected naturally depends on the associated costs and the chance of success. This chapter focuses on how protectionism comes about in practice, particularly as regards administered protection, and the current shapes and forms in which protectionism occurs. The first case study shows that this protectionism can appear in all kinds of forms. In the next chapter we shall seek an explanation for the present protectionism using the political economy approach (and in particular the theory of interest groups).

Case study 10.1 Complaint by American aircraft manufacturers heard at last after many years

During the past decade the previously dominant position of the American aircraft manufacturers in the aircraft market has been substantially eroded. Recently, American producers have faced particularly strong competition from the European aircraft manufacturer, Airbus, a European aircraft consortium which had secured an expanding position in the market, partly with the aid of several European governments. In 1990 Airbus secured 404 firm offers worth a total of $27 billion, thereby increasing its market share to 35 per cent. With the introduction of the new A340, Airbus – which was only set up 21 years ago – is actually trying to achieve a 40 per cent share of the market. This prompted increasing criticism from the Americans about the way in which Airbus production is supported by the governments of four European countries.

The American aircraft manufacturers' criticism centres on the fact that the governments of France, Germany, the UK and Spain have granted Airbus Industrie at least $20 billion in subsidies. This *distortion of competition* enabled the European consortium to increase its world market share to 40 per cent, according to the US, at the expense of American aircraft manufacturers such as Boeing and McDonald-Douglas. In this contest the Europeans threw the ball back into the

---

American court by claiming that Washington also indirectly subsidises its aircraft manufacturers by awarding defence and research contracts. However, according to Washington these are ordinary ad hoc contracts and the companies have to channel back part of any profits to the US government. The conflict which has been simmering between the US and the EC since 1987 on the abolition of *subsidies* for aircraft manufacturers erupted when Washington filed a complaint with the GATT.

As a result, the GATT instituted an inquiry into the Airbus Industrie subsidies. The European Commission deplored the inquiry but nevertheless reluctantly agreed to it. The GATT had never before ventured to conduct an inquiry into the politically sensitive question of *government aid* to the aircraft industry. However, the trade organisation now gave in to a single specific complaint from the Americans, namely that the German government was giving Deutsche Airbus *exchange rate support*. This is in fact an unusual form of aid at which other aircraft manufacturers could only gaze longingly. Let us just see how this form of aid functioned. Aircraft are traditionally invoiced in dollars. If the US dollar is weak in relation to the DM, this can lead to heavy loss of revenue for the German aircraft manufacturers. When the Messerschmitt-Boelkov-Blohm group was taken over by Deutsche Aerospace in 1989, the latter imposed the condition that Bonn should cover the future exchange rate risks. (Deutsche Aerospace is a subsidiary of Daimler Benz and represents just under 40 per cent of the European Airbus consortium.) It was agreed that the German government would cover exchange rate losses if the dollar fell to DM 1.60; if it fell below that rate, Daimler would have to bear the excess losses.

According to the Americans, the German government has already granted Deutsche Airbus over DM 390 million in subsidies under this arrangement. In order to make the unfair competition even clearer, Washington also calculated the subsidy per aircraft: it came to $2.5 million for each Airbus aircraft delivered by the consortium in 1990. The *GATT inquiry* was conducted by the trade organisation's subsidy committee. The EC would have preferred the complaint to be dealt with by the general civil aviation committee 'because that could have yielded a better, more balanced judgment', but did not get its way on this point. The US brought the case in the GATT because bilateral consultation with the EC had come to nothing. Although Washington concentrated on the German exchange rate subsidies, it still left the option of attacking other subsidies later. In fact, in the long term the US wants the abolition of not only all *export subsidies* but also all *production subsidies* to Airbus, and the reduction of *development subsidies* from 80 per cent to 24 per cent.

According to the EC, there is no question of any *export subsidies* and the amounts are also only granted for a limited period. The EC therefore considers the payments to be legal according to the *GATT codes*, which stipulate that specific factors in the aircraft industry (including widespread government support) must be taken into account in the application of the general GATT rules on subsidies.

The case study tells us that there are all kinds of government aid instruments in aircraft manufacturing. Exchange rate support, production subsidies, export subsidies and development subsidies are mentioned; we might also think of examples such as the advantage which can result from government contracts. None of these instruments is presented with the explicit aim of protecting the aircraft industry against foreign competition. However, the ultimate effect is definitely that the national industry is placed at an advantage in relation to the foreign industry, and that it is used as a trade instrument. Hence the dispute between the US and the EC.

Questions which arise on reading this case study are:

1. Which government instruments can be regarded as trade policy instruments?
2. Why and how do such trade instruments come about?
3. Why do governments in both the US and the EC wish to protect the aircraft manufacturing industry?
4. In this context, what is the relationship between industry and government?
5. What is the role of the GATT rules in this?

Questions 2 and 4 will be largely dealt with in Chapter 11, questions 1, 3 and 5 in this chapter. Apart from these questions on the case study, there is also a more general question, namely: if protection is granted by the government, in any form whatsoever, how effective is this for the sector being protected? In other words, how much protection is really necessary, e.g. to achieve a significant recovery in profits or substantial growth of employment in a particular sector? Owing to the importance of this question, we shall examine it first before going into the other questions.

10.2 The effectiveness of protection

In some of the preceding chapters the *effects of protection at national level* were subjected to welfare theory analysis. This is an analysis of the efficiency of protection, or if you like, the national costs and benefits of protection. This was done in Chapters 6 and 7 for trade policy in general and for import tariffs, export taxes and subsidies, (elimination of the effects of) market failures and strategic trade policy in particular. Yet it is natural for protection to have effects at microeconomic level in the last instance. For example, if the American government secures an import restriction on Japanese cars, as has been the case since 1981, or if the Multi-Fibre Arrangement is brought under the GATT rules, it is naturally the car or textile producers and their workforce who will be most interested in knowing what the effect will be on their profits and jobs; the general effects on national welfare are of less interest to them, let alone the effects on global welfare. Similarly, the aircraft manufacturers mentioned in the case study will presumably not care very much about the extent to which the costs of the subsidies which they receive are passed on to national taxpayers or any other group.

That is why the theory pays attention to the *effect of protection at micro level.*

The study of effectiveness or efficiency generally examines whether the objective is achieved; in the case of protection, this concerns primarily the extent to which a company's profit can increase as a result of a given level of protection: this is called the *theory of effective protection*. This theory analyses the effect of the whole tariff structure on a particular industry by taking the additional value added of this industry generated by a particular tariff structure and comparing it to the industry's value added without that tariff structure. One can then check the consequences for propensity to invest and employment, and how effective protection is in safeguarding particular interests.

Let us assume that a company which makes cars sold at NLG 25,000 ex works is threatened by competition from imports. Since this company's market share declines under the impact of strongly competing foreign supplies of comparable cars, the company successfully calls on the government for protection. This then leads to a set of measures which amount to a 10 per cent import duty. Since the country is small, foreign suppliers will not adjust the prices of their cars which, let us assume, also sell for NLG 25,000. Thus, import prices at the border do not change.

However, inside the country the imported cars have become NLG 2,500 more expensive: the import tariff is added to the import price so that the price of an imported car on the home market becomes NLG 27,500. If the domestic car manufacturer is satisfied with a competitive position in relation to the foreign suppliers which is equivalent to the old situation, he can get away with raising the price to NLG 27,500 per car, so that his profit increases by NLG 2,500 per car sold; because there is no reason to assume that costs have changed.

In so far as this additional revenue leads to an increase in the domestic value added of the product process, it will be apportioned among the factors of production and profits, because more generally the value added of a production process is used to pay for the factors of production (such as wages for labour, rent for land and interest for capital), the residue being the profit. The question then is: by what percentage does the value added increase as a result of protection. Let us assume that the car which originally sold for NLG 25,000 contained parts worth NLG 15,000 which were bought in by the company. The value added available to pay for the factors of production and the profit is then NLG 10,000. Protection by a nominal 10 per cent tariff can yield a 25 per cent increase in value added, as the new selling price can go up to NLG 27,500. The parts bought in still cost NLG 15,000. Thus, the value added has risen to NLG 12,500. On the other hand, if the parts bought in had represented NLG 20,000 of the cost price, then the value added would actually have increased by 50 per cent! Clearly, the proportion of the parts bought in (and any tariffs on them: see below) in the value of the final product acts as a lever. This is why the percentage increase in the value added may far exceed that of the increase in the product's price resulting from the tariff.

Obviously, if tariffs had also been imposed on the imported parts, this would have detracted from the increase in value added because these inputs would then have become more expensive. That is why most Western governments arrange their protection structure to protect end products but keep protection to a minimum on imported parts, semi-manufactures and raw materials. As a result, protection on many goods is graduated, increasing at higher stages in product processing. This is also known as *tariff escalation.*

It is not easy to proceed to determine precisely the investment and employment effects, because these depend on a multiplicity of factors which influence the entrepreneurial decision. But for this it is evidently more important to understand the effect of protection on value added rather than to know the actual level of each nominal tariff.

By implication, it is therefore clear that a small degree of protection can still have substantial domestic effects under certain conditions. An understanding of this is naturally also important for those who engage in international negotiations on the abolition of protection.

10.3   The General Agreement on Tariffs and Trade (GATT) and its successor, the World Trade Organisation (WTO)

We have stated that, in theory, there are sometimes arguments for unilateral abolition of tariffs (no negotiation is then required), but in practice we almost always assume reciprocity, i.e. abolition of protection by a country is regarded as a concession and other countries are expected to offer something in return. The *GATT*, which up to 1995 was the main organisation arranging and advising on international trade negotiations (in 1995 the GATT became the World Trade Organisation (WTO) with a rather broader mandate and a somewhat stronger structure), also assumes *reciprocity* in its regulations. This system of reciprocity does not apply to those situations where nothing can reasonably be expected in return, e.g. in the case of developing countries. (These countries sometimes actually receive preferential tariff treatment, i.e. products originating from developing countries are subject to a lower tariff than the same imports from non-developing countries. For an illustration, see Box 10.1.)

The GATT system of reciprocity is defective because of the common negotiating technique, whereby the principal exporters try to do a trade policy deal with the leading customer countries, and the deal is then declared applicable to all participating countries. In practice, with such a negotiating technique one cannot always secure reciprocal concessions equivalent to the amount gained by other countries from the original trade concessions. Thus, one has to accept that there is a high risk of *free riding* here (see also below).

The fact that one participating country's trade concession is then declared applicable to all participating countries is due to another GATT principle, namely that of *non-discrimination*. This principle is expressed both in the *most-favoured-nation* (MFN) *treatment* clause included in trade agreements and in rules based on a system of *national treatment*.

The MFN clause is a provision of an agreement between two countries which states that, if the countries reduce their mutual tariffs, the tariffs which they

191

impose on third countries belonging to the GATT – over 120 countries in practice – must not be any higher. This means that if a country reduces its tariffs in relation to a particular country, that tariff reduction also applies to all other countries enjoying MFN status. As a result, bilateral agreements have multi-lateral effects and countries which are too small or too unimportant to take part in the real GATT negotiations, such as the Dynamic Asian Economies (DAEs) also benefit from the trade concessions which the large countries have extracted from one another. They need offer nothing in return. This is referred to as the GATT *free rider* problem. In recent years there have been increasing calls for reciprocal concessions from successful DAEs.

The national treatment principle means that imported products must be treated in the same way as comparable domestic products on the home market of the importing country. For example, if environmental requirements are imposed on packaging material or technical requirements on products, these must apply in the same way to both domestic and comparable foreign products.

As regards the MFN clause, we might wonder how effective this really is for most of the members to which it applies. Say Japan and Europe conclude mutual agreements to halve import tariffs on video recorders and automatic transmission systems. In that case, under the GATT system these concessions apply to each GATT Contracting Party with MFN status wishing to export these goods. However, countries which do not or cannot supply this type of goods gain nothing from this type of concession. In more general terms, as the post-war abolition of tariffs under the GATT concentrated mainly on industrial products, many developing countries complained that the non-discrimination system still, in fact, discriminated against them because of the composition of their range of export products. If the tariffs on industrial products fell while those on developing country exports had no share in this reduction, there would be a relative deterioration in market access for export products from developing countries.

Box 10.1 Position of the developing countries

During the 1960s, as members of the United Nations set up the Conference on Trade and Development (UNCTAD) in 1964, the developing countries made a joint attempt to secure a special position in the GATT. They considered that they needed a chance to build up their industries under protection before engaging in free trade, without being punished in any way by the GATT system. (See Chapter 6, the infant industry argument for protectionism and the import substitution policy of many developing countries in the 1950s.) To a large extent, the developing countries did actually secure this special position in the GATT:

- they could withdraw or amend concessions on customs duties if this was necessary to build up a new industry which was likely to bring an increase in production and a higher standard of living;
- import restrictions were permitted to maintain the equilibrium of the balance

of payments and secure the necessary foreign exchange to buy goods necessary for implementing development plans; and

- government aid was permitted where necessary to promote the establishment of businesses which could improve the population's standard of living.

From the 1960s in particular, a number of developing countries proceeded apace with exports of manufactured products. As a result, these countries also exerted pressure for freer access to the industrial countries' markets and permission to subsidise their exports. The result was that in 1965 the GATT added an additional part (Part IV) to the text of the General Agreement, specifically aimed at improving the trading position of developing countries. Its principal point was that the non-discrimination principle did not apply to developing countries, so that they could be given preferential treatment on imports of their products into industrial countries. Moreover, the developing countries were not obliged to offer reciprocal trade concessions to the industrial countries.

The addition of the new part to the text of the General Agreement enabled the EC to apply the *Generalized System of Preferences* (GSP) in 1971. The GSP offers 10 year exemption from the MFN clause for developing countries. This exemption meant that industrial countries could grant the developing countries unilateral trade advantages by reducing or abolishing tariffs on their manufactures. Canada institutionalised the GSP in 1974 and, after initial opposition, so did the US in 1976. Other industrial countries also introduced a GSP. It was not until the end of the Tokyo round in 1979 that the GSP was legally incorporated in the GATT. In practice, however, the advantages of the GSP for developing countries proved to be slight.

First, the system imposed all kinds of restrictions on product categories: sectors in which developing countries were traditionally competitive were often excluded from the GSP. For example, textile exports from developing countries were largely kept out of the GSP.

More specifically, in 1957 the US tried to restrict imports of textiles by persuading Japan to apply 'voluntary' export restraint. Other countries, particularly Hong Kong, then took over from Japan as suppliers. The US responded by pressing for an international agreement on trade in cotton. In 1961 a short-term agreement was concluded which was put on to a long-term basis in 1962. Finally, in 1974, this arrangement was replaced by an extensive system of agreements covering all types of textiles: the *Multi-Fibre Arrangement* (MFA). The MFA serves as an umbrella under which importing countries negotiate 'orderly marketing agreements' with exporting countries, with the object of regulating trade in textiles on a bilateral, product for product basis. In 1981 the MFA was extended and is still in force at the beginning of 1994. However, the Uruguay Round did decide on gradual abolition of the MFA agreements, with 2004 as the probable date for termination of the MFA.

Second, the GSP was not very effective because, in practice, it favoured developing countries which were actually already involved in a process of rapid industrialisation. This was due partly to the import quota system commonly applied, consisting of rules whereby preferential treatment in any one year applies only to a small, predetermined volume of imports. In practice, this means first come, first served (i.e. the first to offer imports gains the benefit of the lenient trade rules). The best organised supplier, and especially the one best able to handle the required bureaucratic processes involved in trade, will gain the greatest advantage from this system. These suppliers often came from the most advanced developing countries eligible for the GSP scheme.

An important development in breach of the GATT principle of non-discrimination is the rise of regional integration, whether or not accepted by the GATT. Typical examples are the European Union and EFTA (European Free Trade Association), but also LAFTA (Latin American Free Trade Association) in Latin America, ASEAN (Association of South East Asian Nations) in South-East Asia and the recently established NAFTA (North American Free Trade Agreement) in North America. Although, as we have said, the GATT treaty assigns a central position to the principle of non-discrimination, it was nevertheless acknowledged that if mutual trade barriers are eliminated on a limited, regional scale, this must be seen as a step towards free trade, even if the principle of non-discrimination is not satisfied from a global perspective. That is why bona fide forms of purely regional economic integration such as a customs union or free trade zone, were actually accepted into the system, albeit under certain conditions such as no overall increase in external protection (Art. XXIV of the Agreement).

The exceptions permitted by the GATT to its general principles are clearly contrary to the principle of free trade. Furthermore, in practice governments and businesses often abuse the exceptions granted. In itself, this can lead to a growing tendency towards protectionism, etc. Before we go into this, Box 10.2 offers a brief review of the various rounds of negotiations conducted under the GATT and the results which were or were not achieved.

Box 10.2 The GATT and the rounds of negotiations

The GATT was set up in 1947 when a number of leading trading nations (23 in all) reached agreement on rules to reduce tariffs.

The following important functions were assigned to the GATT:

- Settlement of trade disputes between countries (see Case study 10.1). However, the GATT has no means of enforcing its decisions.
- Defining conditions concerning the trade policy of the contracting parties. For example, these conditions include the MFN clause already mentioned and the ban on the imposition of quotas. The GATT does permit exceptions to these conditions: for example, a quota may be imposed if a country has serious balance of payments problems; regional integration is permitted on a limited scale (the 'preferential trading blocs') provided the mutual trade barriers are demolished for virtually all trade and there is no overall increase in external protection for the region as a result of the integration.

- Promoting tariff reductions; these often take place via multilateral rounds of negotiations, also known as tariff rounds.

So far there have been eight such tariff rounds (see Figure 10.1). The first two, which were held during 1949–51, led to a substantial decline in tariffs. The fact that the US, which wanted liberalisation, had a strong economy while the weak Europe protected its industries was a major factor in this success. The GATT's achievements related mainly to industrial goods made by industrial countries.

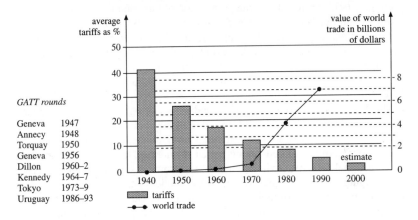

Figure 10.1 Average tariffs in GATT rounds

The next three rounds were far less successful owing to an increase in protectionism in the 1950s.

The sixth round, which lasted from 1964 to 1967, called the *Kennedy Round*, must be seen in the light of US trade policy developments at that time and the rise of the European Community with its protecting agricultural policy. In the US, the Trade Agreements Act (TAA) applied until 1961; the principles which it contained dated back to the protectionist era of President Roosevelt (1934). In 1961 the Kennedy administration decided to liberalise trade and asked Congress for a new trade law. This led to the Trade Expansion Act in 1962. The most important changes which took place under this act were these: negotiations on tariff reductions need no longer be conducted for each product but could relate to several products simultaneously; the concept of injury in the escape clause was given a stricter interpretation. This meant that an increase in imports was no longer automatically deemed to cause injury to the domestic producer; instead it was necessary to prove and investigate whether tariff reduction and the resulting increase in imports actually caused injury to a producer. If actual injury was proved, the solution was no longer to withdraw the tariff reductions, but the businesses and employees concerned were helped to adjust to the new trade situation via 'trade adjustment assistance'. This was a significant initiative for trade policy. The response to foreign competition now was not to grant protection but to set up adjustment programmes (application of the compensation principle).

The Kennedy Round achieved substantial reductions in import tariffs on manufactured goods; this meant that the round mainly concerned the trading interests of industrial countries. Two thirds of these tariffs were reduced by 50 per cent; on average, tariffs on manufactures were cut by 33 per cent.

In 1971 the Nixon administration called for a new GATT round in which the emphasis would be on unfair trade practices against the US and special attention would be paid to the interests of farmers in the US. The president hoped that this would counter calls for protectionism by Congress. At an initial ministerial meeting in 1973 the agenda for the preparation of this round (originally called the Nixon Round but later named the *Tokyo Round*) included the following points: tariff reductions, expansion of trade in agricultural products, reduction of non-tariff barriers, development of codes to prevent unfair trade practices and, finally, the development of special rules for the export products of developing countries. In 1974 Congress gave the president the necessary negotiating powers under the Trade Act.

The Tokyo Round lasted until 1979 and achieved a further average reduction of about a third on most manufactured goods. This GATT round was very successful as regards non-tariff barriers. Codes of conduct were developed in relation to government procurement, border formalities, technical rules on health, safety, national security, environment, etc, government subsidies, import licences and dumping (revision of the existing GATT code). The codes specify in detail what the appropriate government procedures and measures are. In addition, each code provides for a GATT committee to settle international disputes in the areas concerned. However, the Tokyo round made little progress on trade in agricultural products and the position of the developing countries.

The eighth GATT round began in Punta del Este, Uruguay, in 1986 and has since become known as the *Uruguay Round*. The final ministerial conference could not be arranged for the end of 1990 as planned. The Uruguay Round was eventually concluded on 15 December 1993 after difficult negotiations, particularly on the liberalisation of agriculture. The following subjects were very important in this round:

- *Agriculture*. The European agricultural policy was a particularly sensitive subject here. A breakthrough was not achieved until mutual agreements between the EU and the US were adopted under the 'Blair House' agreement, whereby the volume of subsidised agricultural exports will be reduced by 21 per cent in six years. Over the same period total export subsidies will be cut by 36 per cent. The industrial countries will also reduce import tariffs on agricultural products by an average of 36 per cent and developing countries by 24 per cent. Countries with a ban on imports of a particular agricultural product must open at least 3 per cent of the market to foreign goods.
- *The services sector*. International trade in commercial services (tourism, transport, banking, insurance and telecommunication services, etc.) totalled over $850 billion in 1993; that is almost a quarter of the value of international trade in goods, which totalled roughly $3,500 billion in that year. This ratio is now growing by around 2 percentage points per annum. In the past, this sector was disregarded by the multilateral negotiating rounds because trade in

goods was considered more important. As a result, the services sector is still bristling with national barriers, but a framework agreement has now been concluded, namely the General Agreement on Trade in Services (GATS) which stipulates that, in principle, the general obligations and disciplines of the GATT, including the MFN principle and that of national treatment, are also applicable to the services sector. The principal services sectors on which agreements have been made are tourism and professional services, such as accountancy and consultancy activities.

- *Intellectual property.* There has been a sharp increase in trade in imitation products in recent years. Examples include fake Rolex watches, software copies, copies of books and CDs and imitation drugs. Sometimes these are goods which are meant to be passed off as the quality product which they imitate. In other cases it is a question of supplying products without paying royalties or licence fees. These practices are causing increasing annoyance in the industrial countries. The US recently introduced new legislation on that account against countries which tolerate the imitation of brands and products. The GATT is giving developing countries which have no intellectual property protection laws a period of ten years in which to introduce them.
- *A ban on 'grey area' measures.* This concerns mainly 'voluntary export restraints' (VERs). Existing VERs are to be abolished. Each country may maintain such restrictions in only one specific area.

The Uruguay Round again stipulated exceptions for developing countries. Thus, the poorest countries are not subject to the subsidy disciplines and are not under any obligation as regards reducing agricultural tariffs, whereas the developed countries are to reduce import tariffs on agricultural products by an average of 36 per cent, as stated above. The emerging industrial countries regarded the Uruguay round consultations on the services sectors and intellectual property as a direct threat to their sovereignty. As a concession to developing countries, the industrial countries were prepared to undertake a radical review of the safeguard rules (cf. below) and to abolish the MFA, probably in 2004.

10.4   Non-tariff barriers

In the post-war period there was undeniably a reduction in the level of import tariffs imposed by industrial countries, and many import quotas (= quantitative or value restrictions on imports) disappeared; nevertheless, they were simultaneously replaced by many new, often disguised forms of protectionism. From the mid 1970s onwards, in particular, the traditional protectionism in the form of tariffs was largely replaced by all kinds of *non-tariff barriers* (NTBs). This is illustrated in Figure 10.2.

By way of illustration, Table 10.1 shows the NTBs imposed by the industrial countries from 1981 to 1986 in certain sectors as a percentage of imports.[1] Thus,

---

1. The following NTBs are included in Table 10.1: variable levies, seasonal levies, anti-dumping and countervailing measures, import quotas, voluntary export restraints (VERs), non-automatic import licences, import bans and safety and protection measures.

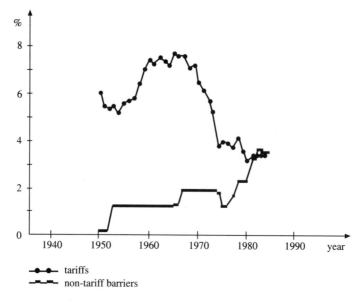

Figure 10.2 The rise of non-tariff barriers
Source: Fig. 18.3 from Magee, Brock and Young, 1989.

in 1986 the industrial countries applied NTBs to 23 per cent of imported goods. If we add the developing countries which generally make more use of NTBs than do the industrial countries, it is reasonable to conclude that probably over a quarter of world trade is regulated by NTBs.

NTBs are protectionist measures which can occur in any form except actual import tariffs. Sometimes, protectionist measures are introduced on the basis of explicit political decisions. Examples are an extension of the Multi-Fibre

Table 10.1 The NTBs imposed by industrial countries in 1981 and 1986 (as % of imports)

	Total NTBs		Quantitive restrictions		Including VERs	
	1981	1986	1981	1986	1981	1986
Agriculture, food stuffs	40.8	42.6	27.3	27.4	0.8	1.8
Agriculture, raw materials	2.8	8.4	1.8	1.8	0.0	0.0
Ore, minerals and metals*	12.7	24.7	4.5	16.8	2.1	14.4
(including iron and steel)	(29.0)	(64.2)	(7.8)	(47.3)	(6.6)	(45.2)
Chemicals	13.2	12.7	8.1	7.6	0.0	0.0
Other manufacturers	18.6	20.5	11.7	12.2	9.2	9.7
All products*	19.6	23.1	12.2	14.4	5.6	7.7

*Non-energy
Source: UNCTAD, 1987.

Arrangement or trade policy directives issued by the European Commission. In many other cases, however, protectionist practices come about on the basis of decisions by bureaucracies and executive agencies without there being any explicit political decision or control at the time of each new protectionist implementing decision. If protectionism comes about in this way, the literature normally refers to it as *administered protection* (AP). In other words, definition of the framework within which protectionist measures may be applied is normally subject to political control; implementation of such a framework often rests with the public authorities which thus in practice have a degree of scope for determining policy, and in some cases that scope is quite considerable.

Forms of AP permitted under the GATT rules include the following measures which national governments may take in order to protect their industries against 'injury'.

1. The adoption of *safeguard measures*. Many countries, including the US, have incorporated escape clauses in their trade laws. These are based on Article XIX of the GATT, known as the safeguard clause, under which temporary import restrictions may be imposed or previous trade concessions withdrawn if imports are causing or threatening to cause serious injury to domestic industries. Under the GATT, such a trade law clause may only be applied without discrimination (i.e. it must apply equally to all trading partners), there must, of course, be proof of the injury and the causative link between the increased imports and the injury, and countries which suffer as a result of the safeguard rules are entitled to mutually agreed compensation. If they receive nothing, then they may take counter-measures themselves. Little use is made of this provision: it was applied 139 times altogether between 1950 and 1990, and 15 times in 1985–90. The reason is that other techniques such as anti-dumping or countervailing duties are preferred because they can be much more accurately targeted (on specific trading partners) and the burden of proof is not so onerous.

   Since the Uruguay Round, the GATT safeguard rules have been tightened up and provide for consultations on compensation and procedures for enforcing its payment.

   In general, safeguard measures may not remain in force for more than four years. Trade policy measures which are abolished automatically after a certain time are covered by the 'sunset clause'.

2. The application of *anti-dumping duties*. Dumping is the sale of products at a price below that in the country of origin and/or below cost. The GATT permits countries to impose tariffs, under certain conditions, on products dumped on the home market. For example, the EU has set out its anti-dumping policy in a regulation whereby:

   - a dumping margin must be established (the difference between the export price and the 'normal value');
   - 'material injury' to EU industries must be established;
   - there must be a causative link between dumping and injury;

- even if dumping is confirmed, it is necessary to ascertain whether intervention is in the Community interest.

Obviously, it takes a complicated procedure to investigate whether and to what extent the four requirements are met. Thus, this kind of rule often leads to lengthy and expensive court actions on the basis of judgments enforced by the complainant country itself, so that there may be variations from one country to another (and certainly not always to the detriment of the complainant, as illustrated by Case study 10.2). This explains the growing popularity of anti-dumping actions and particularly the implementation of provisional measures pending possible, permanent anti-dumping duties. Thus, between 1980 and 1990 the US, the EU, Canada and Australia initiated over 1,000 investigations on whether an anti-dumping duty could be introduced; this resulted in some kind of protective measure in roughly half of the cases. In spite of their large number, anti-dumping practices concern only a limited import value: we know that only about 1 per cent of all EU imports are actually affected by the anti-dumping policy.

3. The imposition of *countervailing duties* (CVDs). If imports are subsidised by the exporting country, tariffs may be imposed on those imports to offset the value of the subsidies in order to protect the national industry competing with the imports. It is mainly the US that makes relatively extensive use of this type of measure (see also Table 10.2).

4. The prevention of *unfair trade*. This can be illustrated by an example. Section 301 of the US Trade Act 1974 provides for the possibility of counter-measures by the US if countries impose unfair restrictions to protect their markets against products from the US. This provision was tightened up in 1988, when the US assumed the right to retaliate against unfair trade by others who damage US exports, under the Super 301 clause. The countries concerned – eight altogether in 1989 – are warned and placed on a 'watch list', which means that sanctions may follow. In practice, the US aims to use this instrument to force other countries to open their borders, which can lead to what the literature calls voluntary import expansion (VIE). A character-istic of these last measures is that, just like the previous one, they do not belong to the sphere of political decision-making but are based on the application of existing national or international laws and regulations.

As remarked earlier, the scope offered by the GATT for legal action is being increasingly used, or abused if you like. In terms of numbers, this concerns mainly CVD and anti-dumping actions. Tables 10.2 and 10.3 show the exact figures for the period 1981–90, with a distinction between the measures taken in expectation of an eventual duty and the actual duty itself. They also show whether the measures were taken against industrial or developing countries.

The picture which emerges from these tables is one of a multiplicity of trade disputes. This in turn reflects enormous activity in the sphere of international consultation, negotiating situations and lobbying. Tables 10.2 and 10.3 also indicate that measures are regularly implemented without eventually leading to

Table 10.2 Anti-dumping actions by industrial countries, 1981–90[1]

		Provisional measures[2]				Final levies			
		US	EC	Canada	Australia	US	EC	Canada	Australia
1981	industrial countries	5	8	17		4	5	13	
	developing countries	3	0	1		0	0	0	
1982	industrial countries	7	1	16		39	5	3	
	developing countries	3	1	7		4	0	3	
1983	industrial countries	15	7	38	21	5	3	28	26
	developing countries	10	2	9	11	2	3	9	12
1984	industrial countries	15	6	27	13	16	5	9	25
	developing countries	20	1	10	9	17	1	3	7
1985	industrial countries	18	7	20	11	18	4	10	9
	developing countries	10	2	9	12	8	2	6	6
1986	industrial countries	11	4	9	15	8	5	12	9
	developing countries	32	2	10	14	17	2	9	9
1987	industrial countries	24	2	11	6	11	3	5	3
	developing countries	26	3	1	9	22	0	3	0
1988	industrial countries	12	2	7	5	16	2	9	2
	developing countries	1	7	12	5	6	2	9	3
1989	industrial countries	21	3	9	4	19	4	3	3
	developing countries	14	4	3	2	9	8	0	4
1990	industrial countries	37	3	1	4	33	3	33	0
	developing countries	27	3	4	6	27	4	29	0

[1]Years from July to June
[2]Provisional measures may be taken in anticipation of final anti-dumping levies
Source: IMF, 1992.

Table 10.3 Countervailing actions by industrial countries, 1981–90[1]

		Provisional measures[2]				Final levies			
		US	EC[3]	Canada	Australia	US	EC[3]	Canada	Australia
1981	industrial countries	1	0	3		0	0	0	
	developing countries	4	0	0		3	0	0	
1982	industrial countries	29	0	0		4	0	0	
	developing countries	17	0	0		5	0	0	
1983	industrial countries	10	0	1	8	13	0	0	0
	developing countries	24	0	0	0	10	1	0	0
1984	industrial countries	3	1	2	7	2	1	0	0
	developing countries	14	0	1	0	9	1	0	0
1985	industrial countries	9	0	1	3	3	1	3	1
	developing countries	30	0	1	0	18	0	0	0
1986	industrial countries	6		1	5	8		0	0
	developing countries	18		0	1	9		1	0
1987	industrial countries	5		2	1	4		2	0
	developing countries	11		1	1	12		0	0
1988	industrial countries	3		1	0	2		1	0
	developing countries	6		0	0	8		0	0
1989	industrial countries	0		0	1	0		0	0
	developing countries	11		1	1	8		0	0
1990	industrial countries	7		0	2	7		2	1
	developing countries	19		2	8	18		1	0

[1]Years from July to June
[2]Provisional measures may be taken in anticipation of final anti-dumping levies
[3]Since 1986 there has been no EC survey on the introduction of countervailing duties
Source: See Table 10.2.

the intended duty. We therefore gain the impression that in a number of cases the procedures set in motion are aimed not so much at a duty but rather at forcing the foreign supplier and/or foreign government to negotiate. This is illustrated by the fact that a number of cases which resulted in a 'voluntary' export restraint were preceded by a great many judicial proceedings against the suppliers: this applied to the restriction on imports of Japanese cars into the US, for example (Case study 4.1), the restrictions on imports of steel into the same country (Case study 6.1) as well as the international agreements on trade in semi-conductors. The EU, in particular, has a strong preference for VERs on the part of suppliers. For instance, of the 270 VERs in existence at the end of 1986, 70 had been 'extracted' by the EU.

Sometimes the abuse of the legal scope is perfectly clear. An example will illustrate this. Although the rule whereby a national (or at any rate European) body decides whether there is 'fair trade' or dumping in an anti-dumping case, in accordance with the GATT rules, there is nevertheless the impression that this arrangement can easily be abused in favour of national producers' interests. First, the abuse of this complaints procedure is hardly ever punished and the costs of the action are often (much) higher for the accused than for the applicant; second, the examination criteria are rather vague; third, the complainants and the judging authority have the same nationality; and finally, the interests of consumers – which are often best served by minimising protection, including protection against dumping – are not taken into account in passing judgment. There are even claims that, before applying for the injury test, some companies actually go so far as to make deliberate cut-backs in production and make workers redundant in order to demonstrate that the unfair competition is actually causing injury to the industry! The CVD imposed on the foreign competitor can then more than make up for the short-term loss resulting from lower production. Action aimed at a CVD is often particularly effective; even just the threat of a CVD can prevent the foreign competitor from adopting an aggressive marketing strategy in a country.

Case study 10.2 shows how the US protected its domestic steel market via AP. In the US it is the trade ministry (Commerce Department) that decides whether or not dumping exists, and to what extent. The International Trade Commission (ITC, a commission set up by American Congress to assess allegedly unfair cases of competing imports in the US) judges whether substantial injury is caused. If so, then the ministry fixes provisional or permanent anti-dumping duties. The whole procedure must not take longer than 390 days. Once this deadline expires, the decision is taken on the basis of the information available at the time. In Case study 10.2 we see that this principle of the 'best possible information' often works to the advantage of the American applicant.

Case study 10.2 Protectionism through paperwork

In recent years procedural protectionism has greatly increased in the US. Anti-dumping cases in the US are particularly notorious for the paperwork involved. If foreign companies become the victims of an anti-dumping case in the US, they have to hand over all their books. Containers full of papers with all transactions, sales figures, prices, analyses and computer tapes are collected. Anyone who, in the ministry's opinion, supplies too little information immediately loses the case. The Best Information Possible principle applies here. If there is just a minor error in some of the defendant's files, the Commerce Department can decide to consider only the facts presented by the accuser.

Thus, in one particular case, the German firm Preussag Stahl AG supplied substantial quantities of data on sales in Germany and America. But the American ministry also wanted information on the types of steel sold only in Germany. On 7 January 1993 Preussag was informed of the deadline for supplying this information: 21 December 1992. Since Preussag was unable to meet this retrospective deadline, the ministry considered only the information supplied by the American competitor in deciding whether or not to impose a duty on Preussag. Not surprisingly, this information was adverse to Preussag and resulted in a duty.

Since foreign firms are subject to stricter rules in anti-dumping cases than the American firms which report them to the Commerce Department, it is the American firms that win in most cases. In January 1993 the ministry imposed heavy import tariffs on foreign steel producers, up to 109 per cent. This kept East European producers out of the American market once and for all. Some other foreign producers had already given up the fight in advance, because they could not face the massive amount of administrative work. In 1993, a Washington lawyer of the Dutch company Hoogovens estimated that foreign steel companies had already spent around $100 million on anti-dumping procedures.

Overall, it is therefore clear that there are a number of shortcomings in the application of anti-dumping duties. First, the procedure disregards the interests of consumers. Second, the anti-dumping duty makes no provision for the economically legitimate case in which a company sells its products at less than cost so that it can at least recoup the fixed costs. In an international economy where products have short life cycles, product quality is difficult to ascertain and more and more initial spending is required on research and development, when marketing a new product, sale at less than cost is actually a logical element in the process of competition. Third, the anti-dumping rules are implemented as if goods were uniform, standardised and not subject to change, and as if foreign competitors are always out to force domestic firms off the market so that they can then secure a huge increase in prices. Fourth, the impression that a firm is dumping its products abroad may be due to the structure of the home market of the firm accused of dumping. If the foreign firm is protected on its home market, e.g. by tariff or non-tariff barriers, it can generate high profits there which can then be used to finance dumping.

Thus, procedures in accordance with these same GATT rules can in practice be abused in order to secure arrangements which are not in fact compatible with the spirit of the GATT. The various national judging authorities play a significant role here. An example of such an authority in the US is the International Trade Commission. For instance, if compliance with an ITC ruling would mean that the government was acting contrary to an existing international trade agreement, the executive agencies can ignore the ITC ruling.

10.5 Summary

The original economic theories predicted that international free trade could lead to the optimum situation for all parties concerned. A practical embodiment of this conclusion is the GATT, which aims to promote free trade. The GATT operates on the basis of the principle of reciprocity and non-discrimination, and this has led to the abolition or reduction of tariffs on industrial products. In assessing the effective degree of protection, one must also take account of the effect of a tariff structure on the value added of an industry. During the post-war period, and particularly from the 1970s onwards, all kinds of new protectionist measures were substituted for tariffs. The reason lies partly in the GATT itself, which leaves considerable scope for protecting markets. Another instance of this is the way in which economic associations between countries and regions are permitted. In addition, the GATT allows trade policy protection in the case of unfair trade, for example, or if free trade causes serious injury to certain industries. However, these rules can easily be abused. The abuse or use of international and national regulations by the bureaucracy or executive agency for the purpose of protecting businesses against foreign competition is known as administered protection.

Bibliography

Magee, S.P., W.A. Brock and L. Young (1989), *Black Hole Tariffs and Endogenous Policy Theory, Political Economy in General Equilibrium*, Cambridge.
IMF (1992), *Issues and Developments International Trade Policy*, Washington D.C.

11 Business, government and lobbying

11.1 Introduction

In international management journals one often comes across tips on gaining access to the bureaucratic machinery in Brussels: Case study 11.1 gives an example. These tips can be valuable to businesses, because various firms often lobby the EU or their national government for trade protection or export subsidies to strengthen their competitive position. Clearly, a successful lobby can influence the competitive position of those firms and thus also trade between countries. The analysis up to Chapter 10 has always adopted the viewpoint of national or international welfare; business interests were subordinate to the general interest. However, it is obvious that the interests of particular businesses need not always coincide with the general interest.

Chapter 10 showed that one of the reasons for the continuing protection, particularly in the sphere of NTBs, lies in the pressure exerted by the business world on officials and politicians to use the scope provided by the GATT/WTO for protection. This pressure may be so great that officials defend themselves altogether against lobbyists by claiming that their hands are tied by the existing rules. On the other hand, government agencies often seem to be not only willing but also resourceful in inventing all kinds of new forms of trade restrictions in order to satisfy protectionist pressure from the business community. This chapter examines why governments give in to pressure from certain interest groups. The politicians' and officials' own objectives often play a part here. This rather strains the assumption of an omniscient government whose objective is to maximise the national welfare, and it should be replaced by the assumptions of political economy, namely that the government consists of various individuals such as politicians, bureaucrats and officials, who are also pursuing their own objectives in taking decisions. This idea recently gave a new boost to the development of trade policy theories, by including the behaviour of the government itself in trade models as an explanatory factor.

11.2 The practice of lobbying: a case study

Case study 11.1 offers an example of the problems which one can encounter if involved in lobbying; it also states the rules one should preferably adhere to.

Case study 11.1 'Getting through to Brussels'

Particularly since the creation of the internal market in the EU, the lobbying of EU institutions has become a fast-growing industry. Over 3,000 professional lobbyists now argue in favour of particular trade interests. Thus, a great deal of time is spent on influencing new legislation, anti-trust measures and merger inquiries. According to a senior official at the Commission, however, 90 per cent of lobbying is pointless. What makes a lobby successful? Etienne Davignon, a former EU Commissioner, advises first forgetting what happens at home. Lobbying in Brussels cannot be compared with what happens at national level: EU officials are generally worried about losing contact with the outside world, so they are much more open to outside contact than most national officials and administrators.

It is important to know how to use this openness in order to get results. The first thing is to 'get through' to the European authorities, i.e. by being received and heard. Once inside, lobbyists can make the long journey to Brussels productive by following some of the ground rules below.

Choose the right objective

This is probably the most important rule, and the one most often violated. Successful lobbying means knowing the right person to talk to about the particular problem. Newcomers to Brussels realise that there is no point in bringing in technical experts to deal with political problems. However, few realise that the reverse is also true. French firms, in particular, often make the mistake of approaching political decision-makers while overlooking the mighty bureaucratic machinery. Politicians are certainly not always receptive to lobbying. For example, one reason why special administrative agencies have been set up in various countries to deal with trade disputes was to avoid politicians being overwhelmed with requests for trade policy protection. In the US, for instance, Congress established the International Trade Commission (ITC), which was to use an 'injury test' to evaluate requests for import protection based on unfair injury due to competing imports, or to decide how to punish the foreign supplier for dumping. In practice, such agencies have a certain amount of discretion in assessing the various cases submitted to them.

Know the process

The easiest way to fail is not to be *au fait* with the complexity of Brussels. The Commission's decision-making process can be influenced at various stages, at both technical and political level, via the Commission, the European Parliament, the EU embassies of member states and national ministries. However, a different approach is needed for each.

Act early

Lobbying in the right place begins with the junior EU officials. These are the people who write the draft regulations on which the discussions are based. Often, the battle is already largely won if you can gain the support of the officials. It is much more effective if the officials can explain their views at the start, rather than having the same officials trying to reverse a decision once it has been taken elsewhere.

Be honest

One reason why EU Commission officials are relatively communicative is their dependence on sources outside the Commission for obtaining background information. The price of this openness is accuracy. According to Paul Gray, a senior official of the Internal Market, Commission officials will never again listen to anyone who once supplied incorrect information.

Avoid overkill

Exaggerated lobbying can be counterproductive.

Watch out for the nationality card

No one will deny that nationalism plays a role in the Commission's decision-making, but waving your passport is one of the least effective lobbying instruments. According to Hans Glatz, head of the Brussels office of Daimler Benz, the reason is simple: 'Even if you've got a commissioner in your pocket, he's got to convince his colleagues.' To convince them requires reasonable arguments and there must be no emotional appeal that cannot be shared by other nationalities.

None of these rules will guarantee success. The work of the Commission often includes resolving two equally strong conflicting interests. But if we know how Brussels functions, this does at least give lobbyists a chance against competitors who have not bothered to find out about the European decision-making process. On the subject of lobbying, the head of the Belmont European Policy Centre and a veteran lobbyist asserts: 'Bad lobbying is commonplace, we see it daily. But when lobbying is effective, chances are you'll never hear about it.'

Source: Sasseen, 1992.

The case study shows that it may be worthwhile for businesses to invest in lobbying for government protection. However, the case study raises the following questions:

1. Why does the government give in to pressure from businesses?
2. Why do consumers not conduct a counter-campaign?

After all, free trade maximises national welfare. If free trade produces winners and losers, the government can compensate the losers via incomes policy. The case study has lifted one small corner of the veil. Fear of losing contact with the outside world makes EU officials accessible to lobbying activities. However, it is unclear why, in the case of the European agricultural policy, for example, the policy-makers sometimes give in to the interests of certain groups when this is clearly at the expense of the economy or certain other groups such as consumers. Political economy can offer a better insight into these problems.

11.3   Political economy: demand for and supply of protection

The world of international trade is not as simple as the trade theories of preceding chapters would have us believe. Even in a democracy where consumers make up the majority of the electorate, the outcome of free trade is not as obvious as one might expect. The interests of voters as consumers generally lie in the abolition of trade restrictions. The reason why this interest is, in practice, often subordinate to the interests of the protected industries can be explained with the aid of *political economy*. According to political economy, protectionism is the outcome of an interaction between various players such as: officials, politicians, businesses and voters. Acting rationally, these players endeavour to maximise their own interests.

Groups of voters can organise themselves if they wish to promote a common interest with politicians, and they do so by lobbying. Since this is a common interest, the *free rider* factor is present. Organising a lobby group takes certain 'investments'; if the group achieves its objective, however, others may also benefit from the advantage gained, i.e. including some who did not join the lobby group. Each individual worker and textile manufacturer benefits from an import tariff on textiles, regardless of whether he contributed to the lobbying for the tariff. As a result, individuals have no incentive to contribute to the costs of organising a lobby group. Free riding plays a more significant role the greater the size of the group and the harder it is to control free riding. Organising an effective lobby group therefore has more chance of success if:

- the number of interested parties is small;
- the group was already formed for another objective; and
- there is a demonstrable advantage in participating in the lobby group (e.g. in the form of particular information or facilities).

In political economy, it is usual to assume that interests are promoted and organised by branch or sector, within which the various sub-groups, such as employees, employers and financiers, work harmoniously together in the interests of the whole group. The basic assumption in the traditional trade theory mentioned earlier is essentially different, because one of the questions then was who would benefit from free trade and who would not, the interest groups being defined on the basis of the different factors of production. Thus, in the HOS model, for example, the factor labour is opposed to capital regardless of the sector in which these factors are located. Which is the most plausible standpoint regarding the dividing lines between interests: the political economic model which distinguishes between sectors or the HOS model which distinguishes between owners of factors of production?

Empirical research is needed to answer this question. In 1980, for example, Magee tried to find the answer by analysing the position of employees and management as regards acceptance of the trade law by the US president in 1973. There were 21 industries pressing for the adoption of this law. The position of the employees and representatives of the capital was identified for each industry. It emerged that in only 2 of the 21 industries did 'labour' adopt the opposite position from 'capital'. Thus, the research supported the political economic idea that interest groups are organised mainly according to industrial branches or sectors.

Protectionism may take all kinds of forms. For simplicity, the rest of the chapter will be based on tariffs, but other protectionist instruments could also be substituted in the text. As we have noticed already in analysing export taxes and subsidies, as well as in the case of the VER of Japanese cars imported by the USA, it can make quite a difference for the welfare implications of protection in whatever particular form protection is taking shape. In this chapter, however, the form of protection is not at stake but merely the issue of how the emergence of protection in whatever form can be explained on the basis of the political and administrative decision-making process.

In order to distinguish between lobby groups, we divide the interest groups roughly into those in favour of tariffs and those against them.

11.3.1   Pro-tariff interest groups

These include national firms competing with foreign firms. They are frequently supported by trade associations active in the same economic sector. This group often has a great political interest in protection since the direct advantages of protection (an increase in output and employment) can be clearly demonstrated for this group. (In this connection, cf. also the effective theory of protection discussed in section 10.2.) These groups will often appeal to national feelings.

11.3.2   Anti-tariff interest groups

Consumers are the first group to come to mind. For them protectionism means a smaller variety of products and higher prices. However, at the same time many consumers are employed in import-competing industries and may have an interest in protection in that capacity. In addition, exporting companies also gain from free trade. Their interests lie in a free trade climate in which they have unimpeded access to foreign markets. Multinationals will also generally be in favour of free trade: they can operate efficiently on the international market and protectionism will often be a hindrance to them. Finally, there are companies which have to import raw materials and semi-manufactures. In the first instance they, too, will gain from free trade. However, these firms are often also in the sector which competes with imports, so that their position is ambiguous.

The pro-tariff lobby group is generally more uniform in character than the anti-tariff lobby, so that the first group can clearly define its common objective: increased profit. In addition, this group is usually relatively small in size, so that the free rider factor is less important. In contrast, the anti-tariff group is heterogeneous. First, consumers in themselves constitute a heterogeneous group so that free riding is very difficult to control. Furthermore, this group includes multinationals and exporters all aiming to protect their own trading interests. Although exporters are against tariffs, they may still lobby the government for subsidies in the form of cheap export credits or export credit guarantees. Multinationals will be more interested in monopoly power. If we apply the interest group theory to these characteristics, we can predict that the pro-tariff interest group contains the elements of a successful lobby group: small size, clear objective, low organisation costs since it is possible to operate from existing organisational structures (such as employers' and employees' organisations, product marketing boards or an Economic Affairs Ministry). For the opposite reasons, the anti-tariff group will find it more difficult to form a successful lobby group.

The conditions under which pro-tariff groups will proceed to lobby and the chance of success are determined by the 'political' market of protectionism. We shall illustrate this on the basis of the demand for and supply of protectionism.

11.3.3 *Demand for protectionism*

Figure 11.1 shows the costs and benefits of lobbying for protection. The horizontal axis indicates the increase achieved in the tariff; the origin indicates the original level of the tariff. The vertical axis measures the costs and benefits of an increase in nominal protection. (The reader will remember from Chapter 10 that the effective degree of protection may deviate from this; for convenience, owing to the complications in translating from nominal to effective protection, we shall work on the basis of nominal protection.) The OA curve indicates the costs of lobbying. We assume rising marginal costs: it becomes increasingly difficult to secure a higher tariff. The OA curve also reflects the willingness of politicians to agree to the request for protection. Thus, the curve indicates the expenditure required for a successful lobby and will be higher:

1. the less well-organised the group;
2. the more inefficient the lobbying; and
3. the more other groups in society disagree with the imposition of the tariff.

Curve OB indicates the lobby group's additional revenue. The greater the tariff increase, the higher the lobby group's revenue until point C is reached; this is the tariff level at which nothing further is imported: the gradient of the curve is horizontal from C onwards. For the curve in Figure 11.1 we assume that the marginal gains (i.e. the additional gain due to one extra unit of tariff protection) decline the higher the tariff. The segment OC shows this. However, the curve could have been drawn differently, namely with rising instead of falling marginal gains. Lobbying is optimalised at tariff level t*, namely the level at which the

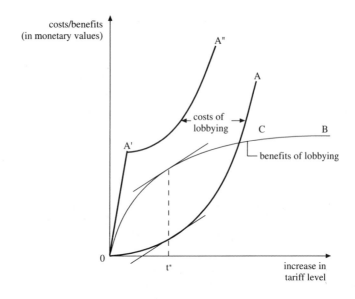

Figure 11.1 Costs and gains of lobbying

marginal gains (represented by the gradient of the tangent to the 'gains curve') are equal to the marginal costs (represented by the gradient of the tangent to the 'costs curve'); because at tariff level t* the gradients of curves OB and OA are the same so that the distance between the two curves, indicating the net advantage for the lobbyists, is at its maximum. If one were to aim for higher protection than t*, then the net gains from lobbying decline until reaching the intersection point from curves OB and OA. To the right of the intersection point the net gains actually become negative.

However, lobbying can sometimes be associated with such high initial costs, a situation represented by curve OA′, that the costs curve OA′A″ lies above the lobby revenue curve. This situation can occur if the costs of organising the lobby are very high; in that case, lobbying can never yield net gains. Thus, Figure 11.1 illustrates what has been said before, namely that a lobbying policy can be profitable mainly if it is based on an existing organisation, e.g. as in the case of curve OA.

11.3.4 Supply of protectionism

In the end, it is the government that decides whether or not to increase tariffs. As we have already seen, this may be due to a combination of executive and legislative power. Of course, the government may be in favour of free trade (liberal attitude) or against it (nationalist attitude) on ideological grounds. However, a government's ideology is constrained by a number of factors, the most important being the elections. The power of the protectionist lobby groups·

may be so great that a government which is strongly in favour of free trade loses the elections. A liberal government which is afraid of losing the elections and wants to govern at all costs will then present itself as a supporter of protectionist trade policy. Furthermore, the policy will often also depend on the government budget and the balance of payments. A country with a trade or budget deficit will be more inclined to pursue a protectionist policy than if the situation were different. In both cases the government is normally subject to criticism and will have to conduct a campaign to let people see that it is doing something about the deficit. Moreover, reducing the government deficit by imposing tariffs often provokes less political resistance than domestic cut-backs or tax increases.

In taking its decision on trade policy, the government will not usually be greatly 'hindered' by consumers. Many voters regard protectionism or free trade as less important than internal policy and economic election issues. People are generally better informed about the level of supermarket prices and the quality of cars, for example, than about various more abstract political topics. Furthermore, it is not rational for voters to invest a great deal of energy in gathering political information on trade policy since they know that they can exert very little influence over the election outcome (*rational ignorance*).

Protectionism also depends on the bureaucracy which prepare, formulate and implement the trade laws. The officials of these agencies often attach importance to their prestige and the power and influence which they can exercise over their clientele, who are frequently from specific business sectors. Officials dealing with agriculture, for example, often have interest groups in the agricultural sector as clientele. Their functions will generally include promoting the interests of their clientele, which often leads to protectionist measures. For this purpose, the officials use the instruments which they can control themselves, and which thus come under 'administered protection'. This means that they frequently prefer NTBs and subsidies to tariffs (see Box 11.1).

The executive agencies have a certain degree of freedom since parliament and government are partly dependent on them, e.g. for obtaining information. Moreover, officials of the executive agencies have access to far more specialist information which may also give them a position of some power. As a result, even under a liberal government a protectionist policy may still be pursued because of the above factors.

Box 11.1 The optimal obfuscation hypothesis

Take a democratic country in which several political parties and lobby groups are active. These lobby groups support the political party which best protects their interests, and they will also support that party in the elections. One political party, say the industry party, promotes the interests of textile industry workers. In return for looking after their interests, this party receives financial support from the textile union. Owing for instance to competition from low-wage countries, wages in the textile industry are fairly low and profits are also suffering. If wages fall too low, it will become increasingly difficult for employers to attract workers; on the other hand, higher wages will damage profits. In order to retain the support of the textile union, the industry party advocates an import tariff on textiles in order to secure higher wages in the textile industry.

As stated in Chapters 6 and 7, trade policy is never more than a 'second best' solution to domestic problems. The most efficient solution in terms of national welfare is a policy which encourages labour and capital to leave the sector, e.g. by retraining workers. Trade policy may be considered as a 'second best' option: the most efficient approach in terms of the sector's welfare is to subsidise the textile workers direct via wage subsidies. If this is not possible, then the government could grant a production subsidy on textiles. Only if this cannot be done either is an import tariff on textiles a solution. After that, one might consider an import quota on textiles.[1] The most inefficient solutions involve non-tariff barriers, e.g. via the Multi-Fibre Arrangement.

In practice, people seem to ignore this ranking based on the efficiency criterion, as indicated by the increase in all kinds of non-tariff barriers such as quotas and VERs (see Tables 10.1 and 10.2).

The *optimal obfuscation hypothesis*[2] can shed some light on this. According to this hypothesis, politicians try to conceal the process of income redistribution by using indirect measures. This makes it very difficult for voters (and economists) to ascertain the cost of these measures. Trade policy is also incomes policy. Protection of certain industries results in a redistribution of incomes in an economy. In the example, income is redistributed from the taxpayers to the textile industry. However, textile industry workers do not form the majority of the electorate. It is therefore in the interests of the industry party and the politicians in power to try to conceal the fact that they wish to transfer income. The price paid for this is the efficiency cost in terms of distortion of consumption and production decisions. The introduction of a tariff is therefore defended by referring to employment, 'unfair competition' from low-wage countries, national support base, regional interests, the environment or health, for instance. Such a veiled presentation thus enables the industry party to secure votes and funds from the textile industry while at the same time limiting the number of votes lost.

However, at a given moment any greater 'obfuscation' on the adoption of measures will nevertheless alienate voters, since there will be more and more economic waste. Moreover, excessive 'obfuscation' can cause the lobby group itself to cease to recognise the positive effects, so that election contributions will fall. The better informed the voters are, the more serious will be the effect of the loss of votes through increasing economic inefficiency and there is then a risk of what is called a *voter information paradox*: if the voters' knowledge of policy on incomes and trade increases, then politicians react with increasingly subtle forms

---

1. For the theoretical argument behind this order or precedence, cf. for example Bhagwati (1971), pp. 69–90.
2. See Magee, Brock and Young (1989), chapter entitled 'Optimal Obfuscation and the Theory of the Second Worst'.

of protection, but these are associated with greater distortions. The switch from tariffs to NTBs in recent decades illustrates this paradox. Over the years, voters have become better and better informed about trade restrictions so that they have come to oppose them. Initially this led to a decline in tariffs. However, the end result was that these lower tariffs were offset by NTBs such as VERs. These trade instruments are less transparent to the voter, but probably cost more in terms of welfare.

11.4 Summary

Thus, this chapter shows that politically efficient decision-making processes do not always produce the results that one might expect on the basis of economic efficiency criteria. With the help of insights from political economy, we can explain how interest groups arise, under what circumstances they can operate successfully and why governments are amenable to lobbies by such groups. For trade theory this meant that the government was no longer regarded as an omniscient, exogenous factor striving to maximise national welfare. Thus, political economic theory could be applied to trade policy. Important assumptions in this theory are that all those concerned aim to maximise their own interests. In the process, interest groups can be formed which exercise such great power that the general interests become subordinate to the interests of pressure group minorities. The rational ignorance of large groups of persons concerned is a major factor here. In spite of rational ignorance, consumers are gradually becoming more aware of the negative welfare effects of trade instruments. According to the optimal obfuscation hypothesis, in order to disguise the income redistribution effects, governments will switch to using more complex NTBs which are less efficient in economic terms.

The Appendix examines the fact that interest groups may have mutually opposing interests and may therefore fight one another; this can be analysed with the aid of a reaction curve model, for example. According to this model, both interest groups invest in lobbying until a certain equilibrium is reached. Investment in lobbying is wasteful from a national welfare point of view.

11.5 Appendix: Competition between lobby groups

Up to now we have assumed that protectionism is determined by the power which one interest group exercises over officials and politicians, namely that of businesses threatened by foreign competition. In reality, the outcome is not always easily predictable, as Case study 11.2 illustrates.

Case study 11.2 The European banana war

When the EU imposed an import ban on cheap 'dollar bananas' from Latin America in July 1993, under pressure from the banana lobby in the former colonies with which the EU traditionally maintained contact, there was considerable protest. The free trade lobbies made a lot of noise about the undesirable increases in banana prices for the consumer. With effect from July 1993, the EU member states together could only import 2 million tonnes of dollar bananas per annum; moreover, the market share of dollar banana importers and traders had to be cut by 33 per cent in favour of dealers/importers selling bananas from European overseas territories and former European colonies. Traders in 'dollar bananas' warned that the measure was liable to make bananas twice as expensive in countries such as the Netherlands and Germany. Thus, there was interaction between groups which were for and against freer imports of 'dollar bananas'. The groups which had lobbied for the EU measure were supported in their campaign by environment and development groups which appealed to sentiments such as the poor working conditions on dollar banana plantations and the fact that the poor, small farmers in other countries could not compete with these plantations. In this case, the protectionist lobby won the day. The German government submitted a complaint to the European Court of Justice in Luxembourg, but without success.

If we leave aside the specific interests of politicians and officials, then according to the ideas of political economy the level of protection is determined by the interaction between interest groups. The following model shows how the interaction between lobby groups determines the level of protection. Here we assume that one factor of production, capital, can only be used in a particular sector; it is no use outside that sector, e.g. for technical reasons. An example might be capital in the form of a highly specialised machine. We assume that the other factor of production, labour, is mobile. This means that labour can easily move from one sector to another if more can be earned elsewhere. The point is that if we apply these assumptions, it will be patently obvious that international trade will yield winners and losers, because international trade can cause one sector to grow while another will have to shrink. The workers' interests are not much affected because in this model labour can easily transfer to other sectors. However, owners of non-mobile capital goods are in a risky position. If the sector expands, the return on their capital investment in that sector will increase, but if their sector shrinks then they will lose. Thus, in this example there are always two opposing parties as soon as there is any debate on whether or not one should give in to pressure for more free trade (or more protectionism): those who own the capital in the export sector which expands under free trade versus those with capital invested in the shrinking sector which is competing with imports. For instance: we are in an economy with the following two sectors: sector 1 producing goods which are also produced efficiently abroad, the import-competing sector; sector 2 where goods are made for export. In this situation, the owners of the capital in sector 1 will therefore lobby for the imposition of a tariff;

in contrast, those who own the capital in the export sector will lobby the government to ensure free trade. The workers have no clear incentive to lobby.

The owners of the capital in both sectors are bound to incur costs if they are to lobby. These costs consist of the organisation costs entailed in forming a lobby group and using it in the lobbying process, and the costs of precluding free riders. The level of 'investment in lobbying' for the two lobby groups together determines the eventual level of protection. We can assume *a priori* that if the amount invested in lobbying by those who own the capital in the export sector is greater than that invested by the owners of the capital in the import-competing sector, protection will probably decline.

We now assume a situation in which the two groups in fact compete with one another (in theory they can also contact one another and make a deal). This can be demonstrated by a simple model based on reaction curves such as those used in Chapters 8 and 9. In such a model the two groups (players) use the same strategy to try to maximise their profits. Each player regards the action of the other party as an established fact and takes it into account in his decisions. In terms of our model, each lobby group decides for itself how much to invest in political campaigning, always assuming a particular level of investment by the other group. Figure 11.2 shows the *investment reaction curves* of the two lobby groups; since we assume that the two groups are identical, both curves are symmetrical about a 45-degree line, PP. Each reaction curve in Figure 11.2 shows how much a lobby group invests in lobbying as a reaction to all possible levels of such investment by the other lobby group. The reaction curves therefore determine the optimum level of investment for one lobby group as a function of the (assumed) action by the other lobby group. Curves 11 and 22 are the reaction curves of the import-competing sector and the export sector respectively; the curves present a positive trend because the more one group invests in lobbying, the more the other will also invest. Curve 11 is flatter (and 22 is thus steeper) than the 45-degree line because we assume that if the opponent invests more, there will be a response, albeit that the additional investment will not be so great.

The point at which these two reaction curves intersect, point A, indicates the equilibrium situation.[3] It is only at this point of intersection that neither group decides to change the level of its investment. This is a stable equilibrium. Let us assume that the owners of the capital in the export sector (sector 2) invest the sum OB in lobbying. On the basis of the export sector's investment level OB, the optimum investment for owners of the capital in the import-competing sector (sector 1) is now OC. The optimum level of investment for owners of the capital in sector 2 has therefore changed; if sector 1 invests OC, the optimum investment for sector 2 is OD. Sector 1 reacts once again and changes its level of investment

---

3. The point of intersection can only be at equilibrium if both curves have a positive trend and if the gradient of 22 is steeper than that of 11; the equilibrium thus obtained is called the Cournot-Nash equilibrium.

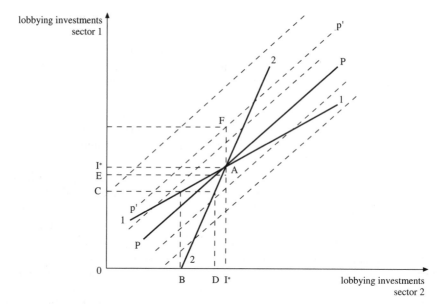

Figure 11.2 Lobbying reaction curves

to OE, etc. Once sector 1 and sector 2 are investing OI*, neither sector will make any further change in its investment decision and equilibrium will have been restored.

Curve PP, drawn through the equilibrium point, is not only the 45-degree line but also an *iso-protection curve*. This curve indicates all combinations of investment levels for the two groups at which the level of protection – the result of lobbying – is the same. Thus, if we move up along the curve, both groups will invest more in lobbying, but because they are neutralising one another's action there is no overall change in the protection. Thus, it is really in their interests to reach agreement on not investing anything (because the result is the same). But as they don't really trust one another, that does not happen.

Such a curve can be given for all kinds of different situations (that need no longer pass through the origin). Some more iso-protection curves are shown in Figure 11.2 (the dashed lines). The dotted curves left of line PP indicate a higher level of protection than the curves to the right of PP. This can be deduced as follows on the basis of the graph.

Say we are at point A on the iso-protection curve PP. This protection curve gives level of protection x. Technological developments abroad then cause the price of imports to decline while at the same time foreign producers' profits increase as a result of higher sales and lower costs. For the import-competing sector, this means a decline in sales on the home market. This generates greater interest in lobbying for protection (at a given level of investment in lobbying by the other party): curve OB in Figure 11.1 moves up, and so does curve 11 in

Figure 11.2. However, rising incomes abroad bring an increase in sales by the export sector on the foreign market. The export sector will make rather less effort to lobby for free trade (given the efforts of the other party); curve 22 therefore shifts slightly to the left. Let us assume that the shift in the two curves is such that the new equilibrium is at point F. The equilibrium is then on a higher iso-protection curve than A, so that protection has increased: sector 1 is investing more in lobbying, while sector 2's investment in lobbying has remained the same. Thus, lobbying by businesses and hence the level of protection depends partly on miscellaneous international developments which they themselves cannot influence.

Bibliography

Baldwin, R.E. (1989), *Measuring Nontariff Trade Policies*, NBER working paper series, no. 2978, Cambridge, May.

Baldwin, R.E. (1992), Assessing the fair trade and safeguards laws in terms of modern trade and political economy analysis, *World Economy*, vol. 15, no. 2, pp. 185–203.

Bhagwati, J.N. (1971), The generalized theory of distortions and welfare, in: J.N. Bhagwati *et al.* (eds), *Trade, Balance of Payments and Growth: Papers in International Economics in Honour of Charles P. Kindleberger*, Noord-Holland, pp. 69–90.

Bhagwati, J.N. (1988), *Protectionism*, MIT Press.

Finger, J.M. (1987), Antidumping and antisubsidy measures, in: J.M. Finger and A. Olechowski (eds), *The Uruguay Round: A Handbook for the Multilateral Trade Negotiations*, World Bank.

Finger, M.J. (1989), Protectionist rules and internationalist discretion in the making of national trade policy, In Vosgerau, H. (ed.), *New Institutional Arrangements for the World Economy*, Studies in International Economics and Institutions, Springer-Verlag, pp. 153–61.

Frey, B.S. (1984), *The International Political Economics*, Basil Blackwell.

Grill, E. and E. Sassoon (eds) (1990), *The New Protectionist Wave*, Macmillan.

Magee, S.P., W.A. Brock and L. Young (1989), *Black Hole Tariffs and Endogenous Policy Theory, Political Economy in General Equilibrium*, Cambridge University Press, Cambridge.

Sasseen, J. (1992), Getting through to Brussels, *International Management* 62–3, March.

Snape, R.H. (1991), International Regulation of Subsidies, *World Economy*, vol. 14, no. 2, pp. 139–64.

United Nations Conference on Trade and Development (UNCTAD), *Protectionism and Structural Adjustment*, Trade and Development Board Paper, no. TD/B/1126, Geneva, 1987.

Vosgerau, H. (ed.) (1989), *New Institutional Arrangements for the World Economy*, Studies in International Economics and Institutions, Springer-Verlag.

12 The importance of international capital flows

12.1 Introduction

The preceding chapters dealt with international flows of goods and the cross-border movement of factors of production. However, in the discussion of the foreign exchange market and balance of payments in Chapters 1 (section 1.5) and 2, it was already made clear that in doing so we are considering only a part of the total of international transactions. More than that, in terms of value it was very evident that flows of goods together with cross-border (primary and secondary) income nowadays form a minority of international transactions. This sounds surprising, especially in view of the great deal of attention usually paid to international trade in goods. That attention consists not only in media reporting on imports and exports and political interest in the national competitive position: it is also apparent in the emphasis on trade in goods in the theory of international economic relations. This is undoubtedly due to the great importance of the export position for essential economic objectives such as growth and employment and the fact that, in relative terms, trade in goods was of far greater quantitative significance in the not so distant past.

At first sight it might appear that the volume of international capital flows is not all that impressive, but on closer examination it certainly is. The reason for such a false impression is that – just as with flows of goods – there is a tendency to take the level of financial flows as the level of the corresponding balance of payments items. However, in contrast to trade in goods, these balance of payments items normally show *net* flows in the sense of the export of a particular type of capital after deduction of imports. A more accurate picture of the volume of capital flows is therefore obtained from the volume of business on the foreign exchange markets. Adjusted for transactions arising from international trade in goods, this indicates foreign exchange transactions relating purely to capital flows. In April 1992 the average daily volume of trading on all foreign exchange markets together was at least $1,000 billion. 'Only' $17.5 billion, or less than 2 per cent of this, was needed to pay for international trade in goods and services, leaving over 98 per cent for international capital movements![1]

---

1. Table 1.6 gives estimates of daily transactions on the world's leading foreign exchange markets. In April 1992 the total volume of business on markets included in the table was over $950 billion. Since the table does not cover a number of smaller markets, it is no exaggeration to estimate the total daily volume of business worldwide at a minimum of $1,000 billion. We can compare this

This chapter will discuss international capital flows in detail, covering the following questions. Their significance is made clear in Case study 12.1.

- What are the motives for international capital movements and, following on from that, what different types of capital movements can we identify?
- What motives and options does a country's government have for influencing the direction or level of international capital flows?
- How are international capital transactions organised?

Case study 12.1 Gasunie's cash

Gasunie is a company with its head office in Groningen, The Netherlands. Its shareholders consist of the Dutch government together with the Shell and Esso oil companies. Gasunie has the sole right to sell Dutch natural gas to many West European customers in countries such as Germany, Belgium, France and Italy. In the context of international capital transactions, the first choice facing the company is whether to promote natural gas sales by providing export credit for customers. If it decides to do so, the Netherlands becomes a capital exporter: this increases claims on other countries and gives rise to a capital account entry, although without any money actually crossing the border and without any transaction taking place on the foreign exchange market. The reason is that the credit is essentially part of a combined transaction involving the export of goods, in this case natural gas. The two associated opposing flows of money cancel one another out, whereby the objective – namely the postponement of payment for the natural gas received – is attained.

Gasunie then has to decide what to do with the cash which comes in when the export credits expire. The company naturally incurs costs, and part of the incoming payments has to cover them. That is why a proportion of the foreign receipts is immediately converted into guilders. But Gasunie also makes a substantial profit, and much of that eventually goes to the shareholders. In the meantime, however, Gasunie has a large amount of cash in hand which naturally has to be invested as efficiently as possible. This benefits the shareholders. The question then is whether there is any advantage in investing at least part of the cash abroad. If so, the next question is which foreign currency that part should be invested in. For example, is it preferable for Gasunie to adopt a passive approach, and invest all incoming German marks in Germany, French francs in France, etc.? That would at least save on the transaction costs associated with international payments, because there would be no need for any foreign exchange conversion, which is a relatively

---

with the average daily volume of foreign exchange business generated by trade in goods, which can be determined as follows: we know from GATT calculations that international trade in goods and services totalled $3,530 billion and $850 billion or $4,380 billion altogether for the whole of 1991. On the basis of an estimated 250 working days per annum, this corresponds to an average daily volume of business on the foreign exchange market of $17.5 billion to pay for goods and services, which is therefore less than 2 per cent of the daily volume of business on the world's foreign exchange markets.

expensive banking transaction. Another relevant consideration is that an asset denominated in a foreign currency entails the risk of that currency depreciating against the guilder. On the other hand, there could of course also be the benefit of an appreciation. Another factor in the choice of currency is that interest rates can vary significantly from one country to another. Gasunie also has to decide on the length of time for which the cash is invested and in what type of asset. The choice ranges between keeping the foreign currency (safe) in a foreign bank for several days, and buying shares in another company (with a very uncertain future value). In other words, Gasunie faces a range of choices. Obviously, it is therefore extremely useful to have sufficient information on which to base those choices.

The chapter is divided into the following sections to answer the above three questions. In section 12.2 we summarise types of international capital flows and give a general review of the various motives. A detailed examination of the motives behind purely financial flows – i.e. capital flows which are *not* linked to real international transactions – such as arbitrage, speculation and portfolio investment, forms the subject of sections 12.3 to 12.5. Section 12.6 focuses on government interference in international capital movements and section 12.7 on the truly international money and capital markets and international financial centres which developed partly in response to this government interference.

12.2   Types of international capital flows

12.2.1   Differing motives

An important distinction in the case of cross-border capital flows is between short- and long-term capital. Capital flows are in fact equivalent to trade in debt instruments, such as bonds and equities, which are sold for their cash equivalent. The dividing line between short- and long-term capital is usually taken as a maturity of one year, measured at the time of issue of the instrument. Placing a sum with a foreign bank for three months is an example of a short-term international capital transaction. Purchase of a (long-dated) bond abroad with a residual maturity of less than one year is thus classed as a long-term international capital transaction, as is the purchase of shares in another country. The motives of the person buying these securities are irrelevant: bonds and equities are classed as long-term capital even if they are sold again, say, one day after purchase, and that was the purchaser's intention from the start.

Another important distinction regarding international capital flows is based on the motive behind the capital flows. Where an international goods transaction is financed with the aid of credit, the motive is naturally to conclude the goods transaction in question. The provision of such credit tends to increase the chance of the transaction coming off. Both the importer and the exporter may decide to obtain credit in connection with the transaction. Credit implies a claim. Any change in the state of a country's international claims, in other words its international capital position, is accompanied by an international capital transaction on the balance of payments – by definition.

Apart from international capital movements connected with the financing of international goods transactions, there are also international capital movements for the purpose of international portfolio investment or foreign direct investment. In the case of international portfolio investment, a country's residents acquire debt instruments in the form of bank credit balances, bonds or equities. Investments in foreign shares are similar to foreign direct investment but there is an essential difference, as already remarked in Chapter 1 (section 1.4). In the case of a portfolio investment the return on the shares is paramount, while in the case of direct investment the primary consideration is the share in decision-making power conferred by the share ownership. So the aim is to act as an entrepreneur. In the case of a foreign direct investment the entrepreneur's motive is evidently to internationalise his production.

The reasons why such an entrepreneur might wish to operate internationally have already been outlined in Chapter 5. As already stated, the motive for granting trade credit is to facilitate international trade flows. This subject was also touched on in Case study 12.1. In view of the practical importance of trade credit for trade it is useful to consider it in rather more detail. This will be done in sub-section 12.2.2 below. The motives for international portfolio investment have yet to be discussed. In contrast to the other two forms of international capital transaction – trade credit and the financing of foreign direct investment – there is no real underlying transaction in the case of an international portfolio investment. It is a purely financial transaction. There are various forms of this kind of investment which can be distinguished according to the type of motive. We can use the following classification: arbitrage, speculation and risk spreading. These forms will be discussed successively in detail in sections 12.3, 12.4 and 12.5.

12.2.2 Trade credit

The most common form of trade credit is export credit, the international form of supplier's credit. The exporter arranges credit in favour of the goods importer to accompany the export transaction. In practice, this means that the importer need not pay for the goods for a certain period of time. Instead of payment the exporter receives a claim on the importer, which often takes the form of a bill of exchange drawn by the exporter on the importer. The bill of exchange is a written payment order accepted by the importer (the drawee) and held by the exporter (the payee). The function of a bill of exchange is to make the credit negotiable. For example, the exporter can sell the bill of exchange to his bank, which then discounts it. Thus the exporter receives his money immediately, i.e. the face value of the bill but minus the discount (payment for loss of interest until the due date of the bill of exchange). The bank keeps the bill in its portfolio until the due date, the date on which the credit has to be redeemed by the importer.

This payment is, of course, made to the holder of the bill of exchange – in our case the exporter's bank – in return for the bill of exchange.

In the case of export credit we have a remarkable phenomenon: an international capital transaction, namely the provision of export credit, which need not actually lead to an international flow of money, or a transaction on the foreign exchange market either. Yet the capital transaction is recorded on the balance of payments. Is this an exception to the rule that every balance of payments entry must be accompanied by a transaction on the foreign exchange market? Certainly not! In this case there are in fact two international transactions taking place simultaneously in opposite directions, both of which are recorded on the balance of payments but cancel one another out exactly on the foreign exchange market. There is no payment, and therefore no transaction on the foreign exchange market, corresponding to the export of goods, but an international claim is created, again without any transaction taking place on the foreign exchange market. The combination of the goods transaction and the change in the international debt position can be regarded as an action consisting of two simultaneous but opposing transactions on the foreign exchange market, both with the exporter and importer as market operators, the payment for the goods transaction being channelled back directly in the form of a payment for the claim (the security). Both transactions are recorded on the balance of payments, but at that time with no effect on the balance of payments balance (in the sense of changes in the official reserves) or on the value of the exchange rate. Naturally, the position is different once the export credit is redeemed.

It is not only the exporter who can provide the importer with trade credit for his goods; the reverse is also possible. In that case the exporter obtains what is known as a buyer's or customer's credit from the importer. This is commonly done in the case of goods which take a long time to produce, such as aircraft and ships. After concluding the contract of sale, the exporter commences production with financial support in the form of credit from the importer. A very common form of short-term buyer's credit is known as documentary credit. This credit is often supplied by a foreign bank on behalf of the importer. It takes the form of a bill of exchange drawn by the exporter on the bank opening the credit. This bank is prepared to accept the bill of exchange against assignment of the documents (bills of lading, insurance certificate, invoice, etc.). Such a bill of exchange accepted by a bank (known as a bank acceptance) can easily be discounted by the exporter. The credit is then in fact provided by the person who discounts the bill. In the case of *confirmed* credit there is agreement with a foreign bank *and* a bank in the exporter's country whereby the latter bank will pay the exporter as soon as it receives the documents. This payment to the exporter is known as documentary cash credit, provided by the national bank. For the exporter, the advantage of this arrangement is the elimination of the risk that payment might not be possible, e.g. because the importer's country introduces restrictions on international capital flows. The exporter's bank charges the exporter a confirmation commission for its payment guarantee.

12.3 Arbitrage

At first glance, the terms 'arbitrage' and 'speculation' look very similar. The object of both activities is to make a profit out of price differences. Arbitrage concerns a price difference or a difference in the rate of return existing at one and the same time. By acting at that moment an arbitrager operates with total certainty, because at that moment all the necessary elements for calculating the profit are known. In contrast, a speculator operates on the basis of a price difference at different times, inevitably acting on the basis of uncertainty. The speculator can only have expectations about the price at the other time, which is in the future.

A simple example of arbitrage is foreign exchange arbitrage, in which a profit is made on the basis of a simultaneous currency price differential on two markets. For example, say the US$ costs NLG 2 on the foreign exchange market in Amsterdam and NLG 2.20 on the foreign exchange market in New York. In that case it is profitable to spend NLG 2 to buy one dollar in Amsterdam and sell this again immediately in New York for NLG 2.20. This transaction yields a 10 per cent increase in the guilders which we hold.

This description of foreign exchange arbitrage prompts two questions. How do we get the dollars so quickly from Amsterdam to New York and do we not need to take account of the costs of the two transactions (in Amsterdam and New York)? Nowadays, speed is not a problem. This type of transaction is usually conducted via the giro or credit transfer system by telephone and banks' interlinked computer screens. Thus, the transactions can be completed within a very short time (a few minutes at most). The transaction costs are indeed an important cost item for non-bank private individuals, so that foreign exchange arbitrage is carried out mainly by banks. Since they have no significant transaction costs they are able to exploit the profit opportunities to the full. As a result of their actions, there will be no substantial differential in the price of the dollar in the world's financial centres. One reason for this is that, taking our numerical example, the banks will not buy just one dollar but a massive volume of dollars in Amsterdam and sell them again immediately in New York. In response to this arbitrage activity, the price of the dollar will rise in Amsterdam and fall in New York via the price-determining process of demand and supply. These price movements will not cease until the dollar prices (expressed in guilders) are the same on both foreign exchange markets, because until that happens there is still scope for a profit and the banks will continue their foreign exchange arbitrage. Since the banks have virtually no arbitrage costs, prices are actually identical down to several figures after the decimal point. As soon as a larger price differential is imminent, the banks go back into action to restore identical prices via the prospect of an arbitrage profit and an actual arbitrage transaction. As a result of foreign exchange arbitrage by banks, we can therefore state that the price of a convertible (i.e. freely exchangeable) currency is the same in all the world's leading financial centres.

Interest arbitrage concerns a difference in the rate of return on investments available simultaneously on different markets, so that a financial transaction may be profitable. For example, say the interest rate on a three-month investment on the Amsterdam money market is 1 per cent – and over 4 per cent on an annual basis taking into account compound interest determination. If at the same moment the rate of interest on a three-month investment in New York is 2 per cent (or over 8 per cent on an annual basis) then, leaving aside transaction costs, it seems advantageous to convert the Amsterdam investment into an investment in New York. However, this is not entirely certain. In order to make this move it is necessary to buy dollars in exchange for the guilders available for investment abroad. At the end of the three-month investment period one will want to convert back into guilders the dollars which were released. It is, indeed, advantageous to convert the investment if, for example, the price of the dollar expressed in guilders does not change during the three-month period. Then the interest rate differential is the only thing that matters and the return in New York would be a lucrative 1 per cent per quarter higher than in Amsterdam.

The outcome of the interest arbitrage would be very different if it were known in advance that the value of the dollar in guilders would fall by 1 per cent during the three-month investment period. This would destroy the profitability of the arbitrage because the profit on the interest rate is now offset by the exchange loss suffered on the dollar. The arbitrager will then be indifferent about the choice of investment location. He will even prefer the investment in Amsterdam as soon as the decline in the value of the dollar exceeds 1 per cent. The interest rate advantage in New York then ceases to offset the exchange loss on the dollar. The converse is true if the decline in the value of the dollar is less than 1 per cent.

The above review of the points considered in interest arbitrage means that the arbitrager compares the interest rate in Amsterdam with the interest rate in New York plus the percentage change in the dollar rate expressed in guilders. One important point needs to be clarified: the rate of the dollar in three months' time is, of course, not yet known. The arbitrager can only guess; he will have an expectation about it. However, such an expectation cannot be an element for the arbitrager in his deliberations because – by definition – he works on the basis of firm prices. However, the arbitrager can also actually avoid the uncertainty by using the forward exchange market. There is a forward market for currencies just as there is for many commodities. This is a market where a product is traded but not delivered until a future date, although the price is fixed when the contract is concluded. There is a forward exchange market for various periods. For instance, forward markets based on 1, 2, 3, 6, 12 and 24 months operate for trade in American dollars. Our arbitrager can use the three-month market to sell now the quantity of dollars which he wants to invest plus the dollars which he is going to receive as interest payment; because he need not deliver these dollars for another three months, this is precisely the amount which he will receive when the invested dollars will again become available, with interest. He also already knows the rate which the forward dollars sold will fetch. If the forward dollar is more expensive than the spot dollar (the dollar delivered immediately), then the dollar is traded at a premium in the forward market. In the opposite case it is at a discount. Thus, in calculating the return on the investment in America as stated above, the arbitrager can now replace the percentage change in the rate of the dollar expressed in guilders by the percentage at which the dollar is at a premium or discount. This means that 'firm' prices are a fact for the interest rate arbitrager.

This results in an equilibrium condition for the interest arbitrager at which the domestic interest rate is equal to the foreign interest rate plus the forward premium on the foreign currency concerned expressed in the domestic currency. The type and maturity of the investment in the two countries must, of course, be identical. This equilibrium condition is known as the covered interest parity. The term 'covered' expresses the fact that the exchange rate risk has been eliminated (or hedged) by using the forward exchange market. Expressed as a formula, the covered interest parity is:

$$i = i^* + (F - E) / E . 100 \tag{12.1}$$

in which i and i* stand for the domestic and foreign interest rate (in per cent) and F and E for the exchange rates on the forward and spot exchange markets.

Any deviation from the covered interest parity prompts activities by arbitragers. The arbitragers will redirect their investments towards the highest rate of return, thus helping to level out that differential. Let us assume that in our numerical example the interest rates are the same as before (1 and 2 per cent in Amsterdam and New York, respectively) and that the forward rate of the dollar is the same as the present spot rate – having previously been at a discount of 1 per cent. It is then profitable to transfer the investments to the US. This means additional demand for dollars on the spot market, and thus an increase in the value of the dollar, and at the same time an additional supply of dollars on the forward market, and hence a fall in the dollar forward rate. As a result of these two price movements, the dollar is at a discount which makes it less attractive once more to invest in the US. The arbitrager ceases to transfer investments to the US as soon as the covered interest parity applies. This means: as soon as the dollar is again at a discount of 1 per cent, because at that moment the profit which made investment in the US so attractive ceases to exist.

Finally, it should be clear that the covered interest parity can only apply as an equilibrium condition if the transaction costs for the arbitragers are extremely low. Once again, as in the case of foreign exchange arbitragers, it is really only banks that satisfy this condition, so it is mainly banks that operate as interest arbitragers. Empirical research shows that the covered interest parity does actually apply in practice for currencies not subject to any exchange restrictions, i.e. currencies which can be freely exchanged: in other words, *convertible* currencies.

12.4 Speculation

Speculation, like arbitrage, is motived by a price differential but now – in contrast to arbitrage – the differential relates to different times, for the same product. The essential characteristic of a speculator is that he adopts an open or uncovered position. This means that he runs the risk of a fall in prices affecting the value of his asset, or a price rise increasing the value of his debt. A speculator operates under uncertain conditions, by definition. For example, a foreign exchange speculator buys dollars at NLG 2 per dollar in the expectation that the dollar will appreciate in the very near future. This means that he has an open position in dollars, because his dollar holding is not equal to his liabilities in that currency. This can produce an exchange rate gain, but also a loss! If, three months later, the dollar should be worth only NLG 1.80, then the foreign exchange speculator can only sell the dollars at a 10 per cent loss.

Like the interest arbitrager, this foreign exchange speculator will take account of interest rate differentials in determining his anticipated profit, because obviously the dollars purchased will be invested at interest for the next three months. Equally, a decision to continue holding guilders would have meant that these would be invested at the rate of interest applicable to the guilder. In the end, the points considered by the foreign exchange speculator are much the same as those for the interest arbitrager, except that where the arbitrager looks at the forward exchange rate, the speculator focuses on what he expects the exchange rate to be on the spot market. The equilibrium condition for the foreign exchange speculator is also expressed in an interest parity, but the uncovered rather than the covered parity. The premium on the foreign currency is replaced by the expected percentage change in the value of that currency. Expressed as a formula, the uncovered interest parity is:

$$i = i^* + (E^e - E) / E . 100 \qquad (12.2)$$

Here, E* is the expected exchange rate.

So far we have assumed that the foreign exchange speculator buys or sells on the present spot market and reverses this transaction on the spot market in the future. This means that the speculator must have the necessary financial resources. This limitation on the scale of the speculator's activities is far less of a factor if the speculator conducts his activities via the forward exchange market instead of the current spot market. An example should make this clear. Say the dollar rate on the forward exchange market for delivery in three months is NLG 2. If the foreign exchange speculator expects the dollar rate on the spot market to be NLG 2.20 in three months' time, he considers it profitable to buy dollars on the forward exchange market now at NLG 2 each for the purpose of disposing of them again immediately at NLG 2.20 each on the spot market at maturity. The expected profit is 10 per cent. The advantage of these two transactions is that the speculator need have hardly any cash. The two transactions are so close together in three months' time that the guilders raised by selling the dollars on the spot market can be used to pay the guilder price of the dollars on the forward exchange market. In practice, however, the financial market, in this case the bank through which the forward transaction is conducted, usually requires the speculator to pay a certain amount by way of security, but far less than 100 per cent. This means that the speculator can use the cash at his disposal to speculate for many times that amount on the forward market. It implies that he increases his leverage substantially.

Banks are not meant to engage in foreign exchange speculation. That is a big difference compared to interest and foreign exchange arbitrage, which are conducted mainly by banks. The reason is that arbitrage is based on certainties which can be calculated. In the case of speculation, uncertainty is the main point: the profits can be huge, but so can the losses. A central bank which exercises supervision over the commercial banks therefore does not permit foreign exchange speculation. That does not mean that, at the end of the working day, a commercial bank has normally covered its foreign exchange position in full. One hundred per cent cover is almost a technical impossibility, though commercial banks are required to keep their uncovered position at a low level; in fact, it should only result from the bank's day-to-day activities on behalf of customers.

12.5   Portfolio diversification

If one has financial resources which one does not wish to use to buy goods, or not immediately, one will wish to invest. That can be done through a bank account on which interest is paid, offering total certainty about the return while the value of the investment is not liable to change. The position is different as soon as bonds or shares are used as investments. Their value is determined daily by supply and demand on the stock exchange. In the case of shares, the percentage of the annual dividend also becomes uncertain. In the long term, this uncertainty appears to be normally offset by a higher average rate of return.

A technique commonly used in the case of investments for risk spreading purposes (portfolio investments) is diversification of the investment portfolio. The aim is to invest in securities (bonds, shares, etc.) with a high return, while at the same time achieving such a combination of securities in the investment portfolio that the risks or fluctuations in the return on the individual securities neutralise one another as far as possible. The return consists of both the annual interest or dividend payment and the change in the value of the principal invested. For example, if it is known that two business sectors tend to have opposite cyclical trends (when one is expanding the other is contracting), it can be attractive to include equities from both sectors in the investment portfolio. This moderates the fluctuation in the return on the portfolio as a whole. The connection (or lack of it) between returns on two different investments is usually expressed in the correlation coefficient of those returns. Figure 12.1 clarifies the

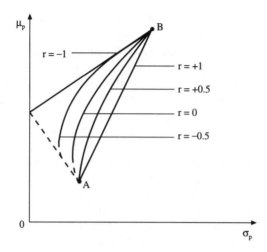

Figure 12.1 The influence of the correlation coefficient on risk: an example
Source: Jager (1990), p. 22.

connection between this correlation coefficient and the fluctuations in or uncertainty surrounding the return on the investment portfolio. That uncertainty is often read as the standard deviation of that return. The standard deviation is a well-known measure of spreading in statistics.

In the figure the symbol r indicates the correlation coefficient, μ_p the average return on the portfolio P consisting of two investments A and B, while the standard deviation of the return on the portfolio, σ_p, indicates the risk concerning the portfolio return. The coordinates of point A give the average return and the standard deviation of the return on one investment, while those of point B do the same for the other investment.

The figure shows that if the value of the correlation coefficient is one, portfolios can be composed of the two investments A and B, with the combinations of the average value and the standard deviation of the return lying in a straight line between the points A and B. If we gradually reduce the proportion of A in the portfolio in favour of B, we follow the line from A to B. The set of portfolio compositions appears to move to the left as the correlation coefficient falls. This shift is actually favourable to the investor, who can then realise average returns on his portfolio at lower standard deviations of the return, i.e. with less uncertainty about the return. The most attractive portfolios are found when the correlation coefficient is minus one. This means that the returns on investments A and B show the exact opposite movements: if one return rises the other falls. The result is maximum return stability. We can see this in the graph at the farthest left position of the line corresponding to r = −1. The point where this line intersects the vertical axis is very special: at this point the portions of the investments are in inverse proportion to the standard deviations of their returns, as we can deduce mathematically. All uncertainty regarding the return has then been eliminated.[2,3]

It is evident from both theoretical and empirical study of investments that the greater the scope for composing a portfolio of more individual investments, the more the uncertainty over the return can be reduced. At this point in the reasoning, international portfolio investments come on the scene. The creation of scope for international portfolio investment increases the number of potential investments and thus promotes a more favourable relationship between the average return on the investment portfolio and the uncertainty of the return. But not only that: in terms of return level and variations, foreign portfolio investments quite often behave significantly differently from national investment opportunities. The business cycle may be in a different phase abroad, and the production sectors also quite often differ from those at home. This introduces shares and bonds with investment qualities which are not issued in the home country. Figure 12.2 illustrates the influence of diversification on the standard deviation of the portfolio return for an American investor. With just domestic investment options the standard deviation of the portfolio comprising upwards of 20 different securities will be roughly half the standard deviation of a single, representative American share. A further decline in this standard deviation ratio to around 25 per cent is achieved if foreign investments are also permitted.

12.6 Foreign exchange regulation

History abounds with examples of countries which felt it necessary to impose a system of rules on their international flow of payments. This means that the government of such a country regulates trade in foreign currencies, or foreign exchange. Such *foreign exchange regulation*, also known as *exchange control*, is usually conducted by the central bank. In practice, such exchange control often means an *exchange restriction* for the country's residents. For those wishing to buy foreign currencies, the effect is that they can buy them only on certain conditions (a quantitative restriction) or at a price which differs from the equilibrium value (price control). In practice, there are also examples of exchange control in which the supply of currency by foreigners for buying home currencies is restricted. Case study 12.2 offers an illustration.

---

2. For three correlation coefficient values the lowest sections of the lines in the graph are broken lines. The reason is that the portfolio compositions which they represent are inefficient: they will not be chosen, because for each point of the section the investor can select a point straight above it. This point is more advantageous to the investor because the average return is higher while the risk remains the same.

3. For a more detailed discussion, see Jager (1990).

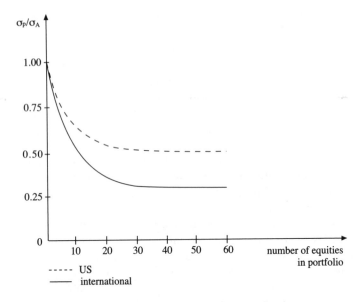

Figure 12.2 Risk reduction by national and international diversification
Source: Lessard (1983), p. 8.2.5.
Note: P stands for portfolio, A for a representative American share. If investment possibilities are confined to American shares, the result is the US curve. If non-American shares are also among the investment possibilities, then the International curve applies.

Case study 12.2 Bond market reopened to foreigners

The bond guilder is to go. Last night the finance ministry announced that the government has authorised the Dutch central bank to abolish the 'bond circuit' with effect from tomorrow, 1 February. From now on foreigners will be able to buy Dutch bonds in the normal way.

The idea of the bond guilder dates from September 1971. The intention was to prevent too much foreign capital and money market material from flowing into the Netherlands when the dollar was weak. Thenceforth, non-residents could only buy Dutch bonds if they could lay their hands on guilders which had resulted from sales of Dutch bonds by other non-residents.

The guilders required for this were known as bond guilders and were more expensive than normal guilders, sometimes by as much as 7 per cent.
From: NRC Handelsblad, 31 January 1974.

In order to apply stringent forms of exchange restriction, the central bank can assume a foreign exchange monopoly in which private individuals are not allowed to hold foreign exchange. On the one hand, all foreign currencies have to be handed over to the central bank, which in turn issues exchange permits or announces the rate at which a currency can be purchased from it for a particular type of international transaction. The bank could take account of the transaction's priority in the national interest both in issuing exchange permits and in setting the scale of exchange rates (known as *multiple exchange rates*). Foreign currencies are scarce and have to be used as effectively as possible. Thus, we might imagine that in the case of imports of basic essentials and medicines, an exchange permit will be issued almost automatically, but will be practically ruled out for the import of a luxury car. If the central bank operates a system of multiple exchange rates, then the currency needed to import essential goods can be obtained cheaply, but that for the importation of the luxury car will be much more expensive (always in terms of the national currency). Clearly, such a form of market intervention will be open to corruption. It is easy for the central bank to favour certain people, as the decisions are taken for each transaction and the system of allocation soon becomes opaque to outsiders.

What are the considerations behind the introduction of exchange regulation? Evidently, the government is not satisfied with the outcome of free currency conversion on the foreign exchange market. For example, free convertibility of the national currency into foreign currencies can give rise to a net private demand for foreign currencies at the given exchange rate. In that case, under a fixed exchange rate system, the central bank has to satisfy the net demand by supplying the required currencies out of the monetary reserves. But the monetary reserves are finite, so that this process cannot continue indefinitely. If nothing changes in the meantime, the country's monetary authorities (the Finance Ministry and the central bank) have to adjust their economic policy. They have a choice of three evils: devaluation of the national currency, change in monetary policy or introduction of exchange restrictions. If a country has opted for a fixed exchange rate, it naturally cannot go for devaluation (but more about this in Chapter 14). The change in monetary policy would then have to consist in tighter monetary policy, causing interest rates to rise, so that investments in the home country become more attractive and net demand for foreign currencies will thus decline. The mechanism behind this process is that of the covered interest parity. However, this approach is usually also unattractive. It was not for nothing that the country had chosen its original monetary policy, which evidently best suited the desired domestic economic objectives such as employment and inflation. Adjustment of this monetary policy would mean that national objectives were subordinate to the foreign objective (a fixed exchange rate), possibly impairing national political autonomy. In such a situation, exchange regulation can be of help: in any case, it would avoid devaluation and an undesirable shift in national monetary policy.

Of course, the third evil, exchange regulation, is not without its costs either. It hinders the optimum allocation of capital and the production of goods. The importation of goods from countries which have a comparative advantage in them may be prevented because no exchange permit for foreign currencies is issued. The same thing can happen to a planned foreign investment. As we saw in Chapters 6 and 7, under certain conditions the thwarting of the optimum worldwide allocation of production is at the expense of wealth, both for the world as a whole and for the two export and import countries directly involved.

Another possible cost factor in exchange regulation is the risk of abuse of the rules and the emergence of pressure groups.

An exchange restriction on foreign currencies supplied, as is raised in the case study, is usually based on one of two considerations. It may be an attempt to support the value of the foreign currencies. It is also possible that the monetary authorities want to counter the additions to the domestic money stock, which is a consequence of the required buying of foreign currencies by the central bank. In the Dutch case both reasons were relevant.

Apart from possible costs, the feasibility of exchange regulation is also undermined by the likelihood that it will be rather ineffectual. Nowadays, the financial world in particular stresses the ease with which exchange restrictions can be sidestepped, especially in the case of capital transactions which are not linked to any real transaction consisting of tangible goods.

To end this section we shall briefly consider the post-war restrictions on currency convertibility. The Second World War totally disrupted the flow of international payments. Immediately after the war there could therefore be no question of restoring currency convertibility. The war had put many factories in Europe out of action, in contrast to the US. It is therefore not surprising that European demand for products focused heavily on the US. Europe was threatened by chronic, substantial deficits on the trade balance. That is why exchange restrictions were introduced in all West European countries immediately after the war. It was not until 1958 that sufficient balance had been restored to international relations that many of these countries decided to make their currency convertible for current account transactions. Until recently, almost all countries had at least some restrictions on the convertibility of their currency for pure capital transactions.

Recent history has also seen some notable restrictions on currency convertibility due to international capital movements. In the latter half of the 1950s Britain still had large trade balance deficits. Although London was the leading international financial centre, the British government felt that it had to restrict capital exports by London banks, in the form of international financing via the pound, in order to relieve the downward pressure on sterling. This was the primary factor which gave rise to the Eurodollar market in those years: more about that in a moment. In the 1960s the American dollar gradually came under increasing pressure, so that in 1965 the American government decided to inhibit the financing of American foreign direct investment from the US by introducing the 'Voluntary Credit Restraint Program'. In the early 1970s, confidence in the stability of the dollar declined to such an extent that there were signs of a flight out of dollars, mainly into currencies whose stability was not in question: the Swiss franc and the Dutch guilder, but above all the German mark. In order to curb the inflow of capital the Netherlands, for example, introduced the Bond Circuit in September 1971. This system is described in Case study 12.2. Belgium reacted differently. It is one of the few industrial countries to have a variant of the system of multiple exchange rates. It had already introduced a dual currency market in 1951: one segment of the market was for all transactions connected with international trade in goods and services, the other was for currency transactions generated by international capital movements. There were therefore two exchange rates for the Belgian franc: a commercial rate for goods and services transactions and a financial rate for capital transactions. The dual currency market prevented the exchange rate applicable to goods transactions from being influenced by sudden fluctuations in Belgium's international capital movements, such as speculative capital flows. This benefited the stability of the commercial rate. It was not until 1990 that Belgium abolished the dual currency market, as a result of EMS obligations (see Chapter 18).

12.7   International capital markets and financial centres

National rules concerning the financial sector, and particularly foreign exchange restrictions, were major factors in the creation and subsequent growth of truly international capital markets. It in fact began with the exchange restriction described above, introduced by the British government in the latter half of the 1950s. This meant that British banks were liable to lose a substantial part of their business. There were signs that a significant number of non-Americans would like to convert the dollars which they held in American banks into dollar holdings outside the US. This mainly concerned East Europeans who were afraid that in the adverse climate of the Cold War their bank deposits in the US might well be frozen or – worse still – confiscated. The British banks and non-American holders of dollars found one another in a financial innovation: *Eurodollars.*

Eurodollars are dollar deposits held at banks outside the US. This term became quickly too narrow, because it was only in the initial phase that the banks outside the US were confined to banks in Europe. The innovation was a resounding success, the activities started by the London banks being taken up by banks elsewhere in Europe, rapidly followed by banks elsewhere in the world. And soon it was not just American dollars that were concerned: similar activities were quickly developed for other currencies. That is why nowadays we talk about the *Eurocurrency market,* rather than the Eurodollar market, and even better the *offshore* currency market. It is tempting to equate the Eurocurrency market with a foreign exchange market, but there is a great difference. On a foreign exchange market currencies are exchanged for one another: currencies are sold. In contrast, on the Eurocurrency market each transaction involves only one currency and a credit, not a purchase or sale.

The claims on banks in for the banks foreign currencies do not have to be owned by foreigners, as was originally the case with the London banks and the East European account holders. Claims on banks in currencies foreign to the bank, held by residents of the country in which the bank is located, are also Eurocurrencies. Table 12.1 shows this and also gives a diagrammatic representa-

Table 12.1 Bank credits ($ billion, end of 1992)

	To residents	To non-residents
In domestic currency	domestic activities	traditional cross-border bank loans 1,282
In foreign currencies	1,154*	6,198*

*Eurocurrency market transactions
Source: The figures were obtained by processing BIS data (1993, p. 99).

tion of the four categories into which banking activities have since been divided. Apart from domestic activities (with residents in the national currency), international activities are divided into traditional international banking activities and banking activities on the Eurocurrency market. So the international character of the activity may relate to both the other party (a cross-border transaction) and the currency (a foreign currency from the bank's point of view). Table 12.1 also quantifies the three international banking activities for 1992, indicating the great importance of Eurocurrency market transactions nowadays. The figures in the table should be qualified by pointing out that interbank loans represent a substantial proportion of the Eurocurrency credits, namely $3,692 billion.

The British government has long since lifted the restriction on the London banks' activities which prompted the launch of the Eurocurrency market. At first sight it is therefore surprising that this market still exists today – and that its volume is so great. Apparently there were other factors which also stimulated this market. That is true. Furthermore, those factors remained when the restrictions on the London banks were lifted. First, from the start it was not only the type of currency that distinguished the Eurocurrency market from the domestic money and capital markets. It is in fact a market for larger operators, because transactions are subject to a minimum level of one million monetary units. Moreover, because of their size the firms operating in this market are usually known to the banks, so that there is no need to check their creditworthiness. These two aspects keep down the transaction costs, as a percentage of the loans, for the bank on this market. That is reflected in attractive interest rates on the Eurocurrency market for both debtors and creditors. As a result, the rate at which the banks can attract capital on the Eurocurrency market (deposit rate) can be higher and the rate at which the banks provide credit (loan rate) can be lower than on the national market for the currency concerned. This feature is enhanced by two other characteristics of the Eurocurrency market. Their relevance requires a short explanation. In principle, Eurodollar trading in London involves two central banks: the Bank of England and the Federal Reserve Board, the system of American central banks. The Bank of England's task is to protect the stability of sterling, but the dollar is not its concern, so neither are dollar liabilities of British commercial banks. Conversely, the American central bank has no legal authority to issue instructions to British commercial banks. Thus, the lack of any regulation gave banks greater freedom of action in regard to their Eurocurrency activities. This was also partly reflected in more favourable interest rates. Moreover, the banks are not tied to any specific location for their activities on this market, or only to a very minor degree. This enables them to take account of tax advantages in choosing that location. The banks can also proceed to pass on these advantages (in part) to customers in the form of more advantageous rates.

Where bonds are concerned, there has been a development comparable to that for bank borrowing and lending activities. The regulations applicable to national bond markets led to the development of 'international bonds'. These are bonds issued outside the country of the issuer. In contrast, ordinary domestic bonds are issued in the country of residence of the issuer. International bonds are further divided into foreign bonds, which are issued in one country only and denominated in that country's currency, and Eurobonds which are issued in several national markets simultaneously. The currency in which Eurobonds are denominated is a foreign currency for all these countries. Foreign bonds are not a recent financial innovation: classic international bond loans were already issued in this form. For example, the construction of railways in the US was financed at the time with European money. While the issue of foreign bonds is still subject to some rules which are imposed by the country in which they are issued, that is no longer the case for Eurobonds. This illustrates the similarity between Eurobonds and credits on the Eurocurrency market. In principle, of course, there is still the difference in the way the interest rate is fixed and the type of repayment obligation, as also applies in the case of domestic bonds and domestic bank loans. A bond has a fixed rate of interest, while repayment does not take place until the end of the bond's life. In contrast, a loan normally has a variable rate of interest and is repaid in instalments over a predetermined period. In practice, the gap between Eurobonds and Eurocurrencies is filled by the introduction of floating rate notes, or FRNs, also known as medium term notes or Euronotes. These are medium-term Eurobonds with a variable rate of interest, based on a reference value such as LIBOR – the London Interbank Offered Rate – plus a certain mark-up, the spread. This serves to cover the bank's costs and risk. The motives behind international bonds are essentially the same as those underlying the uncovered interest parity in equation 12.2, except that the interest rates and exchange rate expectations are now longer term.

There are also marked differences between bank loans and bond issues from the point of view of the commercial banks. In the case of bank loans, the bank continues to be involved even after the loan has been arranged, while that is not the case with bonds, though a group of banks is usually active in the issuing of bonds. Via underwriting the bank also sometimes guarantees the sale of a proportion of the bonds, but the involvement remains temporary in the case of a bond loan.

In the past decade the financial sector has switched extremely rapidly to trading on computer screens. At first sight, this development renders the banks' location irrelevant. In principle, the whole world can be covered anywhere. But there are two forces which encourage banking activities to be pursued from particular centres (in this connection, cf. the Porter diamond discussed in Chapter 3). In the provision of banking services, personal service often plays an important role. This means that personal contact must not be too difficult. Furthermore, external economies of scale are very important in the financial sector. Clustering of the sector in particular centres renders the financial know-how available on demand. That is why we can see a tendency towards the establishment of financial centres in the world.

The location of these international financial centres is not purely a question of chance: tradition plays an important role. Such centres often developed in connection with a high volume of international trade in goods. Once the financial knowledge is established, there is an internal force – separate from the trade in goods – which favours continuation, though without guaranteeing it. Another important point is the economic policy pursued in the country of location. Considerations such as tax policy, the liberalisation of international capital movements, the presence of an independent central bank and exchange rate stability play an important part. For the country concerned it is an attractive proposition to have an international financial centre within its territory: it guarantees high-grade jobs and additional tax revenue via taxes on profits. Examples of international financial centres are New York, London, Tokyo and to a lesser extent Luxembourg and Singapore. In spite of the important conservative role of tradition, there are nevertheless signs of gradual, relative shifts in financial centres. In Europe, Frankfurt is developing; South and East Asia are expanding relatively rapidly; and in the group of developing countries elsewhere in the world we can also see emerging markets.

12.8 Summary

1. In terms of volume, international capital flows tower over international flows of goods and services, though it should be noted that the foreign exchange market transactions are predominantly interbank transactions, i.e. they are conducted between banks.

2. International capital flows are usually divided into five categories according to motive: international trade credit, foreign direct investment, international arbitrage capital, international speculative capital and international capital movements connected with the need for risk spreading. In so far as capital transactions are linked to trade and investment, they are prompted by motives in the real world. The other three categories are based on purely financial considerations.

3. Of the motives derived from the real world, direct investment motives have already been discussed sufficiently in Chapter 5. The same applies even

more so to international trade: almost all the chapters preceding this one covered the subject. This chapter therefore only had to outline the form of trade credits. These consist of export and import credits, often in the form of trade bills of exchange. These credits are therefore negotiable and an exporter, for example, need not wait for his money until their term expires. Documentary credit is a common form of import credit.

4. The commonest forms of international arbitrage in the financial sphere are foreign exchange arbitrage and interest arbitrage. In both cases the focal point is the advantage gained from price differentials which become apparent on different markets at one and the same time. This is the motive behind all forms of arbitrage. Foreign exchange arbitrage concerns the difference in value of an exchange rate on two foreign exchange markets; interest rate arbitrage concerns the difference in the rate of return on a similar financial investment in two countries. These rates of return comprise not only interest rates but also the premium on one of the two currencies on the forward exchange market. On this market, foreign currencies are traded and the price is determined at the time of conclusion of the contract, but delivery and payment do not take place until a predetermined period has elapsed. The covered interest parity is the equilibrium condition for the behaviour of interest arbitragers.

5. The uncovered interest rate parity is the equilibrium condition for currency speculators in so far as they operate on the spot market, where the foreign currency is delivered and paid for immediately. (In practice, delivery takes two working days.) In the uncovered interest rate parity the premium on the forward currency is replaced by the expected relative change in the value of the foreign currency.

6. International capital movements for risk spreading purposes are aimed at achieving a more favourable ratio between the expected rate of return (assessed as positive) and the uncertainty about the rate of return (assessed as neʕ ⁱtive). Research has shown that the possibility of extending capital movements beyond national borders greatly improves the scope for risk spreading by means of portfolio diversification.

7. This is also a reason why governments should minimise the remaining foreign exchange regulations on international capital movements. If all regulations have been abolished on a currency, it is called a convertible (freely exchangeable) currency. The drawback of a convertible currency is that a country is subject to considerable restrictions on the macro-economic policy to be pursued in aiming at a stable exchange rate, as we shall see in Chapter 16.

8. The international capital markets have expanded enormously since the 1950s. This applies to both the diversity of financial instruments and the volume of business. As far as the instruments are concerned, it began with the launch of the Eurocurrency market, where bank credits are made available in currencies foreign to the bank concerned. Various financial innovations were subsequently added, such as international bonds, which

can be sub-divided into foreign bonds and Eurobonds. During those years there were also some moderate changes in the location of the true international financial centres.

Bibliography

Bank for International Settlements (BIS), *63rd Annual Report*, 1993.

Bayoumi, T. (1990), Saving-investment correlations; immobile capital, government policy, or endogenous behavior?, *IMF Staff Papers*, vol. 36, pp. 360–87.

International Monetary Fund (IMF) (1993), *International Capital Markets*, Part I, Washington DC.

Jager, H. (1990), Wisselkoersen, rentevoeten en internationale diversificatie, in H. Jager and E. de Jong (eds), *Internationale Financiering; de theorie en de Nederlandse praktijk*, Stenfert Kroese, Leiden/Antwerp, pp. 13–29.

Kindleberger, C.P. (1988), *International Capital Movements*, Cambridge University Press.

Lessard, D. (1983), Principles of international portfolio selection, in A.M. George and I.H. Giddy (eds), *International Finance Handbook*, vol. II, Wiley, pp. 8.2.3–8.2.19.

Scholtens, L.J.R. (1993), *Het geld en de stad; over de ontwikkeling van internationale financiële centra*, Amsterdam University Press.

13 The exchange rate explained

13.1 Introduction

The term 'exchange rate' has already been mentioned many times in preceding chapters. Chapter 2 described the close link between the balance of payments and the exchange rate. Every balance of payments entry, or every international transaction, leads to a foreign exchange market transaction and therefore influences the price level on that market, namely the exchange rate. All balance of payments entries together therefore determine the exchange rate. Thus, the exchange rate is the result of a large number of determinants: every variable which influences an international transaction also has an effect – albeit small – on the exchange rate. The previous chapter showed that capital transactions unrelated to trade in goods and services dominate the foreign exchange market. They therefore largely determine the exchange rate.

This composite impression of the exchange rate gives only a superficial idea of the economic forces which determine it. This chapter will provide a more detailed picture. It is not sufficient to know that capital movements, in particular, influence the exchange rate. Information about the particular form of capital transaction is required too. Furthermore, it is useful to have some knowledge of the latent forces behind these different forms of capital movement and the precise way in which they affect the exchange rate. Do these latent forces also include determining factors of the international trade in goods and services? Has this international trade perhaps even an independent influence?

Everyone involved in international transactions has a great need for the best possible information on which to base forecasts of the future trend in the value of the exchange rate. In order to ascertain that outlook it is essential to know what factors determine the exchange rate. This applies not only to a company involved in international trade in goods, but certainly also to an international investor and a government which has to decide on its policy. Case studies 13.1 and 13.2 make this clear.

Case study 13.1 Exchange rate uncertainty and the business world

Gasunie, which we met in Case study 12.1, has to contend with exchange rate uncertainty on two fronts. A soundly based forecast of future exchange rate

---

rate values would be very welcome to the company. Gasunie supplies natural gas to various West European countries.

Every contract with a new customer confronts the company with the problem of *exchange rate uncertainty*. A contract on the international market of natural gas is usually expressed in dollars and concerns an obligation to supply natural gas for many years. A large proportion of Gasunie's costs are expressed in guilders. It is therefore important for the company's future profitability to achieve maximum certainty about the future guilder value of the contract to be concluded. As we shall see in Chapter 15, there are financial instruments which a company can use to eliminate exchange rate uncertainty for the first year or two. But such a contract with Gasunie – and with many other exporting companies – often runs for a much longer period than that, usually more like ten years. It is not possible in practice to hedge exchange rate uncertainty for such a long period. It is a matter of making the most accurate possible prediction of the trend in the value of the dollar expressed in guilders. The question then is what to base such a prediction on: expected interest rates in the Netherlands and United States, perhaps, because the exchange rate is so greatly influenced by international capital flows? Or should we look more at real world factors, such as the expected competitiveness of the two countries, in order to obtain an idea of the exchange rate in the more distant future?

Gasunie is also subject to an exchange rate risk on its foreign currency investments. The nature of these investments was outlined in Case study 12.1, where we saw that they are usually short-term in character, so that the risk of a change in the value of these foreign currencies also concerns the short term. As we said, there are ways of hedging this risk, but investors certainly do not always make use of them. One reason is that there are costs associated with hedging facilities. Another reason is that investors can also have clearly defined exchange rate expectations which, if they come true, are more advantageous to the investor than hedging this risk. Naturally, these expectations also apply to the short term, in accordance with the life of the investment. Instinctively, you would think that the forces affecting exchange rate expectations in the short term would be different from those in the long term. But what are those differences? Since those operating on the foreign exchange market can be expected to act rationally, the said forces will tend to be a combination of the theoretical factors determining the exchange rate and empirical phenomena – which are often also already incorporated in the theory. The suggested difference in the forces determining the exchange rate implies that short-term exchange rate theory can sometimes differ from the longer term theory.

Case study 13.2 Determination of the equilibrium exchange rate

Until mid 1994, Surinam officially adopted a fixed exchange rate for its currency, the Surinam guilder. The official exchange rate was such that a Surinam guilder was worth roughly the same as a Dutch guilder. This vastly overvalued the Surinam guilder. A strong indication of *overvaluation* of a currency is the absence of a free foreign exchange market where trading takes place at roughly the official exchange rate. Who would be willing to buy the overvalued Surinam currency? More particularly, in the case of overvaluation, if the central bank wants to give the official exchange rate any practical significance then it has to require all foreign exchange transactions to be conducted through the central bank, as we saw in the previous chapter. An overvalued (domestic) currency means that the central bank has to contend with a demand for foreign currency which exceeds the supply, because the artificially expensive domestic currency makes foreign currencies cheap, prompting strong demand from importers and investors. On the other hand, exporters who earn foreign currency will be very reluctant to offer this currency to the central bank. Essentially, they will get far too little domestic currency in return. It is therefore not surprising that a black market in foreign exchange tends to develop where a domestic currency is officially overvalued. On the black market, exporters can sell their foreign currency at a far more attractive – and realistic – price. The characteristic of a *black market* in foreign exchange is that it is not officially permitted, and is illegal therefore. Such a market is also known by the – rather more neutral – name of *parallel market*. There is in fact such a market in Surinam: in April 1993, for example, the price was 25 to 30 Surinam guilders for one Dutch guilder. By mid 1994 this price had already risen to over 100 Surinam guilders.

In this situation it is advisable for a government to liberalise foreign exchange dealings. A very unrealistic official price causes severe disruption in the domestic economy and also undermines authority. This is exactly what happened in Surinam. The crucial question then, of course, is what the new official exchange rate should be. What is the equilibrium exchange rate at any particular moment in time? What determining factors can be used to estimate that rate?

This chapter which, as we have said, deals with factors determining exchange rates, is arranged as follows. First, section 13.2 will give an idea of the different exchange rate terms and how they are used. The way in which the exchange rate is presented, or listed, in the financial press will also be described. The factors which determine exchange rates form the subject of sections 13.3, 13.4 and 13.5. Section 13.3 describes the macro-economic context of the balance of payments and the exchange rate. This will lead us on to relevant conditions for the balance of payments equilibrium and thus for the equilibrium exchange rate. A coherent chains of causal relations on the essential factors determining the level of the exchange rate is called an *exchange rate theory*. Exchange rate theories can be divided into long- and short-term explanations of the exchange rate. The long-term explanation forms the subject of section 13.4. The key element of such an explanation will prove to be the equality of a currency's internal and external purchasing power. The short-term explanation is discussed in section 13.5: it centres on international capital movements.

An important factor which helps to determine the exchange rate will be disregarded in this chapter, namely: how exchange rates are influenced by international agreements on the international monetary system. The very existence of such an agreement can influence the exchange rate. Moreover, a precisely defined government policy on the exchange rate normally forms part of such an agreement, and that usually influences the level of the exchange rate as well. The next chapter will consider these international agreements.

13.2   Exchange rate concepts and presentation

The exchange rate which we have always been talking about so far is the *nominal bilateral exchange rate*. 'Nominal' because the value of the foreign currency is expressed in terms of money, viz. the domestic currency. The rate is also 'bilateral' because it concerns the relative mutual value of currencies of *two* countries. The price of a foreign currency and with it the price of the domestic currency cannot, of course, be expressed any more precisely than that. This rate tells us much about the bilateral relationship concerned. However, it is less appropriate for other purposes such as ascertaining the position of one currency among others in the world. The nominal exchange rate of a currency also offers only limited information on the competitive position of the two countries concerned. Modified expressions have been developed for that purpose: effective and real exchange rates.

The nominal *effective exchange rate* is a weighted average of nominal bilateral exchange rates. For the economy of a country, the exchange rate of one foreign currency is likely to be much more important than that of another. The level of a country's international trade with its individual partners is a good indicator of that economic importance, which is why that level is normally expressed in the weightings when determining the average of nominal bilateral rates. Thus, the flow of exports to trading partners in proportion to the total exports of the country concerned is used as a factor for weighting the bilateral exchange rates. The share of imports or the sum of import and export flows in proportion to the total volume of imports and exports is also used for weighting. Several effective exchange rates can therefore be constructed for one and the same currency. The bilateral rates cannot just be added together to determine an effective exchange rate. The number of guilders per dollar and the number of Belgian francs per dollar cannot be totalled to find the effective dollar rate. Their dimensions differ. This would be the same mistake as adding together apples and pears. To avoid this mistake, the bilateral nominal rates are first converted to index numbers with a certain base period for which the values of all bilateral rates involved in the calculation are set at 100. If the weighted average of these index numbers of bilateral rates increases, then the average value of the currency (the dollar in our example) rises against that of other currencies (the guilder and the Belgian franc).

The nominal exchange rate is of limited value as an indicator of the *competitiveness* of the country in question. Of course, *devaluation* of a currency makes a country cheaper for the rest of the world. But if this reduction in the currency's value is in response to high inflation in the country during the preceding period, the change in the exchange rate serves only to compensate for that. This already shows us that the exchange rate tells us far more about the country's competitiveness when considered in conjunction with prices at home and abroad. Real exchange rates combining the nominal exchange rate with these prices are therefore constructed to indicate this competitive position. In practice, the *real exchange rate* is produced by taking the nominal exchange rate, multiplying it by the price in one country and dividing it by the price in the other. For example, in the case of the real exchange rate of the dollar against the guilder, with the nominal rate expressed in the number of guilders per dollar, this rate is multiplied by the price level in the United States and divided by the price level in the Netherlands. The numerator then comprises the product of the nominal rate and the American price level, or the American price level converted to guilders. The denominator consists purely of the Dutch price level in guilders. Thus, numerator and denominator provide a very direct comparison (in the same currency) of the price levels in the two countries and hence their relative attractiveness as suppliers of goods and services for the world's consumers. If this real exchange rate rises then the competitiveness of the United States deteriorates in comparison with the Netherlands – and vice versa. In practice the three components of the real exchange rate are first produced in the form of an index number. The real exchange rate itself is then also in the form of an index number.

Like the nominal exchange rate, the real exchange rate can be stated in both bilateral and effective form. The real bilateral rate is a useful indicator of the trend in a country's competitive position, particularly in relation to one other country. As regards a country's competitive position in general, the real effective exchange rate is a better indicator.

Box 13.1 Daily information on exchange rates

Information on the level of exchange rates is published daily in the financial sections of newspapers. The kind of information differs, however. In American newspapers, such as the *New York Times* and the *Wall Street Journal* you will find for the last two working days in New York selling rates for trading among banks in amounts of $1 million and more. These exchange rates are published in dollars per foreign currency and its reverse, the number of foreign currencies per dollar. But the information can be more extensive, especially for retail transactions. For example, in Dutch newspapers each day two price lists are published for nominal bilateral exchange rates: the rate for electronic transfers and the rate for notes. The buying and selling rates for funds transfer (Table 13.1b) apply to payments to and from other countries through bank accounts. The first figure after a foreign currency indicates the price which the bank pays for one unit of that currency, the second figure gives the price which the bank charges for the same unit. The advantageous margin between the two prices does not only yield a profit for the bank but also serves as the necessary premium to cover the risk incurred by a bank

---

in foreign exchange transactions. These funds transfer rates are much more attractive to customers than the buying and selling rates applied by a bank if foreign notes are offered or requested over the counter. This is evident from the figures under the 'banknotes' heading in Table 13.1a. The keen prices for cash-less foreign exchange conversions are due to the larger volume of the transactions and lower labour costs per transaction in comparison with dealing in foreign exchange over the bank counter.

Table 13.1c shows effective exchange rates for a number of currencies. These are both nominal and real rates. 1985 was taken as the base year for the index numbers, the values for that year being set at 100. In the case of the guilder the column shows that, with some fluctuations, the nominal effective rate rose by 22.8 per cent on average from the base date to 1994. However, this does not mean that

Table 13.1 The Amsterdam foreign exchange market

Table 13.1a *Banknotes*
The recommended rates in guilders given below are GWK Bank's buying and selling rates for banknotes in foreign currencies.

	Previous day	29/6
$	1.490–1.610	1.490–1.610
Aus$	1.05–1.17	1.05–1.17
BFr 100	5.29–5.59	5.29–5.59
Can$	1.065–1.185	1.065–1.185
Dkr 100	27.15–29.65	27.15–29.65
DM 100	109.40–113.40	109.40–113.40
£	2.32–2.57	2.32–2.57
FinM 100	35.05–37.55	35.05–37.55
Frfr 100	30.40–33.10	30.40–33.10
Drachma 100	0.60–0.77	0.60–0.77
Hong Kong $ 100	17.50–21.50	17.50–21.50
Irish £	2.45–2.70	2.45–2.70
Israeli sheqel	0.48–0.63	0.48–0.63
Italian lira 10,000	8.55–10.25	8.55–10.25
Yen 10,000	180.50–186.50	179.50–185.50
Nkr 100	23.60–26.10	23.60–26.10
Austrian shilling 100	15.64–16.14	15.64–16.14
Escudo 100	0.96–1.14	0.96–1.14
Peseta 100	1.21–1.37	1.21–1.37
Turkish lira 100	0.0027–0.0047	0.0027–0.0047
S.A. rand	0.35–0.50	0.35–0.50
Skr 100	19.90–22.40	19.90–22.40
Swiss fr 100	132.50–137.00	132.50–137.00

Source: Het Financieele Dagblad, 29 June 1995.

the Dutch competitive position deteriorated to the same degree. The facts confirm this, since the real effective rate of the guilder rose by only 5.6 per cent over the same period. Inflation in the Netherlands was evidently more moderate than in its trading partners. In comparison with its main trading partner, Germany, the Netherlands' worldwide competitive position actually improved according to the table: the real effective rate of the German mark went up by 13.7 per cent over the same period. For countries such as the United States and Japan, the changes are much greater. In both nominal and real terms, the value of the dollar declined by about 25 per cent, while the yen rose by 104 per cent in nominal terms and 70 per cent in real terms. All these trends have continued strongly in 1995. However, these changes should be placed in perspective by remembering that the choice of base period is essential and random here, particularly as the dollar was subject to major fluctuations in the 1980s: at the end of 1985 this currency was still only just past its peak.

Table 13.1b *Funds transfers*
The rates in guilders below, established at 13.15 hours, apply to funds transfers effected by GWK bank

	Previous day	28/6
$	1.54925–1.55175	1.55475–1.55725
Antillian guilders	0.8600–0.8900	0.8600–0.8900
Aus$	1.1060–1.1160	1.1090–1.1190
Bfr 100	5.4475–5.4525	5.4445–5.4495
Can$	1.12675–1.12925	1.13075–1.13325
Dkr 100	28.655–28.705	28.655–28.705
DM 100	111.990–112.040	111.980–112.030
£	2.4565–2.4615	2.4615–2.4665
Frfr 100	31.885–31.935	31.865–31.915
Drachma 100	0.6420–0.7420	0.6400–0.7400
Hong Kong $ 100	19.935–20.185	19.995–20.245
Irish £	2.5250–2.5350	2.5330–2.5430
Italian lire 10,000	9.5050–9.5550	9.5150–9.5650
Yen 10,000	184.500–184.600	183.950–185.050
NZ	1.0380–1.0480	1.0380–1.0480
Nkr 100	25.100–25.150	25.095–25.145
Austrian schilling 100	15.9200–15.9300	15.9200–15.9300
Escudo	1.0400–1.0800	1.0380–1.0780
Peseta	1.2770–1.2870	1.2780–1.2880
SKr 100	21.935–21.445	21.415–21.465
Swiss fr 100	135.495–135.545	135.305–135.355
ECU	2.0585–2.0635	2.0600–2.0650

Source: see Table 13.1a

Table 13.1c *Effective exchange rates*

(base 31.12.1985 = 100)

The nominal effective exchange rate of a currency is established by weighting the currencies of trading partners on the basis of bilateral trade weights. The real effective exchange rate is produced by a weighted adjustment, using the same weights, for retail price index differentials. A rise in the real index reflects a deterioration in the competitive position of the country concerned.

	Netherlands		Germany		UK		US		Japan	
	nom.	real	nom.	real	nom.	real	nom.	real	nom.	real
1985	100.0	100.0	100.0	100.0	99.9	100.0	100.1	100.0	100.0	100.0
1986	107.2	105.1	108.5	105.3	92.1	92.9	84.4	83.7	130.2	128.2
1987	112.5	106.8	115.0	108.6	90.9	93.1	75.8	76.0	144.0	137.4
1988	112.3	104.5	114.7	106.1	96.7	100.8	70.7	71.7	159.9	148.5
1989	111.2	100.2	113.7	103.4	93.5	100.8	72.6	74.0	151.4	136.9
1990	115.1	101.3	118.8	105.2	92.1	103.9	69.5	71.3	139.1	123.1
1991	114.5	99.4	118.1	103.1	92.9	106.0	68.5	69.9	150.1	131.2
1992	117.5	101.6	121.9	106.7	90.0	102.9	68.3	70.1	158.6	136.6
1993	122.0	104.8	127.3	112.5	83.0	93.3	72.0	74.3	188.1	159.3
1994	122.8	105.6	128.2	113.7	83.9	94.1	72.5	75.7	204.1	169.9
Jan. 95	125.3	107.1	131.5	116.5	83.7	93.9	72.3	75.8	207.2	170.8
Feb. 95	126.4	108.1	133.0	117.7	82.6	92.9	71.6	75.1	209.4	171.5
March 95	130.1	111.6	138.2	121.9	81.7	91.9	70.1	73.7	225.1	183.0
April 95	130.9	112.6	139.0	122.2	81.0	91.1	68.3	72.0	241.9	195.1
May 95	129.7	111.6	137.1	120.4	80.5	90.7	68.2	72.0	239.2	191.7
%	6.3	6.6	7.8	6.7	−3.6	−3.7	−7.1	−5.9	18.3	13.7
19/6	129.8	111.2	137.2	121.1	80.5	90.6	68.5	72.0	240.3	195.8
20/6	129.9	111.3	137.3	121.2	80.6	90.6	68.4	71.9	239.9	195.5
21/6	129.8	111.3	137.2	121.2	80.6	90.6	68.2	71.7	240.8	196.2
22/6	130.0	111.5	137.4	121.4	80.5	90.4	68.2	71.7	240.7	196.1
23/6	129.7	111.2	137.1	121.0	80.1	90.0	68.3	71.6	239.6	195.2
26/6	130.0	111.5	137.5	121.3	79.9	89.8	68.1	71.6	240.5	195.8
27/6	130.2	111.7	137.8	121.6	79.3	89.1	68.1	71.6	240.9	196.1
28/6	130.2	111.7	137.7	121.5	79.4	89.3	68.3	71.8	239.8	195.1

%: percentage change for May 1995 against May 1994.

Source: see Table 13.1a

13.3 The macro-economic framework for the exchange rate

The exchange rate is a macro-economic variable par excellence. As argued previously, all sorts of international transactions come together on the foreign exchange market. The starting point for a macro-economic review is the *income identity*. This indicates that a country's domestic production is made up of various components. Expressed as a formula, that identity looks like this:

$$Y = C + I + G + EX - IM \tag{13.1}$$

The meanings of the symbols are as follows: Y is domestic production, C is consumption by residents, I is investment by residents, G is the country's government spending, while EX and IM respectively denote the country's exports and imports. All these economic quantities are expressed in domestic currency units. The sum of the first three variables (C + I + G) on the right-hand side of the identity equation is also known as aggregate spending by residents or *absorption*, A. By deducting imports we arrive at residents' expenditure on domestic products. If we add exports – i.e. foreign purchases of domestic products – we obtain the total expenditure on goods produced in the country. This total expenditure on domestic goods will always correspond to domestic production. If, for example, expenditure is liable to be lower, then companies are forced to stockpile unsold products; however, these stocks are included in investments, voluntary or enforced, so that equation (13.1) still holds true.

By substituting A for (C + I + G) in equation (13.1) and after a minor rearrangement of the remaining variables we arrive at the following identity:

$$EX - IM = Y - A \tag{13.2}$$

This shows that the export surplus (EX – IM), corresponding to the net result on visible and invisible transactions in the balance of payments, is equal in value to the difference between domestic production Y and absorption A. Equation (13.2) is merely an identity. Unlike behaviourial equations it therefore does not indicate any causal relationships. Equation (13.2) merely expresses the fact that a balance of payments problem in the form of an import surplus is necessarily associated with surplus spending of residents. This is the essence of a theory which has become known as the *absorption approach* to the balance of payments.[1] The equation clearly shows that if a country succeeds in increasing domestic production and/or reducing expenditure by residents, this is bound to be associated with an improvement in the balance of visible and invisible transactions of the country in question.

Equation (13.2) can be developed somewhat further. For one thing, the left-hand side comprises only part of the current account balance on the balance of payments. Net income earned abroad by domestic factors of production is still

---

1. The absorption approach became known mainly through the work of Alexander (1952).

lacking, as is the balance of payments item 'net inflow of unilateral transfers'. We therefore add these balances, R, to the left-hand side. If we also add R to the right-hand side, equation (13.2) still balances. We also add taxes, T, twice to the right-hand side: once with a plus sign and once with a minus sign. This does not alter the value of the right-hand side. Finally, if the absorption is replaced by its component parts, we arrive at the following equation:

$$EX - 1M + R = Y + R - T - C - I + T - G \qquad (13.3)$$

Here, (Y + R) is *national income*.[2] Private savings are defined as the part of national income not spent on consumption, investment or payment of taxes. The first four terms on the right-hand side of equation (13.3) are therefore equal to private savings, S. If we replace them by S, the result is:

$$EX - 1M + R = (S - I) + (T - G) \qquad (13.4)$$

The left-hand side shows the current account balance. The first term on the right-hand side gives the difference between private savings and investment. The second term gives the difference between tax revenue and government spending; this is the budget surplus or the government's saving. Equation (13.4) shows that the current account balance is closely linked with private savings surplus and the government's budget surplus. Once again, there is no causal relationship. We can only state that any current account deficit must imply a simultaneous private savings deficit and/or government deficit. We can also state that in order to reduce such a current account deficit it is necessary either to reduce the private savings deficit or the government deficit (or both).

Since all current account entries imply transactions on the foreign exchange market, equation (13.4) contains important information on factors influencing the exchange rate – the real subject of this chapter. If everything else remains the same, changes in the private savings surplus have a direct effect on the value of the currency. If this surplus falls, then the current account balance also falls as a result of the identity, and demand for foreign currency will increase. A decline in the government budget surplus has a similar influence on the exchange rate. These macro-economic relations for the exchange rate are not derived from any specific economic theory. As already stated, the above equations are the outcome of the use of a set of identities without the addition of any behaviourial equations

2. As we know, domestic production is output produced within the national borders. National production is production by individuals who are nationals of that country. National production differs in two ways from domestic production. First, there are individuals with that nationality who produce abroad: that production has to be added to domestic production. Second, individuals with a different nationality contribute to the production process within the national borders. To ascertain national production, that production has to be deducted from domestic production. The balance of the income earned abroad by the factors of production, capital and labour, portrays these two differences. National production is therefore defined as domestic production plus this balance – a balance which may equally well be negative, of course. National income in turn is obtained from national production if 'net inflow of unilateral transfers' and terms of trade improvements are added.

at all.[3] The earnest attention paid to this type of identity in practical policy-making dates mainly from the 1980s. A well-known example is the debate since 1985 on the reduction of the American trade deficit, which was considered to be worryingly large, and the associated macro-economic requirements.

Equation (13.4) does not only give an idea of the macro-economic influences on the current account and the exchange rate; it also forms the foundation for analysing the scale of these influences. If, for convenience, we reduce the current account to visible trade and invisibles by setting R at zero, we can write the left-hand side of equation (13.4) as follows:

$$EX - 1M = P_x.ex - P_m.im = E.P^*_x.ex - E.P^*_m.im \qquad (13.5)$$

Here, P_x is the export price level and P_m the import price level. Addition of an asterisk (*) to a variable indicates that it is denominated not in domestic but in foreign currency. The symbol E expresses the nominal exchange rate and the small letters ex and im represent the volume of exports and imports respectively. E is the number of domestic currency units per unit of foreign currency. In the case of a current account deficit, equation (13.5) shows the variables which can be used to achieve the eventual restoration of equilibrium on the current account via devaluation of the domestic currency. However, in order to effectuate that, we cannot avoid introducing behaviourial assumptions for these variables. In the simplest situation, we assume that prices are determined entirely on the world market: the country in question is merely a price taker and is therefore evidently small in comparison with the world economy. This means that the foreign prices on the far right-hand side of equation (13.5) are fixed.

In the case of the said devaluation we assume a 1 per cent increase in E. This reduction in the value of the domestic currency then causes the current account to deteriorate by the same percentage as the depreciation via variable E in equation (13.5). The export and import prices in domestic currency units both increase by this percentage depreciation (since prices expressed in a foreign currency do not change), so that the same must be true for the balance on the current account. On the far right-hand side of (13.5) the increase in E causes both terms to rise by the percentage devaluation and, thus, their difference too. Consequently, any existing trade deficit will increase by the percentage of depreciation. The desired improvement in the current account will therefore have to come subsequently from volume effects. In terms of domestic currency, the depreciation causes an increase in the price of goods traded internationally. This will inhibit domestic demand and stimulate production. If there is production at home which competes with imports, this will also be boosted by the price increase. All these volume effects of depreciation lead towards an increase in the available volume of exports and a fall in the required volume of imports, in short

---

3. Behaviourial equations describe the behaviour of economic subjects, the private sector and government. It is in the specific assumptions regarding this behaviour that economic theories differ from one another.

to an improvement in the trade balance. Clearly, these volume effects only will more than offset the negative price effect of the depreciation on the current account providing they are sufficiently large. Only then will the depreciation lead to a net improvement in the trade balance. The so-called *Marshall-Lerner condition* describes this requirement: it states the price elasticities of the volumes of exports and imports in relation to the devaluation percentage. The exact form of this criterion depends on both the initial trade balance, the size of supply elasticities, and the degree to which depreciation pushes up import and export prices expressed in foreign currency. In its most simple form the Marshall-Lerner condition requires that the sum of the (absolute) values of the price elasticities of both export demand and import demand exceeds the value one. Only then a devaluation improves the current account.

The right-hand side of both equation (13.2) and (13.4) shows that the Marshall-Lerner condition in fact goes beyond just the balance of trade. If domestic demand for imports and exports is to be reduced by devaluing the domestic currency, then in general absorption must fall in relation to domestic production and the national savings deficit (made up of net private and government's savings) must be reduced. If that does not happen, then the trade balance cannot improve either. In other words, domestic production and demand must offer scope for more exports and fewer imports after the depreciation of the domestic currency. An extension of production of these tradables would be easy in the event of unemployment and spare production capacity. Otherwise, the extension would need a shift of production factors from the nontradable sector.

In addition, other countries will also have to give the country in question the opportunity to improve the trade balance. Thus, it must be possible to exploit the enhanced export potential by expanding foreign sales. Our simplified assumption in the preceding analysis that prices of imports and exports are determined on the world market offers the country that scope for expansion. The reason is that that assumption implies that the country concerned is so small in relation to the world market that the world market can readily absorb changes in this country's demand and supply at current prices. However, if that is not so then the country will be able to sell on the world market only part, if any, of the enlarged supply of exports resulting from the depreciation. The rest will be left unsold and the producer will be forced to stockpile the goods. This will be expressed as follows in equation (13.2). If domestic production is stepped up in order to expand exports, the right-hand side of (13.2) increases. However, the associated improvement in the trade balance does not occur now: the goods cannot be sold on the world market. This leads to an increase in domestic 'investment' in the form of forced investment in stocks. The investments form part of the absorption, so that the right-hand side of equation (13.2) again falls in value by the same amount as the original increase. In other words, the initial tendency towards an increase on the right-hand side is negated by this forced increase in investments. From this it is clear that equation (13.2) expresses a two-way traffic: this corresponds to the earlier finding that the equation does not incorporate any causality.

Up to now the Marshall-Lerner condition has been interpreted as the requirement for an improvement in the trade balance as a result of a reduction in the value of the domestic currency. The significance of the Marshall-Lerner condition goes beyond that. The exchange rate is the price on the foreign exchange market. The question which the Marshall-Lerner condition answers is essentially this: under what exchange market condition will a price change have the effect of restoring equilibrium. In other words, under what condition is the exchange market *stable*. If the equilibrium on the exchange market is disrupted, then a stable market implies that the disruption leads to a price change such that the disruption is rectified. Let us assume that there is a current account deficit. This implies excess demand for foreign currency. If the resulting increase in the price of foreign currency brings that excess demand back down, the market is stable. If it does not, then we have an erratic or *unstable* market. In the case of an unstable exchange market, the forces of demand and supply push the exchange rate further away from its equilibrium value.

In practice, even just from the point of view of current account transactions, the foreign exchange market certainly need not be stable in the short term. This phenomenon has even been given a name: the *J-curve effect*. It ties in with our previous analysis of the price and volume effects of depreciation. The additional assumption is that the price effect takes place immediately after depreciation but the volume effects take some time to appear. This means that the deterioration in the current account based on the price effect is manifest immediately after the devaluation at time t_0. If a country is able to influence international trade prices, import prices will initially tend to rise faster than export prices. This will further aggravate the original deterioration in the trade balance. The positive volume effect on the current account balance will only gradually become apparent. Thus this balance produces a pattern like that exemplified in Figure 13.1.[4] From time t_1 onwards, the volume effects gain the upper hand, after which it is not until time t_2 before the effect of the devaluation wears off. If the prior calculation, which underlies the devaluation policy, was correct, the current account balance will then have attained the desired value B, so that the balance has improved to the amount of AB. In the short term the exchange market is unstable because the depreciation of the domestic currency initially increases the deficit on the foreign exchange market. But in the end it is stable after all, since in the longer term such a depreciation reduces the deficit on the foreign exchange market.

---

4. The name of the curve is easier to understand if Figure 13.1 is turned slightly in an anti-clockwise direction.

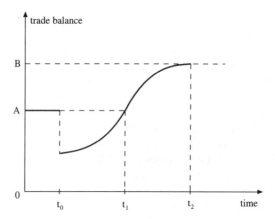

Figure 13.1 The J-curve

13.4 Exchange rate theory: the long term

13.4.1 Purchasing power parity

The oldest theory explaining the exchange rate is the Purchasing power parity theory. The basic idea is found in the *Law of one price*: disregarding trade barriers and transport costs there will be a tendency for a given product to have the same price in different countries. Goods arbitrage is responsible for this result. If prices of the same product are different in two countries, it is profitable to buy the product in the cheaper country and sell it in the dearer one. This buying and selling activity will cause the price to rise in the cheap country and fall in the expensive one. The arbitrage activity ceases once the prices are the same in both countries. A change in the exchange rate can contribute to this price equalisation tendency or may actually be entirely responsible for it, because the prices in two countries are only genuinely comparable if the price in one country is multiplied by the exchange rate to give the price in the other country. International buying and selling also influence the exchange rate in such a way that changes in that rate contribute towards price equalisation. If the prices of goods are rigid in the short term, price equalisation will actually have to come about entirely via changes in the exchange rate.

The retail price index is a weighted average of prices of individual (types of) goods. It is tempting to state that the law of one price also applies to countries' price indices via the concept of price aggregation. The idea then is that if prices of individual goods are the same, a composite set of prices will also be identical. Expressed as a formula, this gives us the following equation:

$$P = E.P* \tag{13.6}$$

This equation expresses *purchasing power parity* or the international equivalence of national purchasing powers. The name in itself indicates – as shown by equation (13.6) – that a certain collection of goods can be bought with a particular sum of money at home, given price level P in that country. However, the same sum of money enables the same collection of goods to be bought abroad at price P* after conversion at the current rate of exchange. If the price level expressed in domestic currency units is higher abroad than at home, demand will switch to domestic goods. This is associated with a decline in demand for foreign currency and increased demand for domestic currency. As a result, the domestic currency rises in value: E falls in value. This engenders the restoration of purchasing power parity. Interpreted in this way, purchasing power parity is an equilibrium condition for the exchange rate:

$$E = P / P^* \qquad (13.7)$$

If the domestic price rises, demand for domestic goods and thus for domestic currency will fall. This will reduce the value of the domestic currency (and E will therefore increase). This contributes to the restoration of equilibrium on the foreign exchange market. The same effect occurs in the case of a foreign price fall.

There are two ways of specifying the purchasing power parity theory of the exchange rate which mitigate some of the drawbacks of the absolute version as given in equation (13.7). In addition to this version of the theory there is also a relative version. The formula for it is this:[5]

$$\Delta E/E = \Delta P/P - \Delta P^*/P^* \qquad (13.8)$$

The practical advantage of this version is that transport costs and trade barriers do not play a part so long as they do not alter significantly during the period in question. Another important advantage is that the baskets of goods on which the price indices are based need not be exactly the same. For the relative version it is sufficient if the relative price increases in equation (13.8) accurately reflect inflation in the two countries concerned.

The other variant of the purchasing power parity theory stresses the facet that the law of one price and goods arbitrage are possible only for goods which can, in principle, be traded internationally. Non-tradable goods include many services such as medical services, the renting of houses and the services of hairdressers. In principle, of course, everything can also be obtained from abroad, i.e. including services or goods which are difficult to transport. But in practice, apart from some rare exceptions, there will clearly be no international transportation of quite a few goods and services, so that no international competition is possible. Elaborating on this idea, purchasing power parity can apply only to

---

5. This formula follows from equation (13.7) by taking the natural logarithms of the left- and right-hand side and differentiating the result. By approximating the differentials by the first differences we arrive at equation (13.8).

goods which can be traded internationally. Taking this view, the exchange rate theory of purchasing power parity looks like this:

$$E = P_t/P_t^*$$

Here, P_t stands for the price of tradables, goods which can be traded internationally.

Case study 13.3 The 'Big Mac' index

Since 1986 *The Economist* has published the Big Mac index every year. This compares the prices of Big Macs in 79 countries. By comparing hamburger prices we can see whether an exchange rate is under or overvalued in relation to its (long-term) equilibrium rate. If purchasing power parity applies, prices of Big Macs expressed in one currency must be identical.

Table 13.2 is taken from the 15 April 1995 issue of *The Economist*. The first column shows the price of a Big Mac expressed in local currency. The second column gives the price of the same Big Mac in dollars which would result when the actual exchange rate against the dollar is used. If we divide the local price of a Big Mac by the American dollar price used in the US we obtain an exchange rate at which the Big Mac purchasing power parity applies. According to this exchange rate, the price of a Big Mac is the same in the different countries. In the table this is the column 'Implied PPP of the dollar'. If we take the exchange rate applicable in the case of Big Mac purchasing power parity and compare it with the actual exchange rate (the fourth column), we can see whether the actual exchange rate is under- or overvalued. The table shows in the second column that the cheapest Big Mac is sold in China and the most expensive in Switzerland. In China a hamburger costs $1.05 and in Switzerland it costs $5.20. According to the fifth column the Chinese yuan is the most undervalued currency and the Swiss franc is the most overvalued currency.

According to the Big Mac index, the dollar is undervalued in relation to the leading currencies. The Big Mac purchasing power parity gives a dollar/yen rate of 169 yen. On 7 April the actual rate was 84 yen. This means that the yen was 100 per cent overvalued against the dollar, or conversely, the dollar was 50 per cent undervalued against the yen. Similarly, the Deutschmark and the Dutch guilder are respectively 50 per cent and 52 per cent overvalued against the dollar. But this indication of an undervalued dollar is countered by the fact that overall in the table there are almost as many currencies undervalued against the dollar as overvalued.

The Big Mac index is a creative way to approach the law of one price. It concerns a homogeneous good: the recipe is the same worldwide. Nevertheless, the index does have its shortcomings:

1. The purchasing power parity theory applies only to tradables and the Big Mac is not traded internationally.
2. The production of Big Macs requires local inputs. They can differ in price because they are internationally traded.
3. Local prices can differ widely as a result of the presence of trade barriers or differences in rates of tax.

Table 13.2 The hamburger standard

Country	Big Mac prices		Implied PPP* of the dollar	Actual $ exchange rate 7/4/95	Local currency under (–)/over (+) valuation†, %
	in local currency	in dollars			
United States§	$2.32	2.32	–	–	–
Argentinia	Peso 3.00	3.00	1.29	1.00	+ 29
Australia	A$ 2.45	1.82	1.06	1.35	– 22
Austria	Sch 39.0	4.01	16.8	9.72	+ 73
Belgium	BFr 109	3.84	47.0	28.4	+ 66
Brazil	Real 2.42	2.69	1.04	0.90	+ 16
Britain	£ 1.74	2.80	1.33††	1.61††	+ 21
Canada	C$ 2.77	1.99	1.19	1.39	– 14
Chile	Peso 950	2.40	409	395	+ 4
China	Yuan 9.00	1.05	3.88	8.54	– 55
Czech Republic	CKr 50.0	1.91	21.6	26.2	– 18
Denmark	DKr 26.75	4.92	11.5	5.43	+112
France	FFr 18.5	3.85	7.97	4.80	+ 66
Germany	DM 4.80	3.48	2.07	1.38	+ 50
Netherlands	FL 5.45	3.53	2.35	1.55	+ 52
Hong Kong	HK$ 9.50	1.23	4.09	7.73	– 47
Hungary	Forint 191	1.58	82.3	121	– 32
Indonesia	Rupiah 3,900	1.75	1,681	2,231	– 25
Israel	Shekel 8.90	3.01	3.84	2.95	+ 30
Italy	Lira 4,500	2.64	1,940	1,702	+ 14
Japan	¥ 391	4.65	169	84.2	+100
Malaysia	M$ 3.76	1.51	1.62	2.49	– 35
Mexico	Peso 10.9	1.71	4.70	6.37	– 26
New Zealand	NZ$ 2.95	1.96	1.27	1.51	– 16
Poland	Zloty 3.40	1.45	1.47	2.34	– 37
Russia	Rouble 8,100	1.62	3,491	4,985	– 30
Singapore	S$ 2.95	2.10	1.27	1.40	– 9
South Korea	Won 2,300	2.99	991	769	+ 29
Spain	Ptas 355	2.86	153	124	+ 23
Sweden	SKr 26.0	3.54	11.2	7.34	+ 53
Switzerland	SFr 5.90	5.20	2.54	1.13	+124
Taiwan	NT$ 65.0	2.53	28.0	25.7	+ 9
Thailand	Baht 48.0	1.95	20.7	24.6	– 16

*Purchasing power parity: local price divided by price in the United States
†Against dollar
§Average of New York, Chicago, San Francisco and Atlanta
††Dollars per pound
Source: The Economist, 15 April 1995, p. 74.

4. Profit margins need not be the same everywhere because of differences in competing substitutes.

Therefore, the Big Mac index only gives a quite rough indication of the long-term equilibrium exchange rate.

Goldman Sachs,[6] an American firm of stock brokers, also calculated the dollar/ yen rate applicable according to purchasing power parity. They arrived at a rate of 185 yen. According to their calculations the dollar is therefore actually even more undervalued than the Big Mac index would indicate.

Empirical research offers only limited support for the purchasing power parity theory. The theory does not hold good in the short term. However, viewed over a number of years there is a tendency towards purchasing power parity. The theory is therefore usually regarded as the essential part of the explanation for the longer term exchange rate.

Of course, the idea comes up immediately whether it is possible to improve the long-term explanation of the exchange rate in the form of the purchasing power parity. Although there is a long-term tendency towards this parity, apparently something is missing. It means that it is realistic to adapt equation (13.7) in the following way:

$$E = \pi . P/P^* \tag{13.9}$$

The variable π functions as a bridge between the values of E and P/P^*. This variable is referred to as the real exchange rate. This can be explained by rewriting the equation:

$$\pi = E . P^*/P \tag{13.10}$$

Now π expresses the ratio of the prices in the countries with the domestic currency as the common denominator. Looking at the dimensions of the ratio, it becomes clear that the dimension of the numerator is: domestic currency per foreign consumer package. The dimension of the denominator of the ratio is: domestic currency per domestic consumer package. Combined, π has the dimension domestic consumer package per foreign consumer package. In other words, π expresses the real price (in units of the domestic consumer package) of the foreign consumer package. This explains π's name: the real exchange rate.

By means of this economic contents of the real exchange rate π, we are able to indicate the economic interpretation of its addition in equation (13.9). Suppose that there is a demand shift from domestic to foreign goods while there is no single change in the two money markets. The latter means that the two price

---

6. *The Economist*, 11 March 1995.

levels will not change, as we will see in the next sub-section. The demand shift nevertheless affects the mutual price of the two consumer packages. The foreign package will become more expensive. This implies an increase in π and, according to (13.9), an increase in the nominal exchange rate E. It is in this way, due to a more expensive foreign currency, that the more expensive foreign goods package manifests itself. Not through a higher price level P*. It turns out that through an explanation of π, we are able to explain an absence of purchasing power parity.

13.4.2　The monetary approach

The beginnings of the purchasing power parity theory date back several hundred years. It was not until the 1920s that the Swede Cassel perfected the theory and gave it its present interpretation. In the latter half of the 1970s the purchasing power parity theory was further developed into the *monetary approach* to the exchange rate: here, the longer term exchange rate is again explained by the ratio of the price levels in the two countries, but this approach delves deeper than the purchasing power parity theory. It does not end with prices as an explanation for the exchange rate: the prices themselves need to be explained. For that purpose the monetary approach uses the equilibria on the money markets in the countries concerned.

The domestic money market equilibrium is as follows:

$$M = P.L\,(y, i) \tag{13.11}$$

M stands for the money supply and L is the real demand for money, so that P.L is the nominal demand for money (in currency units). The widespread assumption is that the real demand for money depends on real income, y, and the (nominal) interest rate, i. If y increases, the demand for money is reckoned to increase because of the increase in the stock of money needed in the country to pay for transactions. Money supply consists of cash and sight deposits at a bank that do not produce interest. If the interest rate in the country increases, it thus becomes more expensive to hold money and people will tend to reduce the amount of money in stock. In this way an increase in the interest rate depresses demand for money. The interest rate can be regarded as the cost of holding money; that does not mean real costs (unless one has to borrow) but the return which one is foregoing by not investing the money at interest. For this reason one usually speaks of the opportunity cost of holding money.

The assumption is that the money market is continually in equilibrium. This is part of the idea that financial markets in general find a new equilibrium immediately (within a few minutes!) after a disruption, by means of change in the price. In this context the money market price is the interest rate. An increase in the money supply (e.g. because of an easing of monetary policy on the part of the central bank) leads to a short-lived excess supply on the money market, but almost immediately this will cause the interest rate to fall. This makes it cheaper to hold money, which immediately increases the real demand for money. The fall in interest rates continues until the money market equilibrium is restored.

The widely accepted assumption is that the interplay of the money supply and real demand for money determines the longer term price level. The idea is that the prices of goods tend to be rigid in the short term, so that money market equilibrium cannot be achieved by adjusting prices in the short run. The interest rate therefore (temporarily) does the job. In the long term, however, the price level is able to perform that function. Thus, in the longer term:

$$P = M/L \,(y, i) \tag{13.12}$$

If there is a permanent increase in the money supply, the price level will ultimately rise if the real demand for money remains the same. Conversely, if there is a permanent increase in the real demand for money (because incomes rise or the interest rate falls), the price level will ultimately fall – at least if the money supply remains unchanged.

Internationally, there is a similar relationship between the price level, the money supply and real demand for money, comparable to equation (13.12). We assume that this equation also applies for the same variables, but with the addition of an asterisk. If we now substitute for P and P* in equation (13.7), we arrive at the following equilibrium equation for the exchange rate in the longer term:

$$E = M/M^* \times L^*/L \text{ in which } L = L\,(y, i) \text{ and } L^* = L^*\,(y^*, i^*) \tag{13.13}$$

This equation shows that if the domestic money supply increases by, say, 10 per cent the exchange rate will also eventually rise by 10 per cent. Eventually, because the equation only holds for the long run. In view of the background to equation (13.13) – and particularly equation (13.12) – the connecting link between M and E here is the domestic price level which eventually also rises by 10 per cent.

13.5 Exchange rate theory: the short term

13.5.1 The uncovered interest rate parity

What can we say about the short-term change in the exchange rate? For that we need a theory. The overriding explanation of the short-term exchange rate is nothing other than the uncovered interest parity already introduced in Chapter 12 and materialised in equation (12.2). For our convenience, it will be repeated here:

$$i = i^* + (E^e - E)/E.100 \tag{13.14}$$

It expresses the fact that a foreign exchange speculator reacts to differences in the expected rate of return on investments in two countries. The left-hand side shows the domestic rate of return consisting only of the domestic interest rate, i, measured as a percentage. The right-hand side expresses the rate of return on an investment abroad. This rate of return has two components: the foreign interest rate, i*, and the exchange gain[7] anticipated during a possible investment abroad. Both components are expressed as percentages. The numerator of the second component indicates the difference between the expected exchange rate, E^e, and the present exchange rate, E. The period to which the expectation applies is the same as the investment period. If we divide this difference by the present value of the exchange rate, we find the expected relative change in the exchange rate. If we multiply it by 100 it becomes a percentage.[8]

Equation (13.14) is the short-run equilibrium condition for the foreign exchange market. It brings the exchange rate together with the three factors which determine it, namely the domestic interest rate, the foreign interest rate and the expected value of the exchange rate. Changes in these affect the equilibrium value of the exchange rate. For example, if the foreign interest rate rises, investment abroad immediately becomes more attractive than domestic investment starting from an equilibrium situation. This prompts a mass tendency to exchange the domestic currency for foreign currency in an attempt to invest abroad. As soon as this tendency is perceived on the foreign exchange market, there is an increase in the value of the foreign currency and thus in the value of E. Given the value of the expected exchange rate, this means that the expected exchange gain declines. This compensates for the more attractive foreign interest rate, so that a new equilibrium is almost immediately reached at a higher value for E. In other words, the domestic currency has depreciated. The influence on the exchange rate of other changes in the factors which determine it can be deduced in the same way. Thus, in the short term the international value of the domestic currency is evidently influenced in a negative direction by an increase in the foreign interest rate and in the expected exchange rate value, and by a fall in the domestic interest rate.

This explanation of the exchange rate in the short term can be easily combined with the long-term exchange rate model as expressed in equation (13.13). This composite model consists of equations (13.12), (13.13) and (13.14) plus the assumptions of national income determined exogenously and a speculator acting rationally. This means that the speculator knows the model and hence sees the consequences of any change in model variables. The consequences still hidden in the future are discounted by the speculator in his expectations based on this model.

This model can explain the remarkable practical phenomenon of over-

---

7. That profit may well be negative, of course, and thus expresses a loss situation.

8. The second component on the right-hand side is only a fair approximation of the expected exchange gain. It concerns only the gain expected on the principal. The expected exchange gain on the foreign interest yield (which is paid out in foreign currency, of course) is ignored. However, this amount is quite small compared to the other components so that its exclusion does not affect the essence of the subsequent conclusions.

9. This variant is not alone here. There are other variants which also produce this phenomenon.

reaction (*overshooting*) by the exchange rate.[9] We shall illustrate this on the basis of the example of a monetary disturbance in the form of an unexpected and permanent 10 per cent increase in the money supply on the part of the monetary authorities. This policy change affects the model in two ways. First, the money market equilibrium is disturbed by this increase in the money supply. Since the price level is sticky in the short term, there is only one variable in equation (13.11) which can restore the money market equilibrium. That is the interest rate, which will fall to the point where equilibrium is restored via a sufficient increase in real demand for money. Second, the expected value of the exchange rate will also increase in response to the larger money supply, because the rational speculator knows that, according to equation (13.13), the permanent 10 per cent increase in the money supply will eventually also lead to a 10 per cent increase in the exchange rate. The speculator will adjust his expectation similarly and notice that his investment equilibrium for interest-bearing assets has currently been upset in two ways: in equation (13.14) the left-hand side has fallen in the form of the lower domestic interest rate while the right-hand side has increased in value as a result of a 10 per cent rise in the expected exchange rate.

The speculator will respond to this two-sided disturbance of the equilibrium with a mass shift from domestic to foreign investments. This causes a huge increase in demand for foreign exchange, so that the exchange rate rises. A 10 per cent increase in the actual value of the exchange rate is not enough to alter the speculator's behaviour: although such an increase does restore the right-hand side of equation (13.14) to its original value (because both the expected and the actual exchange rate have now risen by 10 per cent), there is still no reason for the domestic interest rate to rise again. As a result, the left-hand side of equation (13.14) remains below the original level, so that speculators still have reason to transfer their investments abroad. It is not until the actual exchange rate has risen so far that in equation (13.14) the right-hand side is just as far below its original value as the left-hand side that the speculator is again indifferent as regards the country where he wishes to invest. At that point the excess demand for foreign exchange ceases and the actual exchange rate stabilises.

The trend in the actual and expected exchange rates over time is shown in Figure 13.2. At the present stage of our analysis, the actual rate is at level C. This situation may persist for some time. The length of this period depends on the rigidity of the price level. As said before, the long-term exchange rate model is based on the fact that prices are to some extent rigid. Once the domestic price level gradually begins to rise after a time, the temporary equilibrium with the exchange rate at level C is left. According to equation (13.11), the money market equilibrium is now disrupted again: there is excess demand on the money market. This causes the domestic interest rate to rise. According to equation (13.14), this prompts an inflow of speculative capital, which is accompanied by rising demand for the domestic currency. As a result, the exchange rate begins to fall, keeping pace with the rise in the interest rate – in accordance with equation (13.14). Eventually, the price reaches its long-term equilibrium level. As a consequence its rise and that of the interest rate ceases as does the fall of

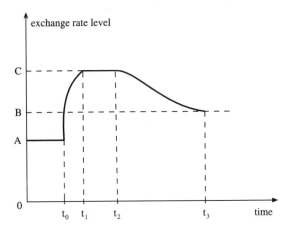

Figure 13.2 Overshooting behaviour of the exchange rate

the exchange rate. It has now reached level B in Figure 13.2, the level which the expected exchange rate had already reached immediately after the monetary disturbance. The pattern of the actual exchange rate over time in Figure 13.2 clearly shows why one states that exchange rate over-reacts.[10]

Case study 13.4 The trend in the principal exchange rates

Figure 13.3 shows the trend in the mutual values of the three leading exchange rates in the world since 1970. Apart from the presence of upward and downward trends, substantial fluctuations are particularly evident. These did much to fuel ideas on exchange rate overshooting. In the 1980s the American dollar, in particular, produced an equally spectacular rise and fall. The explanation put forward for this ties in with the explanation of exchange rate overshooting presented in this section. In response to the continuing rise in inflation in the 1970s, the American central bank, the Federal Reserve Board, introduced a very restrictive monetary policy around 1980. This caused the American interest rate to rise. An expansionary fiscal policy further contributed to this. The greater demand for goods caused an additional increase in the interest rate in the United States. The high American interest rate attracted a large amount of foreign investment capital. The associated strong demand for dollars caused a massive increase in the value of the dollar. To compensate for the interest rate advantage, the value of the dollar had to rise beyond its eventual equilibrium value so that people expected it to appreciate. It was not until the price rises in the United States diminished after a while as a result of the tight monetary policy that the US interest rate could drop back again, and with it the rate of the dollar.

---

10. The name of the American economist, Dornbusch, is associated with exchange rate overshooting. He was the one who first offered a model to explain this phenomenon which so obviously occurred in practice. See Dornbusch (1976).

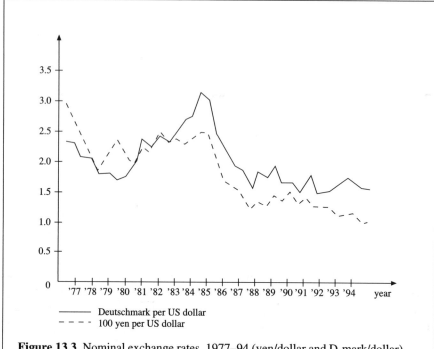

Figure 13.3 Nominal exchange rates, 1977–94 (yen/dollar and D-mark/dollar)
Source: IMF, International Financial Statistics, several issues.

13.5.2 *The portfolio model*

The exchange rate theory was further developed in two ways in the 1980s. In the first, least radical development, the constraint that domestic money can only be in domestic hands was dropped. This led to the *currency substitution model* of the exchange rate. The deciding factor for substitution between domestic and foreign currency is uncertainty about the future value of the exchange rate and, particularly, the direction in which the rate is expected to move. If people anticipate a depreciation, they will put their money into other currencies. The differential between the domestic and foreign interest rates naturally plays no part in this because cash and sight deposits at banks do not yield interest. This expansion of the theory did not produce any important new explanations for practical phenomena, but the theory has interesting practical implications for hyperinflation countries where the national currency is at risk of being displaced by more stable foreign currencies, and particularly the American dollar.

A more interesting expansion of the theory is the *portfolio approach* to the exchange rate. In addition to the monetary approach, this now explicitly incorporates the equilibria on a country's domestic and foreign bond markets.

In the monetary approach, such interest-bearing investments are already an implicit alternative to holding money. This is hinted at by the interest rate in the money demand function owing to the opportunity cost of holding money. However, no distinction was made between domestic and foreign interest-bearing assets. They were implicitly treated as equal, because the foreign rate of return is not presented as a second indicator of the opportunity cost in the money demand function. In the adjustment process following a monetary disturbance, however, there was an incipient distinction between domestic and foreign assets, but only until equilibrium was restored.

The essence of the portfolio approach concerns the desired allocation of the financial assets over the portfolio of a country's private sector. These assets involved are domestic money, domestic bonds and foreign bonds. Changes in the desired allocation occur on the basis of the (expected) rates of return on the financial assets concerned. In the simplest form, the rate of return is zero for money and the relevant interest rates for both types of bonds. But in this approach, these bonds are incomplete substitutes. For example, if the foreign interest rate rises then the (desired) proportion of foreign bonds in private assets will increase at the expense of money and domestic bonds. But despite that the domestic bonds remain desirable in the portfolio, although with a smaller proportion. If the volume of private asset holdings increases, these proportions do not change; demand for and hence ownership of the assets will increase proportionately to the previous asset holdings. On the supply side, the supply of money domestic bonds is assumed to be exogenous as it is considered to be determined by, respectively, the central bank and the government. In contrast, the supply of foreign bonds is endogenous and changes as a result of any current account surplus or deficit on the balance of payments. A surplus means an increase in foreign claims: owing to the simplicity of the model of the portfolio approach, this is entirely in the form of foreign bonds. The domestic supply of foreign bonds does not increase in this way alone; it can also rise as a result of an increase in the value of the foreign currency, because in the model the supply of and demand for foreign assets are denominated in domestic currency units. If the exchange rate rises (so that the foreign currencies become dearer), then the value of the foreign bonds in the portfolios will also rise in terms of domestic currency units.

Case study 13.5 Financial liberalisation in Japan

After the Second World War, Japan's financial system was initially largely closed. The 1973 oil price shock led to a temporary current account deficit for Japan. In response to that, Japan eased restrictions on capital imports to help finance the increased oil account. In subsequent years Japan gradually liberalised its international capital movements more and more. When there seemed to be no stopping to the rise of the American dollar in the first half of the 1980s (see Figure 13.3), President Reagan brought great pressure to bear on the Japanese government to open up its borders still further to financial transactions. The pressure led to the intended Japanese measures, but not to the intended behaviour, as the main result

---

was a sharp increase in Japanese capital *exports*. Since most of these went to the US, the dollar received a further upward boost. But Japanese capital imports also increased, also from the US. The portfolio approach, in particular, can explain such an increase in mutual capital inflows between two countries following the capital liberalisation. In both countries people are adjusting their investment portfolios to the new possibilities which have been opened up.

To ensure a proper understanding of the portfolio approach to the exchange rate, we shall describe the adjustment process which occurs after a disturbance. Say, the central bank increases the money supply. In this model that means more than just an increase in the money supply, because the central bank usually puts the additional money into circulation by buying domestic bonds. The alternative in this model is an exchange of money for foreign bonds. This is in fact a form of foreign exchange market intervention in which foreign currency in the form of foreign bonds is bought by the central bank for domestic currency. This transaction does not alter the level of private asset holdings, but excess supply occurs on the money market and excess demand on the foreign bond market. This excess demand also means excess demand for foreign currency, which leads to an increase in the price of that currency. This means a fall in the value or depreciation of the domestic currency. As a result, there is an increase in the *value* of the supply of foreign bonds, caused not by a larger volume of bonds in the country but an increase in their value in domestic currency. This rise in value also means an incipient increase in the value of the financial assets of private persons in that country. This in turn leads to increased demand for all assets, depressing the excess supply of money and causing excess demand for domestic bonds, resulting in an increase in the value of those bonds and a decline in the domestic interest rate. This in turn generates higher demand for money and a lower demand for domestic bonds. Thus, the markets in money and domestic bonds tend towards a new equilibrium. On the foreign bond market the increased demand leads to a further rise in the *value* of foreign currency, instigating another round of changes, until the financial markets have gained equilibrium.

The financial equilibrium is again disturbed by the fact that the decline in the domestic currency brings a current account improvement over a period of time, and this leads to an increase in the *number* of foreign bonds held by the domestic private sector. This new development implies a surplus of foreign bonds causing the exchange rate to decline. The temporary financial equilibrium was apparently characterised by overshooting of the exchange rate. Under certain realistic assumptions a new equilibrium is eventually reached on all three domestic financial markets. The end result is that the central bank's action causes an increase in the stock of reserves held by the central bank, a fall in the domestic interest rate, a net decline in the value of the domestic currency on the foreign exchange market, and a new current account equilibrium.

The current account is indeed in equilibrium again, but with changed balances of its sub-accounts. As the country experienced a net inflow of foreign financial assets during the adjustment period, the inflow of foreign capital earnings has increased compared to the initial equilibrium. In the new equilibrium the goods and services balance must, therefore, necessarily be unfavourably compared to the initial situation. The new equilibrium is only compatible with domestic goods that have become dearer. This outcome is due to higher domestic prices, whereby relative to the initial equilibrium, the percentage rise of prices exceeds that of the exchange rate. This price increase is a response to higher foreign and domestic demand for domestic goods. The initial cause of this higher demand is depreciation. The permanent cause is an increase in the real value of private holdings of financial assets, being a determining factor of domestic expenditure.

13.6 Summary

1. The exchange rate takes many forms. Normally, when we refer to the 'exchange rate' we mean the nominal bilateral exchange rate. This expresses the value of a foreign currency in domestic currency units. A general idea of the trend in the value of the domestic currency is obtained by determining its nominal effective rate. This expresses the value in relation to a weighted average of foreign currencies relevant to the country's international trade. A better picture of a country's competitive position is provided by its real exchange rate. Here, the nominal exchange rate forms part of a larger whole in which the domestic price is expressed in relation to the foreign price, measured in one and the same currency. This real exchange rate is also available in bilateral and effective form.

2. Exchange rate theories aim to explain the nominal exchange rate. They give an indication of the relevant factors determining the exchange rate. These theories can offer support in attempts to predict the value of the exchange rate. Sound exchange rate predictions are very useful in both international trade in goods and the investment world. The government also finds exchange rate theories helpful in its exchange rate policy where indications of the equilibrium level of the exchange rate are of importance. In this chapter the exchange rate theories have been divided into three categories.

3. The first category of theories is based on economic definition equations. The income identity leads to the absorption approach in which growth of domestic production and a decline in absorption (spending by a country's residents) boost the trade balance surplus and hence the value of the domestic currency. The definition of the current account forms the framework for the Marshall-Lerner condition. This states that the effect of a devaluation on the volume of imports and exports must be sufficiently great to outstrip the detrimental effect of the devaluation itself on the trade balance via higher import and export prices. Only then will a devaluation yield the expected improvement in the current account. In the short term that will not always happen: then the J-curve effect occurs.

4. The second category of theories focuses on explaining the exchange rate in the long term, this means over a number of years. In the purchasing power parity theory there is a close link between the exchange rate and the ratio of domestic and foreign price levels. Apart from this absolute version, there is also a relative version of this theory. Here, the relative increase in the exchange rate is equal to the difference between the domestic and foreign inflation rates. The absolute version of the purchasing power parity forms part of the monetary approach to the exchange rate, in which the exchange rate is linked via the price ratio to the ratio between the domestic money supply and demand compared to that ratio abroad.

5. In short-term exchange rate theories the emphasis shifts from an explanation based on goods to one based on financial assets. The basic assumption is that imbalances in the financial sphere are rectified immediately whereas a longer or shorter adjustment period is necessary where goods are concerned. Thus, the uncovered interest rate parity can serve as the starting point to explain the phenomenon of overshooting, so characteristic of the behaviour of exchange rates. The uncovered interest rate parity is characterised by the complete substitutability of domestic and foreign interest-bearing assets. As soon as that substitution is incomplete, which means that domestic and foreign interest-bearing assets are considered to be different, the portfolio approach to the exchange rate becomes relevant. Apart from markets for domestic money and domestic interest-bearing assets, this approach also distinguishes a market for foreign interest-bearing assets.

Bibliography

Alexander, S. (1952), The effects of a devaluation on a trade balance, *IMF Staff Papers*, vol. 2, pp. 263–78.

Dornbusch, R. (1976), Expectations and exchange rate dynamics, *Journal of Political Economy*, vol. 84, pp. 1161–76.

Dornbusch, R. (1987), Purchasing power parity, in: J. Eatwell, M. Milgate and P. Newman (eds), *The New Palgrave; a Dictionary of Economics*, MacMillan, pp. 1075–85.

Frankel, J.A. and K.A. Froot (1990), Chartists, fundamentalists, and trading in the foreign exchange markets, *American Economic Review*, vol. 80, pp. 181–5.

Frankel, J.A. and H.G. Johnson (eds) (1978), *The Economics of Exchange Rates: Selected Studies*, Addison-Wesley.

McKinnon, R.I. (1982), Currency substitution and instability in the world dollar standard, *American Economic Review*, vol. 72, pp. 320–33.

Taylor, M.P. (1995), The economics of exchange rates, *Journal of Economic Literature*, vol. 33, pp. 13–47.

14 Exchange rate effects

14.1 Introduction

The previous chapter discussed the influence of various factors on the exchange rate. These influences are incorporated in theories to explain the exchange rate. In this chapter the interest shifts from the exchange rate as the *consequence* of certain effects to the exchange rate as the *cause* of economic effects. In other words, the subject matter now concerns the influences produced by the exchange rate itself. We shall see that a change in the value of the exchange rate may have a range of consequences: for the purpose of analysing those consequences, it is reasonable to distinguish between the influence of the exchange rate on economic policy *objectives* and its influence on the policy's *effectiveness*.

The principal economic variables influenced by the exchange rate are international trade in general and bilateral trade flows in particular. These also alter the ultimate underlying economic variables including those which are the target of policy. This does not only concern the balance of payments: the whole set of variables comprising wage rates, business profits and ultimately inflation is also affected, as are the objectives associated with them: domestic production, economic growth and employment. All these influences of the exchange rate form the subject of sections 14.2–14.4.

In macro-economic policy we distinguish between monetary policy and fiscal policy (this is also known as the government's budgetary policy). The government uses these two forms of policy to try to achieve its macro-economic objectives. In sections 14.6 and 14.7 we see that the possibility of changes in the value of the exchange rate is very important for policy effectiveness. This in turn is connected wit' the system of determining exchange rates applicable to the currencies involved in the exchange rate concerned. Before examining that, in section 14.5 we shall therefore consider the various exchange rate systems. As well as describing the systems we shall look at their consequences for exchange rate stability and for the instruments with which a central bank can influence the value of the exchange rate.

14.2 International trade

Variations in the exchange rate add an element of uncertainty to international trade transactions which does not apply to domestic trade, because a foreign trade contract is always denominated in a foreign currency for at least one of the two contracting parties. For example, a Dutch export deal with Australia can be concluded in the exporter's currency (the guilder) or the importer's currency (the Australian dollar), but also in a third currency (very often the American dollar). The currency in which the transaction is denominated is called the *invoice currency*, because that is the one in which the invoice is made out. The choice of invoice currency is influenced by the market position of each contracting party but also by normal practice in the market concerned. A goods trader normally prefers invoicing in his own currency, in order not to be confronted with the uncertain value of a foreign currency in terms of his own. But if, for example, a Dutch exporter is very keen to clinch the deal, then he will be willing to make a concession to the Australian customer by offering the option of the Australian dollar as the invoice currency. If both contracting parties prefer their own currency, then choosing a third currency may provide a compromise. In certain goods markets a particular currency is generally used: thus, contracts on the international oil market are normally in American dollars, whoever the two contracting parties are.

It is usual for a trade contract not to be executed immediately. Once the contract has been signed it is normally some time (often several months) before the goods are delivered. After that it is often several more months before payment is made. In the period between the signing of the contract and the eventual payment the exchange rate may change, sometimes considerably. This may operate in favour of the party who has to cope with a contract in a foreign currency, but it may also be to his disadvantage. Since an international goods trader normally aims to avoid risk, this uncertainty has a negative value for the trader concerned. A national transaction does not entail this foreign exchange uncertainty. That is why we expect increasing exchange rate variations and the greater uncertainty directly associated with them to bring about a shift from international to national trade. This implies failure to make use of the advantages of international specialisation. As we also saw in Chapter 3, this is detrimental to the welfare of the world as a whole and the countries concerned in particular.

In practice, the adverse effect of this type of exchange rate fluctuations and uncertainty on the volume of international trade is far less than expected, as goods traders have the option of *hedging*. This means that they can cover their exchange rate risk, namely via a transaction on the forward exchange market. Say a Dutch trader can look forward to a payment in dollars in six months' time as a result of an export to the United States. The uncertainty about the guilder value of those dollars six months hence disappears if the exporter, immediately after signing the export contract, sells the dollar proceeds at the prevailing forward rate on the six-month forward market. The actual transaction on that market will not take place until a specific date in six months' time, but the rate on that market is already known.[1] Apart from the costs associated with a forward

---

1. We shall examine this market in more detail in the next chapter.

transaction, in this way the international trade transaction is no longer any different from a domestic one. Normally an exporter will pass on the forward market transaction costs in the price. This means that the export price is somewhat higher than the price for a purely domestic transaction. In theory, this effect may to some extent undermine the optimum allocation of production in the world, but it is usually of minor importance.

Possible exchange rate movements in the medium and long term cause more problems. In practice, we are talking about fluctuations in the rate over a period of over one year. There is hardly a forward market for such long periods. Furthermore, the goods trader faces a different problem: international trade is seldom confined to a single, independent transaction. In most cases it forms part of a long series of transactions generated by opening up a trade channel. This usually entails substantial initial investment ('sunk costs') by the exporting country in the country to which goods are to be sold. The nature of this investment may vary from one product to another. Sometimes it is a matter of finding a suitable importer; in another case it is a question of opening up retail sales channels. A further way of 'breaking open' a market is to set up a service network to provide after-sales service. Moreover, launching exports almost always requires a massive local advertising campaign.

It can take years to recoup the costs of the initial investment, so that one must be reasonably certain that the export being launched will continue for a number of years. However, the problem is that a good competitive position now can be turned into loss-making exports in the future just by exchange rate movements. A permanent increase in the value of the exporter's currency has a serious, lasting impact on the international competitive position. There is no way of covering such *exchange rate uncertainty*. This is therefore the source of the real danger of possible exchange rate changes for the exporter. The consequence may be that – owing to the possibility of undesirable long-term changes in the exchange rate – goods traders may still refrain from launching exports even if they are sufficiently competitive on the international market. The initial investment required is then considered too risky. For large companies, in particular, this may mean that direct investment in the target country is the preferred option (see Chapter 5). In this way they set production costs in the foreign currency against the foreign currency income. This will diminish their exchange rate exposure substantially.

Apart from longer term exchange rate uncertainty, there is another link between exchange rate changes and international trade, derived from *protectionism* at the borders. The central idea is that an increase in the value of the domestic currency makes it harder for domestic producers to sell in both the export sector and the sector competing with imports. In the case of a substantial appreciation there will certainly be calls for protection, e.g. in the form of arguments in favour of a temporary import levy and/or a temporary export subsidy. All too often a government gives in to these demands. As soon as the value of the domestic currency reverts to the old level the reason for protection has naturally disappeared. However, the political economics of protection indicates that once

271

preferential rights have been granted it is difficult for the government to withdraw them. Once rights have been acquired they often prove to be structural.[2] If the value of the domestic currency subsequently rises, there are renewed calls for protection which is often granted once again, so that in the end it, too, becomes permanent. The end result of these cumulative protection measures is that, without any net increase in the value of the domestic currency, international trade lags farther and farther behind the level which it would have attained without these exchange rate fluctuations.

The influence of exchange rate uncertainty and protectionism on the volume of international trade flows naturally affects the balance of trade. Since similar effects are at work in other countries, the total net effect on a country's trade balance is uncertain. The influence of an exchange rate change on the value of a country's international trade flows and hence on its balance of trade has already been discussed from the macro-economic angle in the previous chapter. The effects of exchange rate uncertainty and protectionism form an essential part of this. Whether an exchange rate change influenced the trade balance in the expected direction and degree proved to depend on whether the Marshall-Lerner criterion was satisfied and whether the overspending in the country was reduced by the depreciation of its own currency.

14.3 Inflation

There are four ways in which variable exchange rates can fuel inflation in a country and hence in the world as a whole. Little need be said about the first one: it is a consequence of the cost of using the forward exchange market to cover the exchange rate risk. The exporter or importer will pass on these *hedging costs* as far as possible, and thus reflect them in the selling price. If this can be done, then the price of the product rises in the importing country. Since the price of imports affects the general price level in the importing country, this gives an upward boost to that price level.

The second way in which variable exchange rates can stimulate inflation results from the *lack of discipline in government behaviour* which such rates may engender. Permanently fixed exchange rates do not undermine discipline in this way; in other words, such an exchange rate system can promote discipline in economic policy. With fixed exchange rates, the government of a country knows that an expansionary economic policy favouring higher employment can have a boomerang effect. Such a policy can easily stimulate domestic inflation, thus undermining the competitive position on the world market and subsequently reducing employment again as production is cut back in the sector making internationally tradable goods. The system of fixed exchange rates in fact means

---

2. For a more detailed discussion of the political economy of protectionism, see Chapters 10 and 11.

that inflation has to keep in line with that in other countries. We shall come back to this in sections 14.6 and 14.7.

With variable exchange rates, however, the boomerang does not work. Essentially, that is because externally an expansionary economic policy, and the concomitant domestic price rise, will find an outlet in an exchange rate adjustment. In this case the deterioration in the competitive position and the associated lack of demand for the domestic currency on the foreign exchange market is thus offset by depreciation of the currency. The deterioration in the competitive position and the ensuing undermining of employment therefore do not occur if exchange rates are variable, although the depreciation of the domestic currency does give an additional boost to inflation via an increase in domestic prices of internationally tradable goods.

One objection to the discipline effect is that it also works the other way: its effect is symmetrical. Countries which, on account of a tight labour market, wish to pursue a restrictive economic policy leading to lower inflation, are prevented from doing so if exchange rates are fixed. The reason is that lower inflation improves the international competitive position, stimulates domestic production of tradables and hence increases demand for labour. This encourages a labour shortage and thus stimulates inflation. With variable exchange rates, countries advocating lower inflation would not be thus discouraged from achieving their objective. The improvement in the international competitive position can then take the form of a currency appreciation, which in turn leads to lower import prices and still lower inflation.

If the discipline effect is in fact symmetrical, higher average world inflation cannot occur with variable exchange rates. On the one hand there are countries which use the scope to attain a higher inflation situation; but conversely, there will also be countries that use it to reduce inflation. However, what remains is that the range of national inflation rates in the world will be greater than under fixed exchange rates.

The third boost from variable exchange rates to inflation is in some ways related to the preceding one. It is not only the policy-makers in a country who lack a *disciplinary effect* under variable exchange rates. This applies equally to the *private sector*. If exchange rates are variable, it is far less expensive in terms of unemployment for the labour unions to make big wage demands. If the competitive position is impaired at all, depreciation of the country's currency will promptly follow so that employment is not at risk. In that case, though, the point of such wage demands is dubious: they are negated as it were by the higher prices prompted by higher wages plus the more expensive imports resulting from appreciation.

The fourth boost to inflation which may come from variable exchange rates is known as the '*ratchet effect*'. An exchange rate alters because one country has an impending balance of payments surplus and the other a looming deficit. In the country with the depreciating currency, import prices increase because the depreciation makes them higher in terms of domestic currency units. This affects the other prices in the country so that an overall price rise results. If wages are

273

totally or partly index-linked for rising prices, a wage and price spiral ensues. Conversely, however, import prices in the surplus country can and should fall as the currency appreciates, but in practice this often does not happen, or only to a limited extent. Exporters in the depreciating country and/or importers in the appreciating country often prefer to raise their profit margin instead. Thus, prices evidently rise in the country with the depreciating currency, but decline to a much lesser extent, if at all, in the country with the appreciating currency. This empirical result explains the name 'ratchet effect': prices are upwardly flexible but there is a great deal of resistance to price reductions, as if there were a ratchet to prevent them. The end result is that price rises in one country are accompanied by a smaller or zero reduction in the other country, so that there is a net increase in prices worldwide as a result of the change in the exchange rate.

This additional boost to inflation resulting from exchange rate changes is also disputed. On the one hand, people doubt the ratchet effect. There are many cases in which the price of the depreciating country's imports does not actually increase. In the case of an appreciation in their currency, export companies are afraid that their market share will be impaired on those export markets where their products have thus become more expensive. To avoid that they reduce their export prices in terms of their own currency. On the other hand, it is argued that the adjustment process following disequilibrium on the balance of payments under fixed exchange rates does also have such a ratchet effect as a by-product. In order to rectify the imbalance – now that it is not permissible to alter the exchange rate – the adjustment will have to come from a change in spending policy. The country with a balance of payments surplus has to increase its spending to expand imports. This can fuel inflation. The deficit country, on the other hand, will have to reduce spending. This curbs imports. However, only a small price reduction, if any, can be achieved in the case of a downward ratchet effect on prices. Overall, the price level rises in the two countries taken together. This means that the inflationary effect of variable exchange rates need be no greater than that of fixed exchange rates.

So far we have compared variable exchange rates with a situation in which exchange rates are permanently fixed. This may offer a useful basis for comparison, but it is not realistic. In practice, even fixed exchange rates can still be adjusted. Of course, they are kept fixed as far as possible, but if a *fundamental imbalance* develops – often gradually – in the economy concerned, then a one-off adjustment is made in the exchange rate. Every effort is then made to keep the rate fixed at that new level. It is these occasional adjustments to the exchange rate which can equally well stimulate inflation in the manner described above. However, in practice the cumulative exchange rate changes are normally far smaller under fixed than under variable exchange rates.

14.4   Growth and unemployment

The word 'unemployment' has already occurred several times in this chapter. The influence of variable exchange rates on the volume of trade and inflation makes itself felt, through these variables, not only in a country's production and economic growth but also in employment and thus unemployment. If variable exchange rates, via the associated uncertainty or protection, impair the volume of world trade, they also have an adverse effect on world employment. If variable exchange rates stimulate world inflation, perhaps they also stimulate employment in the short term. But in the longer term, inflation could well have the reverse effect on employment: the present view from economic theory tends towards a negative long-term connection between inflation and employment.

Apart from the above indirect links there are also two direct connections between variable exchange rates and unemployment. Let us confine ourselves to the case of a variable exchange rate showing just fluctuations but no upward or downward trend. These fluctuations will also generate similar fluctuations in the competitive position of the two countries concerned. These temporary changes in the competitive position cause part of the production factor labour to move to and fro, over a period of time, between sectors producing tradable and non-tradable goods. In practice we find that, as a result of all kinds of rigidities on the labour market, there are often substantial welfare costs associated with the movement of labour, even within a national economy. This means that a regular movement of labour from one sector to another and back is accompanied by a permanent increase in frictional unemployment. In addition, there is the unemployment which results because some of the firms producing tradables, having been forced out by temporary international competitive pressure, are subsequently unable to return as producers of export goods. To do that they would again have to make initial investments, which can sometimes be too high in comparison with the known profitability of the sector concerned. This combination of factors means that exchange rate fluctuations contribute towards the development of structural unemployment.

This phenomenon of a fluctuation in a variable exchange rate differs from the indirect effect via the volume of world trade, as previously described, in that the latter involves exchange rate uncertainty. Here we are concerned with a situation in which even certainty about the fluctuation in the exchange rate leads to job losses.

A third direct link between variable exchange rates and unemployment concerns the significance of exchange rate uncertainty for foreign direct investments. However, the effect of this link on unemployment is unclear, unlike that in the two previous cases. An exporting firm may respond to exchange rate uncertainty by deciding to switch part of his production to the country where it is sold. In that way, revenue in a foreign currency (assuming that this is normally the invoice currency for export contracts) can be set against costs in the same currency. The attraction of this is that it reduces the influence of exchange rate changes on the profitability of foreign sales. This transition to a position as a multinational reduces employment in the home country but increases it in the host country. Worldwide, this need have no effect on unemployment: employment is merely reallocated between countries. It is also unclear which countries will suffer and which will benefit in terms of economic welfare from this reallocation.

14.5   Exchange rate systems and policy

Before discussing the influence of the exchange rate on the effectiveness of economic policy, it is necessary to describe the different exchange rate systems which a country can choose. The extremes as far as exchange rate systems are concerned are floating and fixed exchange rate systems, i.e. totally free-floating exchange rates and totally fixed exchange rates. In practice, people are often inclined to talk about floating and fixed exchange rates although they are concerned not with the extremes but with modified, intermediate forms. The reason is that floating or fixed exchange rates hardly ever occur in practice in their pure form. A system of floating exchange rates is also often called a flexible exchange rate system.

In the case of *floating exchange rates*, the monetary authorities of a country make no attempt to influence the level of the exchange rate of their currency. This means that they refrain from *foreign exchange market intervention.* Normally, among a country's monetary authorities, it is the central bank that intervenes in the foreign exchange market. For that purpose it holds a stock of international monetary reserves.[3] The bulk of these is usually made up of gold and freely convertible currencies held by the central bank. International monetary reserves are simple, easy and cheap to sell for domestic currency.[4] By selling reserves on the gold or foreign exchange market in exchange for domestic currency, a central bank supports its own currency. This is because the demand which it creates for its own currency drives up its price against that of other currencies. Conversely, a central bank can also have a demand for components of the international monetary reserves. Paying for them in domestic currency causes the latter's price to fall. Thus, a central bank has the power to influence the value of its own currency in both ways in relation to that of foreign currencies and possibly, if desired, to stabilise that value.

We refer to *fixed exchange rates* if the rate can only fluctuate within a small margin around a par value, also known as peg, parity or central rate. The reason for permitting such a margin is that it is technically impossible to keep the exchange rate totally fixed. A central bank cannot react to every small change in the exchange rate by making an adjustment. A small margin of fluctuation for

---

3. There are many similar names used for these, such as international reserves, monetary reserves and international liquidities. For a more precise definition of this term, see Chapter 2.

4. Nowadays, gold is the odd man out. Its position in international monetary reserves dates back to the days of the gold standard (see Chapter 17), when gold was central to the international monetary system. It has now lost that position altogether.

the exchange rate does not cause any problems as regards certainty for international goods traders either. Thus, we can certainly refer to a fixed exchange rate if the rate fluctuates only within a margin of, for instance, just a few percentage points on either side of the par value. The par value is the officially fixed relationship between two currencies.

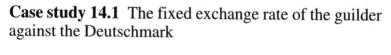

Case study 14.1 The fixed exchange rate of the guilder against the Deutschmark

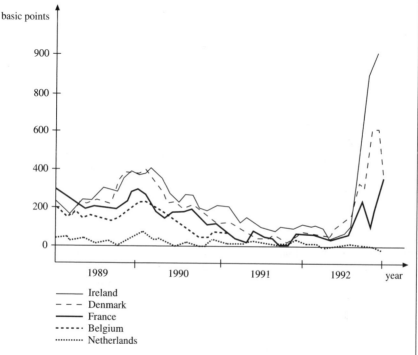

Figure 14.1 Interest rate differentials in the ERM*
* A line shows the national interest rate's deviation from the German rate, both on three-month interbank deposits. A positive value means a higher non-German rate.
Source: 'The ERM in 1992', *European Economy*, no. 54, 1993, p. 148.

One of the few fixed exchange rates in the world is currently the guilder/ Deutschmark rate. Although until August 1993 under the Exchange Rate Mechanism (ERM) of the EMS (see Chapter 18), a fluctuation margin of 2.25 per cent on either side of the central rate was formally agreed for the exchange rate (i.e. a total fluctuation band of 4.5 per cent), the Netherlands aims at a 1 per cent margin on either side of the central rate. Since March 1983 the central rate for the guilder/ mark has been fixed at NLG 1.12 per mark.

It is noticeable, but not surprising, that such a fixed rate is associated with interest rates in the Netherlands and Germany which apparently hardly deviate from one another. Other countries in the Exchange Rate Mechanism do not have interest rates which are so close to those in Germany. The explanation lies in the uncovered interest rate parity, shown in equation (13.14). If financial market traders are convinced that the guilder and the Deutschmark are permanently and irrevocably linked, the expected change in the exchange rate for these currencies will tend towards zero. According to equation (13.14), this leads to a strong convergence of the two national interest rates. Figure 14.1 illustrates this.

Intervention in the foreign exchange market is not the only instrument, and not even the most powerful one, which the central bank has at its disposal for defending a fixed exchange rate. In general, interest changes have a greater influence on the exchange rate. Furthermore, the advantage of interest rate adjustments over exchange market intervention is that there is virtually no limit to the use of the interest rate instrument for defending a flagging currency. Both these statements need explaining.

The stock of international monetary reserves is, of course, limited. World-wide, the value of these stocks totalled $1,538 billion at the end of 1994. In April 1992 the figure was $1,278 billion.[5] On those dates the foreign currency component of the monetary reserves was respectively $1,120 billion and $898 billion. Compared with the daily turnover on the world's foreign exchange markets, estimated at over $1,000 billion per day in April 1992, according to Chapter 2, these figures are of the same order of magnitude. This leads to the important conclusion that in terms of size, the reserves are a minor instrument for resisting a wave of speculation against particular currencies. Once the reserves have been used up, the central bank has no ammunition left. True, in such a case a creditworthy country can borrow additional reserve funds from other central banks or on the international capital market itself, but that does not alter the fact that there is little scope for foreign exchange market intervention to counter sentiment on those markets.

With interest rate changes the situation is different. A country can, in principle, raise the interest rate to a very high level – and in practice that does happen. In the industrial countries, a central bank occasionally actually raises the short-term rate to several hundred per cent in order to defend the exchange rate! Naturally this is done for only a limited period because the aim is to discourage foreign exchange speculators, who mostly work on a time-scale of a few weeks maximum.

The theoretical basis for using the *interest rate instrument* is the uncovered interest rate parity, as shown in equation (13.13). Here we see that if foreign

---

5. This figure was obtained by calculations based on information from the IMF, *International Financial Statistics*, September 1992 and May 1995. The gold in the reserves is valued at market price – not the official gold price.

exchange speculators believe a currency will depreciate, the term 'expected relative change in the exchange rate' has a high value. The central bank in charge of the currency concerned will have to set the interest rate differential with the other country at the same level as this value to create an opposing force. Only then will there be no speculative flow of capital out of that currency. A very high interest rate may then be necessary, as we see from Case study 14.2.[6]

Case study 14.2 The interest rate weapon against capital flight

In a system of fixed exchange rates it is understandable that central banks will often still adhere grimly to the fixed exchange value when rates are out of balance. It is not immediately apparent whether the imbalance is a transitory or permanent disruption of the equilibrium. And only in the latter case should an exchange rate adjustment be considered. Another reason for this immobility is the fear that devaluation will cause loss of prestige for the country. The imbalance in the value of the exchange rate can then be aggravated, and in that case the tension will have to be released sooner or later. It is common to see a flight of capital out of an overvalued currency. This flight is encouraged by the expectation that the value of the currency concerned will shortly diminish. Where there is a large increase in the imbalance over a time, it is quite conceivable for the currency to be overvalued by, for example, 10 per cent. Say a foreign exchange speculator thinks there is an 80 per cent chance of the fixed rate falling within four days, as a result of speculative pressure. The flight out of the threatened currency – with the intention of returning as soon as the devaluation has taken place – provides the speculator – according to his own expectations – with an average exchange gain of $0.8 \cdot 10\% + 0.2 \cdot 0\% = 8\%$ within four days. Converted to an annual basis, a profit of 8 per cent in four days based on a 360-day year is equal to $360/4 \times 8\% = 720\%$! If a central bank is to resist such speculators' expectations, then we must think in terms of a short-term interest rate of at least 720 per cent on an annual basis. Only at such a level can a foreign exchange speculator be indifferent between a four-day investment abroad or at home. Obviously, a policy like this, due to disruption on the domestic money market, can only be maintained for a short time. And the speculator knows that too, so that it may be a question of who can hold out longer: the monetary authorities or the speculators.

The uncovered interest rate parity also shows that once the fixed exchange rate policy becomes credible, interest rates in the countries concerned will have to be virtually the same; because the term 'expected relative change in the exchange rate' in the parity is then in fact reduced to zero, so that the difference between the domestic and foreign interest rate must also have disappeared

---

6. In section 14.3, spending policy appeared as an instrument for supporting the exchange rate. It is not mentioned here because it is not a responsive policy instrument. Both the decision to use it and its implementation take quite a long time. Spending policy is therefore not a suitable means of temporary support for an exchange rate.

entirely. A small variation between the two interest rates immediately prompts a large flow of private capital in the direction of the higher interest rate, and that could yet undermine the fixed exchange rate. The high credibility of the fixed exchange rate between the guilder and the Deutschmark explains the minimal difference remaining between Dutch and German interest rates in Case study 14.1.

The monetary authorities also keep an eye on the 'expected relative change in the exchange rate' in their foreign exchange market intervention policy. For their part, foreign exchange speculators do not know everything, and are only too well aware of it. If they are hesitant in certain situations, then they are susceptible to signals from the central bank. If in such a situation the bank takes firm, convincing action to support the currency by market intervention, that will affect the expectation of the speculators about a change in the exchange rate. Foreign exchange speculators may back off as a result of this *signalling effect*. They then use the central bank's (presumably) good insight into the future exchange rate to justify the revision of their own behaviour. The tendency to follow central banks will be all the greater if several central banks decide on joint, *coordinated intervention* in the foreign exchange market to support a currency which is under pressure. This is the psychology of intervention, and with good timing it can certainly be very important for the market. The signalling function of intervention lacks this psychological effect, or even works the opposite way, if market intervention appears to be unfounded. If the central bank loses the 'game' with the speculators and the value of the currency falls in spite of the (coordinated) support operation, then the central bank has once again lost some of its credibility in the eyes of the foreign exchange speculators. Intervention on the foreign exchange market then loses its signalling effect.

If a fixed exchange rate can no longer be defended with the aid of market intervention and interest rate changes, then the only real recourse left to the monetary authorities in the country with the overvalued currency is to adjust the value of the exchange rate. An exchange rate system which permits such a one-off adjustment in the central rate is called an *adjustable peg system*. After the Second World War this system was used throughout the world and still holds a prominent position, namely in the European Monetary System (EMS). It is a genuine intermediate form between floating and fixed exchange rates. The basic pattern of an adjustable peg system is illustrated in Figure 14.2.

The par value (the broken line) is adjusted at times t_1 and t_2. This means that the rate, including the fluctuation band (the distance between the two continuous horizontal lines) moves to a new level. The exchange rate can move freely within the fluctuation band. There is then no formal need for any intervention in the foreign exchange market, although *intramarginal intervention* (intervention while the rate is within the margins) may actually make sense: a central bank can thereby avoid being cornered as the limits of the fluctuation band are approached. On the other hand, in the case of a rather broad fluctuation band there can be advantages in letting the rate move to the limit of the margin: in that situation the foreign exchange speculator gambling on a devaluation is exposed

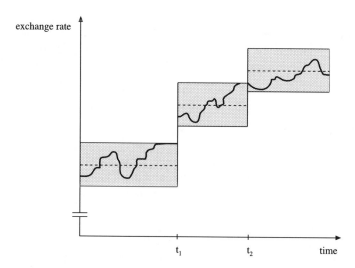

Figure 14.2 An exchange rate system with an adjustable peg

to a substantial exchange rate risk. If a currency which is under pressure recovers after all, it can soon gain several percentage points in value within the band. This danger will moderate the speculator's activity.

Three other exchange rate systems found in practice are the target zone, the crawling peg and the managed floating exchange rate. The *target zone* has attracted considerable attention in recent years in plans for establishing a new adjustable peg system throughout the world. The idea is a cautious form of adjustable peg system with a fluctuation margin of 10 per cent on either side of the central rate for the world's leading currencies. A *crawling peg* is an adjustable peg whereby parity adjustments are made regularly in small stages. The system became notorious because it was applied by various developing countries in Latin America with very high rates of inflation. The large inflation differential with countries such as the United States forced these countries to make a great many adjustments to the central rate. But under more moderate conditions such a system may certainly have its attractions. If the exchange rate changes are small, it is possible that the fluctuation bands will partly overlap as a result of the frequent parity adjustments. That is the case in Figure 14.2, for example, with the adjustment at time t_2. Such situations generate uncertainty among speculators because even if the rate adjustment which they expect is actually made, they can still suffer a foreign exchange loss. This in fact occurs in Figure 14.2 at t_2, because immediately after the adjustment – when the speculative pressure is over – the exchange rate recovers so that, in spite of the new par value, it remains below the old level of the upper intervention bound for quite a time.

A *managed floating exchange rate* exists if the spontaneous movements of the floating rate are toned down from time to time. The central banks enter the foreign exchange market on occasion, using intervention to resist the expected imminent (further) change in the exchange rate. If the domestic currency is weakening, it is supported by selling foreign currencies, while conversely a strengthening currency is countered by the purchase of foreign currencies. This rather free intervention policy is known as 'leaning against the wind'.

14.6 Monetary policy

When we refer to the effectiveness of economic policy, we always mean the sensitivity of domestic policy objectives to a particular change in the intensity of that policy. The level of domestic production is normally in the forefront of domestic policy objectives.

The effectiveness of monetary policy is supported by a variable exchange rate, as may be seen from the following example. Say the government of a country believes that the economy is temporarily bogged down and needs stimulating. It decides on a temporary increase in the money supply. This monetary expansion leads to a decline in interest rates at a given level of demand for money. In the absence of free international capital movements, we can assume that this will stimulate investment and consumer demand, prompting an increase in domestic demand. This is followed by an increase in domestic production.

However, in the case of freedom of movement for international capital, the picture is different. To make a proper assessment of the relevance of international capital movements to this adjustment process after a change of policy, one should remember that nowadays most Western industrial countries' international capital movements are highly liberalised. In that situation, by virtue of the uncovered interest rate parity, the cut in the domestic interest rate will first discourage domestic investment in favour of investment abroad. In the case of free international capital movements, the result is a massive outflow of capital, manifested on the foreign exchange market as a large increase in both the supply of domestic currency and demand for foreign currency. When the exchange rate is *floating*, both factors contribute to a substantial depreciation of the domestic currency. Owing to the high mobility of international capital and the speed of operation by players in these markets, this effect will be rapidly and clearly felt.

The tendency toward depreciation is further encouraged by the subsequent gradual change in the current account on the balance of payments. Higher domestic production stimulates national income and hence also the demand for imported goods and services. The resulting deterioration in the current account also means an increase in demand for foreign currencies. As a result of the depreciation of the domestic currency, the price of home-produced goods and services becomes more attractive than that of foreign products. This stimulates exports while also causing part of the demand for imports to be switched to domestic production. With the lapse of time, these changes in demand together give a second boost to domestic production. Overall, it is clear that the possibility of exchange rate changes is a major factor in the substantial effectiveness of the expansionary monetary policy.

In practice, monetary policy is seen mainly as a temporary instrument for countering the economic effects of cyclical fluctuations. When applied in the longer term, an active monetary policy aimed at the economic cycle becomes far less effective and eventually has no effect at all. The reason is that, over time, monetary expansion affects the price level. Although prices are rigid in the short term, in the longer term they may change. Monetary expansion is therefore followed in the intermediate term by a price increase of comparable relative size. The two immediate effects of monetary expansion mentioned earlier, the decline in interest rates and depreciation, which initially stimulated domestic production, thus appear eventually to become totally negated. The reason is that the eventual price increase will lead to greater demand for money, so that the initial fall in interest rates is reversed. The advantage of foreign investment is also lost. Moreover, the price increase destroys the initial improvement in competitiveness: depreciation of the domestic currency is now followed by a domestic price increase which neutralises the improvement in competitiveness. Thus, in the longer term, domestic production gains no real effect at all from the original stimuli. Breaking this relationship with the price level is the only way for an expansionary monetary policy, and equally a depreciation, to have a permanent, positive effect on domestic production.

If the exchange rate is *fixed*, monetary policy aimed at domestic production has little hope of being effective. Actually, this is already true in the short term. In the previous example, the fall in interest rates is initially maintained for a time as a result of monetary expansion under a fixed exchange rate. But with international capital mobility the subsequent adjustment process is fundamentally different. Through the capital outflow, the fall in the rate of interest threatens to lead to depreciation of the domestic currency. But in a system of fixed exchange rates, that is not permitted, so the central bank has to avoid the threatened fall in the exchange rate. The primary instrument for that purpose is central bank intervention in the foreign exchange market. By selling monetary reserves in exchange for domestic currency, the central bank increases the supply of foreign currency while at the same time reducing supply of its own currency. Both changes support the value of the domestic currency against foreign currencies. However, in so doing the central bank takes money out of circulation, thus counteracting and even totally neutralising the initial monetary expansion. The monetary stimulus is cancelled out – if not immediately then after a time – by the rules of the fixed exchange rate system. Only then the domestic interest rate regains its original value at which there was no capital outflow.

In many cases under fixed exchange rates the monetary boost will not even produce a fleeting effect. Certainly if the country in question is small in comparison with the rest of the world and capital movements respond immediately to yield incentives, the prompt reaction by international capital movements means that the slightest tendency towards declining interest rates will disappear immediately owing to the required intervention on the foreign exchange market which we have just described. This in fact means that the domestic money supply and domestic interest rate do not really get the chance to change, since the central bank has to buy up exactly the same quantity of domestic currency as it initially created via monetary expansion. Only then will the interest rate ultimately remain unchanged. As a result of the need for a fixed exchange rate, there is therefore nothing left of the monetary expansion, and hence no effect at all on domestic production will last. Under fixed exchange rates, autonomous monetary expansion, independent of other countries, is not really possible, even in the short term. In any case it has no effect!

Case study 14.3 Dutch exchange rate policy

In March 1983 the Netherlands devalued the guilder by 2 per cent against the Deutschmark. Opinions on this were clearly divided among Dutch policy-makers. The Finance Ministry was in favour of the devaluation, the central bank was against it. The Ministry hoped that, by improving the competitive position in relation to the principal trading partner, Germany, the devaluation would help to reduce unemployment in the Netherlands. According to the central bank, devaluation would at best have only a temporary effect on employment, whereas a constant guilder/mark rate would have a permanent, positive effect on employment. The Dutch central bank got its way to some extent in that the Finance Minister promised that this devaluation would be the last. So far that promise remains unbroken.

The Dutch central bank's position was – and still is – based on the following view. In the Netherlands, wages were at that time totally index-linked. Devaluation will produce a general price rise via an increase in import prices. In the situation of index-linkage, wages react to this, initiating a wage/price spiral. The resulting price increase soon destroys any competitive advantage initially gained from a devaluation. In that respect – except in the adjustment period – nothing is gained in comparison with a situation without devaluation. However, there is a great advantage in refraining from devaluation. Then the financial markets notice that the guilder is a strong currency, in that it can keep pace with the Deutschmark. As a result, like the mark, the guilder acquires the aura of a currency with a tendency to revalue. In the context of the uncovered interest rate parity, this means that the expected value of the guilder increases. This makes it more attractive to invest capital in the Netherlands, and gives the Netherlands scope to cut interest rates. As a result, domestic demand for investment and consumer goods receives a permanent boost and that in turn promotes employment, or so the argument goes.

The disadvantage for the Netherlands of this exchange rate policy is that monetary policy cannot continue to be used to provide a (temporary) stimulus for the economy and hence employment. Since the exchange rate of the guilder is irrevocably linked to the Deutschmark, the Netherlands cannot afford to let interest rates decline in relation to those in Germany. It would immediately lead to a massive outflow of capital. Dutch monetary policy is therefore used entirely to keep the Dutch interest rate in line with the German – for better or worse. That was also true in the early 1990s when the interest rate was maintained at a high level in Germany because of the economic consequences of German reunification. The economic situation in the Netherlands made it desirable to cut the Dutch interest rates, but that was not permitted by Dutch exchange rate policy. Figure 14.1 has already shown how Dutch and German interest rates move in parallel. We also see that the *nominal* interest rate in the Netherlands is among the lowest for the EMS countries shown, thanks to this exchange rate policy.

14.7 Fiscal policy

Just as we did for monetary policy, we shall first analyse the effectiveness of fiscal policy under floating exchange rates and then under fixed exchange rates.

An expansionary fiscal policy is reflected in an increased difference between government spending and tax revenue. This policy may take the form of higher public spending, but also a cut in taxes. In the latter case, growth in demand for goods comes not from the government but from the private sector, where lower taxes mean a higher disposable income.

Let us take an increase in public spending as an example of an expansionary fiscal policy. In a situation where the factors of production are not fully utilised, this will stimulate domestic production. But not only that: it also increases the demand for money, since the public wishes to hold a larger amount of cash for the purpose of transactions. For a given money supply, this will drive up interest rates. The increased demand for goods will be directed partly at domestic goods, but also partly at foreign goods. Higher imports will cause a deterioration in the trade balance. However, in the case of free international capital movements, this effect on the balance of payments via demand for imports is nothing like as great as the influence of the higher interest rate on the capital account. By virtue of the uncovered interest rate parity, a slight increase in the interest rate immediately attracts huge volumes of capital from abroad.

With *floating* exchange rates, this means an immediate increase in the value of the domestic currency because of the dominant effect of capital movements, causing a deterioration in the competitive position. This prompts a shift in demand at home and abroad in favour of foreign goods at the expense of demand for domestic production. The initial increase in demand for domestic goods generated by the increase in public spending is therefore cancelled out by the exchange rate effect. This depresses domestic production. The concomitant fall in demand for transaction funds brings the domestic interest rate back down from its initially higher level. This adjustment process continues until the increase in the value of the domestic currency has reduced demand for and production of home-produced goods sufficiently that the upward movement of money demand and thus interest rates is totally neutralised. For this, the decline in demand must be equal to the original increase in demand brought about by higher public spending. Demand for domestic goods is then back to the original level, so that domestic production has also reverted to the original level. Overall, the expansionary fiscal policy has therefore forfeited all influence over the level of production. In other words, fiscal policy is ineffective under floating exchange rates.

In a *fixed* exchange rate system the adjustment process following an expansionary fiscal policy will differ from the process described above as soon as the value of the domestic currency threatens to rise. Since under fixed exchange rates that is unacceptable, the threatened rise has to be resisted. To this end, the central bank has to counterbalance the huge supply of foreign currency on the foreign exchange market (in order to be able to acquire the domestic currency). For the central bank, this means buying foreign currencies – in favour of the bank's international monetary reserves – in return for domestic currency. This increases the quantity of money in the hands of the private sector (being non-banks) and hence the domestic money supply. The effect is a reduction of the interest rate. This domestic cut in the interest rate gives a second boost to domestic demand. Just as under floating exchange rates, this process continues until the domestic interest rate has returned to its original level. Only then is there an end to the inflow of capital necessitating foreign exchange market inter-vention. International capital movements combined with fixed exchange rates are thus essentially the reason for the second boost to domestic demand. We can therefore conclude that, in a system of fixed exchange rates, an expansionary fiscal policy is extremely effective. Not only does this expansion in itself stimulate domestic production: the increase in the money supply resulting from the obligatory foreign exchange market intervention is another contributory factor.

14.8   Summary

1.   In this chapter we saw that exchange rate fluctuations can:
   (a) permanently inhibit international trade;
   (b) promote domestic inflation; and
   (c) aggravate unemployment.
2.   The negative influence of variable exchange rates on trade is exerted via greater exchange rate uncertainty and stronger demands for protection on the part of domestic producers. The level of protection can sometimes have a downwards, ratchet effect so that there is the danger of a structural increase in protection in spite of symmetrical exchange rate fluctuations – without any trends in the exchange rate movements.
3.   A variable or flexible exchange rate stimulates domestic inflation via the cost of hedging the exchange rate uncertainty and the absence of the disciplinary effect produced by a fixed exchange rate. It is not only the policy-makers who lack discipline but also the economic subjects in the private sector, such as the trade unions. Another factor stimulating domestic inflation is the ratchet effect, whereby depreciation of the currency generates

higher inflation but an increase in its value produces a much smaller fall in inflation.

4. A variable exchange rate causes more unemployment via the said effects on international trade and inflation, but also via an increase in frictional unemployment and the asymmetrical reaction to devaluations and revaluations on account of the initial investment (sunk costs) which a company has to make in order to launch new exports.

5. A variable exchange rate also has an influence on foreign direct investment via the associated exchange rate uncertainty. It causes a direct shift in employment from the home country to the host country of the companies concerned. In a worldwide context there is probably hardly any employment effect.

6. Exchange rate systems vary greatly, with purely floating and fixed exchange rates as the two extremes. In the latter case the central bank is responsible for the currency concerned, and is obliged to defend the fixed rate. For that purpose it has the interest rate weapon and international monetary reserves which it can use to intervene on the foreign exchange market. Such intervention does not only have a direct effect on the exchange rate, but also has a signalling effect on the foreign exchange market: by their intervention central banks express their view of the equilibrium value of exchange rates. If foreign exchange speculators and other market operators believe in the central banks concerned – and hence in their view – they will be guided by the rate advocated by the central banks. This holds true particularly when the private speculators are uncertain themselves about the future exchange rate movements. In following the central bank's view, speculators will in fact support the bank's intervention activity via their buying and selling behaviour. Other relevant exchange rate systems are based on: the adjustable peg, the crawling peg and the managed floating exchange rate (in order of increasing exchange rate freedom).

7. Under fixed exchange rates and free international capital movements – the latter is quite commonly the case nowadays – *monetary policy* cannot influence domestic production in either the short or the long term; in other words, monetary policy has no effect. In contrast, under floating exchange rates monetary policy is very effective in the short run. In the longer term that effectiveness declines and eventually is also lost as monetary policy makes its influence felt on wages and prices.

8. In the case of *fiscal policy*, the effect on economic activity is precisely the opposite: with free capital movements this policy is effective in influencing domestic production under fixed exchange rates, but not under floating rates.

Bibliography

Bergsten, C.F. and J. Williamson (1983), Exchange rates and trade policy, in W.R. Cline (ed.), *Trade Policy in the 1980s,* Institute for International Economics.

Froot, K.A. and P.D. Klemperer (1989), Exchange rate pass-through when market share matters, *American Economic Review,* vol. 79, pp. 637–54.

Goldstein, M. (1984), The exchange rate system: lessons of the past and options for the future, *IMF Occasional Paper,* no. 30, Washington D.C.

Grauwe, P. de (1989), Exchange rate variability and the slowdown in growth of international trade, *IMF Staff Paper,* vol. 35, pp. 63–84.

Jager, H. (1979), The impact of the exchange rate system on the effectiveness and implementation of stabilization policy in the Netherlands, *De Economist,* vol. 127, pp. 143–86.

Krugman, P.R. (1987), Pricing to market when the exchange rate changes, in S.W. Arndt and J.D. Richardson (eds), *Real-Financial Linkages among Open Economies,* MIT Press, pp. 49–70.

15 International risks: forms and cover

15.1 Introduction

Business is associated with uncertainty and hence with risks. For that, the entrepreneur does not even need to trade internationally. Even if he operates exclusively in his own country, he is subject to various business risks. However, there are grounds for arguing that internationalising transactions increases the business risks. Both the types of risk and the level of the risks already applicable to the home country normally increase as a result. An apt example of the first, which relates to the preceding chapters, is the exchange rate risk. This can only occur if a company has international transactions, i.e. if it is involved in a form of international trade, foreign production or international credit. An example of the increase in risks which also apply at home is the risk of default. Since some part of the customers is now located abroad, there is perhaps a greater risk of being caught out by defaulting debtors. In most cases a supplier has less information on foreign than on domestic customers.

This chapter describes the expansion and intensification of the business risks at financial level ensuing from the internationalisation of a company's activities. The argument is based on the financial risks incurred by a company at home. What are they and what does internationalisation add to them? In this chapter we shall use the term 'company' in a broad sense: sometimes it applies to an industrial company, or a financial business such as a commercial bank. Another time it is an investment company. We shall review a range of risks such as credit or debtor risk and market risk in the case of purely domestic transactions, and country risk, political risk or sovereign risk, policy risk, transfer risk, exchange rate risk, transaction risk, economic risk and translation risk in the case of typical international business activities. We shall see that for a good understanding of these types of risks it is important that the description be set in a clear framework so that the mutual connections and differences become apparent. After the description of the risks, this chapter reviews the options available to an entrepreneur for reducing these risks – and perhaps eliminating them altogether.

15.2 Country and exchange rate risks

The most obvious financial risk for a company lies in the possibility that interest on and redemption of an outstanding claim will not be paid in accordance with the original agreements. This is the *credit* or *debtor risk*. The agreed annual sum for redemption and interest payment together is known as the debt service. Breach of the original agreements may concern only the interest payment or the redemption of the principal, but it may also concern both debt service components at once. The international dimension of the credit or debtor risk is in one way merely an extension of the creditworthiness of individual foreign debtors, but there are additional complications. Different practices and customs, and different views of business ethics abroad, can easily cause misjudgment of the foreign contracting party. Moreover, in a typical international transaction one encounters additional risks due to particular legal, social and political developments in the debtor's country. These risks, which are obviously specific to particular countries are collectively known as country risk or sovereign risk.[1]

One aspect of the *country risk* is the risk of war, revolution, expropriation of foreign property (with compensation) and confiscation (seizure) of foreign property; this is expropriation without compensation. In these cases we refer to the *political risk*. It is also possible that, under the macro-economic policy of the debtor's country, the debtor may be unable to service his debt. A common danger is the *transfer risk*; this occurs if government restrictions on the use of foreign exchange prevent the foreign debtor from converting the funds available for the debt service from domestic currency into a payment in foreign currency to another country. The transfer risk forms part of the much larger area of what we might call *policy risk*. This covers all government economic intervention which may have the side effect of influencing the value or payment of the foreign debt service. For example, a highly restrictive government policy will seriously damage economic growth in the debtor's country. As a result, the debtor's business may get into such great difficulty that the debtor defaults. Finally, the country risk also comprises the *legal risk*. This includes the risk that legal rules abroad may be less favourable for the position of a creditor than in his own country. For an exporter, recovery in the case of default is often much more difficult than in his own country. The principal difference between a national and an international claim is that the first implies a legal obligation to repay which can be enforced through the courts. That is not the case for an international claim. The means by which a foreign debtor can be made to meet his financial obligations are only indirect. Thus, one can try to exclude the unwilling debtor from international (export) credit in future. Experience in a country may even show that court rulings tend to be unfavourable to foreigners. That is another aspect of the legal risk.

To sum up, we can state that the country risk forms part of the credit or debtor risk. The country risk can in turn be broken down into the political risk, the policy risk (including the transfer risk) and the legal risk.

The holder of financial assets is subject not only to a credit or debtor risk on

---

1. It should be pointed out that the specific content of the risk terms which follow may vary from one author to another. The meaning attributed to the terms here is dictated partly by the need for clear distinctions and logical coordination of the content with the name.

these assets, but also a market risk. *Market risk* applies if the price of these assets may change. The amount of wealth tied up in the financial assets is then liable to change. We are familiar with this in the case of equities and bonds; their market prices are constantly changing. On the other hand, bank deposits are not subject to market risk. The holder of foreign financial assets faces an additional element of market risk, namely the *exchange rate risk*, also known as the *currency risk*. In the case of a foreign investment, the asset holder sees the price change not only if there is a change in the price of the asset expressed in the foreign currency. Also if there is a change in the exchange rate linking the foreign currency concerned to the currency of the asset holder's country of residence, for the asset holder the asset price will change. As a result of the exchange rate risk, also a person holding a foreign bank deposit is subject to a market risk although there is no change in the value of the credit balance expressed in the foreign currency concerned. It is then only the exchange rate that causes uncertainty over the value.

Exchange rate risk occurs in three forms: transaction risk, economic risk and translation risk. These are the subject of the next section. For simplicity, the exchange rate risk will be considered from the point of view of a firm exporting goods or services. However, the exchange rate risk – in all three forms – applies equally to other international economic activities.

15.3 Forms of exchange rate risk

15.3.1 Transaction risk

For an exporter or importer, the most obvious variant of the exchange rate risk is the *transaction risk*. This concerns the possibility that the financial outcome of a transaction may ultimately differ from the initial expectation as a result of an exchange rate alteration in the period between commencement and completion of the transaction.

In the case of an international transaction, both exporter and importer naturally prefer the price to be expressed in their own currency, because that avoids the transaction risk. At the start of the transaction they know exactly how much of their own currency they will receive or have to pay. However, either the exporter or the importer will be unable to have his preference: the price on the invoice can only be stated in one currency at a time. The other party is then saddled with the transaction risk. The choice of invoice currency depends on the market position of exporter and importer. If the entrepreneur has market power, it will be very easy for him to impose his own preference. Roughly speaking, around one third of international goods and services transactions are invoiced in the exporter's currency and one third in the importer's currency. At first sight this seems strange, because the currency of the exporter or importer appears to be the obvious choice. But then the shares would have to add up to one. The explanation lies in the widespread use of a third currency for pricing and invoicing international transactions. In the majority of cases it is the US dollar. The reason for this choice is that the daily volume of trading in the US dollar is very great so that this currency can easily be bought or sold – without any detrimental effect on the exchange rate: the dollar market is deep and therefore liquid. The dollar also has an exceedingly well-developed system of supplementary financial markets, such as forward, option and futures markets. It is therefore very easy and relatively cheap to hedge the exchange rate risk on the dollar in comparison with that on other currencies.

Thus, in the case of an international transaction, a transaction risk arises for at least one of the parties involved. This risk may endure for a long period, as there is often a considerable time lapse between the start of the transaction, when the contract is signed, and the end of the transaction when payment is made. Usually it takes some time before an order (or the signing of the contract) is executed by the delivery of the goods. Not only does it take time to transport the goods; a firm often also produces to order, so that the production time has to be taken into account. It is customary for the seller to tempt the buyer with supplier's credit (in the case of an international transaction, this is export credit). The credit period begins on delivery of the goods and ends on the date of payment. From the signing of the contract to the date of payment, a contracting party is exposed to a transaction risk, at least in so far as the contract price is stated in a foreign currency.

For large transactions such as the supply of capital goods (ships, aircraft and the like) and the execution of infrastructure work (constructing airfields, ports, etc.), the signing of the contract is preceded by a period in which the transaction risk already exists. This type of transaction begins when the exporter submits a tender, including a quotation. As soon as the tender has been submitted, this exporter is subject to a transaction risk. In the period up to acceptance of the tender by the importer the exchange rate may change to the disadvantage of the potential exporter. A factor which complicates tendering is that the exporter is not certain that this risk will actually arise, because that depends entirely on the importer's eventual decision whether to accept the bid. As we shall see in sub-section 15.5.2, this kind of uncertainty makes it more difficult but not impossible to hedge the transaction risk in this phase.

15.3.2   Economic risk

Following on from the transaction risk there is a second variant of the exchange rate risk, namely the *economic risk*. Future exchange rate changes may not only have an adverse effect on revenue from current transactions, they may actually impair the profitability of all a company's future export revenue. We call this the economic risk. It thus extends further than the transaction risk and now also concerns unknown future transactions. The essential point is the possible effect on the international competitive position of the business in question in the future. Of course, this risk not only applies to an exporter. It may even apply to a company producing solely for the home market, which constantly has to contend with the threat of foreign competition on the home market. In fact, this kind of risk holds true for producers of all goods which can be traded internationally. In this case, appreciation of the domestic currency means a deterioration in the competitive position of the company concerned, which will have to expect a lower price in terms of the domestic currency and/or a lower volume of sales. Production costs expressed in domestic currency, however, are often more or less fixed. The appreciation of the domestic currency then damages the profitability of the company. This is a common form of economic risk.

As was already argued in section 14.2, the real bane of the exchange rate risk lies in this economic risk. The company's management has great difficulty in controlling this risk, because it cannot be hedged. The future period to which it relates is too long and the size of the sum at risk is too uncertain. There are many problems in attempting to quantify the economic risk, as may be seen from the following questions, which an exporter needs to answer in order to quantify the risk:

- How is the exchange rate going to move in future? This concerns not only an accurate prediction of the exchange rate against the currency of the country to which goods are being exported, but also against the currencies of competing suppliers on this market.
- How sensitive is foreign demand to an increase in the price of our products compared to those of competitors?
- How sensitive is the cost side of the business to the appreciation of the domestic currency? Each component of the production costs (wages, financing costs, raw materials, semi-manufactures) then has to be considered.
- How quickly and to what degree can the cost side be restructured in the case of permanent appreciation of the domestic currency? The restructuring must then be such as to reduce the proportion of costs in domestic currency: that is the only way of reducing the impact of the appreciation of the domestic currency on the company's profitability.

The reduction of the share of the domestic currency costs in total production costs can be brought about along two lines: cutting the costs at home and increasing the use of foreign inputs in the production process or extending foreign subsidiaries which provide for part of that process. That such a restructuring of production can be realised successfully even if massive adjustments are required, is illustrated in Case study 15.1.

Case study 15.1   Japanese restructuring in response to the high yen

Since the peak in the value of the US dollar in February 1985, the currency has shown a steep fall against the other major currencies in the world. Figure 15.1

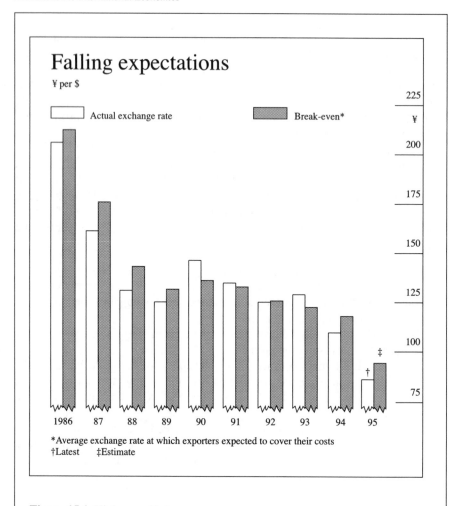

Figure 15.1 High-yen efficiency
Source: The Economist, 8 April 1995, p. 67.

displays the development of the dollar falling against the Japanese yen. Quite remarkable in this figure are the rapidly diminishing Japanese production costs. They keep pace with the fading dollar. This implied that the fall in Japanese production costs expressed in yen roughly equalled the fall of the dollar (in percentages). Japanese firms managed to achieve this through a combination of downward pressure on domestic production costs, outcontracting parts of the production to foreigners (specifically in East and South-East Asia), and setting up new firms abroad.

15.3.3 *Translation risk*

The third and last variant of the exchange rate risk is the *translation risk*. This concerns the possibility that, for a company preparing its annual balance sheet, the values of the assets and liabilities denominated in a foreign currency change on translation into the reporting currency (usually the domestic currency) under the influence of exchange rate changes during the reporting year. A company operating internationally often has a range of assets and liabilities denominated in foreign currencies, most commonly claims and debts. Other familiar forms of assets and liabilities in foreign currencies are foreign branches and foreign subsidiaries. The composition and volume of a company's assets and liabilities in foreign currencies are constantly changing. Even if the volume and currency breakdown remains the same as on the previous balance sheet date, the company still incurs a translation risk, because that risk is present as soon as the company has an *open position* in a specific foreign currency. This is the difference between the values of assets and liabilities in one and the same foreign currency. On one moment in time, a company may thus have more than one open position. The amount for which a company is exposed to the exchange rate risk, i.e. the open positions for all foreign currencies together, is known as *exposure*. In this specific case concerning the consequences for the balance sheet it is called translation exposure.

A particular characteristic of the translation risk is that its influence on the balance sheet has no connection with the operating result in the period between the balance sheet dates. Nevertheless, it influences the company's equity or profit and loss account. Another characteristic is that there are various methods of handling the valuation of the exchange rate, often with widely varying effects on the amount for which the company is exposed to the translation risk. The valuation methods allowed are linked to the principles for valuing a company's assets and liabilities. Two accounting standards are available for the non-monetary assets and liabilities (such as fixed assets, participations and stocks of goods): the closing rate method and the temporal method. According to the former the items are valued against current cost (in fact replacement costs), in the latter against historical cost. For the monetary assets (claims and debts) there is only a current cost evaluation.

In accordance with the historical cost method of valuation, a company could decide to use the historical exchange rate for its non-monetary assets and liabilities expressed in foreign currencies for the purpose of preparing the balance sheet. This defines the size of the translation exposure, because choice of this method means that business premises located in the United States, for example, and bought in a period when the exchange rate was four guilders to the dollar (roughly the position at the beginning of 1985) are now still valued at this exchange rate for the purpose of preparing the balance sheet. Thus, the effect of choosing the historical exchange rate method is that the company does not in fact incur any translation risk on foreign assets: there is no uncertainty over the exchange rate to be applied. But uncertainty does exist if the company, by analogy with the current cost method of valuation, uses the closing rate of exchange for preparing the balance sheet. The closing rate method means taking the actual exchange rate at the end of the reporting period. At the end of 1994 the exchange rate was about 1.75 guilders to the dollar. On the balance sheet date, 1 January 1995, the premises in the United States would then be valued at this exchange rate, which would mean that the value of the premises had dropped by more than 50 per cent, in terms of guilders, against the purchase price (beginning of 1985). This realistic example makes it sufficiently clear how enormously the effects on the balance sheet can vary according to the choice of exchange rate valuation method. At first sight, it is an attractive option for a company to select each year the exchange rate translation method which shows the balance sheet in the most favourable light. But that is not allowed. The company has to choose a method at a given moment and is, in principle always obliged to use the same one. A country also has guidelines on the method to be used, as Case study 15.2 shows.

Case study 15.2 Determination of the translation risk in the Netherlands[2]

In the Netherlands, the Council for Annual Reporting has issued guidelines on the exchange rate value to be selected in valuing balance sheet items. In the case of a company's foreign subsidiaries, it is important whether the activities involved are an extension of the company's own activities or whether the subsidiary is independent. In the first case the guidelines state that the temporal method should be used. This means that the reference date for the exchange rate value corresponds with the valuation principles. If a non-monetary asset is valued at historical cost, then the historical exchange rate should also be used. If an asset is valued at current cost, then the closing rate is the translation exchange rate for that asset.

Exchange rate variations between successive reporting periods have to be shown in the profit and loss account. Companies find this a serious drawback because it means that their results in the reporting year can be depressed by adverse exchange rate movements. However, this obligation does not apply in the case of independent subsidiaries. Then the instructions are to use the closing rate for all balance sheet items. But adverse changes in the exchange rate in the interim then merely have to be charged to the equity. It is partly because of this business preference that the temporal method is very rarely applied in practice. Around 90 per cent of Dutch companies use the closing rate method, and the worldwide proportion appears to be similar.

---

2. With thanks to Henk P.A.J. Langendijk for supplying the information.

15.4 Hedging the country risk

The country risk does not really seem to be capable of measurement – although attempts are made to adopt a criterion for it. Experts nevertheless agree that this type of risk is very great in various cases. As a result, the government plays an important role in insuring this risk in industrialised countries. Case study 15.3 underlines this practice.

Case study 15.3 Nederlandsche CredietverzekeringsMaatschappij (NCM – Dutch Credit Insurance Company)

In the Netherlands, the government's involvement in insuring the country risk takes place through the Nederlandsche CredietverzekeringsMaatschappij (NCM) in Amsterdam. NCM is a private insurance company which has had a reinsurance agreement with the Dutch state since 1932, reinsuring country risks and larger commercial risks. The cover provided by NCM is total: in the case of export credits, international agreements stipulate a minimum cash down payment of 15 per cent, whereas NCM offers a maximum of 95 per cent cover for an export credit (worth a maximum of 85 per cent of the selling price). In certain specific situations the country risk may be so great that the state restricts the countries for which it will provide cover. If a country's stability improves, cover for transactions with that country can be restored. In principle, the insurance premiums which Dutch enterprises have to pay to the state via NCM for country insurance are meant to cover the costs. Of course, the premiums are set in advance and any benefits are only paid out later, so that there is never any guarantee that the Dutch state will not lose money in the end. Thus, it happened that up until 1983 the balance of premiums received and claims paid out for the period since 1945 was positive for the state, while at the end of 1983 that balance was suddenly negative (Hoobroeckx, 1984, p. 90). Other bad years followed, which naturally had everything to do with the worldwide debt crisis in the 1980s (cf. Chapter 17).

Since the country risk insurance premiums are steep, a business has to consider whether to estimate the risk itself and then only insure the major risks with NCM. This approach is not usually popular with NCM, which is then landed just with the problem countries, so that the risk for NCM and hence the state naturally increases, inevitably leading to a higher insurance premium.

To estimate the country risk, a business can simply use the credit rating institutes which constantly monitor countries and give them a particular credit rating on the basis of a set scale. A business can, of course, make its own attempt to determine the creditworthiness of a country to which it plans to grant credit.

Any estimate of the size of the country risk can only be approximate: too many national aspects play a part. Particularly for the country in question there are too few cases of default to establish a statistically reliable relation between the country risk and variables which might explain it. It is therefore impossible to develop criteria which can subsequently be applied automatically, so that every assessment of the country risk has to be made individually and is therefore labour-intensive. A great deal of information plays a part in such an assessment. Banks used to make country risk assessments and do use standard assessment forms for the purpose. Case study 15.4 offers a simple example.

Case study 15.4 Assessing the country risk

Table 15.1 illustrates the considerations deemed important for determining the country risk. The weightings assigned to them are rather subjective.

The information in fact consists of a series of isolated data and ratios. Non-economic data (categories A and B) account for roughly one third of the assessment. As one would expect, the actual situation and the economic outlook (category C) are viewed mainly in the light of the current account positions, the overall balance of payments and a country's debt position. Possible reasons for a current account deficit are the growth of national product, a government budget deficit and excessive money creation. They are all incorporated in the form. On the other hand, low unemployment provides an indication of the government's freedom of action for reducing the current account deficit: at least the set of policy instruments need not also be used to tackle unemployment. The seriousness of the financial problems can be seen most directly in the level of debt and – more precisely – the debt service in relation to the value of the country's exports, both on an annual basis. This ratio expresses the percentage of the annual export revenue of the debtor country which has to be set aside to pay the financial charges associated with the foreign debt. The country cannot use that proportion of the foreign exchange revenue for the often desperately needed imports. In practice we find that the greater a country's financial problems, the less the statistical information is made available, either deliberately or due to circumstances beyond the country's control. That explains the presence of that item on the form.

In a country assessment, the options available to a country for correcting an existing, undesirable balance of payments position and for confronting unexpected adverse influences seem the most important factors. These options are assessed using information on such aspects as the country's flexibility for increasing exports, the degree of diversification in its imports and exports and the economic growth rate. One essential question, however, concerns the reason for the current account deficit. For example, if it is due to excess spending on viable investments, the funding of the deficit certainly need not be regarded as loss financing. South Korea is an example of growth financing in recent decades. It can still be worth granting credit to a country confronted by only a cyclical current account deficit or where a deficit is accompanied by a credible adjustment policy. However, in the case of structural excess consumer spending and non-viable investments, we can say that losses are being financed by foreign credit. The form in the table is inadequate to detect these situations.

Table 15.1 A country risk assessment form

	approximate weighting (%)
A Legal considerations	10
B Political considerations	25
C Economic considerations	
– Power of the government (e.g. a Danish-type minority government which finds it difficult to introduce unpopular measures compared with a British first-pass-the-post system).	6
– Assessment of current plans for the economy. Feasibility of development plans, main bottlenecks, etc. Resource base: natural and human resource, etc.	15
– Recent events and present state of the economy	
GNP growth	0.3
rate of inflation	0.6
government budget position	0.6
money supply growth	0.3
current account balance of payments	0.3
unemployment	0.6
level of external debt	1.2
debt service ratio	1.2
latest date of published statistics	0.9
	6
– Future prospects for the economy if present trends and policies continue	
GNP growth	0.7
rate of inflation	1.3
government budget position	2.0
money supply growth	0.7
current account balance of payments	2.0
unemployment	1.3
level of external debt	2.5
debt service ratio	2.5
	13
– Ability of the country to correct adverse implications of present binds and to withstand unforeseen shocks (vulnerability)	
imports as a proportion of GDP	0.7
exports as a proportion of GDP	0.7
diversification of imports by category and by geographical area	4.6
diversification of exports by category and by geographical area	4.6
compressibility of imports (i.e. extent to which imports consist of non-essentials)	6.4
vulnerability of the economy to changing prices of main exports and imports. Energy dependence	8.0
	25
	100

Source: The Banker, January 1981, p. 74.

Determining the creditworthiness of a country on the basis of an assessment form as in Case study 15.3 merely means forming an opinion on the basis of unrelated information and ratios. Another estimating method is econometric: it uses statistical techniques to link a country's level of defaulting to measurable variables – often selected from those in Table 15.1. These are used as factors determining the risk of default. Although this method looks sound at first sight, it has also been subject to criticism. For a country which has defaulted on only a few occasions, if any, in the past, the study will use the information on other, comparable countries. Moreover, the method implicitly assumes that 'history repeats itself', although every situation is different. That is why this method is also too unreliable, although it can form one useful element of a country risk study.

15.5 Reducing the exchange rate risk

15.5.1 Traditional instruments

Exchange rate risks exist virtually as long as money is in circulation. Two national monetary systems are enough for that. It is therefore not surprising that there is a long tradition of reducing these risks, because although a risk can ultimately yield advantages and disadvantages, the prevailing need in business is still to reduce the exchange rate risk. People are risk-avoiding in that uncertainty has a negative value. The traditional instruments limiting the exchange rate risk include: leading and lagging, netting, the borrow-deposit technique and use of a forward exchange contract. These will be discussed in this sub-section. Instruments introduced more recently form the subject of the next sub-section.

Leading is the early collection of claims or payment of debts in foreign currencies; *lagging* is the opposite, namely delayed collection or payment. A contract often permits either option. If a British importer who has obtained export credit in a foreign currency from a foreign exporter expects that currency to be revalued, it may be advantageous to pay off the credit early, i.e. before the revaluation. Conversely, if the importer expects the foreign currency to be devalued, he will try to postpone paying off the loan until after the devaluation.

Netting is a useful instrument available mainly to multinationals or companies with financially autonomous divisions. If various subsidiaries of the same multinational have a complex network of mutual claims and debts in foreign currencies, frequent multilateral clearing, e.g. through the multinational's central treasury, has financial advantages for all parties concerned. Not only does this netting avoid using the foreign exchange market and the costs associated with it for the financial transactions concerned. They also achieve a lower exchange rate exposure and thus reduce the exchange rate risk for each subsidiary.

Netting may also extend to the subsidiaries' claims and debts in relation to other companies. By arranging for the exchange rate risk on claims to be covered by that on debts at central level, it is possible to achieve a substantial reduction in the multinational's exposure to exchange rate changes. The subsidiaries also gain by it. For example, say a French subsidiary A has a claim worth $1 million on an American company, while another French subsidiary B owes $2 million to a Brazilian company, both with a term of three months. By agreeing that in three months' time B will take $1 million from A to pay off B's debt at the exchange rate valid now, both A and B incur a lower exchange rate risk. They avoid the market and therefore do not have to pay transaction costs either.

A traditional instrument used by multinationals and investment companies operating abroad is the *borrow-deposit* technique. In order to limit the exchange rate risk, institutions then finance assets in foreign currencies so far as possible by creating debts in the same currencies, e.g. by issuing shares or bonds in those currencies, or via a bank loan in the currency concerned, using the proceeds to buy the assets. This rules out the translation risk in particular.

Another instrument which has long been in widespread use is the *forward exchange contract*. This is an external instrument because a company has to apply to the market for it, in this case the forward exchange market, and that entails bank charges. In a forward exchange transaction already described in Chapter 12, agreement is reached on the delivery of a specific amount of foreign currency at a particular date in the future at a price which is also fixed now in the contract. That price is called the forward exchange rate. Because they aim to make a profit, the activities of foreign exchange arbitragers in both the spot and the forward markets mean that the covered interest rate parity applies. (See section 12.3 for the form this takes and the background to it.) Firms can cover the exchange rate risk on both their claims and their debts by this method. If the claim is made available by the debtor in foreign currency at a specific moment in the future, say in three months' time, the recipient company can sell that foreign currency now on the three months' forward market. The forward rate for delivery of the foreign currency in three months' time is indicated by a bank on request. Thus, the recipient company already knows how much domestic currency it is going to receive for the foreign currency claim.

The advantage of a forward exchange transaction is the flexibility in the amount of the transaction, because the forward exchange market supplies to order so that it is possible to do a deal on any desired amount. It is therefore possible to cover the exchange rate risk in full. One disadvantage is the lack of maximum flexibility as regards maturities (half-month periods, and full-month periods for maturities in excess of three months). Forward transactions for periods in excess of two years are uncommon, so that these markets are thin and therefore quite illiquid. In order to counteract this problem of the restricted maturities for forward transactions, national credit insurance companies often offer companies facilities for concluding long-term exchange risk insurances.

15.5.2 Recent financial innovations

The following instruments are much more recent ways of reducing the exchange rate risk: currency futures, parallel loans, currency swaps and currency options. We shall now review them.

Currency futures were introduced in 1972 on the Chicago Mercantile Exchange. Chicago had over a century's experience in futures for cereals and other commodities. A currency future is very similar to a forward exchange contract and can be regarded as a standardised forward contract. It is denominated in round sums, available for a limited number of currencies and, like a forward contract, has a set maturity; the number of maturities available is strictly limited. This standardisation makes a futures contract relatively cheap: for example, in the UK it costs less than 1 per cent of the value of the underlying transaction, compared with 20–25 basis points in the cash market. Standardisation also means that it is readily negotiable. It is perhaps less useful to a commodities trader because of the fixed amounts of currency futures, since a contract in commodities seldom comes to such a round figure. On the other hand, the foreign exchange speculator will appreciate a futures contract particularly for its good negotiability, as that greatly increases the speculator's room for manoeuvre.

In the case of futures contracts, the principle of 'marking to market' applies. This means that at the end of each day's futures trading the holder of a futures contract has to take his profit or loss. That is one reason why the holder is obliged to keep a margin with a clearing house. For example, say a holder has one futures contract in Deutschmarks (for DM 125,000 the initial margin required is $1,400). If the DM rises by $0.01 on the first day's trading on the futures market, then $1,250 (125,000 × $0.01) is added to the holder's account at the end of the day. Moreover, the original futures contract lapses and is replaced by a new contract stating the futures price of the mark at the end of that day's trading. Using this technique, the risk of serious consequences resulting from the holder's insolvency is very small on a futures contract, as the holder's losses are written down immediately. If the margin has become too small because of previous losses, then the holder has to top it up again. If he cannot, then the clearing house and the other party still do not suffer financially since the holder's losses up to that time have already been paid for. Arbitragers ensure that a close link is maintained between the prices of the two related financial instruments: futures and forward exchange contracts.

A *parallel loan* is an attractive instrument for a parent company wishing to lend money to a foreign subsidiary in the currency of the country where the subsidiary is located. During the term of the loan the parent company is exposed to an exchange rate risk. This can be avoided if there is another parent company with a subsidiary and the countries of location are exactly reversed, if here, too, the parent wishes to make a loan to the subsidiary. The two parent companies can agree to lend a particular amount to one another's subsidiaries. The great advantage of this is that the parent companies make the loan in their own currency so that there is no longer any exchange rate risk. At the end of the maturity of the loans the principal is simply paid off in the same currency in which it was lent. Another advantage is that the parent companies can thus sidestep any restrictions on capital exports and imports, because they are not exporting any capital, even though their subsidiary receives a loan; they are merely making a domestic loan. The drawback of such an arrangements is its legal complexity because four parties are involved.

Two market parties can enter into a mutual *swap contract* for currencies: this is in fact an agreement for the temporary exchange of currencies. The reason for it can be clarified by an example. Say party A would like to take out a loan leading to periodic payments of interest and repayments of principal (together called the debt service) in dollars, while another party B also wants a loan but with a periodic debt service payment in Deutschmarks. The respective currencies preferred will depend on how the two parties expect exchange rates to move and their different exchange rate exposures. For example, A has a large amount of assets in dollars and B in marks. Obviously, banks in dealing with their customers will quite commonly be facing foreign currency exposures. It will therefore not come as a surprise that the swap market mainly covers inter-bank transaction. But also for goods traders a currency swap can offer advantages. For instance, firm A could borrow directly in dollars and B in marks: then they would not need each other. However, it may be that A can borrow on more advantageous terms than B in marks and, conversely, B can borrow on better terms in dollars. This may be because A is a German company and B an American company. On their home market they are well-known – and respected – operators and can therefore extract a certain interest rate advantage. It is also possible that capital restrictions prevent A and/or B from borrowing in foreign currencies. Be that as it may, in this situation it is mutually advantageous if A takes out a loan in marks and B a loan in dollars, after which the two parties swap the two loans, including the financial obligations. Currency swaps date from the mid 1970s.

Currency options were first traded on the European Options Exchange (EOE) in Amsterdam at the end of 1982, followed by the Philadelphia Stock Exchange early in 1983.

A currency option is a financial instrument that entitles – and expressly does not oblige – the holder to buy or sell a stated amount of foreign currency at an agreed price. The right to sell is called a put option; the right to buy is a call option. There is also a distinction between an American and a European option. An American option can be exercised at any time up to a specified date. A European option confers this right on the specified date only. A currency option is a useful instrument for companies operating in a sector where tendering is the norm, such as contracting and the production of capital goods. If a Swiss company submits a tender in dollars to an American company, the Swiss company is exposed to a particular type of exchange rate risk during the period for which the tender applies. The tender may be accepted and the Swiss contractor will receive his dollars after expiry of a period stated in the tender, but that is totally uncertain because the tender may also be rejected. For the Swiss entrepreneur a forward exchange contract is then in fact too risky, because it would oblige him to supply the dollars on expiry of the term, dollars which he may not receive if the tender is not accepted. A currency option is the appropriate instrument in that case, because a put option offers the option holder the right, but not the obligation, to supply the dollars.

Like futures contracts, currency options come in standard sizes which may vary from one stock exchange to another; they are also similar in size to currency futures. The buyer of an option has to pay an option premium to the other party, the option writer. The size of the premium depends on various aspects, not least the difference between the spot rate and the strike price stated in the contract. For example, in the case of a call option for dollars, if the strike price (the price at which dollars can be bought with the option) is NLG 1.80 and the spot rate at that moment is NLG 2.00, then the option is 'in the money'. If the option holder were willing and able to exercise (i.e. use) the option at that moment, then he could buy the dollars from the option writer for NLG 1.80 and sell them immediately for NLG 2.00 on the spot market, which would be a profitable deal. This profitability potential is reflected in the level of the premium. A strike price of NLG 1.80 for the option is riskier for the writer than a strike price of, say, NLG 2.00 – or even more extreme – NLG 2.20 (then the option would be 'at the money' or 'out of the money' respectively). However, in almost all cases the premium is a few per cent, which means that currency options are expensive in comparison with currency futures. But they do have an attractive return profile for speculators, because one can hardly make a loss by holding an option. The worst conceivable situation is the case in which the holder does not exercise the option: he has then lost the premium paid on purchasing it. On the other hand, the potential profit associated with holding an option is unlimited. The higher the spot rate above the strike price on the strike date, the greater the exchange gain for the holder of a call option.

The financial innovations in foreign exchange dealing described above are classed as *derivatives*. These are contracts which give one party a claim on an underlying asset at a specified future time, the other party having a corresponding obligation. In the cases described in this section the underlying asset is of course a foreign currency. The explosive growth of derivatives in recent years has worried the central banks, as the scope for supervising this trade is limited. Moreover, derivatives cannot reduce the overall risk in the international financial system – although they can be used effectively to reduce the risks for an individual. Derivatives merely transform and reallocate the risk. There is even some concern that the risk is being concentrated in the leading commercial banks via the trade in derivatives (cf. for example Capital Market Division, 1994, p. 49). These banks are very active in some derivative markets. This makes it possible that the total risk for the financial system (*systemic risk*) will ultimately have increased.

The two graphs in Figure 15.2 give an idea of the growth of these markets in derivative instruments and the proportion of these derivatives with foreign

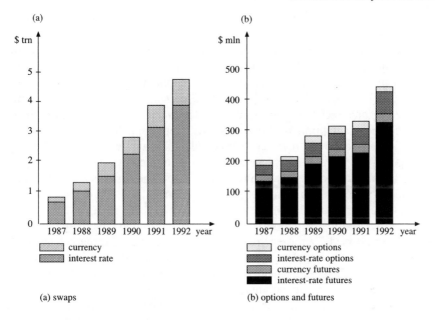

Figure 15.2 Volume of trading in derivatives
Source: The Economist, 14 May 1994, p. 22.

currencies as the underlying asset. The issue of swaps has increased five-fold in the space of five years, while trading in options and futures has roughly doubled over the same period. Derivatives in foreign currencies represent less than 20 per cent of the total in both graphs.

15.5.3   Exchange rate predictions

A company also has much to gain if the uncertainty associated with the exchange rate risk can be reduced to a calculated risk. As an alternative to the hedging instruments mentioned, it can therefore obtain an exchange rate prediction including an indication of the corresponding margin of uncertainty. Firms have three possibilities here which can also be used simultaneously.

The first possibility is to conclude a contract with an agency specialising in predicting exchange rates. This is quite an expensive proposition, while the results are generally rather disappointing. A second possibility is to have its own staff produce predictions on the basis of a qualitative or quantitative study of exchange rate fundamentals. The former may be a macro-economic analysis of the two countries concerned in the relevant exchange rate. An econometric or quantitative study examines exchange rate determinants in greater depth. If these determinants are then predicted, it is possible to produce a prediction of the exchange rate using the regression equations obtained. This method is known as *fundamental analysis.* This approach does not produce very satisfactory results either at the moment.

A third possibility is to have one's own staff producing predictions on the basis of *chart reading.* This is a method for which the only input is long time series of the actual exchange rate concerned: economic theory is not involved. It is a purely *technical analysis.* This type of study centres on the patterns produced by the exchange rate over time. This naturally concerns time in the past, and the assumption is that history will repeat itself (this applies to all statistical and economic research, incidentally). Trends, e.g. in the form of a moving average, form the simplest pattern. Other important concepts used by the 'chartists' are a support level and a resistance level. The first is seen as the lower limit of an ongoing downward trend in the exchange rate, while the resistance level is the upper limit which the market does not expect a rising rate to exceed. These market sentiments are also of psychological importance: if the assumed barriers are crossed by the exchange rate after all, then the market normally interprets this as a breakthrough, after which the trend in the rate is accentuated. Chart reading is successful mainly in making short-term predictions. A recent survey of the use of technical analysis and chart reading by foreign exchange dealers in the world's leading centre – London – appears to confirm this. In the case of exchange rate predictions of up to one month ahead, chart reading is often more widely used in practice than studying the fundamentals. Where longer prediction periods are concerned, fundamentals gain the upper hand.

The foreign exchange market is often regarded as an efficient market. One of its features is that all the relevant information on the market at any given time is always already reflected in the market price. Taking that view, historical information should not offer the opportunity to make on average an extra profit out of trading. Such information could not help to improve the market price prediction, as the relevant information is deemed to be already known to the market participants. Chart reading and technical analyses are therefore at odds with the assumption of an efficient foreign exchange market!

15.6 Summary

1. Financial risks for the business world can be divided into two broad categories: the credit or debtor risk and the market risk. Companies operating internationally do not only face these two types of risk to a greater degree than at home: the risks also appear in new forms.
2. The specifically international form of credit risk is the country risk. This concerns uncertainty due to the specific country of the debtor, and may impede the payment of outstanding claims. The country risk can be divided into the political risk (which includes the transfer risk), the policy risk and the legal risk.
3. The specifically international form of the market risk is the exchange rate risk (or currency risk). Again there are three variants: the transaction risk,

the economic risk and the translation risk. The main problem is the economic risk. The translation risk causes the least difficulties.

4. The government often plays an important role in insuring the country risk. In the Netherlands that is done via Nederlandsche Credietverzeker-ingsMaatschappij (NCM), the premium being intended to cover the costs. It is very difficult to ascertain the level of country risk because the circumstances in which a country gets into payment difficulties are not systematic. Nevertheless, quantitative and qualitative analyses of the country risk are widely used.

5. The exchange rate risk has long been countered by the use of instruments which hedge this risk in whole or in part. The traditional instruments include: leading and lagging, netting, the borrow-deposit technique and the forward exchange contract. More recent instruments are currency futures, parallel lending, currency swaps and currency options. In spite of their dynamic growth, trading in this type of derivative on the foreign exchange market still accounts for less than 20 per cent of total volume of trading in this type of instrument on the financial markets.

6. Exchange rate predictions are also widely used in an attempt to counteract the exchange rate risk. The point of such predictions is contrary to the idea that the foreign exchange market is a particularly efficient market. In that case historical information could add no useful knowledge for predicting the rate: all information is deemed to be already discounted in the current price.

Bibliography

Capital Market Division (1994), Banks and derivatives markets; a challenge for financial policy, *IMF Survey*, vol. 23, 21 February, pp. 49–51.

Committee on Banking Regulations and Supervisory Practices (1988), International convergence of capital measurement and capital standards, in De Nederlandsche Bank, *Kwartaalbericht, 1988*, no. 2, pp. 37–50.

Eaton, J., M. Gersovitz and J.E. Stiglitz (1987), The pure theory of country risk, *European Economic Review*, vol. 30, pp. 481–513.

Frankel, J.A. and A.T. MacArthur (1988), Political vs. currency premia in international real interest differentials; a study of forward rates for 24 countries, *European Economic Review*, vol. 32, pp. 1083–121.

Giddy, I.H. (1994), *Global Financial Markets*, D.C. Heath.

Hoobroeckx, J.W. (1984), Grenzen der kredietverzekering, in NIBE Jaardag, *Grenzen der kredietverlening*, NIBE publication no. 48, Amsterdam, pp. 85–125.

Meierjohann, W. (1984), Charting a course through the waves, *Euromoney*, July, pp. 157–65.

Taylor, M.P. and H. Allen (1992), The use of technical analysis in the foreign exchange market, *Journal of International Money and Finance*, vol. 11, pp. 304–14.

Torre, J. de la (1988), Forecasting political risks for international operations, *International Journal of Forecasting*, pp. 221–41.

16 International monetary cooperation

16.1 The motives

International economic relations imply a mutual economic influence between countries: exports of goods, international capital flows or changes in one country's economic policy will always influence another country to a greater or lesser degree.

International economic cooperation is prompted mainly by this mutual influence which countries have via their economic policy and subsequently through their international transactions. The 'spill-over' of one country's economic policy on the economies of other countries is usually an unintentional side effect. In welfare theory it is called an *external effect*. The consequence of such an external effect is that, from the point of view of total world welfare, the country pursuing this economic policy is not applying the correct dose, because it is concerned only with the costs and benefits which it will itself derive from that policy. These determine the exact form and extent of the policy devised. The ensuing costs and benefits in another country are ignored. If the policy-maker were to take these into account as well, then he would have undoubtedly devised a different optimum policy as being the optimum policy.

The aim of international economic cooperation is that national economic policy decisions should also take account of these effects on other countries' economies. This seldom if ever seems to happen spontaneously. National governments obviously focus mainly on their own country. That is what they are for, because that is the location of the electorate who will ultimately decide whether to re-elect the policy-makers.

International economic cooperation therefore almost always needs to be organised, and that organisation is the subject of this chapter. It deals with both the possibilities and the facts as they have unfolded in the past few decades. This chapter will remain confined to international cooperation in the monetary sphere only, though we shall see that too strict a division between monetary and economic policy is not generally practicable. It would detract too much from international monetary cooperation in its real form. That is why this chapter will also touch on fiscal policy and trade policy in so far as they are important at that point for a better understanding of international monetary cooperation.

The chapter is arranged as follows. Section 16.2 describes the various forms of international economic cooperation and examines in greater depth the theoretical concepts just touched on. This section also deals with the practical problems facing international economic cooperation. Practical aspects of international monetary cooperation are divided into three sections in this chapter. Section 16.3 examines international monetary cooperation up to the end of the Second World War, followed by 16.4 on international monetary cooperation between 1945 and 1973, a year which was notorious for the world economy on two counts: OPEC initiated the first oil price shock between October and the end of the year, and the post-war system of fixed exchange rates collapsed in March of that year. Section 16.4 will also include an account of the International Monetary Fund, the main post-war international organisation in the sphere of international monetary cooperation. Since 1973 exchange rates have in fact been floating on a global scale, but monetary cooperation is still in evidence. This is the subject of section 16.5.

Specific questions which this chapter will answer in this connection are:

- What different forms of international economic cooperation can be identified?
- In what ways does harmonisation differ from coordination as being forms of international economic cooperation?
- What is the function of the widespread phenomenon of groups of countries such as the G-3, G-5, G-7 and G-24?
- Is international monetary cooperation a post-war phenomenon?
- Why did the world system of fixed exchange rates collapse in 1973?
- What is the point of studying exchange rate systems from the past?
- Why is intervention in the foreign exchange market normally coordinated nowadays?
- What is the current role of the International Monetary Fund (IMF) in regard to the exchange rate system?
- Why did the IMF introduce SDRs in 1970 and what are the principal characteristics of SDRs?
- Is there a reason for the decline in the use of the dollar as an international reserve asset and a medium for private investment?

16.2   Forms of international economic cooperation

There has been some degree of international economic cooperation for hundreds of years. Often it was in a very moderate form, namely the exchange of information on the state of the countries' own economies and on their plans for future national economic policy. It was not until this century that international economic cooperation became more or less permanent. At the end of the Second World War it actually gained momentum.

Since the Second World War the *exchange of information* on national economic policy has been incorporated in the work of the Organisation for Economic Cooperation and Development (OECD), which has its secretariat in Paris. Government representatives regularly meet there to exchange ideas on the economic situation in their country and forthcoming economic policy. With the information thus obtained, a country's government is in a better position, when preparing its policy, to take account of the expected policy in other countries and the influence which that is likely to have on the economy of the home country. For example, if it is apparent that Germany is preparing for an expansionary policy, the governments of countries such as Belgium and the Netherlands can react by moderating any plans which they have for expansion. They can expect that via the increased German demand for imports, stronger growth in Germany will have an expansionary influence on their economies, which traditionally send a substantial percentage of their exports to Germany.

A closer form of international cooperation is *policy coordination*. All countries involved in the coordination have their own preferences as regards the future values of their economic policy objectives. They are aware of the mutual influence exerted by national economic policy. The ultimate aim of policy coordination is that individual countries should adjust their policy instruments in the best interests of all the economic objectives of the countries concerned. In theoretical form: the econometric model containing all the countries concerned includes all national economic objectives and economic policy instruments; there is also an objective function comprising all countries and containing all national objectives, each in relation to the target value for that objective, with a specific weighting which expresses the importance of the objective concerned. The aim is to maximise the objective function under the condition of the econometric model. This process yields the optimum value of each of the national policy instruments, in the best interests of the group of countries concerned – although it cannot be precluded that the result of this optimisation is that some countries' welfare declines.

Since the mid 1970s, international policy coordination has taken place mainly in the G-7. This is the group of seven leading industrial countries: the US, Japan, Germany, United Kingdom (UK), France, Italy and Canada. Since 1976 these G-7 members have held annual meetings of the heads of state or government leaders of the participating countries.[1] The agreements made at these meetings are general in character, aiming, for instance, to reduce the American budget deficit, cut taxes in Japan and produce a more expansive government policy in Germany. There is no retrospective monitoring or evaluation. The agreed policy often fails to be implemented because, according to the country concerned, new developments during the year necessitated interim adjustments of their policy intentions.

---

1. The first of these meetings was held in Puerto Rico. The previous year the first five countries had met as the G-5 in Rambouillet (France). After a great deal of political pressure, Italy – followed by Canada – were eventually also allowed to attend these meetings.

Case study 16.1 The G-7 summit in Halifax in 1995

In 1995 the leaders of the seven principal industrial countries held their annual meeting in the Canadian town of Halifax. The meeting took place from 15 to 18 June. The usual final economic and political declarations contained recommendations which were unusually specific. The main reason for this was that in the New Year the world had been unpleasantly surprised by a serious financial crisis in Mexico which once again shook the foundations of the international financial system. This was the reason for recommending that the IMF be enabled to develop an early warning system for such crises. For that purpose, monitoring by the IMF of its 179 member countries needs to be tightened up, and an effort should be made to supply more open information better and faster. If a financial crisis were nevertheless to break out in a country, then the IMF must be able to provide a large amount of support more quickly than hitherto through an 'Emergency Financing Mechanism' to be created at the Fund. It was proposed that this could be financed by increasing the amounts available under the General Arrangements to Borrow (GAB). (For an explanation of the GAB, see sub-section 16.3.2.) Under these arrangements, the G-10 countries and Saudi Arabia can provide the IMF with a maximum of $27 billion. The summit conference recommended doubling this figure and asking other countries – such as the developing Asian countries and the Scandinavian countries – to join in the GAB as well.

The final declarations also referred to the multilateral aid developing countries. The global institutions working in that field should concentrate their policy more on the poorest countries and on combating poverty. Another recommendation was that the World Bank and the IMF should develop new mechanisms for reducing countries' debts to these institutions. The G-7 countries also expressed their support for the new World Trade Organisation, the WTO, and undertook to guarantee an efficient and well-respected mechanism for settling trade disputes.

Various other groups of countries have developed in addition to the G-7. These also aim at coordination, but in regard to a specific aspect of economic policy. Thus, the G-10 has been in existence since 1962. It consists of the G-7 countries plus the Netherlands, Belgium and Sweden, with the addition of Switzerland in 1964.[2] This group became involved in the IMF's liquidity position on the initiative of the US; section 16.4 will examine this in more detail. Since 1972 there has also been a G-24 comprising a large group of developing countries. The number of members rapidly grew to far more than 24. This group discusses international monetary issues and tries to arrive at common positions before the annual meeting of the IMF, so that the developing countries can speak with one voice and thus have more say at that meeting. There have been periods in which a G-5 looked likely to develop as a permanent consultation agency. This group consisted of the G-7 without Italy and Canada. However, the G-5 now

---

2. Japan also joined in 1964. Although the group has 11 members the name has never been changed.

seems to have had its day. Instead there is a tendency to establish a G-3 consisting of the US, Japan and Germany, or a variant in which Germany is replaced by the European Union (EU). The G-7 coordination meetings could then become a matter for the G-3.

Another form of international economic cooperation is international *policy harmonisation*. We usually talk of harmonisation if the object of cooperation is to achieve a degree of convergence in policy intervention in the various countries. Thus, harmonisation does not so much concern macro-economic policy but rather policy intervention which influences the international competitive position of national enterprise, e.g. the setting of rates of tax – particularly indirect taxes such as VAT rates – and government regulations aimed at protecting the safety and health of consumers. This has been attempted in the EC, in particular, in recent years. As regards VAT, so much progress has been made that all countries impose their indirect taxation on the basis of VAT and a minimum level has been set for both the low and high rates of VAT. This system combats price advantages which are not based on low production costs but on something else than comparative advantage such as favourable rates of tax.

The most radical form of international economic cooperation is total *integration* or *unification* of economic policy in the countries concerned. Obviously, such an economic policy is *supranational* in practice. This means the existence of economic control at a higher than national level, mapping out and implementing economic policy for the countries involved in the unification. Another form of supranational decision-making is majority decisions by participating countries. This form of cooperation combines well with democratic decision-making, though this requires a supranational parliament. The plans for an Economic and Monetary Union (EMU) in the EU clearly contain supranational elements and thus constitute an example – albeit far from complete – of economic policy unification (cf. Chapter 18).

We can therefore identify four forms of international economic cooperation. In ascending order of closeness, these are: exchange of information as the least radical form, coordination, harmonisation and unification as undoubtedly the closest form of international economic cooperation. For each of these a further distinction can be made according to the scope of the cooperation, which ranges from strictly sectoral (e.g. international cooperation on trade policy for the textile sector only, in the form of the Multi-Fibre Arrangement) to fully integrated economic policy. There is also a geographical differentiation in scope: from small-scale, regional cooperation (e.g. by Belgium, the Netherlands and Luxembourg in the Benelux) to truly global cooperation (as in the IMF).

As stated in section 16.1, the advantage of international economic cooperation is undeniably that the effects on other countries' economies are taken into account in determining national policy. However, in economics there are no advantages without disadvantages; it remains a science based on weighing up costs and benefits, and international economic cooperation is no exception to that. The disadvantages of international cooperation can be divided into: the sacrifice of national autonomy in policy-making; the complexity of implementation; the risk of cheating; and free riders. These four disadvantages will now be explained in more detail.

Loss of national autonomy in the implementation of economic policy is often in itself a psychological disadvantage for a national government. Independence and autonomy are usually regarded as positive attributes. But optimum international economic cooperation ought to lead to maximum economic welfare for the whole co-operating region. However, one cannot rule out the possibility that part of the region, e.g. one of the co-operating countries, will nevertheless suffer a loss of welfare or gain hardly anything at all. Much depends on the weightings given to that country's economic objectives in the overall economic welfare function. Those weightings will be small if the country in question is of minor importance in the overall co-operative framework. In economic terms, it is the largest countries which have the power. They have very little interest in cooperation since their economy is relatively little influenced by other countries. For small countries the exact opposite applies. As a result, the large countries will be able to impose the most demands, and they will do so.

International economic cooperation in the form of policy coordination is *difficult to implement*. It is in fact even more difficult to implement than national economic policy. In formal terms, ascertaining the outcome of optimum international policy coordination demands a knowledge of a number of elements which are particularly difficult to quantify. One is the combined welfare function for the countries taking part in the coordination. Another is the composition of national models considered to give a good quantitative description of the participating economies. At national level this information is already hard to come by, and people continue to disagree on the correct form. Where several countries are concerned, the level of disagreement can clearly increase significantly. One complication here is that simulation results of econometric models for policy coordination indicate that use of a model which, on closer examination, proves to be incorrect or unsatisfactory as a reflection of the economy involved, can easily more than negate the positive result of coordination.

The last issue in connection with policy coordination concerns the fact that (potential) participants withdraw from the agreements or from the cooperation as a whole. In this case, the cooperation is undermined by participants *cheating* or behaving as *free riders*. Once the form in which the coordinated economic policy is to be implemented has been decided by mutual consultation, it can be to the advantage of a participating country to fail to carry out its own part. The other countries' policy will in itself make a positive contribution to the desired economic development of the country in question. One reason for trying to avoid participating in the implementation of the policy may be that the country's own intended contribution to the coordinated policy entails costs for that country. One example is the implementation of an expansive fiscal policy which has to be financed on the capital market by issuing government bonds. Failure to meet obligations, or cheating, cannot be avoided altogether; at best the risk can be reduced. In this connection, retrospective legal action serves no practical purpose, because there are no legal rules for this type of international agreement, although failure to comply with agreements will be less attractive if such policy coordination is not an isolated instance but continues from year to year. Cheating in any one year then entails costs for the country concerned, in that it is bound to be excluded from the policy coordination in subsequent years – and hence also from the important phase of devising the common policy! The risk of cheating can be further reduced if the policy for countries taking part in the cooperation is laid down in an agreement and if an organisation is set up to supervise compliance with the rules.

The free rider issue concerns the fact that a country can withdraw not only from implementing the coordinated policy but also from devising it. In short, the country remains totally outside the international economic cooperation. Such an attitude combined with the expectation that the country will actually benefit from the common policy of the remaining group of countries – in the form of an improvement in economic development – makes the country into a free rider. Nothing can be done about this problem apart from bringing political pressure to bear on the free rider. A single free rider will not block international policy coordination. However, if a number of mainly larger countries thus stay out of range, this can mean the end of the attempt at coordination.

16.3 International monetary cooperation prior to 1945

In about 1870, most of the leading economic powers of the day went over to a monetary system based on gold: the *gold standard*. For having a gold standard it is not necessary to have gold coins in circulation with a gold content which determines the value of the coins via the price on the international gold market. Nevertheless, such a gold coin standard did initially exist. In the course of time the gold exchange standard gradually came into use. Its characteristic was that the gold became concentrated at the country's central bank, which instead of solid gold coins circulated *fiduciary money*, money with a value based on the users' trust in it. This essentially means trusting that the central bank will at all times be prepared to materialise its obligation to exchange the fiduciary money at a fixed price for gold (under the gold standard), or trusting that the central bank will not undermine the purchasing power of the fiduciary currency by issuing too much of it. The essence of a gold standard is the central bank's exchange obligation. If such an obligation no longer exists in the case of fiduciary currency, we refer to a *paper standard*.

If two countries use the gold standard for their monetary system, then it follows that their currencies are linked by a fixed exchange rate. The value of the exchange rate corresponds to the relationship between the gold value of the central currencies of the two countries. For example, if the value of the Dutch guilder is equal to the value of two grammes of gold and the dollar is worth four grammes of gold, then by definition the dollar is equal in value to two guilders. Thus, the global adoption of the gold standard in around 1870 indirectly meant acceptance of fixed exchange rates at world level. This system was therefore associated with the known advantages and disadvantages of fixed exchange rates: the advantage of certainty for international trade and investment, but also the disadvantage that a situation of a permanent deficit on the balance of payments combined with high domestic unemployment cannot be rectified by devaluing the currency. Although this was formally possible by reducing the gold content of the currency (under the gold standard) or the compulsory exchange of fiduciary currency for a smaller quantity of gold by the central bank (under the gold exchange standard), this possibility was hardly ever used in practice.

The gold standard worked excellently from 1880 to 1914. However, when the First World War broke out countries abandoned the gold standard *en masse* and did not return to it until the early 1920s. This restoration of the gold standard appeared to be short-lived. As is well-known, 1929 brought the world economic crisis. It began as a financial crisis with a crash on the New York stock market. Unemployment soared to massive levels soon after. In 1931 this prompted the UK to abandon the gold standard and hence the fixed exchange rate in favour of a depreciating pound sterling. The pursuit of an internal macro-economic objective, namely low unemployment, was accorded precedence over the external objective of a fixed exchange rate. Other countries did the same, though in many cases reluctantly. Thus, the Netherlands did not switch to a floating exchange rate until 1936. The 1930s then saw competitive devaluations between countries attempting to improve their own employment: if one currency was devalued, other countries then followed suit by devaluing their currency. This caused the first country to devalue once again, and so on. Countries also introduced exchange restrictions, and trade policy intervention was used, too, to provide additional support for domestic producers. All this was naturally at the expense of employment in countries which did not devalue, or which devalued their currencies by less than their trading partners: the countries which rapidly devalued their currencies thus 'exported' their unemployment to their trading partners, often neighbouring countries, which is why such a process of competitive devaluation is called a *beggar-thy-neighbour* policy.

A period of intense disunity and hardship provides favourable conditions for stepping up cooperation. The final days of the Second World War were no exception. First, in the 1930s the world had witnessed the disintegration of the global economy into inward-looking countries; this was followed by the ravages of war from 1940 to 1945. When the end of the war was in sight, the leading countries met at Bretton Woods (US) in July 1944 in an attempt to lay the foundations for a restored world economy once the war was over. It was decided to set up a number of international economic organisations which would control world economic cooperation in later years. These were the International Monetary Fund (IMF), the World Bank (officially known as the International Bank for Reconstruction and Development, or IBRD) and an International Trade Organization (ITO) which was later to function in truncated form as the General Agreement on Tariffs and Trade (GATT). Eventually this trade agreement was incorporated in an international trade organisation: the World Trade Organisation or WTO. This organisation only started functioning on 1 January 1995.

315

The basic idea behind the attempt to restore international economic cooperation in the post-war world was to avoid a repetition of the economic chaos of the 1930s and to promote international trade and hence world economic growth via the ensuing certainty and freedom. This would undoubtedly be accompanied by a large increase in economic welfare and high employment. For this purpose, people thought that the primary requirement was stable and therefore predictable exchange rates. Fixed exchange rates would clarify the pattern of comparative advantages and therefore contribute to the optimum allocation of production in the world. Apart from stable exchange rates, maximum efficiency in production naturally also required the absence of both exchange controls and trade barriers.

In the light of this approach, the new international economic institutions were assigned specific tasks. The IMF was to promote exchange rate stability without countries retreating into foreign exchange restrictions. For this purpose the Fund was enabled to provide members with short-term credits as balance of payments support. This allowed those countries to protect the fixed value of their currency against market disruption by intervening in the foreign exchange market. Where a balance of payments problem required a structural solution rather than a temporary one, the IMF credits gave the country at least the flexibility to spread the required adjustment of the domestic economy over a number of years.

The World Bank was assigned the task of supporting the post-war process of economic development and growth. Unlike the IMF, it was given the scope for this by freedom to raise capital on the international financial markets on the basis of guarantees from creditworthy member countries. This capital is then lent on to members needing it for the purpose of stimulating their economic development. Since the World Bank has an excellent credit rating owing to the guarantees from member countries, it can raise capital at a relatively low interest rate. This benefits the far less creditworthy developing countries to which the World Bank lends money. The functions of the IMF and the World Bank have gradually come to overlap. The problems afflicting the countries to which the IMF grants credit require such a long adjustment period that the IMF has extended in the course of time the maturity of some of its forms of credit. On the other hand, since the mid 1980s the World Bank has shifted the emphasis of its activities in the direction of support for solving macroeconomic problems rather than project aid. This interweaving of spheres of activity is acknowledged, witness the passage in the final communique of the summit conference of heads of state and government in Halifax in June 1995: 'the IMF and the World Bank should concentrate on their respective core functions (broadly speaking, macro-economic policy for the IMF and structural and sectoral policy for the World Bank).'[3]

The IMF and the World Bank were set up at the Bretton Woods conference:

---

3. Note that this wording is conspicuously less specific. But that problem, as we have said, is inherent in the way the G-7 works. In this connection it is more important that the G-7 is paying attention to the matter: that indicates the seriousness of the problem.

not so the third cornerstone of the post-war world economy, the GATT. As we have already seen, the GATT – which came into force in 1947 – was to help reduce restrictions on trade. The agreement proved extremely successful in this respect. Of these three cornerstones of the post-war international economic system, only the IMF has a substantial role in international monetary cooperation. This institution will therefore be examined in more detail.

16.4 International monetary cooperation between 1945 and 1973

16.4.1 The IMF: its organisation and credits

The IMF was able to start work at the end of 1945 when a sufficient number of 29 countries had signed the Articles of Agreement. In mid 1995 there were 179 member countries. The group of members was expanded by fits and starts. Particularly in recent years the number of members has increased greatly as a result of the accession of many former planned economies, including the countries which emerged from the collapse of the Soviet Union and Yugoslavia. The organisational structure of the Fund consists of a Board of Governors, a Board of Executive Directors with 24 members and the Managing Director, since 1987 the Frenchman Camdessus. The Board of Governors normally meets twice a year. Each member country has a seat on this Board. Eight member countries each have their own representative on the Board of Executive Directors. These are the G-5 countries plus Russia, China and Saudi Arabia. The other executive directors represent voting groups of countries. The day-to-day management of the IMF is handled by the Board of Executive Directors headed by the Managing Director.

On joining the IMF, a country pays a subscription which gives it a corresponding IMF *quota*. In principle, the size of the subscription depends on a number of economic characteristics of the country in question, particularly the volumes of its domestic production and international trade. Periodically, i.e. about every five years, the IMF increases the quota. This is because the Fund uses the subscriptions to provide loans to members which so require on account of their balance of payments deficit. Since international payments and hence balance of payments deficits expand over the years, the IMF considers that it should also be able to increase its loans by the same degree. This means that the subscriptions have to be adjusted upwards from time to time. The ninth general quota revision took place at the end of April 1993: on that occasion the total quotas were increased by 50 per cent from SDR 91.2 billion to SDR 144.6 billion. The SDR (Special Drawing Right) is the accounting unit used by the IMF.[4]

---

4. At the beginning of July 1995 the SDR was worth 1.57 US dollars. The SDR has the character of a composite reserve currency and was introduced by the IMF as such in 1970. For more details see sub-section 16.4.3.

A country has to pay in 25 per cent of its subscription in the form of reserve currencies and the remaining 75 per cent in its own currency. This rule also applies to payment of the periodic increases in the quota. The payment burden is in fact negligible for a country, because in return for the payment in reserve currency it is entitled to draw on the IMF for the same amount in the form of withdrawals in convertible currencies as soon as it encounters balance of payments problems. Thus, in essence, the payment of 25 per cent of the quota means that a country is exchanging some components of its international monetary reserves: the loss of reserve currency is offset by a corresponding increase in the country's (unconditional) general drawing rights on the IMF. Payment of the 75 per cent in its own currency is not a burden at all for a country. If need be, this can be done simply be creating money. Access to IMF credits is an unmitigated benefit of IMF membership. Over the years these credits have developed into an ever larger, multi-faceted system. Via the miscellaneous IMF credit facilities, a member country with serious balance of payments problems can obtain loans of more than six times the value of its quota. Apart from the first 25 per cent, which were already mentioned before, the loans are subject to economic policy conditions formulated by the staff of the Fund. The next chapter will give some idea of the different credit facilities and the part they play in IMF credits.

On a number of occasions, the IMF's own resources proved insufficient for lending purposes. As we have said, the IMF's own resources consist of the members' subscriptions. The periodic quota increases were sometimes too late or simply too small to cope with the world's balance of payments finance requirement. In such cases the IMF sometimes successfully called on members to make money available in the form of a loan to the Fund. Some of the IMF's credit facilities are financed in this way, as we shall see in the next chapter.

The lending arrangement organised by the IMF with ten industrial countries in 1962 is a very special form of financing. The countries concerned subsequently formed the G-10, and the loan agreements were known as the General Arrangements to Borrow (GAB). These arrangements form a network of bilateral credit facilities between the participating countries. They were introduced when the UK threatened to make heavy demands on the IMF on the grounds of serious balance of payments problems, and the IMF's resources at the time would have been insufficient for the purpose. The countries concerned then agreed that in such cases they would in future make substantial amounts available to one another on a temporary basis. The GAB exists to this day, the maximum amounts of the arrangements have been periodically increased and since 1982 they have also been made available to the IMF for other difficult situations. In 1982 the world debt crisis (see Chapter 17) imposed a huge strain on the international financial system. For that reason it was decided that the money available under the GAB could also be offered to non-members. However, the country concerned is then also subject to IMF conditionality (see the next chapter). Since that time an associated arrangement has been in operation with Saudi Arabia which, as a rich OPEC country, was also prepared to make credit available to other countries. The current maximum available under the GAB is SDR 17 billion (excluding SDR 1.5 billion for the associated arrangement). As we saw from Case study 16.1, the G-7 summit conference called on members of the GAB and other countries to double the resources available under the GAB.

16.4.2 *The exchange rate system: an adjustable peg*

The shape of the post-war international monetary system was designed at Bretton Woods. For the first time in history, there was thus in fact a deliberately constructed international monetary system. Previous arrangements had always been spontaneous, resulting from the countries' individual decisions about their national monetary system. The post-war system again assigned an important monetary role to gold, although more indirectly than before. Gold was again given a fixed price, but expressed only in US dollars. The other participating currencies were then assigned a fixed price in terms of dollars. This system of dollar parities meant that all other currencies were indirectly tied to gold once again, via their link with the dollar. Essentially, the fixed gold price meant that there was still a gold standard. This price was maintained by the American central bank (the Federal Reserve System) which was obliged to honour requests to exchange dollars for gold at the fixed gold price of $35 per troy ounce. At Bretton Woods it had been the American negotiators, in particular, who wanted to preserve this central element of the gold standard.

As was already mentioned in Section 14.5, it is not possible to keep the exchange rate to one exact value, that of the parity. The parity was therefore assigned fluctuation margins within which the exchange rate must remain. This gave rise to a band width within which an exchange rate could fluctuate. The outer limits of this band were 1 per cent above and below the parity. The IMF permitted a currency's par value to be adjusted from time to time. The creation of this scope was a clear departure from the traditional gold standard. In that case the fluctuation band naturally moved too. This gave us the adjustable peg system already explained in Section 14.5 and shown in Figure 14.2. The IMF allowed the parity to be adjusted if a country faced a structural balance of payments deficit and also had an economy in fundamental disequilibrium. This vague concept only gradually acquired the more specific meaning whereby *fundamental disequilibrium* is present if a balance of payments deficit could only be rectified by a domestic policy adjustment encouraging an even greater domestic imbalance. In most cases, that imbalance means unemployment. This adjustable parity satisfied the British concern at the time of Bretton Woods that there should be no return to the rigidity of the gold standard.

The exchange rate system designed in Bretton Woods has never really worked well. Initially, until the end of the 1950s, the central banks did not permit European currencies to be freely converted into American dollars, not even for balance of payments current account transactions. The reconstruction of Europe following the devastation of the world war gave rise to a chronic shortage of dollars, because the United States constituted the main area of the world where production facilities had not been destroyed, and hence was the focus of demand for goods. It was not until the latter half of the 1950s that the European economies had recovered sufficiently to have any hope of balancing the current account at the set rates of exchange. Convertibility was therefore restored at that time, albeit only for current transactions. Currency convertibility in the case of capital transactions came about (much) later and in totally different ways, with countries successively dismantling their capital restrictions.

It was not long after 1958 before the exchange rate system came under strain. The American balance of payments began to move into deficit. Revaluations of the Deutschmark and restrictions on American capital exports in the first half of the 1960s did not, in the end, provide a structural solution. In the early 1970s capital began to flee the United States because the owners considered the dollar overvalued and feared a depreciation of the currency. In May 1971, West Germany and the Netherlands in particular ceased to intervene in the foreign exchange market to support the dollar. In fact, in so doing they abandoned the adjustable peg system of exchange rates in favour of a floating rate.

The guarantee of a fixed gold price for private individuals was already abolished in 1968, as the central banks were no longer able to defend the gold price in dollars on the free gold market at the figure set at the time of Bretton Woods. The dollar might have been allowed to fall in value in relation to gold. However, the Americans felt that this would have damaged the essence of the Bretton Woods system, and therefore found an alternative: a dual gold market, one for official gold and the other for private gold transactions. The official gold price was maintained for official gold only. On the private market the price of gold was left free, whereupon it increased substantially. In August 1971 it was necessary to take another step backwards: the United States actually had to suspend the convertibility of official gold against dollars. The suspension subsequently proved to be a final abolition of convertibility. The dollar parity of all currencies was left free for a time. Although this was a significant breach of the agreement reached at Bretton Woods, it would be going too far to say that it meant the end of the Bretton Woods agreement, as in Case study 16.2. That agreement consisted of more than just an exchange rate system. In December of that year, 1971, the adjustable peg system was restored, including for the mark and the guilder, with new values for the dollar parities. In order to add flexibility to the exchange rate system, the fluctuation margin was increased to 2.25 per cent on either side of the parity. This was known as the *Smithsonian Agreement*, but it proved to be just a temporary reprieve: in February/March 1973 these new parities also proved indefensible, after which in March 1973 the industrial countries allowed their currencies to float against the dollar. That situation persists to this day.

Case study 16.2 Nixon halts gold sales

Yesterday evening, in a twenty-minute speech, President Nixon launched a major package of economic measures which he himself called 'the most important for forty years'. Among other things, the President announced that the United States were suspending the facility whereby other central banks could exchange their dollars for American gold at a price of $35 dollars per ounce. This means that in the countries with the strongest currencies in Europe and Japan, central banks need no longer support the dollar, so that the exchange rate will float and the currencies concerned will have to be revalued, which in those countries amounts to devaluation of the dollar. This ends the system of fixed exchange rates as we knew it and also the Bretton Woods Agreement on which the international payments system has been based since 1944. Nixon also announced that a 10 per cent duty would be imposed immediately on all imports into the United States.

Source: NRC Handelsblad, 16 August 1971.

Retrospective analysis shows that a combination of factors was responsible for the collapse of the Bretton Woods exchange rate system.

1. The American government was never prepared to place more emphasis on external objectives (the system of fixed exchange rates and balance of payments equilibrium) than on internal economic policy objectives (inflation, growth and employment). It was too attached to its political autonomy. As a result, the European countries in particular had to contend with the importation of higher American inflation via the fixed exchange rate obligations. However, European flexibility as regards restrictions on political autonomy also had its limits.
2. International capital movements expanded more rapidly than international flows of goods. The reasons for those capital movements are quite different from the reasons for international trade. As we know from Chapter 13, one of the factors determining capital movements is the expected change in the exchange rate. When, at a given moment, depreciation of the dollar looked imminent, there was a massive capital flight from the United States to Europe. This was the final blow for the exchange rate parities of the time.
3. Timely parity adjustments might have been a solution, but time and again the IMF members were far too cautious. It was not the exchange rate system itself that proved unsound but the way in which it was implemented. Thus, in the final phase of the system the stumbling block proved to be whether the depreciation of the dollar should take the form of a lower gold value for the dollar or a higher gold value for the other currencies – a political question which is totally irrelevant from the point of view of economic theory. The significance of the debate was purely psychological: arranging for the other party to change the gold parity was an attempt to imply publicly that the other party was also responsible for the imbalance – and therefore to blame.

16.4.3   The liquidity issue

In the post-war monetary system, gold was not only given a leading role by linking the value of this precious metal to the dollar. Gold was also a reserve asset used by central banks to pay one another. However, the great drawback of gold in this capacity is that the supply is unpredictable and subject to fluctuation. Moreover, gold is also used for non-monetary purposes in the private sector. It is used for industrial purposes and making jewellery, but above all for speculative purposes. As a result, the supply of gold for monetary purposes fluctuates sharply. For example, if speculators rush into gold, this causes strong upward pressure on its price, and vice versa. The central banks then have to defend the fixed gold price in dollars.

Another important source of international monetary reserves was – and is – the American dollar, because this currency had a central role, along with gold, in the post-war international monetary system. In the 1960s the American balance of payments produced substantial deficits, on average. The United States could simply finance these deficits with its own currency, i.e. by creating money. In this respect it was in a unique position: virtually no other country was able to do that. Other countries first had to obtain monetary reserves, after which they could use them to finance the balance of payments deficit. By financing their deficits with dollars, the American monetary authorities introduced increasing quantities of their currency into the international financial system. Some of it ended up with foreign monetary authorities and thus added to their monetary reserves. Another part was absorbed by the private sector. The dollar was also heavily used as a means of payment and investment in the private sector, but there was a limit to the periodic international circulation of new dollars. So long as demand persisted there was no problem. But that demand was not self-sustaining and was fuelled partly by confidence in the dollar elsewhere in the world. Ultimately, confidence in the value of the dollar was determined by the gold backing which the United States had to give for dollars in circulation under the IMF Articles of Agreement. However, the said balance of payments deficits caused a gradual reduction in the percentage of cover. Initially it was well over 100 per cent, but in the 1960s it dropped well below that. The American balance of payments deficits gradually undermined confidence in the dollar. People therefore realised that the American government would have to rectify these deficits in the foreseeable future, even though this would dry up an important source of supply for the world's international monetary reserves.

Thus, in the end, both gold and the US dollar proved to present problems as reserve assets. The international monetary system needed an alternative to gold as a reserve medium, because its supply was variable. A supplement to the creation of reserve assets was also desirable since it was foreseen that the supply of American dollars would dry up. This justified a serious search for the alternative. The IMF therefore introduced a new reserve asset: the *Special Drawing Rights* (SDRs) created on paper, after years of discussion. The advantage of this asset is that the IMF creates it (out of nothing) as the need arises for more international monetary reserves in the world. The SDR became a unit of account as well as a reserve asset.

As a *unit of account*, the SDR was initially given the same value as the US dollar; but that formula was soon dropped and the SDR was given a value based on a group of national currencies. At first, sixteen currencies were used but in the end a simpler formula was adopted in which the value of the SDR was equal to a basket of the world's five leading currencies: the American dollar, the Japanese yen, the Deutschmark, the British pound sterling and the French franc. Every few years the proportions of the different currencies in the basket are reviewed on the basis of differences in the economic development of the countries to which the five currencies belong. In 1995 the basket was made up as follows: $ 0.57; DM 0.45; yen 31.8; Ffr 0.80; £ 0.081. In view of the prevailing exchange rates, the shares of the currencies in the basket were distributed as follows at that moment in time: 40% $, 21% DM, 17% yen, 11% Ffr, 11% £.

The method of creating SDRs as a *reserve asset* is as curious as it is simple: once the IMF Board of Governors believes that new SDRs need to be placed in circulation to ensure satisfactory growth of the world's monetary reserves, all member countries taking part in the SDR Department are allocated an additional quantity of SDRs on their SDR account. The allocation is in proportion to the countries' IMF quota and is free of charge. At first this seems odd, but on closer examination it is not. These SDRs can only be held in the official sector. A country can itself only use the SDRs indirectly, not directly, to finance balance of payments deficits. If it needs SDRs for balance of payments purposes, it has to ask the IMF to designate a country – also participating in the SDR scheme – which is obliged to accept the first country's SDRs in exchange for currency reserves. As soon as a country uses SDRs assigned in this way, it has to pay interest on them. This SDR interest is in turn a weighted average of the market interest rates in the five home financial centres of the currencies which make up the SDRs. The weights are the basket shares. The country that accepts the SDRs receives interest on them at a rate linked to the SDR rate. Thus, the allocation of SDRs is essentially an unconditional right to borrow reserve currencies. That makes it easier to understand why the allocation of SDRs is in itself free of charge.

The SDRs were created under adverse conditions and everything has always been against them. When the first SDRs were allocated in 1970, there was no shortage of international monetary reserves at all, contrary to expectations. Quite the reverse. The American balance of payments deficits had persisted and were even increasing. In 1981 SDRs were again allocated, but again there was no real need. SDRs were also introduced in the private sphere, though of course they were not the same as those circulating in the official sphere. In the private sphere an accounting unit was devised with the same formula for determining its value and the interest rate as that used for the official SDRs.

On the face of it, the SDR formula looks attractive. Giving the SDR a value and an interest rate corresponding to a weighted average of the world's five leading currencies makes that value and interest rate agreeably stable. The reason is that there is a good chance that increases in the exchange rate of one currency in the SDR basket will be (partly) offset by a simultaneous fall in the rate of one of the other component currencies. If uncertainty is undesirable, this is an attractive characteristic. Nevertheless, the central banks did not prove keen to hold SDRs and the SDR was never more than a marginal phenomenon in either the official or the private sphere. For the official sphere, this is clear from Table 16.1. From time to time the IMF does attempt to give 'its' currency a more prominent place in the international monetary system, because originally the aim was actually that the SDR should develop into the world's principal reserve asset – and that is still the formal objective. Table 16.1 shows that the SDR is a long way from becoming that. By far the largest category is now the 'foreign currencies' component, and the trend for this component is still upwards. In contrast, the share of gold in the reserves is declining.

16.5 International monetary cooperation after 1973

As we saw in the preceding section, post-war international monetary cooperation increasingly had to contend with an adjustment problem (reluctance to adjust exchange rates), a confidence problem (the position of the central currency, the dollar, was increasingly undermined) and a liquidity problem (the supply of monetary reserves became more uncertain). These problems were automatically resolved by the switch to worldwide floating exchange rates in March 1973. The phenomena persisted in part but no longer represented a problem, as we shall see in this section.

Post-1973 policy on exchange rates between the dollar, the yen and the European currencies can best be defined as a system of managed floating exchange rates. In this connection the term 'manage' refers to the occasional need to adjust the trend in the rate to some extent by foreign exchange market

Table 16.1 The composition of the world's monetary reserves (end of year, %)

Type of asset	1982	1984	1986	1988	1990	1992	1994
Reserve position in the IMF	3.5	5.9	4.9	3.4	2.7	3.7	3.0
SDRs	2.5	2.3	2.7	2.4	2.3	1.4	1.5
Foreign currencies	39.5	49.6	50.4	59.4	66.6	70.4	72.8
Gold*	54.5	42.2	42.0	34.7	28.5	24.5	22.7
Total (as %)	100.0	100.0	100.0	99.9	100.1	100.0	100.0
(Same in bln SDRs)	(721)	(705)	(722)	(831)	(892)	(918)	(1,052)

*Gold reserves have been valued at London market prices
Source: IMF, *Annual Report*, various issues.

intervention. Demands for intervention arose in particular if the rate changes were large and totally out of line with the trend in the exchange rate fundamentals, i.e. the fundamental forces which determine the equilibrium value of the exchange rate. These are in fact the exchange rate determinants discussed in Chapter 13. The first complaints of an alleged imbalance in the exchange rate often come from the private sector, especially internationally oriented businesses in the country with a currency which has appreciated strongly. The opposing force to foreign exchange market intervention comes mainly from the theorists. In the 1970s, in particular, they argued that pure foreign exchange market intervention (or sterilised intervention) was pointless. Sterilised foreign exchange market intervention is neutral in its effect on the domestic money supply. The view is that intervention will not moderate the exchange rate movement unless it affects the domestic money supply (by reducing or increasing it). But then it is in fact the monetary policy associated with the intervention that affects the exchange rate. The monetary approach to the exchange rate, discussed in sub-section 13.4.2, clearly portrays this influence of monetary policy on the exchange rate: it does not allow for sterilised intervention affecting the exchange rate.

The end of fixed exchange rates worldwide deprived the IMF of an essential function: the pursuit and support of such a system of rates. This was confirmed when the IMF Articles of Agreement were revised in 1978. Members were formally permitted to operate any desired exchange rate arrangement, although the IMF did take on the role of surveillance over members' exchange rate policy. Since then the Fund has endeavoured to give this role some practical significance, but the IMF's activities in this respect (in the form of annual consultation with each member country) do not appear to have been very relevant so far.

It was only in 1985 that clear signs of a revival in international monetary cooperation emerged. In the preceding years the *adjustment problem* dating from the period prior to March 1973 seemed to have turned into a surfeit of exchange rate changes. Figure 13.3 illustrated this for the leading exchange rates. After a gradual decline in the initial phase of floating exchange rates, the dollar fell to an all-time low in 1980. In the first half of the 1980s the dollar reacted strongly and rose above the level it had held at the time of the Bretton Woods exchange rate system.

The reason for this rise of the dollar was a change of course in American macro-economic policy around 1980. In 1978 and 1979 the world economy suffered the effects of a second oil price shock, which gave a new boost to the inflation which had already been rising gradually for the preceding decade, with a tremendous transitory acceleration during and just after the first oil price shock. The American monetary authorities saw the new inflationary stimulus as a decisive reason for a drastic change of policy. They switched to a highly restrictive monetary policy. After an initial running-in period, interest rates in the United States soared, making investment in that country highly lucrative so that a vast volume of capital flowed into the United States: an unintentional effect, caused by a lack of international policy coordination. This inflow of capital caused the dollar to rise sharply. The interest rate increase was further reinforced by the effect of the expansive fiscal policy – known as Reaganomics – inadvertently introduced by President Reagan in the early 1980s. He believed that tax cuts would automatically be recovered. This proved incorrect, so that the American budget deficit expanded rapidly, and so did calls on the capital market. This further boosted the American interest rate.

Although President Reagan was attached to the free market principle, in the end he could not avoid government intervention in the foreign exchange market. American macro-economic policy had driven up the value of the dollar, but there was another force at work. In the first half of the 1980s, in an attempt to curb the rise of the dollar, Reagan successfully brought pressure to bear on the Japanese government to liberalise the Japanese financial markets. He hoped and expected that better market access would encourage Americans to start investing in Japan, which would weaken the dollar. However, the result was the exact reverse: the financial liberalisation in Japan gave the Japanese the opportunity for international investment diversification. They rushed *en masse* into investments in the United States, i.e. in the dollar, and this simply reinforced the upward trend in the dollar. The resulting high price of the dollar placed American exporters in an extremely poor competitive position, along with American producers competing with imports. In the United States there were calls on all sides for protectionist measures by the American government. In choosing between these two evils, Reagan opted to bring the dollar down by government intervention in the foreign exchange market rather than extend trade protection.

This explains the at first sight surprising positive attitude of the American government to coordinated exchange market intervention around 1985. In September 1985 the G-5 countries decided on this approach in the Plaza Agreement. The object was to reduce the value of the dollar by intervening in a coordinated way on the foreign exchange markets. People believed that by coordinating the intervention of the G-5 countries, and thus always intervening jointly at the same time and in the same direction, they could be much more convincing in regard to the foreign exchange markets. Perhaps the expected dollar value could be reduced by the psychology of intervention, and perhaps dollar investments could thus be discouraged according to the uncovered interest rate parity. This idea subsequently proved correct: the dollar had already peaked at the end of February 1985 and by September of that year it had fallen (slightly). But since the Plaza Agreement the fall of the dollar continued.

A second agreement followed in February 1987: the Louvre Accord. It set out the principles of coordinated intervention, but aimed to keep the dollar at the much lower value which it had now reached. The Louvre Accord was an agreement concluded by consultation in the Group of Seven. It was apparently also decided to apply a weak form of exchange rate agreements and fix a target zone for the dollar. The IMF was not involved in these agreements. In the years following 1987 coordinated intervention to counter the fluctuations on the foreign exchange market seems to have weakened. In those years the aim of stabilising the exchange rate at an equilibrium value also proved subordinate to interest rate policy for domestic economic purposes in the leading industrial countries.

At the time of the floating exchange rates the *confidence problem* regarding the dollar naturally persisted, in principle, but it no longer imposed a strain on the monetary system, because after March 1973 the dollar rate no longer had to be defended! As we have just described, there were renewed periods when the dollar was in demand as an investment currency: the first half of the 1980s is a clear example. The reasons then were the high American interest rate, the tendency of the dollar to appreciate and the need for diversification which was able to manifest itself in Japan. In spite of the revival of interest in the dollar during this period, the dollar was nevertheless becoming less attractive than other currencies. This is evident in the allocation of international investments among the various currencies. For example, Table 16.2 shows that the proportion of the American dollar in the foreign currencies component of monetary reserves fell from 67 to 61 per cent worldwide between 1980 and 1993. The decline in the share of the dollar was offset by an increased share for the yen and the category 'other currencies'. Surprisingly, there was hardly any increase in the share of the Deutschmark.

Monetary reserves are only a poor indicator of demand for a particular currency. The central banks' objectives go beyond obtaining a good return on their stock of monetary reserves. Particularly when a currency is weakening they will tend to hold an increasing proportion of that currency in the stock of reserve currencies, because it is that currency which is being bought by the central banks to support its value. If a currency is strengthening, the opposite tendency will apply.

Private investment behaviour gives a better idea of the attractiveness of a currency in the investment sphere. Table 16.3 provides an indication: it shows the percentage breakdown of the annual issue of international bonds by currency of denomination. We see that the share of the dollar slumped from 64 to 37 per

Table 16.2 The composition of the foreign exchange reserves: all IMF member countries (end of year, %)

Currency	1980	1982	1984	1986	1988	1990	1992	1993
US dollar	67	70	70	67	65	58	63	61
Deutschmark	15	12	13	15	16	19	14	16
Yen	4	5	6	8	8	9	9	9
Sterling	3	3	3	3	3	3	3	3
French franc	2	1	1	1	1	2	2	2
Swiss franc	3	3	2	2	2	1	1	2
Dutch guilder	1	1	1	1	1	1	1	1
Other currencies	3	5	5	4	5	7	7	6

Source: IMF, Annual Report, 1988, p. 68; Annual Report, 1994, p. 158.

Table 16.3 The currencies in which international bonds are denominated (end of year %)

Bonds denominated in	1982	1984	1986	1988	1990	1992	1993
US dollar	64	64	55	37	35	38	38
Yen	5	6	10	10	13	12	12
Deutschmark	7	6	8	10	8	10	11
Sterling	–	–	5	11	9	7	9
Swiss franc	15	12	10	12	10	5	6
ECU	–	–	3	5	8	6	2
Other currencies	9	12	9	15	17	21	22

Source: Allen (1989), p. 85 and Goldstein (1994), p. 66.

cent in the brief period from 1982 to 1988. From then on the dollar share appears to have been stabilised. The share of the Swiss franc also declined considerably. 1993 saw a sharp fall in the ECU. The yen and the mark, but particularly the 'other currencies' category, made clear gains. Bond loans were obviously being distributed more widely among the currencies.

The *liquidity problem*, which was still such an important factor at the time of the exchange rate system of Bretton Woods, faded away under (managed) floating exchange rates. An essential point was that this change of exchange rate systems totally eliminated the obligation to intervene in the foreign exchange market in order to keep the national currency within the fluctuation margins. In essence, in the case of pure floating exchange rates, no international monetary reserves are therefore needed at all. Though given the current practice of impure or managed floating, reserves are still needed for ad hoc intervention. But because there is no obligation to intervene, there cannot really be a reserve shortage. However, the possession of reserves can enable the monetary authority to give an impression of power, which may be necessary to give some force to its own pronouncements on the correct level for the exchange rate, because a point of view is powerless without a solid instrument.

It should be borne in mind that, although the dollar, mark and yen are floating against one another, many of the less important currencies have (had) a fixed rate of exchange with one of these three currencies after 1973. Monetary reserves continue to be relevant in the case of such exchange rate arrangements, although it is often very easy to borrow on the international capital markets to make up for a shortage of reserves. There are no signs that the world is short of reserves in the current period. Nevertheless, people in the IMF are calling for a new allocation of SDRs. The argument is threefold: in the early 1990s countries joined the IMF but have never yet been allocated any SDRs: that was before their time as members. The IMF also mentions a shortage of reserves in the world, though without offering any evidence. The last argument – put forward with caution but perhaps the main argument in the IMF – is that a long period with no SDR allocations undermines the position of the SDR as a reserve asset.

16.6 Summary

1. International economic cooperation makes sense if national economic policy has external effects on the economies of other countries. Such cooperation can then take account of these effects in shaping national policy.
2. The following forms of international economic cooperation can be identified, in ascending order of closeness: exchange of information, policy coordination, policy harmonisation and total integration of economic policy. The ultimate aim of international policy coordination is that, by consultation, countries should adjust their policy instruments individually in the best interests of all economic objectives of the cooperating countries. In the case of international policy harmonisation, the countries concerned try to achieve convergence of their national policy intervention in the economic process.
3. The grouping of countries for the purpose of international cooperation often combines the exchange of information and coordination. The group of the seven leading industrial countries, the G-7, is an apt example. Groups are also often used for the purpose of speaking with a single voice at international conferences, in order to be heard better. This is the central aim of the G-24, a large group of developing countries.
4. In practice there are four drawbacks to international policy coordination. It means a certain loss of national political autonomy. Psychologically, that is a problem in itself. Owing to a severe shortage of information, it is difficult to determine the right form of coordinated policy, and that also makes the policy difficult to implement. By cheating, participating countries can also undermine the jointly devised policy. Finally, coordinated policy suffers a serious loss of power and continuity in the case of free riders: countries which have an interest in – and hence often an effect on – the attempt at coordination, but do not wish to take part.
5. International monetary cooperation came about mainly after World War II in the form of the introduction of the post-war monetary system mapped out at the Bretton Woods conference in 1944. Its central feature was the IMF and the adjustable peg system of exchange rates. This differed from the fixed exchange rate system in that the fixed parity could be changed, with the consent of the IMF, in the case of a fundamental imbalance in a country's economy.
6. The exchange rate system of Bretton Woods collapsed in 1973. A primary reason was that the US considered exchange rate stability less important than internal economic objectives. Another reason was the vastly increased international mobility of capital, which means that economic divergences between countries have an immediate impact on exchange rates via huge capital movements. This experience is an important, rather discouraging lesson for other attempts at implementing an adjustable peg system of exchange rates.
7. In the present 'non-system' of floating and sometimes managed floating exchange rates between the world's leading currencies, the IMF has a very

329

limited function in relation to the exchange rate system. According to its Articles of Agreement, the IMF has a surveillance function, but this remains rather vague.

8. In 1970 the IMF introduced the first SDRs, which were allocated to the member countries wishing to take part in the SDR scheme. The IMF thought that this would allow the world's stock of monetary reserves to be better coordinated with requirements. As there was initially an excess supply of reserves in the world, this aim came to nothing. As an accounting unit, the SDR has a reasonably stable value and interest rate because it is based on a basket of currencies. Nevertheless, the SDR has never really become accepted in that function.

9. As a result of large fluctuations in value around a declining trend, the dollar has become less important as an international currency. Nevertheless, the dollar still has a much greater share in all the functions of an international currency than do rising currencies such as the mark and yen.

Bibliography

Allen, E.A. (1989), International capital markets; developments and prospects, *World Economic and Financial Surveys*, IMF.

Corden, W.M. (1994), *Economic Policy, Exchange Rates and the International Monetary System*, Oxford University Press.

Curry, D. (1990), International policy coordination, in D. Llewellyn and C. Milner (eds), *Current Issues in International Monetary Economics*, MacMillan, pp. 125–48.

Frankel, J.A. (1988), Obstacles to international macroeconomic policy coordination, *Princeton Studies in International Finance*, no. 64.

Goldstein, M. and D. Folkerts-Landau (1994), International capital markets: developments, prospects, and policy issues, *World Economic and Financial Surveys*, IMF.

Grauwe, P. de (1989), *International Money: Post-War Trends and Theories*, Clarendon Press.

International Monetary Fund (1976), *Articles of Agreement*.

International Monetary Fund (1995), G-7 offers proposals to strengthen Bretton Woods Institutions, *IMF Survey*, vol. 24, 3 July, pp. 201–5.

Jager, H. (1991), The global exchange rate system in transition, *De Economist*, vol. 139, pp. 471–96.

McKinnon, R.I. (1993), The rules of the game: international money in historical perspective, *Journal of Economic Literature*, vol. 31, pp. 1–44.

Tavlas, G.A. (1991), On the international use of currencies: the case of the Deutsche mark, *Essays in International Finance*, no. 181, Princeton University.

17 The international monetary system, international debt and economic development

17.1 Introduction

12 August 1982 is a notorious date for the international financial world. On that day Mexico announced to the world that it could no longer meet its financial obligations arising from its international debt of over $80 billion. In the end, Mexico proved to be the first in a long line of countries. The associated cumulation of international defaulting jeopardised the stability of the entire financial system even though – or perhaps precisely because – the banks were from then on extremely reluctant to offer the large debtor countries further credit. This was one factor which forced the heavily indebted countries to implement a stringent austerity programme. Thus, an important feature of the 1980s was a combination of an extremely fragile international financial system and declining economic welfare mainly among heavily indebted third world countries.

The central question in this chapter is the role played by the international monetary institutions in avoiding global financial collapse and in shaping and implementing the necessary adjustment policy in the countries which had borrowed heavily. Following on from this we shall discuss the lessons which can be drawn. In particular, we shall ascertain the extent to which this might benefit the former centrally planned economies whose position is now reminiscent of that of the heavily indebted countries of the recent past. This will answer the question whether the international monetary system is cut out for the international issues of today, and in particular whether it is making the optimum contribution to world economic growth – an objective given prominence in Article 1 of the IMF Articles of Agreement, for instance.

For this purpose, section 17.2 will first review the causes of the outbreak of the world debt crisis in the early 1980s. The range of adverse developments which caused financial problems for many countries is divided into external causes, or causes outside the sphere of influence of those countries, and internal causes which can be attributed to the countries themselves. Section 17.3 then examines the set of instruments which the IMF can use to both provide financial support and to extricate countries from a debt crisis. Next, we look at the way in which these instruments were used in the 1980s. Section 17.4 focuses on the development of the debt crisis in the past decade and the progress achieved. After outlining the position regarding the debt question, section 17.5 will transfer its attention to the former centrally planned economies. What was the economic position of these countries when communism came to an end? What support did the internationally monetary system proceed to give these countries, and what are the prospects for their economic development?

17.2 The causes of the debt crisis

Where economic problems are concerned, it is usually possible to indicate several causes which are to varying degrees interconnected. This empirical rule certainly applies to the debt problem. We can make a distinction between internal and external causes. External causes are those occurring outside the country, which sees its debt increase beyond manageable proportions; i.e. they are causes exogenous to the country, which has no influence over them. Furthermore, these are causes which, in practice, are common to the heavily indebted countries, generated by developments in the world economy, though the intensity of the impact varies according to the country. On the other hand, internal causes arise in the country itself, and are due to factors controllable by the debtor country. Thus, these are causes of the debt crisis which the country could have avoided; i.e. they are endogenous causes. This section will examine the external causes first before dealing with the commonest internal causes.

17.2.1 External causes

1. The *oil price shocks* of the 1970s. At the start of that decade there was a remarkable shift of power in the oil sector. Up to that time, power had been in the hands of the large oil companies. The Seven Sisters – a group of seven large oil companies – had hitherto ruled the world oil market. They were able to fix the price of crude oil, although this was formally done during periodic talks with the oil-producing countries.

To their own astonishment, when these countries broke off such talks unilaterally in October 1973 and went their own way, they proved perfectly capable of imposing their will on the oil companies. Prices proposed by the oil-producing countries, united in OPEC (the Organisation of Petroleum Exporting Countries) were supported by an OPEC boycott of the United States, the Netherlands, South Africa and then Rhodesia. The boycott was used as a means of coercion in the brief war between Israel and its neighbours in October 1973. It dramatically boosted speculative demand for oil, which always makes itself felt in times of instability when there is a tendency to build stocks. It was mainly the ensuing rise in the free market price of oil that caused the oil importers to accept the contractual price increases with OPEC.

As a result, the price of crude oil increased five-fold between October 1973

Table 17.1 Current account balances, 1973–88 (billion dollars)

	1973	1974	1975	1976	1977	1978	1979	1980
Industrial countries	18.1	–13.2	16.2	–2.1	–5.1	30.8	–23.3	–62.0
Developing countries*	–11.3	–36.9	–45.8	–32.1	–28.0	–36.2	–62.0	–86.2

	1981	1982	1983	1984	1985	1986	1987	1988
Industrial countries	–20.0	–22.1	–22.0	–61.7	–54.7	–9.3	–17.9	–25.0
Developing countries*	–111.9	–90.7	–56.3	–40.9	–43.9	–34.5	–41.6	–34.9

*Non-oil exporting developing countries
Source: IMF, *World Economic Outlook,* May 1980, p. 95; April 1987, p. 151; April 1987, p. 154.

and January 1974. This naturally meant a substantial increase in the oil account for oil importing countries. The industrial countries reacted by cutting expenditure in a successful attempt to neutralise the negative effect on the balance of payments. Table 17.1 shows that they were eminently successful within the space of just one year. By 1975 the balance of the industrial countries' current account was back to its 1973 level. In 1974 there was an intermediate decline to a deficit of around $13 billion. However, the non oil-exporting developing countries gave precedence to continuing economic growth as their objective, leading to a permanently deteriorated current account of the balance of payments. They, too, succeeded in their plan, according to Figure 17.1. During the 1970s these countries maintained their annual economic growth at a level of about 5 per cent, in stark contrast to the rich countries where growth was much lower on average, and also much more fickle. In fact, the developing countries were the driving force of world economic growth in the 1970s.

Once the OPEC balance of payments surplus had melted away in 1978, the OPEC countries repeated their price trick in 1978–9, again successfully. This time they used the pheaval on the world oil market caused by the revolution in Iran, which temporarily halted Iranian oil exports. Since Iran supplied around 10 per cent of the world's oil exports at the time, this pushed up the oil price. Once again this influence was greatly enhanced by speculative oil purchases. The effects for the oil-importing countries were comparable with those of the first oil-price shock. Once again the developing countries' current account suddenly deteriorated, while the level of economic growth was maintained initially in 1980. In the industrial countries, economic growth again declined, though less sharply than after the first oil shock. On the other hand, the current account of these countries taken together did not recover as in 1975.

Current account deficits on the balance of payments have to be financed. The oil-importing developing countries achieved this by borrowing abroad. The corollary is, of course, the associated debt service burden (the sum of annual repayments and interest charges). Although an annual increase in the debt was accompanied by an annual increase in the debt service, this was not at first sight

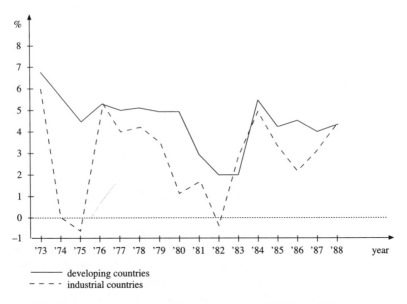

Figure 17.1 Growth of gross national/domestic product, 1973–88 (%)

Source: IMF, *World Economic Outlook*, May 1980, pp. 86/87, April 1985, pp. 205, April 1987, pp. 203, May 1990, pp. 123.

worrying to the oil-importing developing countries. The value of the exports of the countries concerned also grew in the 1970s, so that the debt service ratio hardly increased at all during this period. As stated in Chapter 15, the debt service ratio is the percentage relationship between the debt service and the value of a country's exports, both on an annual basis. It is in fact the most important indicator of a country's creditworthiness. Table 17.2 gives an impression of the trend in this ratio during the period 1973–86, which was so important for the developing countries. Until 1981 the increase in the debt service ratio for all developing countries together was still very small: from 15.9 to 17.3 per cent. However, the table also shows that this aggregate figure conceals large regional variations. For both Africa and the developing countries of the Americas, the ratio increased sharply during that period, but at the time hardly anyone knew about it: There was a chronic lack of quantitative information on the trend in international debts.

2. In the period 1974–9 the world's financial markets were a *borrowers' market*. These markets which had ample supplies of money while demand for new credit was low in the industrial countries. In such markets with a constant threat of excess supply, the borrowers are in a position of power. The supply on the financial markets had initially come from the current account surpluses of the oil-exporting countries. As we have said, the large increase in oil revenues also surprised the oil-exporting countries. Their spending plans were not yet geared

Table 17.2 Debt service ratio, 1973–86 (%)

	1973	1974	1975	1976	1977	1978	1979	1980	1981	1982	1983	1984	1985	1986
Developing countries	15.9	14.4	16.1	15.3	15.1	18.7	18.9	17.3	20.9	24.6	22.2	22.5	23.1	22.0
Including interest payments	6.1	6.1	6.7	6.0	5.8	7.2	8.2	8.9	11.9	14.3	13.5	13.5	12.7	11.4
Africa	8.8	6.7	8.0	8.5	11.9	15.6	15.0	14.4	16.7	20.9	23.7	28.3	30.0	27.7
Asia	9.6	7.8	8.5	7.7	7.9	9.8	8.9	8.1	9.6	11.3	10.7	10.9	11.2	11.0
America	29.3	27.9	32.2	31.4	28.7	37.8	38.9	33.5	41.5	51.6	41.1	39.4	40.5	40.0

Source: IMF, *World Economic Outlook*, several issues.

to that. It took some years for them to adapt to their greatly increased financial resources. In the meantime they offered the oil dollars to the international banking system in an attempt to invest them at a profit. A second source of supply on the international financial markets consisted of the United States' annual current account deficits. At first sight, it is surprising that such deficits can also contribute to the supply on the international financial markets, but in the case of the United States it is true. The US can finance the deficits with its own currency because the dollar is a currency in international demand. Hence no external finance is needed, so long as the international financial markets are able to take the dollars offered by the US and channel them in sufficient volume to those who want them. The recession conditions which prevailed in the industrial countries after 1973, evident from Figure 17.1, made this difficult.

Thereupon, the international banks tried – successfully – to avoid the imminent surplus credit on the international financial markets by offering a low interest rate and adopting a less critical attitude towards borrowers. As a result of the keen competition between the banks as regards lending money, the real interest rate was actually negative in the period 1973–8 and the spread charged was too low for the banks to build up substantial reserves to cover the debtor risk. The real interest rate is defined as the nominal rate minus expected inflation. If the real interest rate is negative, this means that the debtor's borrowings are declining in purchasing value by more than the interest burden. For example, if the interest rate in a given year is 5 per cent and the expected inflation is 10 per cent, then the real value of the principal will fall by an expected 10 per cent while the interest on it is 5 per cent. The interest which a country has to pay on an international loan consists of a basic rate for all countries plus a surcharge specific to the country. The basic rate is equal to the interest rate charged to one another by well-known banks in major financial centres, usually the LIBOR (London Interbank Offered Rate). A surcharge, called the spread, is added according to the debtor. The spread includes a risk premium as well as a number of cost components. The risk premium is specific to the borrowing country in question, and depends on the country's credit rating.

The excessively low interest rate and spread were important factors in the vulnerability of the international financial system. The oil-importing developing countries had easy access to loans, even for projects which were barely viable, if at all. This was a major contributor to their high, stable growth during those years. And that was not a problem given the prevailing negative real interest rate, but such a negative rate is rather the exception to the rule. In addition, the banks did not do enough to build up their defences against future bad debts. Their reserves were too small. Where the banks had good, quantitative information on the creditworthiness of debtor countries, they often took the country risk too lightly. It was said that countries could not go bankrupt because their assets, such as mineral resources, still totalled many times their debts. In other words, countries almost always remain solvent. But a lack of assets capable of being converted quickly into cash, in other words a lack of liquidity, can be enough to render countries incapable of meeting their international financial obligations at a given time.

3. In the mid 1960s the American banks introduced a form of credit on the Eurocurrency market which became known as *roll-over credit*. This form of credit was also commonly used for loans to oil-importing developing countries in the 1970s. In essence, it is long-term credit *with a variable interest rate*. For example, the interest on such long-term loans is adjusted every six months in line with the prevailing short-term rate (LIBOR). The reason was that the banks were developing the practice of financing long-term credit with cash offered to them on a short-term basis. This enabled the banking system to balance out threatened shortages and surpluses for differing maturities on financial sub-markets. The banks had to pay the short-term interest rate on the funds raised. By always charging the long-term borrower the short-term interest rate (plus a mark-up), the banks were protected against the risk of unexpected interest rate hikes which they had to pay to the financiers when interest rates were rising. The risk of such increases was thus passed on to the borrowers, who in most cases had the additional advantage that the short-term interest rate was normally lower than the long-term rate, giving them cheap access to long-term credit.

4. In view of the colossal loans required by the oil-importing countries, the banks began arranging them co-operatively. Such a loan in which many banks participate is called a *syndicated loan*. A bank is asked to act as lead manager, after which it forms a group of interested banks with which agreements are made on each one's share in the loan. The advantage of this type of loan is that the risk is spread over many banks. By participating in various syndicated loans, a bank shares and thus reduces the risk, which enables it to expand its total lending. However, this creates the real danger of over-lending. Moreover, the banks which participated in syndicated loans were not so particular about examining the creditworthiness of the borrower. This was cheerfully left to the lead manager, but the latter also had only a small share in the loan. The risk was aggravated by the fact that elements such as fashion and sense of honour affected the banks' decision to take part in a syndicated loan. Banks are certainly not insensitive to prevailing trends, and if it is 'the in thing' to take part in syndicated loans and enter on the path of international lending, people sometimes consent too readily. Moreover, many smaller banks deemed it an honour to be invited to take part by a major bank acting as lead manager for a loan. Such feelings can also distort one's view of the true risks.

5. In October 1979 the United States adopted a *stringent anti-inflationary monetary policy*. The second oil shock in 1978–9, which gave a further strong boost to inflation, brought about this change of policy. Other industrial countries were not unwilling to follow the US change in policy stance to a certain extent. While inflation in the industrial countries had always been less than 4 per cent in the years up to 1969, it averaged 5 per cent from 1969 to 1972. According to Table 17.3, inflation remained at just under 4 per cent for the industrial countries in the decade to 1973. The first oil shock caused inflation to peak at over 13 per cent in 1974. It subsequently dropped back, though only to about 7–8 per cent in the next few years. The second oil shock pushed inflation back up to over 9

Table 17.3 Inflation,* 1963–88 (%)

	Average 1963–72		1973	1974	1975	1976	1977	1978	1979
Industrial countries	3.9		7.7	13.1	11.1	8.3	8.4	7.2	9.0
Developing countries**	9.1		20.4	27.1	27.9	24.2	27.1	23.6	24.7

	1980	1981	1982	1983	1984	1985	1986	1987	1988
Industrial countries	11.8	9.9	7.5	5.0	4.8	4.1	2.4	3.0	3.3
Developing countries**	31.6	30.6	30.9	43.2	50.5	54.7	36.1	37.1	36.2

*Measured by the weighted average of the countries' consumer prices
**Non-oil exporting developing countries.
Source: IMF, *World Economic Outlook*, several issues.

per cent in 1979 and almost 12 per cent in 1980. The prevailing belief among the monetary authorities of the industrial countries was that inflation was subject to a downward ratchet effect: while inflation could easily rise, reductions were difficult to achieve, as if inflation encountered resistance, a ratchet, in a downward direction. The monetary authorities considered that a stringent anti-inflation policy was needed to overcome this ratchet.

The anti-inflation policy consisting of a restrictive monetary policy was, as already remarked in the previous chapter, instigated by the United States. That country was also the most energetic in implementing this change of policy. The result was a sharp rise in interest rates worldwide, but particularly in the United States. These differential increases in world interest rates also led to a strong appreciation of the dollar as capital flowed towards the highest interest rate. To make matters worse, the higher interest rates worldwide caused a sharp decline in economic growth in the industrial countries, and hence in their imports. Traditionally, it is particularly the exports of developing countries with a strong emphasis on commodity which is suffering from such a negative development.

These three effects of the industrial countries' anti-inflation policy (higher interest rates, higher dollar and decline in the value of imports, especially from developing countries) was highly detrimental to the financial position of the world's debtor countries. This is illustrated particularly clearly by the structure of the debt service ratio. The appreciation of the dollar increased the repayment burden expressed in the debtor country's own currency, since most loans were denominated in dollars. The interest rate and with it the interest payments rose sharply because of the world increase in interest rates. The rate went up not only for new loans but also for existing ones because of their roll-over character. Slower growth in the industrial countries' imports tends to affect the exports of the developing countries in two ways: by slower growth in the volume of exports and a fall in the export price. In 1980 and 1981 the slow-down in growth was so severe that the volume of imports by industrial countries over the two years fell by almost 4 per cent. It goes without saying that the increase in the two components of the numerator and the simultaneous fall in the denominator of the debt service ratio had a disastrous effect on the ratio's value. Table 17.2 shows that for all the developing countries together it went up from 17.3 to 24.6 per cent between 1980 and 1982. This means that in 1982 the developing countries had to spend almost a quarter of their export revenue on servicing their debt. Again, there were substantial variations in the value of this ratio within the group of developing countries from one region of the world to another. Thus, in 1982 the figure for Asia was 'only' 11.3 per cent while for Latin America it was 51.6 per cent! The increase of the interest payments among the components of the debt-service ratio is impressive in particular: between 1978 and 1972 this component (also expressed as a ratio to exports) doubled in value.

17.2.2 Internal causes

As if these external causes were not enough, various internal causes can also be shown to have contributed to the outbreak of the debt crisis in 1982.

1. At that time the developing countries certainly had poorly developed and, moreover, strictly *regulated financial markets*. Regulation often meant that the government kept interest rates artificially low with the aim of promoting domestic investment, while also gaining cheap access to loans for itself in this way. Naturally, the problem with such a regulated market is that easing is not spontaneous: demand for loans always exceeded the supply of capital, because saving was discouraged by the low interest rate. Inevitably the government had to restrict demand for credit via a licensing system.

2. Governments in developing countries are more inclined than those in industrial countries to have *substantial budget deficits*. The governments are weaker and, in order to remain in power, they are more willing to give in to demands from pressure groups, demands that usually cost public money. Because of the limited scope for using the (usually badly developed) domestic capital market, third world governments often resort to financing by money creation or by taking on foreign debts – in so far as they wish to make purchases abroad. The latter form of financing naturally contributes directly to the growth of foreign debts.

3. In many developing countries, the *monetary financing* of budget deficits is the main source of domestic inflation. This is one reason why various third world countries actually face hyperinflation (several hundred per cent or more per annum). Understandably, high inflation prompts calls for index-linking of wages and prices in an attempt to avoid the loss of purchasing power caused by inflation. Compliance produces a fossilised economy in which wage flexibility and the adjustability of relative prices virtually disappears. Wages and prices therefore cease to reflect the underlying relative scarcities, at the expense of efficiency in the economy.

4. Many developing countries suffered from an *overvalued currency*. In some cases this was deliberately encouraged by the government, while in others it was an unintentional effect of the application of the chosen exchange rate system. In its efforts to favour certain population groups, a government would often assist town-dwellers with an overvalued currency, because overvaluation means relatively cheap imports. And in third world countries, imports include many products (luxury consumer goods and food) which are sold in the towns. A second common reason why governments maintain an overvalued currency is to combat inflation. The price of both imports and exports is kept down in terms of domestic currency, and this will help to curb domestic inflation. However, the disadvantage of an overvalued currency is that exports (with prices often fixed in foreign currency on the world market) bring in relatively little domestic currency. This also applies to domestic production which competes with imports. In many cases, exports include minerals and agricultural products produced in the countryside.

Apart from the government's behaviour, the exchange rate system is also a potential source of overvalued currencies. The crawling peg system is frequently used in developing countries. As outlined in Chapter 14, when applied correctly, this entails many but small devaluations or revaluations of the domestic currency. Thus, the exchange rate can always take on its equilibrium value. However, in the case of high inflation – say a double-digit rate per month – the parity adjustments have to be very frequent in order to offer adequate compensation for the loss of purchasing power of the domestic currency against foreign currencies. The necessary frequency of parity adjustments is also often underestimated because the current rate of inflation is an underestimate of future inflation. In that case, the country in question also has to contend with an exchange rate which is constantly lagging behind reality, leading to a permanently overvalued domestic currency. In addition, many developing countries had (and have) a fixed exchange rate in relation to one leading currency such as the US dollar or the French franc. This means that their currency moves up and down with the currency of an industrial country. That movement may be totally counter to the trend in the equilibrium value of the currency of the developing country concerned, and thus cause serious imbalances in the national balance of payments during many years. This adverse effect was seen in the last decade in the case of African countries whose currencies were linked to the French franc: as a result, those African currencies eventually had to be devalued by 50 per cent at the beginning of 1994.

Clearly, an overvalued currency is bad for the country's competitive position, prompting current account deficits and hence rising foreign debts. Economic growth is also at risk. For example, the fact that the new industrial countries of Asia produced much stronger growth than those in Latin America is often attributed in part to the exchange rates. In the first group they were roughly at their equilibrium value, while in the second they were grossly overvalued.

Common side effects of an overvalued domestic currency are flight of capital to other countries and a black market in foreign currencies. An overvalued currency means that the real price of a foreign currency expressed in domestic currency units is below the equilibrium value. Speculators believe that such a difference cannot be maintained permanently because there are economic forces which will ultimately level out the difference. The expected appreciation of the foreign currency is an attractive source of income: by buying the foreign currency now with relatively little domestic money and expecting to sell it again in the near future for a larger amount of domestic money, the speculator is likely to make an exchange rate gain. This will generate massive demand for foreign currencies: speculators 'flee' into foreign currencies. (Here we see again the working of the uncovered interest parity.) This process normally takes the form of the creation of foreign bank credit balances or the purchase of foreign securities such as bonds, equities and property. Since the central bank's monetary reserves in the country with the overvalued currency cannot cope with such demand for foreign currencies, the central bank faces a choice: either to decide on immediate devaluation of the domestic currency or to cease to honour the demand for foreign currencies. In the latter case the central bank effectively imposes foreign exchange restrictions: some requests for foreign currency will still be honoured, but not others. This last category naturally includes requests for the sole purpose of capital flight.

Since foreign exchange speculators cannot be caught out, it is usual for them to arrange a black market in foreign currencies in a situation of imminent capital flight plus exchange restrictions. On the black market there is free interplay of demand and supply, resulting in a free price. In our particular case, the black market price of the foreign currency will be higher than the official market price. People offering foreign currency on the black market include exporters who are able and willing to sell their foreign exchange earnings at the higher black market price. Their willingness to do so will naturally depend very much on the punishment meted out by the government for black market traders.

5. Contrary to what is often thought, third world countries generally have *high trade barriers*, or in any case higher than the industrial countries. Import tariffs and quotas for industrial products are often so high as to bring about import substitution. By imposing import levies which make foreign semi-manufactures and final products expensive on the domestic market, the government stimulates domestic production, thus boosting industrialisation. It is also not unusual for the government of a developing country to impose an export levy on agricultural products and commodities for export. This depresses the domestic price of agricultural products, thus lowering the cost of living. In this way it helps to reduce inflation and also aids the industrialisation process via lower wage demands. Furthermore, it must be remembered that for governments in developing countries, import and export levies are an important source of revenue which they can hardly do without. Other forms of tax necessitate a well-developed administrative machinery which is often lacking in developing countries. The principal objection to all these forms of protectionist policy is of course that it frustrates the optimum allocation of production and consumption, with the known resulting loss of economic welfare.

17.3   The IMF and the debt problem

17.3.1   Lending

The IMF seemed the appropriate body to help finance the balance of payments deficits caused by the first oil price shock. As we saw in section 16.4, the IMF was assigned an essential function as regards balance of payments financing, but in practice, what happened in the 1970s was very different. The IMF was relegated to a secondary position by the private banking system. Between 1974 and 1978 less than 4 per cent of the current account deficits in oil-importing developing countries were covered by IMF credits.

In the 1970s there was a spontaneous division of functions between the IMF and the private banks, the latter providing loans for the most creditworthy countries while the other oil-importing developing countries had to apply to the IMF as a last resort. Moreover, the IMF had the thankless task of offering a helping hand to countries in the first group if their balance of payments difficulties became acute, because at that point the banks promptly dropped out altogether. In short, this meant that the problem cases were left to the IMF. Paradoxically, the reason lay in the required policy conditions attached to IMF credits. Countries have a great abhorrence of foreign intervention in their policy: it impairs their political autonomy, which is obviously very important to governments.

Box 17.1 Nature and use of IMF credits

The IMF offers its members a range of credit facilities, which are summarised in Table 17.4. The table also shows the year of introduction for each facility, plus the maximum level of credit for an IMF member. That maximum is related to the country's IMF quota. The table is intended to give an impression of the complex system of IMF credits which has developed over the years. It would take too long to describe each form of credit, simply because every form has its own policy conditions. We shall therefore confine ourselves to a few individual comments.

The IMF classes the Stand-by arrangement and the Extended arrangement as the two regular credit facilities. A member can draw on these in tranches or segments of 25 per cent of its quota. Drawing in the first credit tranche is subject to the IMF condition that the country must be able to show that it is making a reasonable attempt to correct its balance of payments problems. Drawings in higher credit tranches usually take the form of a Stand-by arrangement. Resources are then made available periodically in instalments, depending on whether, at that moment, the economy of the country in question satisfies the predetermined performance criteria. These criteria relate to ceilings for domestic credit creation and the government budget, targets for the stock of international monetary reserves and the level of foreign debt, and restrictions on international payments for current account transactions. If the IMF reaches agreement with the country, funds are borrowed from the IMF over a maximum of two years, after which the loan has to be repaid within three years.

Table 17.4 IMF credits (% of a country's quota)

Start	Type of credit	Maximum
1947 and 1974	Stand-by and Extended arrangements	
	annually	68
	cumulative	300
1963	Special facilities	
	Compensatory and contingency financing facility (CCFF)	
	fall in export earnings	30
1981	excessive costs of cereal imports	15
	other	145
1969	Buffer stock financing facility	35
1993	Systemic transformation facility	
	cumulative	50
1986	SAF and ESAF arrangements	
	Structural adjustment facility (SAF)	
	first year	15
	second year	20
	third year	15
	cumulative	50
1987	Enhanced structural adjustment facility (ESAF)	
	three-year access	190

Source: IMF Survey; Supplement on the Fund, August 1994, p. 13.

Credit facilities under the Extended Arrangement are intended to finance adjustment programmes in the medium term, in the case of structural problems. Drawings are made over a period of three or sometimes four years, after which they can be repaid over the next six years. Performance criteria are again applicable.

The Special Facilities include the Systemic Transformation Facility. This is a temporary form of IMF credit intended for Russia and other economies in transition from a centrally planned economy to a market economy. The SAF and ESAF shown in the table were developed by the IMF for low-income members. These are loans on easy terms (with interest at only 0.5 per cent) for countries with permanent balance of payments problems. In this, the IMF collaborates with the World Bank.

Figure 17.2 shows that the two regular credit facilities of the IMF represent the bulk of IMF credits. It also shows that the IMF only really began to extend credit on a large scale after the outbreak of the 1982 debt crisis. In 1985 the outstanding loans reached a (temporary) peak of almost SDR 40 billion. The decline in subsequent years was more or less predictable because the repayment period commences about three years after the start of the credit.

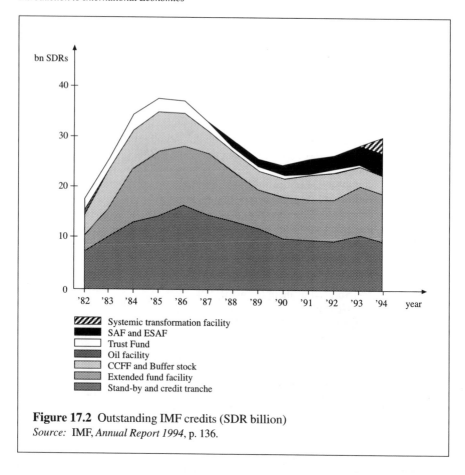

Figure 17.2 Outstanding IMF credits (SDR billion)
Source: IMF, *Annual Report 1994*, p. 136.

The IMF has demonstrated great flexibility in adjusting the nature of the credit facilities to circumstances. Thus, immediately after the first oil shock the Oil Facility was introduced, followed a few years later by the Trust Fund (1976) and the Supplementary Financing Facility (1977), also known as the Witteveen facility after the then Managing Director, the Dutchman Witteveen. Funds for this were made available by individual member countries so that the IMF's regular resources were not affected. When, in the 1980s, it became clear that restoration of balance of payments equilibrium would require more long-term solutions, the Fund produced the Structural Adjustment Facility in which the drawing period was extended to three years and the repayment period to ten years. As a result, the IMF became much more of a competitor for the World Bank. After a period of rising tension between the two international organisations, they now seem willing to resolve this question of overlapping spheres by closer cooperation.

As already noted in section 16.4, the IMF first allocated SDRs in 1970 to members which joined the IMF Special Drawing Rights department in that year. SDRs are in fact a form of indirect credit. As we said in that section, the holder can use them to acquire unconditional credit. Under its Articles of Agreement, the IMF is entitled to create additional SDRs 'to meet the need, as and when it arises, for a supplement to existing reserve assets'. It was therefore not surprising that a link was soon proposed between the possibility of allocating SDRs and financial assistance for developing countries. The underlying idea was: if additional international monetary reserves have to be created for the benefit of the world economy, it is highly efficient to serve a second objective at the same time, namely development aid. However, this link between the issue of SDRs and the provision of development aid never came about. After lengthy discussion in the 1970s, the subject was dropped from the agenda. The main objections put forward by opponents of the link proposal were as follows:

- 'the need for a supplement' concerns the need for additional SDRs on a worldwide scale, not the needs of just one group of countries;
- in the 1970s, inflation certainly increased in the developing countries too. A supplementary allocation of SDRs could easily reinforce increasing inflationary tendencies in the developing countries;
- international monetary reserves are resources held for possible temporary use for balance of payments and exchange rate purposes. As time goes by, a country will top up its reserves again after use. Thus, in essence they are 'reserves to hold' and not 'reserves to spend'. If SDRs were to be used for development purposes, then they would undoubtedly fall into the second category. The developing countries would use them up once and for all. It was thought that this would seriously impair the character of the SDR as a reserve asset, and would most certainly undermine its position as such.

In practice, we find that many developing countries did in fact use up their SDR allocation almost immediately, and that they were hardly ever in a position where they had to buy back the SDRs used in an earlier period. When the debt crisis broke out, the SDRs therefore played no part in financing the balance of payments deficits.

17.3.2 IMF conditionality

The IMF provides temporary credits for members with balance of payments deficits. They are meant to prevent a country from being forced to reduce a balance of payments deficit very rapidly owing to a shortage of monetary reserves. According to definition equation (17.1) – which is the same as equation (13.2) – current account equilibrium, or CA equals zero, means that a country's domestic production, Y, must be equal to the residents' demand for goods, or absorption A.

$$CA = Y - A \qquad (17.1)$$

In the short term, it is only demand for goods that can be changed significantly;

production is more or less fixed. This means that a current account deficit (CA is negative) can only be rectified immediately by squeezing demand. Residents' demand for consumption and investment then have to decline sharply. That can lead to distressing situations, certainly in a poor country. There is therefore much to be said for giving the country the chance to spread the balance of payments adjustment over several years. This offers the opportunity to raise domestic production so that the demand squeeze can be less severe. The country can achieve this by raising loans abroad, including IMF loans.

IMF conditionality is intended to make use of such temporary balance of payments financing as a means of pressurising the country in question to arrange the efficient adjustment of the balance of payments disequilibrium. Another reason for imposing conditions is to protect the IMF resources to have this money available for re-use after a time. If a country were unable to repay the IMF credit, then the IMF would be unable to re-use the money for subsequent lending to other member countries. In other words, IMF loans are revolving in character. The IMF conditions also prove successful on occasion in persuading the member country's government to pursue the policy which it would really have liked to adopt even without the IMF, but which was not possible because of domestic political forces. If the country concerned is subject to the IMF conditions, then the government attains a position where it can blame the IMF. For a weak government it can be an advantage to suggest that the IMF forced it to adopt the policy, thus remaining beyond reproach itself.

According to the IMF, conditionality is individually designed: the policy conditions are tailored to the country applying for a credit. But there is a clear thread running through the IMF conditions, as set out in the following five points.

1. In by far the majority of cases, the country has to carry out a *large devaluation*, often before the IMF agrees to the policy eventually proposed by the country. The devaluation also appears to be mainly a sign of goodwill. The object of devaluation is of course to rectify the overvaluation of the national currency. Devaluation affects the composition of both demand and supply in the country. In economic terms, a developing country is usually so insignificant to the world economy that it cannot influence the world market price of its tradables. That price is therefore set for the country, so that devaluation normally means a substantial increase in the domestic price of these goods, corresponding to the percentage devaluation. As a result, part of the domestic demand for these goods is transferred to non-tradables – which remain cheaper. This shift in demand releases goods for exports and also reduces demand for imports. On the supply side, the reverse shift takes place. The more expensive tradables attract domestic producers in so far as they can transform their production at the expense of non-tradables and in favour of goods which can be traded internationally. This transformation releases more goods for export and will again reduce the country's net demand for imports. Devaluation therefore improves the balance of

payments via both the demand and the supply side of export and import goods.

2. The IMF often considers the excessive growth of the country's money supply to be at the heart of a balance of payments problem. It fuels inflation and undermines the country's competitive position. *Credit ceilings* are therefore prominent among the IMF policy conditions.

3. In developing countries, the government is often the main source of money creation. As already stated, the government often finances a substantial part of the budget deficit by placing money in circulation. The IMF therefore almost always requires a *sharp reduction in the government's budget deficit*.

4. As we have seen, developing countries are often subject to considerable price distortions. The government subsidises many things (such as energy and basic essentials), fixes artificially low prices (such as the interest rate) and intervenes via trade policy in the pricing of tradables. The IMF is fervently opposed to this and therefore demands a *reduction in protectionism* and urges *the lessening of subsidies*. The latter also helps to cut the budget deficit. In practice, the abolition of subsidies on basic essentials causes uproar in countries which bring in the IMF.

5. Only part of the increase in the price of tradables can be passed on in wages and prices of other products. This is meant to avoid creating a *vicious circle*. In economics, that means the chain of cause and effect started by devaluation, through higher inflation at home – via imported inflation combined with domestic wage and price indexation – leading to the need for another devaluation, and so on.

In the past the IMF's policy conditions have been much criticised. In the early 1980s, given the deregulation advocated by the Reagan administration in the US, the IMF was accused of ignoring the supply side of the economy. The IMF defended itself by drawing attention to the influence of devaluation on the supply side. A decade later the main reproach was that the IMF disregarded income distribution in a country, so that the poorest sections of the population, in particular, suffered as a result of the IMF policy. The IMF responded that it had no right to interfere in domestic affairs. The IMF's mandate did not extend beyond the balance of payments objective, for which a rough macro-economic framework was sufficient. Nevertheless, the Fund did accept the criticism in practice and in later years, wherever possible, its policy recommendations placed greater emphasis on those aspects which had previously been the subject of outside criticism.

17.4   The debt crisis

When the debt crisis broke out in August 1982, the great significance of international organisations watching over the interests of the world economy became apparent. The first reaction by the private banks was to call a total halt to further lending to the debtor countries, and to extricate themselves as quickly as possible from outstanding claims on those countries. If all the banks had actually done that, all the debtor countries would have been heading for default. In 1981 and 1982 the net inflow of capital to those countries was still $50 and $38 billion. Such an abrupt reversal as the private banks wanted was therefore totally impossible. Even if the net inflow of capital to these countries had been zero, credit would still have been necessary, in the form of a gross inflow of capital, to enable the debtor countries to finance the required principal repayments and interest charges.

If credit is cut off altogether, collective defaulting or worse debt repudiation, ceasing to acknowledge the debts, is an attractive alternative for heavy borrowers. However, such a reaction would have been disastrous for the international financial system. The private banks' equity would have been totally inadequate to bear such losses. By way of more than an example, take the situation of the nine largest US banks operating internationally. At the end of 1982 they had outstanding claims totalling $57 billion in the 15 countries with the largest debts, while their equity (share capital and reserves for bad debts) was $29 billion (Morgan Guaranty, 1987, p. 3). In other words, their outstanding claims on these debtor countries were almost double their equity! If an individual bank had a more favourable ratio than the average, it was still so closely intertwined with the other banks by extensive inter-bank lending that it would undoubtedly have been dragged down too if they had gone bankrupt.

Consequently, after the outbreak of the debt crisis all private banks taken together were very anxious to continue providing credit in such a way that the debtor countries would not default. But an individual bank cheerfully opted for the role of free rider: it would no longer grant credit itself in the hope that the majority of the other private banks would carry on doing so. This threat of inconsistency in banking behaviour was prevented in 1982 and subsequent years by the action of international organisations. On the initiative of the Bank for International Settlements in Basle, with the support of a number of the world's central banks, Mexico was granted a short-term loan in August 1982.[1] This tided the country over until the IMF was able to reach agreement on credit facilities with Mexico.

Suddenly, the IMF was very much back on the scene. It was the only one prepared to continue granting credit to the debtor countries, under the usual policy conditions. However, the resources available to the IMF for that purpose were far from sufficient to meet the credit requirement. The IMF therefore

---

1. The Bank for International Settlements (BIS) was set up in 1930 as a clearing centre for the German reparations payments resulting from the First World War. Its headquarters is in Basle. The Bank's general objectives include promoting cooperation between central banks and providing supplementary facilities for international financial operations. The bridging loan for Mexico in 1982 ties in well with this. The resources temporarily required for the purpose came from central banks which the BIS asked to participate in the loan. Since then this form of bridging loan has been used by the BIS on several occasions.

adopted a tactical approach and acted as a catalyst for continued lending to debtor countries. The formula was this: first the IMF tried to reach agreement with a debtor country on the policy conditions under which the IMF was willing to lend money to the country. The resulting agreement was then subject to the important supplementary condition that the private banks with outstanding claims on the country in question would continue to extend credit facilities, even if only to refinance maturing credits. Thus, the banks were actually placed in a dilemma: the IMF policy conditions would certainly help to give the banks a chance of recovering the money already outstanding, but they would not be implemented unless the banks came up with more finance. During the 1980s this form of coercion worked extremely well.

Apart from the provision of supplementary finance, debts were often rescheduled. In practice, this actually always meant postponing principal repayments on loans by a number of years and extending the repayment period. Governments of industrial countries were also active in rescheduling the debts of developing countries, because they were often involved in such debts, sometimes directly in the form of outstanding official debts and sometimes rather more indirectly by issuing government credit guarantees to banks and businesses. The Paris Club was used for the multilateral official debt reviews. This 'club' consists of the group of creditor countries and the debtor country for a specific rescheduling case. It implies that its composition varies. The club usually decides the exact form of debt rescheduling at a meeting in Paris, hence its name.

Thus, in the end, the great achievement of the 1980s was that gross lending to major debtor countries was maintained so that the debt crisis was kept under control and a financial collapse of the world economy was avoided. Although the developing countries initially saw an increase in the size of their foreign debt and the associated debt service, these variables gradually declined in relation to the value of exports after peaks in the period 1982–6. In 1986 the figures for the ratios were 178 per cent and 22 per cent; by 1993 they were 'only' 118 per cent and 15 per cent. Naturally, regional variations within the group of developing countries remained as large as ever, but the same tendency of improvement was evident for almost every regional group, although only barely in Africa's case. The ratio between the outstanding bank claims on debtor countries and bank equity improved even more sharply. At the end of 1986 this ratio had already dropped to 121 for the American banks referred to earlier. Since then the decline has continued, so that the ratio was well below 100 per cent by 1990. The risk of a wave of bankruptcies in the banking system caused by collective defaulting on the part of debtor countries is therefore a thing of the past.

The adjustment of the debt situation described above was certainly not painless. The developing countries, in particular, suffered. The required macroeconomic adjustment policy, spurred on by the IMF's policy conditions, caused economic growth in those countries to slow down substantially. But that was inevitable. At the end of the 1980s many large developing countries had a lower per capita income than at the beginning of that decade, which is why people tend to refer to it as a lost decade (for the developing countries). But that is not entirely correct. Even at first sight, this picture is dubious. Figure 17.1 shows that the developing countries did see an abrupt decline in their growth rate in 1981–3, but that since then the growth figures are nearly as high as in the 1970s. Almost without exception, they beat the industrial countries year after year in this respect. Moreover, on closer examination we see efficiency improvements in the economy of many countries. The positive trends apparent in many of these countries in the past few years bear that out. It is only the continent of Africa that is still ailing.

Once the banks had reduced the ratio between their outstanding claims and their equity below 100 per cent, they were able to adopt a much more flexible approach to taking losses on outstanding loans, which until then they had only suffered on paper. In this period, banks started to sell part of the debt instruments of the debtor countries on the secondary market which had recently developed for these instruments. The resale prices were, of course, lower than the face value of the debts. This was how the banks took their losses. The cut-price debt instruments were bought up in particular by companies wishing to invest in such a debtor country, thus acquiring a debt instrument for the country at low cost. These companies are not interested in getting the debt paid out in dollars, but want the underlying value in the local currency because they wish to invest locally. For the country concerned, supplying the local currency is naturally not a problem in itself. It need not be earned first, so it is not scarce. In practice, such a transaction in which a foreign company converts a debt instrument denominated in dollars into shares in local firms (hence the name: debt-equity swap) is often financially advantageous for both the company and the government concerned. Of course, someone also has to be the loser in such a debt-equity swap, but we have already considered that: namely, the bank that sold the debt instrument for a reduced price. In their newly acquired financial position, the banks did not opt exclusively for the secondary market. Other, more direct methods of writing off bad debts were used, as illustrated by Case study 17.1, a news article which dates from 1989.

Case study 17.1 'Tequila sunrise'

The Latin American debt crisis began in Mexico seven years ago and the beginning of a solution is now emerging there. At the weekend, Mexico reached agreement with its private money-lenders on a substantial reduction in its foreign debt. For the first time since Mexico became bankrupt in the summer of 1982, the banks have formally agreed to reduce the debts.

That is a breakthrough, but it is not the end of the debt problem; because the agreement reached between Mexico and the banks after long drawn-out and difficult negotiations concerns part of the debts of just one country. The debt reduction applies only to Mexico's long-term bank debts, which come to $54 billion out of a total foreign debt of $107 billion. The direct cash advantage,

---

a reduction in interest payments worth $1.5 billion per annum, is also not that dramatic. Mexico pays out many times that each year to its creditors.

Nevertheless, the agreement sets a precedent; it is an example to other debtor countries and a reward for Mexico's economic reform policy.

Source: NRC Handelsblad, 25 July 1989.

In March 1989 the American Treasury Secretary launched a debt alleviation plan. Christened the Brady plan, this implied official recognition that full repayment of all outstanding debts was impossible. Brady proposed a reduction in commercial bank debts, offering the banks various options for reducing outstanding claims. Of course, it was no coincidence that this plan was put forward at about the same time as the banks were restored to a position in which they could write off their claims, as described in the preceding paragraph. Mexico was the first country with which such a debt reduction agreement was concluded (see Case study 17.1). Banks with claims on Mexico were obliged to exchange old claims for new ones. With respect to these new claims they had a choice of three evils: at lower interest, with a lower face value or with the promise of supplementary loans. The attraction of the new loan was that it had a repayment guarantee via a transaction with the American government. An IMF adjustment programme for the debtor country in question also formed part of the Brady plan, plus the possibility of letting the debtor country use IMF and World Bank funds to buy back debts on the secondary market.

Mexico was always in the forefront of the debt problem, alternating between success and disaster. 1994 brought another serious setback: at the end of the year, Mexico faced a major financial crisis which shook the foundations of the international financial world. A massive rescue operation led by the United States in collaboration with the IMF was needed to avoid Mexico's financial collapse and restore the financial world's confidence in Mexico to some degree. Essentially, the situation was far less alarming than in 1982. The Mexican economy did not actually demonstrate any fundamental imbalances, but this event does show that the process of adjustment to a stable economic situation still has its vulnerable moments. This is illustrated by Case study 17.2.

Case study 17.2 The fragile exchange rate anchor

The exchange rate as an inflation-stabilising anchor was central to the adjustment policy pursued by Mexico from the end of the 1980s. The exchange rate policy was aimed at devaluing the Mexican peso by less than the differential between the (higher) Mexican inflation and American inflation. Thus, Mexican inflation could be curbed by moderating the imported inflation. In the first years, this policy was successful. Inflation dropped from over 100 per cent at the start of the adjustment policy to 7 per cent per annum at the beginning of 1994. High inflation is usually accompanied by a high nominal interest rate, and this was also true in Mexico. Since the peso was not expected to devalue so sharply, investors could anticipate a higher return on investments in Mexico than in the United States. Via the uncovered interest rate parity (equation (13.14)) this prompted a substantial inflow of capital into Mexico, so that the value of the peso within the fluctuation band maintained with the dollar was consistently high. As a result, Mexico had no trouble at first in keeping to moderate devaluation of the peso.

However, this use of the exchange rate as an anchor to curb inflation has an inherent instability. The country's competitive position deteriorates, perhaps gradually yet unmistakably, causing a constant worsening of the current account. This pattern was quite obvious for Mexico in the years 1990–4. It gradually undermines confidence in the exchange rate policy: after all, the current account is one of the fundamental forces behind the exchange rate. In that situation, once events which are relatively trivial in economic terms begin to undermine confidence in the country, large-scale speculation against the country can result. In 1994 Mexico suffered two such events. First, a presidential candidate was murdered in March 1994 and then at the end of the year renewed riots broke out amongst the Indians in Chiapas, directed against the government. This was too much for the fragile exchange rate anchor. Capital flight caused a shortage of monetary reserves. In response, the fixed exchange rate for the peso was abandoned at the end of 1994. The peso went into free fall, rapidly depreciating by double-digit figures. On the Mexican stock market, shares lost more than half their value, on average.

Application of the adjustment policy by heavily indebted countries has revealed a relatively new problem. Not only is the overall package of adjustment policy components important to its success: the *sequencing* of those components is also essential. The wrong sequence can wreck the adjustment policy. We are concerned with adjustment packages which include among others: liberalisation of the labour market, the goods markets and the financial markets. The liberalisation of the last two market types bear upon both the domestic and the international transactions. Preferably, the domestic economy should be tackled first before international liberalisation of the sector concerned. The reverse sequence can cause the domestic factors stimulating international flows to work in the opposite direction from that of eventual equilibrium. Liberalisation of the labour market takes longest, so this should come first in the liberalisation process. Next, the government's usually large budget deficit must be reduced. To prevent this deficit from providing the wrong stimulus on a liberalised financial market (a real interest rate higher than the eventual equilibrium rate), priority should be given to reducing this deficit. This is followed by liberalisation of the goods markets, both internally (cutting subsidies) and externally (eliminating trade barriers). Only then does it really become clear which are the efficient production sectors in the economy. If the domestic financial sector is not liberalised until then, capital immediately floods into these efficient goods sectors to the detriment of the obsolete sectors, resulting in optimum allocation of capital. Following domestic financial liberalisation, the domestic interest rate settles at its equilibrium level. Only then can international capital movements be liberalised, because from that point on it is clear how the country in question fits into the pattern of relative capital scarcity in the world.

17.5 Transition to a market economy

After the Second World War the communist countries of Eastern Europe, including the Soviet Union, constructed their own economic 'world'. Production was based on plans and mutual trade was increased, again on the basis of an economic plan. This mutual trade took place officially under Comecon (an acronym for Council for Mutual Economic Assistance). The countries concerned placed great emphasis on the economies of scale in production specialisation, so that giant companies developed which sometimes actually covered the whole Comecon area without any significant competition. As a result of the planned economy with its emphasis on quantity, manufactured goods proved difficult to sell in the West because of their mediocre quality. The principle of barter trade was necessary to sell any industrial products at all in the West. Products which did find a ready market in the West were raw materials and particularly crude oil from the Soviet Union.

When great cracks began to appear in the centrally organised production and planning system of the Comecon countries at the end of the 1980s, the countries concerned were in an extremely vulnerable situation. They turned *en masse* to the Western market, but with industrial products which could not compete. Even if the prices were reduced, the goods were extremely difficult to sell in the West. The quality was inadequate and the products were not sufficiently tailored to consumer requirements. In retrospect, it might perhaps have been very useful for the mutual trade between the Comecon countries to be maintained. But political freedom from the Soviet yoke plus the decision by the Soviet Union to charge the ex-Comecon countries the world market price for oil – whereas the price had previously been much lower – destroyed these trade flows. As a result, the East European countries, with the exception of the Soviet Union, suffered a substantial deterioration in the terms of trade as well. Within a few years these countries therefore saw a massive slump in both the volume of exports and domestic demand – and in domestic production as a result of these two factors. With the exception of Romania, the Eastern Bloc countries had already acquired substantial foreign debts at the beginning of the post-communist period. The current account deficits caused by the switch to a market economy greatly exacerbated this situation.

This made the Eastern Bloc countries similar in many ways to the heavily indebted developing countries in the post-1982 period. The adjustment policy recommended for those countries therefore also seemed appropriate to the Eastern Bloc. But the plight of this last group of countries was essentially far worse: they suddenly had to conduct a large-scale privatisation – markets were virtually non-existent and so were private commercial banks – and the social and legal infrastructure necessary for a market economy to work well had to be built up from scratch. Thus, while the macro-economic adjustment programme could be borrowed from the developing countries, more was needed, and it really ought to be done before the adjustment programme.

Privatisation by the issue of vouchers to every individual, permitting the purchase of shares in state enterprises under the privatisation programme, seems to be a reasonably effective instrument in practice. In any case, in the country concerned it generates widespread political support for rapid privatisation. The Czech Republic at least has used it successfully. Private banks which can play a constructive role in the case of bankruptcies, or better still in preventing them for businesses which are viable in principle, are essential and are now beginning to get off the ground in many of these countries. According to some people, the trauma of adjustment is so great that there is no sense in an optimum sequence of adjustment phases. The prevailing idea is that, for these countries, shock therapy is more useful than the 'graduality' advocated for developing countries, and at least offers the reasonably early prospect of light at the end of the tunnel. Be that as it may, it seems that the former planned economies will have to endure an economic abyss in their efforts to make the transition to a market economy. There are signs that, for countries which apply the shock therapy, the abyss is no deeper, but in terms of time it is narrower than for countries which advocate a gradual process. Case study 17.3 is an illustration.

Case study 17.3 The Polish shock therapy

12 September 1989 is a historic date for Poland. That was when Solidarity came to power, led by Lech Walesa. It meant the definitive end of forty years of communism in the country. The centrally planned economy had to be converted into a market economy. For that purpose, a Polish version of the IMF stabilisation programme was developed and then introduced on 1 January 1990. The principal objectives of the programme were to reduce inflation and achieve equilibrium in the markets. To this end, prices had to be largely liberalised and the government budget must be balanced. In addition, three nominal anchors were introduced to curb inflation: a restrictive wage policy, a restrictive monetary policy and a fixed exchange rate. Various institutional changes were also planned to support the policy measures.

In practice, prices were totally liberalised on 1 January 1990. A radical restriction on subsidies and an increase in taxes reduced the government deficit. At first, wages were not liberalised but fixed according to a particular system of indexation whereby they could not rise by more than a certain percentage of inflation. A key aim of the restrictive monetary policy was to achieve a positive real interest rate to inhibit demand for credit and stimulate savings. The exchange rate was not fixed until after the currency, the zloty, had been devalued. The fixed

---

exchange rate was expected to moderate inflation and ensure that international competition exerted great pressure on the efficiency of the Polish producers.

Once these measures were introduced, inflation initially soared, causing a sharp drop in real wages. After a while, the high inflation made the fixed exchange rate untenable, and in October 1991 a crawling peg system was adopted. The loss of purchasing power led to a sharp decline in domestic demand; owing to the collapse of Comecon, foreign demand for Polish products also slumped. Industrial production suffered a particularly sharp drop and unemployment constantly increased. The budget deficit remained high, mainly because of the lower than expected revenue. The recession meant a shortfall in tax revenue, whereas the proceeds from privatisation were less than forecast.

Three years after the introduction of the shock therapy, Poland was the first East European country to bring the decline in production under control. The principal reasons for the restoration of growth were the expansion of exports to the West and the growth of the private sector. Over half the economy was already in private hands!

17.6 Summary

1. The debt crisis which broke out in August 1982 and brought many heavily indebted countries and a very large number of banks operating internationally to the brink of ruin dominated the world economic scene in the 1980s. There were many apparent causes for the debt crisis.

2. External causes of the debt crisis include: the two oil-price shocks in the 1970s, the fact that the international financial markets were a borrowers' market in those years, the fact that the oil-importing developing countries made heavy use of bank roll-over credits with variable interest rates, the banks' large-scale participation in syndicated lending and the strict anti-inflationary policy of industrial countries from the end of 1979.

3. For the countries with large debts, the following are regarded as internal causes of the debt crisis: tightly regulated domestic financial markets, large government deficits, high domestic inflation greatly stimulated by the monetary financing of the government deficits, an overvalued currency and domestic price distortions caused by government intervention and international trade barriers.

4. Although the IMF has a range of credit facilities to offer its members, the Fund played only a modest role in the period prior to the debt crisis. Balance of payments deficits were largely financed by recycling oil dollars through the international banking system. The new IMF credit facilities created in response to the first oil shock and the introduction of the SDR did little to change this. However, in those years the IMF's resources were very important to countries unable to obtain commercial credit.

5. The policy conditions imposed by the IMF as a requirement for the granting

of credit were decisive in dissuading many countries from involving the IMF before the debt crisis.

6. After the outbreak of the debt crisis, however, these developing countries did have to reach agreement with the IMF because the commercial banks called an abrupt halt to international lending. It was thanks to the energetic intervention of the BIS and the IMF, in cooperation with a number of central banks, that credit for major debtor countries did not dry up altogether. Essentially, these international monetary institutions thus avoided the collapse of the international financial world.

7. The fragile balance consisting of IMF loans under policy conditions which compelled the commercial banks to provide supplementary credit helped the debt crisis through the 1980s. This gave the commercial banks the time to put matters in order as regards the initial imbalance between their equity and the outstanding claims on doubtful international debtors.

8. At the end of the 1980s an acceptable financial position had been restored on many bank balance sheets, which gave these banks the scope for dealing realistically with their bad debts. Debt instruments for countries with heavy debts were sold at a loss by the banks on the secondary market. Debts were also rescheduled, not only by extending the period of repayment but also in the form of partial remission. This process enabled heavily indebted countries to achieve a substantial improvement in their debt service ratio.

9. The former planned economies of Eastern Europe and the ex Soviet Union are now making a very painful transition to a market economy. Their problems are similar to those of the heavily indebted developing countries in the 1970s. But there is also a major difference: the former planned economies have to contend with the immense issue of privatisation as well. Some people therefore see shock therapy as the only way for these countries to make the adjustment, while the developing countries could at least still carry out a gradual adjustment process, although the ideal sequence of both internal and external liberalisation of their economy was crucial.

Bibliography

Aghevli, B.B., M.S. Khan and P.J. Montiel (1991), *Exchange Rate Policy in Developing Countries: Some Analytical Issues*, IMF Occasional Paper, No. 70.

Bakker, A.F.P. (1995), *The International Financial Institutions*, Longman.

Bank for International Settlements (1995), *65th Annual Report*, Basle.

Frankel, J.A., M.P. Dooley and P. Wickham (eds) (1989) *Analytical Issues in Debt*, IMF.

International Monetary Fund (1994a), *Annual Report 1994*, Washington D.C.

International Monetary Fund (1994b), *IMF Survey: Supplement on the IMF*, 23.

Morgan Guaranty (1987), *World Financial Markets*, June/July.

Sachs, J.D. (ed.) (1989), *Developing Country Debt and the World Economy*, University of Chicago Press.

18 Regional monetary integration

18.1 Introduction

The system of fixed exchange rates ceased to exist worldwide in 1973 when the system of that type accepted at Bretton Woods in 1944 was shattered. However, there are still some 'islands' in the world where it has been maintained. In certain regions of the world, countries continued to operate fixed exchange rates even after March 1973, though they had their ups and downs. That uneven progress is the subject of this chapter.

Fixed exchange rates are closely connected with the concept of monetary integration, which can refer to both a situation and a process. A situation is a stage which has already been reached, possibly *en route* to full monetary integration. As a process, monetary integration expresses the movement towards more intensive phases of monetary integration. *Full monetary integration* is the final stage in which the countries concerned have rigidly and irrevocably fixed mutual exchange rates (without fluctuation margins) for their freely convertible currencies. Countries participating in monetary integration are usually also required to have abolished their restrictions on mutual capital movements. If countries have tied their currencies together in this way, then they really might as well opt for a single, joint currency. That is also known as full monetary integration.

Clearly, depending on the degree of exchange rate stability, we can identify a number of less advanced stages of monetary integration. Thus, Corden (1972) refers to the adjustable peg system of exchange rates (i.e. including a fluctuation margin) and currency convertibility for balance of payments current account transactions only as the stage of *pseudo-monetary integration*. Obviously, the process of monetary integration affects other aspects of macro-economic policy, such as the liberalisation of capital movements and also the coordination of monetary and fiscal policy for the countries concerned.

We speak of *regional* monetary integration if integration is confined to just one group of countries in the world. By far the best known case of regional monetary integration is the current adjustable peg system in the European Union (EU). The description of that system therefore takes up much of this chapter, namely in sections 18.2 to 18.5. Another interesting case is the French franc area in Africa. A large number of former French colonies in that region have mutually fixed exchange rates. This is the outcome of an agreement whereby the currency of each of these countries has a fixed rate of exchange with the French franc. The case is interesting because here, in contrast to the EU, we have a group of developing countries. This fixed exchange rate area in Africa is described in section 18.6.

The question whether, for a particular type of country, maintenance of genuinely fixed exchange rates is important or not brings us to the optimum currency area theory. This sets out criteria for examining whether it benefits the economic welfare of certain countries if they have mutually fixed exchange rates. As we shall see in section 18.7, this theory is certainly not perfect and is difficult to apply.

18.2 The Snake

The process of monetary integration in the EC (European Community, the forerunner of the EU) was launched at the European summit in The Hague in December 1969. This meeting of European heads of state and government decided to set up the Werner Committee which was given the task of examining the feasibility of monetary integration in the EC. The committee's report was completed in October 1970 and contained a plan whereby the EC – in those days a customs union – would be further integrated into an economic and monetary union (EMU), to be achieved by about 1980. A *monetary union* is a form of cooperation in a group of countries involving full monetary integration. An *economic union* additionally means that the countries concerned coordinate their economic policies to the extent required for efficient operation of the monetary union.

At the time, the principal motive for monetary integration was political: to give a new boost to the European integration process. There was also an economic motive derived from a problem in the EC's common agricultural policy. In the latter half of the 1960s that policy had suffered serious problems because of the realignments of the European currency parities – still in the Bretton Woods system at the time. Agricultural prices were fixed each year in a common accounting unit (currently the ECU); this was and is done at the beginning of the crop year. If exchange rates were adjusted during the year, so that the value of the national currency was generally also realigned in relation to the common accounting unit, then agricultural prices in the national currency would have to be adjusted at the same time. The governments of the EC countries did not want this: they preferred their producers to receive agricultural prices which were fixed in terms of the national currency, or were at least as stable as possible. However, this would cause differences between agricultural prices in the EC expressed in the common accounting unit, bringing the risk of distortions of competition. With adjustable exchange rates this necessitated the reintroduction of trade policy measures between EC countries, as illustrated by Case study 18.1. This protection was naturally a major breach of the customs union, which explains the fundamentally positive attitude at that time in the EC towards a process which would lead to full monetary integration. Another background factor, of course, was the argument that greater exchange rate stability would promote mutual trade in the EC; because it would further reduce uncertainty for that trade, making intra-EC trade still more like domestic trade.

Box 18.1 Monetary compensatory amounts

In 1967 the pound sterling was devalued, followed by the French franc in 1969; in 1969 the Deutschmark was revalued. Increases in the domestic prices of agricultural products (in the national currency) during the crop year in the United Kingdom and France, as a logical consequence of devaluation, were considered unacceptable in both countries from the point of view of controlling inflation and the desired effectiveness of the devaluations. For Germany a price fall for farmers consequential upon the revaluation of the mark was not acceptable. At the end of the 1960s the EC therefore adopted a system of monetary compensatory amounts in agriculture. The principle implied acceptance of the fact that domestic agricultural prices (i.e. expressed in the national currency) must not change as a result of realignment of the exchange rates during the crop year. It was acknowledged that the full effect of exchange rate changes on these prices could only be passed on gradually, over a four year period. In regard to competition in the EC, this means that when exchange rates are realigned, national agricultural markets must also be kept separate for several years. This was done by using trade policy instruments between the EC countries in the form of import tariffs (called levies in agriculture) and export subsidies (called refunds in agriculture) for countries with a revaluing currency and export duties and import subsidies in case of a devaluing currency. Thus, use of these instruments meant that there was no longer a common agricultural market in the EC: just as before the EC existed, there were again national agricultural markets separated by trade barriers.

To illustrate this need to reintroduce trade policy we take the example of the Deutschmark being revalued by 10 per cent against sterling. After 1979 the ECU was the accounting unit for the EC, and thus also for agricultural prices. Like the SDR, the ECU is a basket of currencies. It comprises all national currencies in the territory of the EC, although their weightings vary. To give an arithmetical example, say both the mark and the pound represent 20 per cent of the value of the ECU at the time of the exchange rate alteration. We also assume that it is agreed that 10 per cent of the exchange rate adjustment will take the form of revaluation of the mark against the ECU by 5 per cent and devaluation of the pound by 5 per cent with respect to the ECU. Choosing these percentages leaves the value of the ECU unchanged in relation to the other EC currencies: the increase in the value of the ECU due to revaluation of the mark is exactly offset by the downward effect on the ECU's value resulting from devaluation of the pound.

As we have said, an exchange rate adjustment does not alter agricultural prices in ECU in the current crop year. Without additional measures the intervening exchange rate adjustment would cause agricultural prices in Germany to fall by 5 per cent (expressed in marks) and to increase by 5 per cent in Britain (expressed in pounds). With the monetary compensatory amounts, Germany and the UK are entitled to leave domestic agricultural prices unchanged for the time being. If the borders with other EC countries were to remain open for agricultural products, then Germany and the UK would be unable to achieve this. The prices of agricultural products from countries such as the Netherlands and France, would fall by 5 per cent on the German market, in domestic currency terms, following revaluation of the mark, and prices of such products from the UK would actually fall by 10 per cent. In order to avoid price undercutting on the home market, Germany can introduce a 5 per cent import levy. On the other hand, in order to maintain the competitiveness of its agricultural exports in the EC, Germany is entitled to grant them a 5 per cent export subsidy.

Conversely, following devaluation Britain can only keep domestic agricultural prices unchanged by imposing a 5 per cent duty on exports to the EC and granting a 5 per cent subsidy on imports. These agricultural levies and subsidies which resulted from a change in the exchange rate in the EC during that period were known as monetary compensatory amounts (MCAs). They ensured that, although the actual exchange rates changed, national agricultural prices in domestic currency were left temporarily unchanged. The ratio of agricultural prices in the EC countries is called the green exchange rates. From the start it was intended to phase out the MCAs within four years following the exchange rate adjustment. But devaluations and revaluations marched swiftly, so that the MCAs were piled up rather than gradually reduced. The system of MCAs was abolished in this form on 1 January 1993.

The above-mentioned Werner plan for the formation of an EMU in the EC was not a success. This had nothing to do with the design structure. A three-stage process was planned for achieving monetary integration in the EC. Each stage was described in detail. Perhaps the plan might have become reality in this form if it had not been thwarted by the collapse of the Bretton Woods system in March 1973. This caused such turmoil on the foreign exchange market that almost all exchange rates came under pressure. The first oil price shock at the end of 1973 further exacerbated the worldwide foreign exchange upheaval. The recession of the mid 1970s in the industrial countries, greatly intensified by this oil shock, completed the highly adverse conditions under which the Werner plan was to be implemented. It is therefore not surprising that this plan was shelved.

However, just before the foreign exchange crisis of early 1973, the EC did succeed in establishing its own exchange rate system which to some extent withstood the collapse of Bretton Woods. This EC system was known as the Snake arrangement, and came into effect in May 1972.

The reason for introducing the Snake arrangement can be traced back to the Smithsonian agreement, dated December 1971, which restored the Bretton Woods exchange rate system after a brief period of floating exchange rates from May of that year. As we saw in section 16.4, this restoration did not mean a total return to the old situation. True, the IMF members' currencies were again linked to the dollar, but no longer via the dollar to gold. Nixon, the American president of the day, had suspended the US obligation to exchange dollars for gold in August 1971. That suspension has never been lifted. More important to Europe was the enlargement of the margins within which the exchange rate could fluctuate around the dollar parity from 1 to 2.25 per cent on either side of this parity. In other words, the fluctuation band was increased from 2 to 4.5 per cent of the parity value. However, it should be clear that if two currencies from the EC area have such a fluctuation band in relation to the dollar, the result for the exchange rate of the two EC currencies is a fluctuation band of twice 4.5 per cent, i.e. 9 per cent altogether. That maximum exchange rate alteration of 9 per cent occurs if: at any time one currency is at the upper limit of the fluctuation band against the dollar and the other currency is right at the lower limit; and at a subsequent moment the positions of the two EC currencies against the dollar are exactly the opposite. In other words, one currency moves from a position on the upper limit to one on the lower limit, both against the dollar, while the other currency does the exact opposite. One currency has then fallen by 4.5 per cent against the dollar while the other has gained 4.5 per cent against the dollar. The bilateral change in the value of the EC currencies is thus the sum of these changes, namely 9 per cent.

A bilateral exchange rate alteration of 9 per cent for EC currencies was considered unacceptable for a customs union. It was agreed that these currencies should have a maximum fluctuation band of twice 2.25 per cent, i.e. a total band width of 4.5 per cent under the Snake arrangement. Thus, the fluctuation band against the dollar would no longer be narrower than against an EC currency participating in the Snake. Indirectly, this imposed a further limitation on an EC currency's freedom to move against the dollar. The upper and lower intervention points against the dollar often were no longer reached because the fluctuation band against other EC currencies was frequently more constricting. It was usual for the group of EC currencies as a whole to move up and down like a snake within the wider fluctuation band against the dollar.

In May 1972 this Snake arrangement came into operation for currencies of the countries which then belonged to the EC, plus the currencies of the United Kingdom, Denmark and Norway (followed by Sweden's currency in March 1973). Several currencies remained in the Snake for only a short time. After just one month the pound sterling dropped out, soon followed by the Italian lira. The French franc also had to leave the arrangement at one point, but rejoined it, only to be forced out once again. The central banks for these currencies proved unable to maintain the fixed exchange rate against the other EC currencies, given the domestic economic objectives. Over the years the Snake increasingly degenerated into a kind of Deutschmark area which, apart from the mark as the central currency, comprised only the less important currencies of Germany's small neighbours.

18.3 The Exchange Rate Mechanism of the European Monetary System

In 1978 Germany and France clearly emerged as the backbone of European unification. (A power bloc which, initially very much against the will of the other EC countries, gradually became increasingly dominant in EC affairs.) After mutual consultation, the Federal German Chancellor Schmidt and the French President Giscard d'Estaing produced the plan for closer European monetary integration. The outcome was the European Monetary System (EMS), launched on 1 March 1979.

The EMS has three components. The most important is an adjustable peg system of exchange rates, again with a fluctuation band of 4.5 per cent, within which participating currencies may move against one another. It differed from the Snake only in that all EC currencies except sterling took part. The UK was too worried that its political autonomy might be undermined. A second component consists of a system of credit facilities which members are willing and obliged to provide for one another. The very short-term credit facilities with no upper volume limit are intended, in particular, to finance temporary balance of payments deficits. In that sense, these facilities are specifically meant to discourage speculative international capital movements. Introduction of the ECU (European Currency Unit) with official monetary functions is the third component of the EMS.

Although the UK decided to join the EMS, it was not prepared to take part in the EMS Exchange Rate Mechanism, known as the ERM. In the first few years of its existence the ERM worked only moderately well. As we can see from Table 18.1, there were numerous parity adjustments during that period. In the EMS these are usually referred to as exchange rate realignments. The first few years of the EMS bring to mind the analogy with a crawling peg system of exchange rates. At first, the only real achievement of the ERM was therefore that none of the currencies left the system – in contrast to what happened with the Snake.

Table 18.1 also shows that the Deutschmark is the strong currency in the EMS, in that if exchange rates are adjusted – or realigned – the mark never devalues against any other EMS currency. The net revaluation of the mark by the method set out in the table is 25.25 per cent. After the March 1983 realignment, the guilder joined the mark as a strong currency. Overall, the guilder remained 4 per cent below the mark. The Italian lira underwent the largest net devaluation among the currencies taking part in the ERM from the start, its parity falling by almost 31 per cent to mid September 1992, even though the lira, together with the Irish punt, had initially been assigned a wider band width of 12 per cent. Such fluctuation margins also applied to the currencies which did not join the ERM until later: the Spanish peseta in June 1989, sterling in October 1990 and the Portuguese escudo in May 1992. In January 1990 Italy swapped the broad band for its currency for the narrow band of 4.5 per cent.

The year 1985 represents a clear break with the past for the ERM. The frequency of realignments declined markedly after that year, as Table 18.1 shows. Although inflation differentials between the EMS countries had still not disappeared, the level and frequency of the devaluations against the Deutschmark did decline. Given the continuing inflation differential compared with Germany, this led to the appreciation of the real exchange rates of currencies such as the lira, initially the French franc and later the peseta. In other words, the

Table 18.1 Realignments in the EMS, 1979–91 (in % against the ECU)[1]

	24 Sep. 1979	30 Nov. 1979	23 Mar. 1981	5 Oct. 1981	22 Feb. 1982	14 Jun. 1982	21 Mar. 1983	22 Jul. 1985	7 Apr. 1986	4 Aug. 1986	12 Jan. 1987	8 Jan. 1990
Belgian and Luxemburg franc	−2.9				−8.5		+1.5	+2.0	+1.0		+2.0	
Danish krone		−4.8			−3.0		+2.5	+2.0	+1.0			
Deutschmark	+2.0			+5.5		+4.25	+5.5	+2.0	+3.0		+3.0	
French franc				−3.0		−5.75	−2.5	+2.0	−3.0			
Italian lira			−6.0	−3.0		−2.75	−2.5	−6.0				−3.7
Irish pound							−3.5	+2.0		−8.0		
Dutch guilder				+5.5		+4.25	+3.5	+2.0	+3.0		+3.0	

[1]Percentage changes vis-à-vis the group of currencies whose bilateral parities remained constant during the realignment, except for those of 21 March 1983 and 22 July 1985, in which all currencies were realigned. A plus sign means a revaluation of the currency concerned.
Source: Ungerer (1990), p. 55; De Nederlandsche Bank, *Annual Report*, 1992.

competitive position of the countries with these currencies deteriorated against that of other ERM participants. This appears to have resulted from a deliberate policy. By letting devaluation lag behind the inflation differential, countries such as Italy and France ensured that the rise in import prices was less than the domestic price increases. This enabled them to moderate the increase in the consumer price index – the main indicator of domestic inflation.

The deteriorating competitive position of these countries could have wrecked the anti-inflation policy, because foreign exchange speculators could have taken this deterioration as a sign of imminent devaluation of the currencies concerned. However, there was no speculation against these currencies. The explanation is sought in a phenomenon defined as 'borrowing the credibility of the German anti-inflation policy' via membership of the ERM. Over the years, the German anti-inflation policy is recognised as having been highly successful. By now opting in principle for a fixed link between their currency and the Deutschmark via ERM membership, the other ERM countries signal to the (foreign exchange) market that they are also committed to a macro-economic policy which supports this link. If the policy patently fails to offer that support, the market will be unconvinced of the stability of the prevailing rates of exchange and foreign exchange speculation will readily break out. However, once the supporting policy does become apparent, it will immediately gain considerably in credibility owing to membership of the ERM, and there may be no foreign exchange speculation.

Ironically, in the case of borrowing German credibility, market sentiment can easily work the other way, so that in the longer run tension again occurs in the ERM. The essence of this problem is that in a high inflation country the monetary policy supporting the fixed link to the Deutschmark must be visibly restrictive. That policy will contain excessive inflation so that the competitiveness of the high inflation country is not further damaged in the longer term. A restrictive monetary policy is associated with a high interest rate, certainly in comparison with that in Germany.[1] Increased confidence in the supporting macro-economic policy greatly reduces expectations regarding future devaluations of the currency against the Deutschmark. If we combine these two elements – the relatively high interest rate and low expectations of devaluation – in the uncovered interest rate parity (equation (13.14)), the surprising outcome is that the interest rate advantage for an investment in a high inflation country is greater than the expected exchange rate loss. Thus, the investment recom-

---

1. Another explanation for high interest rate in a high inflation country, which supports this argument, links the level of interest to the expected rate of inflation. The premise is that someone who temporarily hands over his money, i.e. invests it, wants appropriate remuneration for it. He needs a certain reward, called the real interest rate, for postponing spending his money. Furthermore, the person in question will be aware of the intervening decline in the value of money in the case of inflation. The investor wants full compensation for that as well.
The result is that the nominal interest rate in a country is equal to the sum of the real rate and the expected inflation. Assuming that real interest rates are the same in comparable countries, such as the industrial countries, the nominal interest rate will be higher in a high inflation country than in a low inflation country.

mendation will be: swap investments in Germany (and other low inflation countries in the EMS) for investments in countries which are in the ERM but have higher inflation. The resulting inflow of capital to the latter category of countries strengthens the currency of a higher inflation country, which therefore tends to revaluation rather than devaluation!

At first, the situation just described promotes exchange rate stability in the ERM, but there is an inherent instability. If this situation of unchanging exchange rates persists for some time, the equilibrium becomes increasingly unstable, certainly if inflation is only gradually brought under control and if the deterioration in the competitiveness of the high inflation country depresses employment there. The foreign exchange speculators will then of course also perceive that one of the exchange rate fundamentals, namely the competitive position, is increasingly tending to move against the prevailing value of the exchange rate. There can then suddenly come a time when, in the eyes of foreign exchange speculators, this latent imbalance crosses a certain threshold so that this fundamental becomes decisive for market sentiment. Foreign exchange speculators then move en bloc against such a currency – often encouraged by the bandwagon effect. The resulting capital flight then makes devaluation virtually inevitable.

Such a situation can also easily arise without relatively high inflation. It also occurs if the attainment of an economic objective such as full employment is an issue. For politicians, unemployment can be unacceptable, especially if elections are approaching. It is then very tempting to suspend the anti-inflation policy and temporarily give precedence to curbing unemployment and that also means reducing interest rates, of course. However, this can prompt an outflow of capital, fostered by a deviation from the uncovered interest rate parity (see equation (13.4)). In practice we find that even suggestions of a future cut in interest rate, in the form of a wish expressed by a policy-maker, can be sufficient to reverse market sentiment and hence international capital movements.

In September 1992 and subsequently in August 1993 these dangers to the ERM became reality. The September 1992 foreign exchange crisis was greatly reinforced by the gradually developing differences in the competitive position of the countries in the ERM. Figure 18.1 indicates these differences for a number of West European countries. Except for Sweden, all the countries take part in the ERM. Here it should be pointed out that, after much hesitation, the UK eventually joined the ERM in October 1990, with a fluctuation band width of 12 per cent. Before that, sterling had more or less shadowed the ERM for several years. This means that a currency is not a formal participant but in practice the monetary authorities concerned do actually make a serious effort to keep their currency in line with those in the exchange rate mechanism. Sweden with its currency, the krona, also shadowed the ERM for years but never joined during that period. Nor could it, as Sweden was not a member of the EC until 1995. In practice, the Swedes linked their currency to the ECU. Taking 1987 as the base year, there are some countries which have seen an improvement in their competitive position according to their real (effective) exchange rate (left-hand side of the graph) while other countries faced a marked deterioration (right-hand side).

Moreover, on the right-hand side of Figure 18.1 it is clear how the adjustment of the rates in September 1992 brought about a recovery in the disrupted competitiveness of the countries shown. From 1987 onwards there was actually an over-reaction, as the real rates, except those for Spain, had fallen below 100 at the end of 1992. The September 1992 rate adjustment concerned a 5 per cent devaluation of the peseta, though the currency did remain in the ERM. In contrast, the lira and sterling left the ERM on that occasion. Since then they have been floating. This is particularly disappointing for the lira, because that currency was in the ERM right from the start and at the time of the latest realignment of exchange rates in the ERM in January 1990 had even swapped the broad 12 per cent fluctuation band for a narrow one of 4.5 per cent. Trouble on the exchange rate front also persisted: in November the peseta and escudo were forced to devalue 6 per cent. In 1993 the problems continued: in February the Irish punt was devalued by 10 per cent and in May the peseta and the escudo by 7 and 3.5 per cent respectively.

Tension between EMS members on the monetary policy to be adopted ushered in the foreign exchange crisis of early August 1993. As usual, Germany attached great importance to combating inflation. In German terms, domestic inflation was high at around 4 per cent. This caused the emphasis to be very much on a restrictive monetary policy with a relatively high interest rate. In

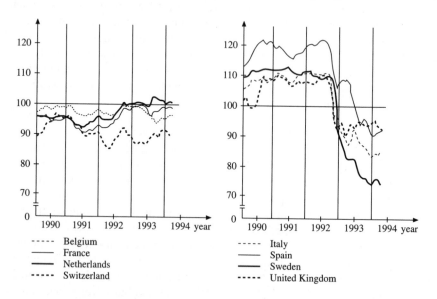

Figure 18.1 Real effective exchange rates,[1] 1990–4

[1]Based on relative unit labour costs in manufacturing. Monthly averages; 1987 = 100.
Source: BIS, *64th Annual Report*, Basle, 1994, p. 83.

countries such as France and the Netherlands, inflation was lower at about 2 per cent to 3 per cent, but unemployment was much higher than in Germany. France and the Netherlands thus faced the familiar, characteristic situation of the eternal triangle: fixed exchange rates, free international capital movements and national political autonomy cannot all be achieved simultaneously. In this connection we should also bear in mind that, since mid 1990, capital restrictions had virtually disappeared between the original EC member states. In this situation, opting for fixed exchange rates also implies following the economic policy of the central country in the exchange rate system, in this case Germany, even if that is contrary to the desired national policy. France openly protested and actually took steps to cut interest rates. This seems to have been the reason that at the end of June market sentiment turned against the French franc. The feeling on the foreign exchange market was that the chance of interest rate cuts in France and Belgium was a real one, whereas the German interest rate appeared to have reached its lowest point. International capital flows turned against the French franc, in particular. In spite of foreign exchange market intervention on a massive scale, in which the German central bank was also closely involved, the exchange rate values proved untenable. Yet instead of a formal devaluation, the very surprising decision was that the ERM fluctuation margins should be substantially widened. At the beginning of August 1993 these were expanded to twice 15 per cent, i.e. a total of 30 per cent, for the participating currencies with the exception of the guilder/mark rate. We are entitled to wonder whether an exchange rate system with such a band width can still be referred to as an adjustable peg system. The old band width was maintained for the guilder/mark rate.

Although everyone expected the ERM countries to use this increased exchange rate freedom to pursue a more independent monetary policy, what happened in practice was different: interest rate cuts hardly deviated from those in Germany, and monetary policy was not relaxed either. The result was that, after dropping slightly at first, the values of the currencies which had been given a 30 per cent fluctuation band rapidly recovered. After a few months both the Belgian and the French francs were back within the old band width of 4.5 per cent in relation to the German mark. Nevertheless, in mid 1995 the monetary authorities still did not feel that the time was ripe for restoring the old band width against the Deutschmark for currencies other than the guilder. That is quite understandable. After too long a period of exchange rate instability since 1987, all kinds of foreign exchange tensions had built up in the ERM, erupting in 1992 and 1993 in the form of large-scale speculative capital movements.

This indicates that an adjustable peg system of exchange rates is equally vulnerable to realignments which are too frequent or too sporadic. In 1979–85 we saw the first problem in the ERM, in 1987–91 the second. Evidently, the operation of such a system nowadays, with such massive and mobile capital movements, demands such sophisticated management that the system has in fact become difficult to apply.

18.4 The ECU

18.4.1 The basket currency

The ECU has attracted great attention as a financial innovation. That attention was perhaps somewhat exaggerated: the basic idea was not new and the functions assigned to the ECU did not amount to much in terms of monetary techniques.

The ECU was created along the lines of the SDR, and is also made up of a basket of currencies, namely all those in the EMS. Table 18.2 shows the history of the composition of the ECU. The ECU basket contains a fixed amount of each national currency of EMS countries. At the start, the amount was fixed in such a way that the share of a national currency in the value of the ECU corresponds to the economic size of the country concerned in relation to the EC as a whole. That size is defined by means of economic variables such as national product and trade with other EC countries in relation to the value of these variables for the whole of the EC. Clearly, if there is a fixed quantity of each national currency in the ECU basket, the shares of the national currencies in the value of the ECU will change as soon as mutual exchange rates in the EC are adjusted. Then the share of a revaluing currency in the ECU basket increases while that of a devaluing currency falls. In order to prevent gradually revaluing currencies from eclipsing the share of a devaluing currency in the ECU basket, provision was made for revising the composition of the ECU basket every five years. And that was always done from the introduction in 1979 up to the September 1989 revision. These revisions also provided the opportunity to incorporate the

Table 18.2 Composition of the ECU

	National currency units			Weights (%)		
	13 Mar. 1979	17 Sep. 1984	21 Sep. 1989	13 Mar. 1979	17 Sep. 1984	21 Sep. 1989
Deutschmark	0.828	0.719	0.624	33.0	32.0	30.10
French franc	1.15	1.31	1.33	19.8	19.0	19.00
Sterling	0.0885	0.0878	0.0878	13.3	15.0	13.00
Italian lira	109.00	140.0	152.0	9.5	10.2	10.15
Dutch guilder	0.286	0.256	0.220	10.5	10.1	9.40
Belgian franc	3.66	3.71	3.30	9.3	8.2	7.60
Luxemburg franc	0.14	0.14	0.13	0.4	0.3	0.30
Danish krone	0.217	0.219	0.198	3.1	2.7	2.45
Irish pound	0.00759	0.00871	0.00855	1.1	1.2	1.10
Greek drachma	–	1.15	1.44	–	1.3	0.80
Spanish peseta	–	–	6.89	–	–	5.30
Portuguese escudo	–	–	1.39	–	–	0.80

Source: Ungerer (1990), p. 61.

currencies of new EMS members in the ECU basket.

Sterling has formed part of the ECU basket from the start, as the UK was always a member of the EMS although it remained outside the ERM until October 1990. In the 1980s Greece (1981) and Spain and Portugal (1986) joined the EC. Since they also signed the EMS agreement at the same time, they immediately became members of the EMS. As we have already seen in the case of the UK, that does not necessarily mean that the countries take part in the EMS exchange rate mechanism as well. The new EMS currencies were added on the next occasion on which the ECU basket was revised. For the Greek drachma, that was in 1984; for the two Iberian peninsula currencies it was 1989.

In 1994 there was another opportunity to adjust the ECU basket, but it was passed by. It was also decided that the composition of the basket would no longer be changed on the basis of interim exchange rate adjustments or changes in the relative economic positions of the EMS countries. The reason was to foster the aim to maximise the strength of the ECU's position as money. An important function of money is as a medium for hoarding, including temporarily retaining purchasing power and postponing expenditure. This function is greatly encouraged if the type of money is attractive as a medium for investment. In turn, that attraction depends very much on the stability of its value – or better still, a gradual increase in its value. This was the idea behind the development of the SDR and later the ECU as a basket currency, i.e. in the form of a weighted average of national currencies, because this promotes the stability of the value of the composite currency.[2]

The decision to halt the periodic revisions of the composition of the ECU basket was intended to promote the strength of the currency with its stable composition. In the past, adjustments to the ECU basket had always led to strong currencies, i.e. currencies with a tendency towards revaluation, being partly displaced by the weak currencies in the basket. In this way, the shares of the currencies in the value of the ECU were restored to the level corresponding to the size of the economies to which the currencies belong. In Table 18.2 we see that the quantity of Deutschmarks and Dutch guilders in the ECU basket in fact declined over the years in favour of an increase in the quantity of the weaker currencies lire and French franc. But this meant, of course, that the trend in the value of the ECU, in the long run, lagged behind that of the national currencies which were acknowledged as strong, such as the mark and the guilder. Freezing the composition of the ECU basket from this point on rectified this.

---

2. Section 16.4 develops this idea somewhat further for the SDR. It also applies to the ECU.

18.4.2   Functions of money

Under the EMS agreement the ECU was assigned various functions which essentially correspond to those attributed to money. However, the functions are confined to the official sphere, which means the circuit of monetary authorities of the member states and, if they desire, international monetary organisations. The functions are those of a unit of account, a store of value (or reserve asset) and a means of payment. In the private sphere there is now also an ECU defined in the same way as the official ECU. However, it developed spontaneously, via market forces, though the actions of the EC institutions strongly supported the development of the private ECU. For example, as we saw in Table 12.3, the ECU bond rapidly gained an important position in the international bond market. However, this table also shows that the ECU bond loan is already past its peak (for now).

For the ECU, its function as an official unit of account meant that all financial positions and transactions in which the EC has been involved since March 1979 are expressed in ECUs. The ERM currency parities are also expressed in ECUs. Bilateral parities for the national currencies are then fixed on that basis. However, the ECU's role in the ERM is primarily symbolic, intended to make the ECU seem important. Technically, of course, the parity of a currency could equally well be expressed directly in the other ERM currencies.

Immediately after its introduction the ECU became an important reserve asset in volume terms. The EMS central banks were now obliged to conclude three month swaps with the European Monetary Cooperation Fund (EMCF).The swap has the character of a temporary exchange of reserve assets. A central bank gives up 20 per cent of its dollar and gold reserves for three months in exchange for the same value in ECUs. Thus, these ECUs appear on the central bank's balance sheet, while its gold and dollar holdings are reduced. The artificiality of this swap is illustrated by the fact that the central bank in question does not actually transfer the gold and dollars. It manages them for the EMCOF. Even the exchange rate gain and the interest revenue continue to be paid to the central bank concerned in the usual way. Every three months the swap is renewed. If a central bank's holdings of gold and dollars have changed in the meantime, the size of the swap will naturally also change, as will the central bank's temporary holdings of ECUs.

The ECU acts as a means of payment in that ECUs obtained via the swap can be used as a means of payment in transactions between the EMS central banks. This possibility arises, in particular, if one central bank has to pay off a loan from another not taken out in ECUs. A central bank cannot make use of a loan in the form of ECUs: the official ECU can only be held by monetary authorities and thus specifically not by private individuals – including commercial banks. A central bank therefore cannot use ECUs to intervene in the foreign exchange market, so that there is no point in taking out an ECU loan from another central bank for that purpose.

The EC institutions support the development of the private ECU because it is expected that, in the case of full monetary integration in the EC, the ECU will be the intended common currency. For that purpose it has to perform the functions of money in the private sphere. In itself, it would have been more efficient to designate a national currency as the common currency. The prime candidate would have been the Deutschmark, which is essentially the anchor currency of the EMS. Such a solution would have been more efficient because the currency is already fully developed and, for example, is prominent in the various markets for derivatives. However, the major objection to such a solution is that it is not a politically neutral option: other countries, certainly large countries like France and the United Kingdom, would feel that their currency was considered inferior. Hence a neutral but more expensive solution in the form of development of a new currency like the ECU.

18.5 European Economic and Monetary Union

In June 1988 the European summit in Hanover decided to set up a committee chaired by the then French President of the European Commission, Jacques Delors. It was instructed to examine practical measures and make proposals for setting up an Economic and Monetary Union (EMU) in the EC. This new monetary momentum in Europe came from the spreading mood in favour of change in the EC, created by the closer integration of the goods and services market by means of the project 'Europe 1992'. The Delors committee produced its report in April 1989. Like the Werner committee report twenty years earlier, the Delors committee decided in favour of achieving EMU in three stages. There were further striking similarities between the content of the two reports, though there were differences too, of course. Thus, the Delors committee went further in the direction of a system of central banks independent of the Finance Ministers. In its day, the Werner committee had suggested greater centralisation of fiscal policy in the EMU. In June 1989 the European Council of Ministers accepted the proposal for the first stage in the Delors committee report. This stage began on 1 January 1990.

In December 1991 an intergovernmental conference was held in Maastricht, chaired by the Netherlands, which decided on both the EMU and an European Political Union (EPU) in the EC. An intergovernmental conference was necessary because these decisions required amendments to the Treaty of Rome, the treaty establishing the European Economic Community. The agreements on EPU remained bogged down in a great many generalised principles.[3] That subject is beyond the scope of this book. The EMU treaty agreed in Maastricht is totally in line with the Delors report, though the ideas are often developed in more detail, such as the specific timing of the launch of stages 2 and 3.

---

3. The general wording still could not prevent the emergence of great differences in the aims of EC countries. So much so that the UK and Denmark refused to sign part of the treaty.

Ratification of the Treaty of Maastricht was completed on 1 November 1993, so that the treaty could enter into force on that date. From then on we usually refer to the European Union (EU) as the successor to the EC.

Stage 1 of EMU was intended to give way to stage 2 on 1 January 1994; and that is what happened. In stage 1 all participating countries had to switch to the narrow fluctuation margin already in operation. As we have seen, nothing came of it. For most countries the fluctuation margin was actually increased to 30 per cent. The possibility of realignment was to be retained in the first stage, but all capital restrictions had to be abolished. Denmark, France, Italy and Belgium had already done this on 1 July 1990. Germany, the United Kingdom and the Netherlands had preceded these countries in that respect.

In stage 2, exchange rate realignments can only take place under exceptional conditions, and central bank financing of the public sector is prohibited. The European Monetary Institute (EMI) was to commence its activities at the start of stage 2. This requirement is also on schedule. The functions of the EMI concern examining the conditions which have to be imposed on a European Central Bank (ECB) which is yet to be set up, and making recommendations concerning the monetary policy and economic policy coordination of the participating countries. After a long tussle, Frankfurt became the headquarters of the EMI. Its first president is the Belgian Lamfalussy. In stage 2 the convergence of the economies will also have to be considerable. Convergence criteria were formulated at Maastricht, together with EMU reference values for each of these criteria. These reference values are the critical values which each country must satisfy if it wishes to be able to join the third stage, or actual EMU, at the end of stage 2. Box 18.2 sets out these criteria and also gives quantitative information on the country positions so far.

Box 18.2 EMU convergence criteria

Table 18.3 shows the convergence criteria for measuring the countries' degree of convergence. The note relating to the table specifies the convergence criteria and the structure of the reference values.

The choice of inflation and interest rates as convergence criteria is understandable in the light of exchange rate theory. According to purchasing power parity and the uncovered interest rate parity, an invariable exchange rate requires inflation and interest rate differentials between countries to be small, at the very least. The convergence requirements in the note relating to the table look arbitrary, and they are up to a point. A critical value of 1.5 per cent could equally have been 1 per cent or perhaps 2 per cent.

The criteria derived from public finance have a rather less direct connection with an invariable exchange rate and are therefore also more subject to criticism. The motive for these criteria seems to have been fear that an invariable exchange rate – and thus certainly a single currency – would enhance the effectiveness of fiscal policy, as we saw in section 14.7. This takes place through the effect of mobile international capital. The greater effectiveness of fiscal policy could

---

Table 18.3 Convergence in stage 2: a half-way house

	Inflation		Long-term interest rate		Budget deficit		Government debt	
	1993	1994	1993	1994	1993	1994	1993	1994
EMU reference value	3.3	3.1	9.3	9.8	3	3	60	60
Belgium	2.8	2.4	7.2	7.7	−6.6	−5.4	139	140
Denmark	1.3	2.0	7.3	7.8	−4.4	−4.3	80	78
Germany	4.2	3.0	6.4	6.8	−3.3	−2.5	48	51
France	2.1	1.7	6.8	7.2	−5.8	−5.6	46	50
Greece	14.4	10.9	21.2	19.0	−13.3	−14.1	115	121
Ireland	2.0	3.2	7.7	8.0	−2.5	−2.4	96	89
Italy	4.5	4.0	11.3	10.5	−9.5	−9.6	119	124
Luxembourg	3.6	2.3	6.9	6.4	1.1	1.3	8	9
Netherlands	2.6	2.7	6.4	6.9	−3.3	−3.4	81	78
Portugal	6.5	5.2	12.2	10.4	−7.2	−6.2	67	70
Spain	4.6	4.7	10.2	10.0	−7.3	−6.7	60	64
United Kingdom	3.0	2.4	7.4	8.0	−7.9	−6.9	48	50
Finland	2.2	1.1	8.2	8.5	−7.2	−4.7	62	73
Austria	3.6	3.0	6.6	7.0	−4.1	−4.4	64	65
Sweden	4.6	2.2	8.5	9.6	−13.3	−11.7	77	88

Explanatory note: The italic figures indicate compliance with the relevant convergence requirements, given a certain interpretation of the criteria. As there is as yet no full agreement on this interpretation, assessment of compliance with the criteria is tentative. The EMU reference values (maximum values) are: for inflation (annual average, %): 1.5 percentage points in excess of the inflation rate of 'at most' the three best performing countries in terms of price stability (interpreted here as the average inflation rate in the three best performing countries in this respect); long-term interest rates (annual average, %): 2 percentage points in excess of the interest rate in 'at most' the three best performing countries in terms of price stability (interpreted here as the average interest rate in the three best performing countries with regard to inflation); budget deficit (total government net lending, % of GDP): 3%; government debt (gross total debt, % of GDP): not more than 60% (or showing a satisfactory decrease). Moreover, the currency must have shown a sufficient degree of exchange rate stability by staying within the normal fluctuation margins of the EMS exchange rate mechanism without devaluation, for two years. (This last requirement is met by Belgium, Denmark, Germany, France, Ireland, Luxembourg, the Netherlands and Austria.)
Source: De Nederlandsche Bank, *Annual Report 1994*, Amsterdam, 1995, p. 105.

prompt countries to make imprudent use of it, which would naturally not be in the interests of the countries in the future EMU, who intend to pursue a less profligate fiscal policy. An expansionary fiscal policy in another member state would have the effect of driving up interest rates there. Since there will be only one integrated capital market in the EMU, interest rates on that market would rise. The other member states naturally regard this as detrimental. There is also the fear that a country whose government has heavy debts will exert strong pressure in order to be permitted, in that case, to finance the large government debt by monetary means as a one-off rescue operation. This would boost inflation, very much contrary to the wishes of the other countries.

A last criterion not mentioned in the table states that a country must not have devalued its currency in the last two years preceding stage 3. The criterion was undoubtedly introduced on the basis of the width of the fluctuation band at that time. Only Germany and the Netherlands are therefore able to satisfy this criterion so far. However, it seems very likely that the wide fluctuation band will be accepted in judging a country's performance. The Dutch central bank already refers to the 30 per cent band width as the 'normal EMS fluctuation margins'.

Almost without exception, the member states in the table have drawn up convergence programmes stipulating when and how the EMU criteria are to be fulfilled. However, the picture which emerges from the table is rather gloomy: at the end of 1994, only Germany and Luxembourg satisfied all the convergence criteria for EMU membership.

Stage 3 is synonymous with joining EMU. A common currency will then replace the individual national currencies. End 1995 the intended common currency was renamed from ECU in euro. The launch date for stage 3 is not certain. If a majority of the EMS countries satisfy the convergence criteria before 1 January 1997, they will be jointly absorbed into EMU on that date. If that majority is not achieved, the starting date will be 1 January 1999. The EMS countries which have met the convergence criteria will then form EMU. This may therefore be a minority of the EMS countries. Here we see that monetary integration at varying speeds has actually been programmed into the Maastricht Treaty. Only in the highly unlikely case that all EMS countries satisfy the convergence criteria in time will they make the transition to EMU *en bloc*.

18.6   The French franc zone

There are other countries which, like those in the ERM, maintain fixed exchange rates. The US dollar, the pound sterling, the French franc and the SDR are the primary currencies against which exchange rates are fixed. This is done unilaterally and does not involve the countries of the anchor currencies concerned. The specific feature of the ERM is that the countries deliberately maintain fixed exchange rates within the group. Africa is the only other place in the world where we see anything similar.

Thirteen African countries have mutually fixed exchange rates. They are former French colonies so it is not surprising that the French franc is the peg for this exchange rate system. The thirteen countries can be divided into two groups, one of seven and one of six countries, each with a joint central bank and a common currency. These are therefore two monetary unions – a close form of integration towards which the EU is still progressing. The group of seven countries is in West Africa and comprises Benin, Burkina Faso, Ivory Coast, Mali, Niger, Senegal and Togo. They form the West African monetary union (WAMU). The full name of their currency is 'franc de la Communauté financière d'Afrique', abbreviated to CFA franc. The other group consists of six Central African countries: the Central African Republic, Equatorial Guinea, Gabon, Cameroon, the Congo and Chad. Together they form the CAMA and their common currency is the 'franc de la Coopération financière en Afrique centrale', also abbreviated to CFA franc. Exchange rates in these two groups are extremely stable. After 1948 the rate of exchange between these two CFA francs and the French franc was not changed for many years. It was only recently, in January 1994, that the first adjustment took place: the CFA francs were devalued by 50 per cent against the French franc, so that the rate of exchange went up from 50 to 100 CFA francs to the French franc.[4]

The structure of the link between the CFA francs and the French franc is based on an account held by each of the two African central banks with the French treasury. That is where the bulk of the international monetary reserves are kept, and interest is paid on them. On the other hand, the account holders can also go into the red, in which case France charges interest. International capital movements with France are free. If a central bank's balance falls below a specified amount it has to restrict lending. The African central banks are also subject to an upper limit on the monetary financing of budget deficits: they may finance up to a maximum of 20 per cent of the previous year's government revenue in that way. This is a degree of financial discipline rare in developing countries. Up to the mid 1980s, the effects were correspondingly good. From 1970 to 1984 inflation in the CFA franc area averaged 10 per cent and growth of gross domestic product 4 per cent. The corresponding figures for surrounding countries were 18 and 2.5 per cent.

However, from the mid 1980s there was a dramatic deterioration in the economic situation in the CFA franc zone. The principal reason was a significant deterioration in the international terms of trade for this group of countries, because of a slump in the world market price of many of the primary products exported by the group (see Figure 18.2). Since the countries export different products, there were also stark variations between countries in the deterioration in the terms of trade. Another problem was that in the latter half of the 1980s the dollar fell sharply, including against the EMS currencies, one of which is the French franc. This caused the CFA franc to appreciate substantially against the currencies of many of its world market competitors. Apart from the negative price effect (deterioration in the terms of trade) on the export side, this also had a negative volume effect on both the export and import side of the balance of payments. For several years, devaluation of the CFA franc looked unavoidable. In view of the liberalised capital movements, that expectation naturally led to

---

4. This was in fact a 50 per cent devaluation, because the rate changed from CFA 1 = Ffr. 0.02 to CFA 1 = Ffr. 0.01, so that the percentage change amounted to $(0.01 - 0.02)/0.02 \times 100\% = -50$ per cent.

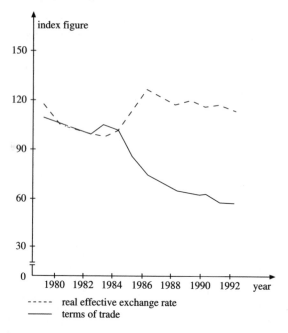

Figure 18.2 The terms of trade and the real exchange rate in the CFA franc zone[1] (index numbers, 1985 = 100)

[1] An upward movement in the real effective exchange rate is an appreciation, a downward movement in the terms of trade is a deterioration. The country weightings are based on the 1985 figures for gross domestic product.
Source: Clément (1994), p. 11.

capital flight, which placed even more strain on the position of the CFA franc.

The devaluation of the CFA franc against the French franc in January 1994 was therefore inevitable. Given the seriousness of the economic upheavals, the size of it (50 per cent) does not seem at all large.

18.7 The optimum currency area theory

In view of the above attempts by Europe and Africa to achieve a monetary union which works well, it seems obvious that such a form of cooperation is advantageous to the countries concerned. Theoretical support for this is not unequivocal. It is the optimum currency area theory which is concerned with this question, constituting a textbook example of a cost/benefit analysis – the driving force of economics.

The benefits of participation in a monetary union are considered to be the known advantages of a fixed exchange rate system. In the case of regional monetary integration, of course, the advantages are rather more limited in scope than in a global system, because they extend only as far as the geographical boundaries of the area of monetary integration. The following changes which occur as a result of the establishment of a monetary union with a common currency can be regarded as benefits:

- Exclusion of the exchange rate risk in transactions within the union.
- Elimination of currency conversion costs in this type of transactions.
- Enlargement of the area in which a single unit of account is used; existence of such an accounting unit in use over an extended area will make markets more transparent in that area.
- Greater liquidity on the foreign exchange market and the markets in currency derivatives. A liquid market means that there is a high volume of trading. The advantage is that transactions can be concluded at all times and without affecting the market price because of the large size of the market. Increased liquidity is brought about by the markets for the national currencies of the participating countries being combined into a single market for the common currency.
- The possibility of using the financial markets of the anchor currency, such as that of the French franc by the African countries in the CFA franc zone. As a result of the fixed link with the French franc, the currency risk in those countries can equally well be covered on the French financial markets.
- Exclusion of the possibility of speculative capital movements within the monetary union. If there are no longer any national currencies, there can also no longer be any capital flight from one national currency to another.
- Reduced need for international monetary reserves, since they are no longer required to finance imbalances in payment flows within the monetary union.
- The institutions of the monetary union can make a substantial contribution to the anti-inflation policy, something that it would be much harder for a country to achieve on its own. In particular, if the anchor country has built up a reputation in the monetary union as a low inflation country, this is a considerable advantage.
- For a participating country, fiscal policy becomes more effective. This follows from what we learnt in section 14.7, that fiscal policy is ineffective under floating rates but effective if exchange rates are fixed.

The disadvantages of monetary union are fewer in number than the advantages. But this does not, of course, tell us anything about the eventual outcome of weighing up the costs and benefits for a particular area. A single disadvantage can be more important than numerous advantages! In fact there are only two drawbacks to (membership of a) monetary union, namely: loss of monetary policy as a national instrument, because it is transferred to the central level – namely the central bank of the monetary union; loss of the exchange rate as an adjustment instrument.

The optimum currency area theory develops several criteria which can supposedly be used to assess whether it is worth joining a monetary union. The benefits are accepted as a fact, which is not entirely fair as the size of the benefits will actually depend on the specific composition and size of the monetary integration area. All the criteria referred to focus on the cost side of membership, which is why we shall examine the costs in greater depth here.

For small countries, centralisation of monetary policy is not in itself a cost item. Even if monetary policy were to remain decentralised, its effectiveness would wane under fixed exchange rates. For that loss a common currency is not needed. We have already seen this in section 14.6. Moreover, the loss of monetary policy as an instrument is only a cost factor if the country in question has a business cycle which is out of step with that of the other members. Only then will the country need to retain national monetary policy as an instrument for moderating the cycle, even in a monetary union. If a downward movement is perceptible throughout the area of the monetary union, then an expansive monetary policy will be implemented centrally to compensate for it. In that case, the outcome for an individual country will probably not differ greatly from that of an independent national monetary policy under floating exchange rates. Finally, it should be expressly pointed out that we were only referring here to a cyclical movement, because we have already seen that in the long term monetary policy has no effect on economic growth.

The criteria for assessing the costs of joining a monetary union are all a reaction to the loss of the exchange rate instrument for an individual country. If the whole union suffers economic disturbance, then of course the exchange rate of the common currency against currencies outside the union is still available for adjustment to counteract the effects of the disturbance. The problem for an individual country does not arise until the monetary union suffers economic disturbances in a specific country. For example, this occurs if demand for goods shifts from country A to country B, while both countries form part of the monetary union. If there was full employment in both countries, this shift in demand means unemployment in country A and a labour shortage in country B. The absence of the possibility of an exchange rate adjustment is still not a cost item for a country so long as wages and prices in both countries are flexible. Wage and price moderation in one country and rising wages and prices in the other can then restore the equilibrium in both countries at full employment level. However, if wages and prices are rigid – as is almost always the case to some extent in practice – then an adjustment problem occurs on the (goods and) labour market unless there is high mobility of labour between the two countries. In the case of high labour mobility the damage is not too great, because labour moves to the country where there is a shortage and full employment is thus restored via the supply side of the labour market. The only long-term problem may then be that the size of population in the two areas of the monetary union becomes an issue. An exodus from one area in favour of another may be undesirable, e.g. because of the wider adverse effects on the economic structure.

This description of the scope for adjustment in an economy without using the exchange rate instrument brings us to the first two criteria for joining a monetary union according to optimum currency area theory. The compound criterion is this: the greater the countries' wage and price flexibility or mobility of labour, the more sense there is in joining a monetary union. Clearly, the two characteristics are complementary: wage and price flexibility combined with high mobility of labour mitigates the objections to joining a monetary union even more.

According to the third criterion, the diversification of the economy also affects the costs of joining a monetary union. The argument is that economic shocks to an economy are often product-based. In a highly diversified economy, disturbance of the market in one product will have relatively little impact, including on the total international trade of the country concerned. Often it will partly be compensated by opposite developments in its other products. The instrument of exchange rate adjustment is therefore less necessary than if exports are heavily concentrated on a few products.

A fourth criterion concerns the similarity of the economic structures of the intended participants in the monetary union. The more similar the countries' production structures, the more similar will be the impact of an economic shock. They will then all have greater need for the same adjustment to the exchange rate, which can readily be combined with possession of a common currency and economic policy on the union level.

A fifth criterion states that monetary integration is more worthwhile the more advanced the integration of public spending in the countries concerned. The reason is that then countries touched by an adverse economic shock can be compensated financially by transfer payments from other union countries. Taking our previous example of the international demand shift: as a result of higher economic growth, country B starts to pay more taxes which then end up as unemployment benefits in country A. Adjustment of the exchange rate of the national currency is then less urgent.

A last widely used criterion is whether the country has an open economy. The basic idea is that an adjustment of the exchange rate in an open economy will have a large impact on wages and prices, because devaluation leads to imported inflation, boosted an increase in the consumer price. This increase is greater the more open the economy. The wage/price spiral which follows then pushes inflation in the country to an even higher level. In an open economy, much of the improvement in competitiveness gained by devaluation is lost in this way. In an open economy the exchange rate is therefore not very effective as an instrument of adjustment, so that it can be abandoned at very little cost.

In principle, plans for joining a monetary union can be assessed in economic terms on the basis of the above summary of the benefits and costs of membership of a monetary union. Naturally the usefulness of forming a monetary union can also be judged *retrospectively*. By way of illustration, we therefore offer some comments on the benefits of the European and African monetary unions.

Mutual trade in the countries of the CFA franc zone is estimated at less than 10 per cent of their total exports; in the EU the figure is well over 50 per cent. The advantages of eliminating the exchange rate risk and conversion costs are thus hardly significant in Africa, but very important in the EU. However, if we consider that, via the link to the French franc, the African countries can also regard the ERM area as part of their area of fixed exchange rates, then this argument changes dramatically. This larger area is also the focus of over half the trade of the countries in the CFA franc area.

Almost all European countries already have well-developed foreign exchange markets, so that the increase in the liquidity of those markets is not such an important factor. In contrast, the African countries gain an enormous advantage from monetary integration because of the resulting opportunity to cover their international risks on the French franc market. In Europe, wages and prices are rather rigid while the mobility of labour is low. Both are disadvantages for a monetary union. In this respect, Africa is in a better position. On the other hand, as regards diversification of the national economy and similarity of production structures, Europe again scores much higher than Africa. One point is clear from this, namely that the eventual decision on joining a monetary union will depend very much on the importance one attaches to the different costs and benefits which such a step will bring.

18.8   Summary

1. Both Western Europe and Africa have an advanced form of regional monetary integration. The European Union (EU, the new name of the European Community (EC) since November 1993) is in the process of monetary integration and on the way to the final stage of full monetary integration. This stage features a permanently fixed exchange rate with no fluctuation margin, or even a common currency. Total liberalisation of capital movements between member states is usually also regarded as a feature of full monetary union. In Africa, the CFA franc zone has been in this final stage of monetary integration for decades.

2. The process of regional monetary integration in the EU is now far advanced. It actually began with the introduction of the Snake arrangement in May 1972, in which the fluctuation margins for bilateral exchange rates were halved in comparison with the rules of the Bretton Woods exchange rate system, as revised under the Smithsonian agreement in December 1991. However, the Snake arrangement soon foundered and in the end consisted only of the Deutschmark and the currencies of a few small neighbouring countries.

3. Introduction of the European Monetary System (EMS) in March 1979 again prompted greater activity among all EC countries relating to monetary integration. All these countries joined the EMS, but not all were prepared to take part in the EMS Exchange Rate Mechanism. This has the same form as the Snake, with additional support in the form of a system of mutual credit facilities.

4. The ECU is also a product of the introduction of the EMS. The ECU fulfils all three functions of money in the official sphere. However, it would be going much too far to state that it is generally accepted in those functions,

though that is certainly a condition for a fully developed currency. The ECU was given a basket formula on the lines of the SDR. This promotes the stability of its value. The attraction of the ECU as a medium for hoarding (or a reserve medium) was increased recently by halting the five-yearly adjustments to the composition of the basket. Apart from the effect of any new EMS members, the basket will keep the same composition from now on.

5. For various high-inflation member countries, the EMS was a means of helping to curb inflation at home, though this function of the EMS contributed to the increasingly unstable balance in this system. This was partly why the system actually collapsed in August 1993. Only the guilder/ Deutschmark exchange rate still meets the original requirement of a 4.5 per cent fluctuation band. The other exchange rates either have a 30 per cent band width (what de facto means floating) or they are floating.

6. Nevertheless, the integration process is making steady progress in Western Europe, and most of the EMS countries are on their way to Economic and Monetary Union (EMU). The Treaty of Maastricht, of December 1991, laid the legal foundation. The convergence of the economies of the EMS members is now the focus of interest. It does not look as if the transition to EMU will take place before 1999. Only countries meeting all the convergence criteria are entitled to join.

7. Full monetary integration in the form of the CFA franc area suffered a serious setback in January 1994 when, for the first time in its life, the CFA franc had to be devalued against the French franc. This devaluation was caused by two external factors (a deteriorated terms of trade and a strong French franc) causing serious economic disturbance in the area from the mid 1980s onwards.

8. The optimum currency area theory which forms the theoretical basis for regional monetary integration puts forward many points for and against such integration. The theory offers various criteria which have been developed for judging whether it is worthwhile for a country to participate in regional monetary integration. They all concern minimising the costs of such participation; the benefits are accepted as a fact. Individually, the criteria cover only a small part of the question. They show that joining a monetary union becomes more worthwhile the greater the labour mobility in the area, the greater economic openness and similarity of economic structures between the intended union partners, and the more advanced the international integration of public spending in the area. Wage and price flexibility and a diversified range of exports for the intended partners also help to minimise the costs of integration. Taken together, the criteria provide a good indication of whether participation is worthwhile, though there is then the inevitable problem that the criteria need not all point in the same direction, so that the policy-makers still face a subjective process of weighing up the considerations when it comes to deciding whether or not to join a monetary union.

381

Bibliography

Corden, W.M. (1972), Monetary integration, *Essays in International Finance*, no. 93.

Clément, J.A.P. (1994), Striving for stability: CFA franc realignment, *Finance and Development*, vol. 31, no. 2.

Bank for International Settlements (1994), *64th Annual Report*.

European Monetary Institute (1995), *Annual Report 1994*.

European Commission (1990), One market, one money; an evaluation of the potential benefits and costs of forming an economic and monetary union, *European Economy*, no. 44.

Grauwe, P. de (1994), *The Economics of Monetary Integration*, 2nd ed., Oxford University Press.

Gros, D. and N. Thygesen (1992), *European Monetary Integration: From the European Monetary System to European Monetary Union*, Longman.

De Nederlandsche Bank (1995), *Annual Report 1994*.

Ungerer, H. (1990), *The European Monetary System: Developments and Perspectives*, International Monetary Fund.

Index